The Remains of the North

Liberalism, History, and Legal Theory

Adekemi Odujirin

University Press of America,® Inc.
Lanham · New York · Oxford

4720 Boston Way
Lanham, Maryland 20706

PO Box 317
Oxford
OX2 9RU, UK

Printed in the United States of America
British Library Cataloging in Publication Information Available

ISBN 0-7618-2518-5 (paperback : alk. ppr.)
ISBN 978-0-7618-2518-0

™ The paper used in this publication meets the minimum requirements of American National Standard for Information Sciences—Permanence of Paper for Printed Library Materials, ANSI Z39.48—1984

To

The woman whose steadfastness ensured
that I received the rudiments of education

Adawi Abeni Odujirin

Though a scholar must have faith in his master, yet a man well instructed must judge for himself: for learners owe to their masters only a temporary belief, and a suspension of their own judgment till they are fully instructed, and not an absolute resignation or perpetual captivity. Let great authors, therefore, have their due, but so as not to defraud time, which is the author of authors, and the parent of truth

Francis Bacon, *The Advancement of Learning*

But I did not get my picture of the world by satisfying myself of its correctness; nor do I have it because I am satisfied of its correctness. No: it is the inherited background against which I distinguish between true and false.

Ludwig Wittgeinstein, *On Certainty*

With the life forms into which we were born and which have stamped our identity we take on very different sorts of historical liability. For the way we continue the traditions in which we find ourselves is up to us.

Habermas, *The New Conservatism*

Contents

Preface

Institutional legal and political theorists take for granted the sociopolitical and economic structures that make possible the practice of professional legal and political scholarship. Institutional structures themselves are products of change over time, and history is a continuing process. But scholars do not suffer law and politics to move perpetually with the ebb and flow of time. At some stage, reflection stabilizes law and politics by constructing some ideal legal and political system from the totality of past experience. The resultant streamlined behavioral patterns and institutional practices shape subsequent legal and political consciousness, which, in turn, engender distinctive legal and political intellectual traditions. Carriers of an intellectual tradition may or may not identify with its overarching morality, but they tend to perceive the polities, principles, and policies the tradition underwrites almost exclusively from the vantage ground of its beneficiaries.

This book is concerned with certain aspects of liberal analytic intellectual traditions as seen through the eyes of a learner intellectually domiciled in 'the north' but existentially situated in 'the south.' I have divided liberal intellectual traditions into two broad categories: old and modern. The former denotes classical and pre-modern political philosophy and their contemporary republican offshoots; the latter denotes rights-based political theories and their democratic ideals. Now, 'the south' is simultaneously a beneficiary and a victim of these intellectual traditions in a number of ways that cannot be spelled out here. It suffices to say that 'the south' is a beneficiary because acquaintance with these intellectual traditions played no small measure in the struggle of 'the south' for and eventual attainment of political independence. But 'the south' was also, and still is, a victim because, as this book argues, the intellectual universe fashioned by these intellectual traditions banish 'the south' to the base of the world pyramid. No matter how closely related 'the south' is to 'the north,' liberal analytic intellectual tradition offers little succor to the former. Unless 'the south' somehow lifts itself up with its own bootstraps, it is destined for the lower rungs of the 'the great chain of being.'

In these circumstances, the resuscitation of liberal analytic political and legal *theories* that counsel representational clarity and coherent elaboration of cultural institutional norms, principles, and rules promise at best a resurrection of the legal and political ideals fostered by the historical processes that earlier culminated in liberal analytic intellectual traditions. As those traditions did not originally contemplate 'visible' minorities and 'the south', this renewal tends to revamp the type of intellectual sensibility that has almost always invariably enabled, in J.S. Mill's words, 'those who begin by being strongest' to use 'their strength to keep the others weak,' without – and this is the crux of the matter - being aware of such a state of affairs.

Nevertheless, just as previous liberal analytic intellectual activities led to the recognition of the existence of 'the south,' whether within or outside 'the north', the current renaissance may yet have its own unintended positive intellectual consequences. The thesis of this book is that an enlarged historical consciousness and cognitive clarity might sharpen awareness of the inherent theoretical and practical limitations of liberal analytic intellectual traditions. Specifically, untrammeled history might enable learners to descry the extent to which the dominant intellectual traditions are permeated by truncated historical awareness that makes scholars pursue objectivity without universality or vice versa.

This book consists of three chapters. The first and second chapters identify and elaborate on the limitations of liberal analytic intellectuality vis-à-vis 'the south' while the third focuses on the limitations of analytical jurisprudence as a philosophy of law. All three have something in common, namely, that 'localism' pervades liberal analytic intellectual traditions. By 'localism' I mean the unarticulated belief that the task of political and legal theory is simply to clarify and systematize or interpret or idealize the cultural (ethical) experience of a people. Put differently, the inadequacies of liberal analytic intellectual traditions identified in this book are the result of the process through which cultural conceptions of liberal and normative legal concepts have been wrapped in philosophic and analytic forms.

This book had a gestation period that spanned more than a decade, and many people read portions of it at one time or another. I wish to thank, without implicating, the following. (1) Professor Ken Norman, whose catholic mind and protestant intellect introduced me to the theoretical tropes of liberal democracy. (2) Professor Bruce Chapman and Denise Reaume, for reading and commenting on portions of the first and third chapters, (3) Professor Jim Phillips, for seeing value in my study and use of history. And last, but not the least, (4)) Dr. Dotse Tsikata, who first suggested, and with whom I discussed, certain portions of the second chapter.

I thank also my resident family - Adenike Toluani, Abeni Adeyinka, Adedotun Abayomi, and their mother, Adunni Oluyemisi - who, in the face of acute shortage of space, put up with my unconventional working hours.

Adekemi Odujirin

Chapter 1

Inside the Lighthouse

> The beginnings of Philosophy were in a very Obscure Dawn, and perhaps it is yet scarce Morning with it. And therefore what we cannot find among former inquirers we are to seek in the Attempts of more Modern Men, and in the Improvements of nearer Ages[1]

Introduction

Since the end of the Second World War, there has been continually renewed interest in the theoretical basis of law and politics. Until the 1960s, however, political philosophers were primarily concerned with descriptive theories of law and politics. That changed in the 1970s. The first challenge to descriptive theorists of law and politics came from rights-based political philosophers. John Rawls[2], Ronald Dworkin[3] and Robert Nozick,[4] among others, represent this school of thought. In that encounter, rights-based theorists triumphed.[5] The second challenge to descriptive theorists of law and politics came from proponents of republican political philosophy. Michael Sandel,[6] Alasdair MacIntyre,[7] Leo Strauss,[8] among others, represent this school of thought. There is no end in sight yet to the debate between these two schools of thought.

This chapter does not participate in the debate between rights-based and contemporary republican political theorists. Rather, it focuses on certain aspects of the intellectual tradition that underpins rights-based and republican political theories. It does this from two seemingly distinct perspectives, namely, the points of view of 'visible' minorities within liberal democracies, and 'the south'. However, it is neither a racial nor an ideological critique of rights-based and republican political theories. Its thesis is that, from the standpoint of visible minorities and the south, all the theoretical work 'that has been done under the sun is calamitous.'[9] Contemporary rights-based and republican political theorists can respond adequately neither to the sociopolitical and economic straits of 'visible' minorities nor to the anemic socioeconomic and political conditions of 'the south'. I will use the term 'modern liberalism' to denote rights-based political theories, and 'old liberalism' to denote ancient and contemporary republican political philosophy.

However, this chapter is disproportionately concerned with modern liberalism, for three reasons. First, while the contest between modern and old liberalism is not a David-and-Goliath encounter, I hold that modern liberalism is superior to old liberalism. There are several reasons for this, but it suffices to mention the most important, namely, that, qua philosophy, modern liberalism is apolitical and a-historical. This does not mean that modern liberalism lives in a no man's land. Rather, it means that modern liberalism *can* focus on the individual as individual in contrast with old liberalism that focuses on the individual as a member of this or that polity or historical people/group. Secondly, certain aspects of old liberalism that are particularly germane to the thesis of this book are considered in the second chapter. Thirdly, and perhaps more pertinently, although I hold that modern liberalism is superior to old liberalism, I believe at the same time that contemporary modern liberalism suppresses the very quality that makes it superior to old liberalism. To make this point requires extended discussion of the theoretical limitations of and institutional constraints on contemporary modern liberalism.

Contemporary modern liberalism is extremely sophisticated. Yet, at bottom, it is quite content with analyzing and constructing theories of justice from the history of certain preferred political societies. It then deploys the resultant ideals to justify, to a larger or lesser extent, existing political structures and practices. But, history yoked with theory tends to paralyze the intellect. The practice in liberal constitutional polities and the ideals to which they lead fall short of the liberal idea that 'every member of the commonwealth must be permitted to attain any degree of status ... to which his talent, his industry, and his luck may bring him.'[10] More specifically, liberal constitutional democracies have been and continue to be tenaciously partial to the majority, in the practice of freedom and equality. The result is that theoretically excellent or seemingly neutral political principles fail in practice to accord equal protection to very 'visible' minorities within liberal constitutional polities.

Unlike the swarm of books and commentaries that identify with either 'old' or 'modern' liberalism, and which then strengthens the one by exposing incoherence and contradictions in the other, this book takes a different tack. It eschews the optative mood. Rather, it sees both 'old' and 'modern' liberalism as aged lighthouses. Even when they eschew comprehensive philosophy of life, many a modern liberal political theorist professes to see the individual and society '*sub species aeternitatis*';[11] thus subtly claiming to speak, if not the final, at least the rational word. But we should be wary of such claims, for philosophy is paradigmatically a perennial human activity, and philosophers are not immune from error. In short, we should keep close in mind that philosophy is not an arena where God speaks, or if it is, the possibility that 'God has not yet spoken.'[12]

The structure of this chapter is as follows. Part I outlines the history of political philosophy from its beginning in Hellas over two thousand years ago to the turn of the twentieth century. Part II traces the thread that links contemporary modern liberalism with its predecessors by placing three leading contemporary modern liberal theorists in a historical continuum. Part III interposes a crucial but seldom explicitly articulated point that the modern liberal constitutional polity requires an incipient or crystallized cultured elite committed to procedural democracy and the modern liberal ethos. It adds that such an elite is non-existent in 'the south' generally and ex-colonial African polities in particular. Part IV argues that contemporary modern liberal theorists espouse menopause forms of the liberal idea. It suggests that contemporary modern liberal political theorists need to find a way of resuming the childbearing capacity of liberal political philosophy. It identifies four offspring that modern liberalism would have to conceive and suckle in order to be able to address the plight of 'the south' and minorities within liberal constitutional polities. Part V highlights the 'school-philosophy' orientation of contemporary 'old' and 'modern' liberalism, and points out that both hold and proffer forms of political knowledge that are antithetical to the advancement of liberal learning vis-à-vis visible minorities and 'the south'.

I

BIRTH AND PROGRESS OF POLITICAL PHILOSOPHY

In intellectual history, the Greeks stand out tall among the peoples of the ancient world; an adequate account of political philosophy must begin with them. Of course, it is rash to attempt to sketch the history of political philosophy within the compass of a few pages. Yet, the effort is both necessary and worth making for the purpose of this chapter. What follows might be described as a precis of the history of political philosophy.[13]

Long after the Greeks had become civilized there arose among their remote descendants an intellectual movement whose members were known as the Sophists.[14] The sophists were teachers of rhetoric, the art of persuasion. They professed to impart political virtue, among others, to their pupils. This implied that political virtue was a skill, know-how or technique that could be acquired by anyone who could afford the fees charged by its professed teachers. And, anyone who acquired that skill could become a city leader, which implied that education rather than birth made leaders. Specifically, it meant that nobody was born to rule or be ruled such that city-leaders could come from any segment of a political society. However, the sophists were not levelers. Ontologically, the sophists were nominalists; philosophically, they were positivists, ethically, they were utilitarians. This triad – nominalism, positivism, and utilitarianism – made the sophists a formidable assailant of the traditional *structure* of the Greek *polis*.

The sophists' teaching threatened the *stability* of the typical Greek *polis*. This, in part, provoked the reaction of the Socratics – Plato and Aristotle. The socratics were convinced not only that there was a natural order after which the state could be modeled, but also that certain elements of traditional Greek political structure closely approximated the natural order. They denied that virtue was a teachable skill, a commodity that could be bought or sold. In opposition to the sophists, the socratics conceived virtue generally and, specifically, political virtue as a gift – an integral part of the soul – which God or Nature bestowed on favorites. It followed that only those who had that attribute of the soul had it, and only those who had it could and should rule. In short, the socratics hypothesized a *natural right* to rule. The socratics' exposition of this concept is scattered in the dialogues of Plato, particularly *The Republic*, and the works of Aristotle, especially *Politics*. Ontologically, the socratics were realists; philosophically, they were anti-positivistic; ethically, they were anti-utilitarians. This triad – realism, naturalism, and anti-utilitarianism – made the socratics a formidable protagonist of the *traditional* structure of the Greek polis. It goes without saying that the socratics too were not levelers.

However, the socratics were neither egalitarian republicans nor conventional democrats. As philosophers rather than politicians or statesmen, they did not defend an actual or historical Greek republic. Rather, their object of love was an *ideal* republic, a Greek cosmopolis. The Greek republic would be a polity permeated by heroic virtues but devoid of such vices as the exclusion of women from political life. It would eliminate the notorious fragmentation and organization of Greeks into rival city-states with the attendant incessant internecine warfare, and the consequent enslavement of Greeks by Greeks. Internally, the ideal Greek polis would be a peaceful, harmonious, republic encompassing *all* Hellenes and characterized by a natural division of labor. That is, a polity in which individuals engaged in the activity to which they were best fitted by God or nature, and ruled by the law. Further, in the ideal Greek polis, there would be no slaves, or, more accurately, only barbarians, that is, non-Greeks would be slaves. Externally, the ideal Greek polis would be an interface of Homeric gods and warriors, a powerful republic protected by Platonic guardians, and able to strike terror into the hearts of other republics. Unsurprisingly, in giving philosophic form to that political ideal and, incidentally, creating a place for philosophers within the polis, the socratics crafted their thoughts and couched their conclusions in the language understood by educated Greeks. They used the apt but potentially misleading Homeric war imageries; they portrayed the polis as the pageant of the gods. Such was the birth of political philosophy in Hellas.

Since then the history of political philosophy has been a succession or ascension of men or groups of men (and their theorists) laying claim to the right to rule. Romano-Christian political philosophy terminated in the divine right of kings. Post-renaissance political philosophy culminated in the natural right of the gentry to a share in, and ultimately monopoly of, political power. The commercial expansions of the modern period and the industrial revolution produced the modern merchant and entrepreneur, and the utilitarians asserted their right to a share in, and eventually control of, the political institutions. As well, the industrial revolution saw the emergence of 'the proletariat', and ideologues idealized, in the guise of a classless society, rule by their intellectual spokesmen.

The socratics had pointed to an inexhaustible source when they made nature the fulcrum of political philosophy. From classical times down to the Renaissance, political philosophers anchored their ideas on nature. Throughout that long period, however, political philosophers made little appreciable advance on the socratics' conception of natural right. The men of the renaissance returned to the Greeks, but it was to the philosophical positivism of the sophists rather than the philosophical naturalism of the socratics.[15] At the beginning of the modern period in the seventeenth century, however, political philosophers returned afresh to Nature. Instead of 'the ancients' notion that the polis was a natural, hierarchically structured entity in which individuals merely find their own places, 'the moderns' came up with a 'state of nature' populated by free and equal individuals. The transition from the 'state of nature' to political society was effected through the medium of the 'social contract'.[16] The advent of 'philosophical contractarianism'[17] marked the abandonment of the philosophical naturalism of the ancients. Instead of the ancients' concept of a natural right to rule, the moderns fashioned the concept of a right to rule based on the social contract, that is, consent. Philosophical contractarianism heralded the birth of modern liberalism.

In the eighteenth century, the 'state of nature' was demoted to the status of a mere presupposition, and the 'social contract' was ultimately branded as an unnecessary fiction. The result was the transformation and preservation of the modern concept of a right to rule shorn of its metaphysical foundations. The development of modern political institutions in the nineteenth century and the emergence of procedural democracy in the twentieth century, rendered otiose the question, 'who should rule?'[18], which was the spur for the dialogues that laid the intellectual 'roots of political philosophy'.[19] As well, by delimiting the scope of governmental power vis-à-vis the individual – in a word by settling the problem of sovereignty or autonomy - modern liberalism banished the principal source of constant bickering and revolutions in the past, namely, the perennial issue, 'how not to rule'. In other words, historical struggle was replaced by institutional technology; the 'revolutionary' ardor was quelled and dammed into the 'reformatory' channels. Imperceptibly, constitutional law displaced political philosophy.

It may well be that that is how it should be, but constitutional law seems to have failed to satisfy all constituencies. This has led to the resurrection of political philosophy that, in turn, has forced the old issues into the forefront once more. However, the 'interpretive turn'[20] in contemporary modern liberal political philosophy lures contemporary advocates of modern liberalism to be content with interpretive constructions of cultural liberal political practices. This dilutes the philosophic force of modern liberalism. What is more, it imperils the oldest creature in the liberal ontological zoo, namely, free and equal individuals. But before going further, it is necessary to outline the continuity and link between the founders of modern liberal political philosophy and contemporary modern liberalism by situating three leading contemporary modern liberal theorists in an historical continuum.

II

LOCATING CONTEMPORARY (MODERN) LIBERAL THEORISTS

(a) The Font

Modern political philosophy started about the middle of the seventeenth century. Before then Rene Descartes had inaugurated, in his *Discourse on Method*, a new intellectual orientation. This is the practice of starting an inquiry *de novo*, in the hypothetical sense, that is, as if one had no intellectual predecessors. Thomas Hobbes was the first to adopt this procedure in political philosophy. Whatever may be the position as regards modern liberalism, modern political philosophy surely began with Hobbes' invention of 'the state of nature' in which the thoughts and acts of free and equal individuals were unconstrained by any political authority. Hobbes' state of nature was characterized by anarchy, the war of all against all. Hobbes constituted political society by inventing the social contract through which individuals relinquished their lawless freedom to a political sovereign, the Leviathan. This logic led Hobbes to propound a seemingly absolutist political theory according to which all legal rights are positive rights.

John Locke was the next outstanding theorist in the social contract tradition. Although Locke worked in the same metaphysical forge as Hobbes, Locke's anvil molded a social contract that issued forth the right to life, liberty and estate – generically called 'property'. Unlike Hobbes' construction, this right was immune from the ambulatory powers of the political sovereign. Far from being the source of right, political society was constituted to ensure the peaceful enjoyment and continued exercise of the natural right to life, liberty and estate. As Locke puts it, 'the great and chief end ... of Mens uniting into commonwealths, and putting themselves under government, *is the preservation of their property*'. And, whereas in the state of nature 'the measure of property [estate] Nature has well set, by the extent of *Men's labour and the conveniency of life*,' in the political society, and since the advent of money, which both induces and makes it possible for any man to appropriate more than is necessary for his sustenance, 'it is plain, that Men have agreed to disproportionate and unequal possession of the earth.'[21] The *raison d'être* of political society was the protection of the right of the individual to life, liberty, and estate. With this short background, we can attempt placing three leading contemporary modern liberal theorists, namely, John Rawls, Robert Nozick, and Ronald Dworkin.

(b) John Rawls and Robert Nozick

Rawls was steeped in the modern intellectual tradition. Rawls started afresh by positing 'an original position' in which individuals enjoyed equal liberty. Additionally, the individuals in the original position neither knew nor did they have a way of knowing what would be their actual position in real life. Hence, they were able to operate in a state of 'reflective equilibrium'. In that state, they deliberated on the procedural devices by which to constitute a 'just' society. With these background assumptions, Rawls proceeded to deduce the primary principles of political justice that rational individuals - persons behind the 'veil of ignorance'- would perforce choose.[22] In short, Rawls theorized with a conceptual being; he peeled several layers of the onionskin, so to speak, up to and including the last, and so had only a notional 'onion' left. The 'self' he deals with is a disemboweled entity. Yet, the peep into the resultant crystal ball yields principles that closely mimic the practice in twentieth-century constitutional welfare democracies. In other words, the 'original position' and the 'veil of ignorance' are magician's hat from which one could extract only what has been previously fed into it.[23]

While the 'original position' parallels the 'state of nature' in the philosophical contractarian tradition,[24] there is a difference between how the classic social contract philosophers used these structural tropes and the purpose the 'original position' and 'the veil of ignorance' served in Rawls' scheme. In spite of its now recognized limitations, Locke and others put the social contract construct to *reformatory* use; it is that fact, among others, that accounts for the continued intellectual appeal of their writings. In Rawls' scheme, however, the 'original position' was avowedly designed for a different purpose. Rene Descartes, who originated the modern intellectual tradition of pursuing an inquiry *de novo*, proceeded first to destroy all his former opinions. Although Descartes had his own political interests,[25] and although he explicitly disapproved of schemes to remake the state all over,[26] he was not a political philosopher. In short, as far as political philosophy was concerned, Descartes was not a modern. But the shift in epistemological procedure precipitated by his radical intellectual methodology entailed the realization that 'reason' takes its flight from 'experience'.

The moderns took 'experience' seriously. Relying on 'experience', they promptly discarded the assumption made by 'the ancients,' namely, that man was naturally a political animal. Hobbes wove into his political theory materials that emphasized and captured the tempers and sentiments of men in the phenomenal world,[27] and Locke closely observed and paid attention to the wiles of the men of his time.[28] But while 'the moderns' rejected the assumption that man was naturally a political being, and despite all talks about the state of nature, neither Hobbes nor Locke performed the rationalist ritual of first destroying all their former opinions.

Rawls exhibits the same empiricist prejudice. Although Rawls started afresh, he neither caviled at nor queried the fundamental assumptions about man and society on which rested modern liberal political philosophy. First, Rawls postulates an atomistic political society. Second, he assumes or rather accepts the correctness of the concept of political justice espoused by the founders of modern liberalism. Third, he aims strictly at rationally reconciling the principles of modern liberal political philosophy with the canons of the modern welfare state. In short, Rawls' did not inject any new values into his theory.

Nozick's political theory is an updated reinstatement of Locke's political thought, especially as it relates to largeness of 'estate'. Nozick points out that a book of political philosophy typically involves 'philosophical exploration of issues ... which arise and interconnect when wc consider individual rights and the state.' That, of course, is a characteristically modern way of posing the question. However, we must immediately rejoin that the resultant theory of justice is nevertheless political. Hence, while one must take seriously Nozick's explicit disavowal of the intention of writing a political tract, one cannot overlook the inherently political character of the result of his philosophical exploration. Nozick aimed primarily at providing theoretical underpinning for a pure form of the dominant sociopolitical and economic system. Although he confessed that his theoretical conclusions are 'callous towards the needs and suffering of others,' Nozick avoided the guilty plea by maintaining that he had grown so accustomed to a libertarian perspective that he proffered 'natural responses which fit the [callous] theory' of justice he propounds.[29]

Nozick could be likened to the journeyman who, at the commencement of his rounds, stood on the bridge over the river, looked down and carefully noted the water level. After several days of peregrination, he returned to the same spot. Again, the journeyman looked down to check the water level; the water level was the same as when he first checked. He then concluded that no water had flown pass since he set out on his journey! Nozick simply assumes that nothing transpired since the triumph of Locke's political theory. Nozick's thesis is that the system of holdings (or rather, the rules underlying the system of holdings) that emerged between the seventeenth and nineteenth centuries is the acme of distributive justice. The modern welfare state dilutes and throws into disequilibrium the ideal state of distributive justice. And so, Nozick bids us return to the so-called nightwatchman state of the nineteenth century. In short, Nozick's rights-based theory is devoid of new values. Both Rawls' and Nozick's theories are new, but the contents of their respective theories are old. Specifically, while Rawls' materials came from the second half of the twentieth century, Nozick's materials came entirely from the heyday of laissez faire in economics, politics, and law.

The nineteenth and the twentieth centuries represent a period when, largely because of the demise of the metaphysical foundation of modern liberalism, modern liberal political philosophy reached its nadir. It is a period characterized by what one commentator rather misleadingly termed 'ideological homelessness'.[30] Contemporary modern liberal theorists embrace 'right' without 'nature.'[31] They resolve the question of the limits of state action into the issue of political morality, of political right. Perhaps that is as it should be. But by disowning the first part of the equation, that is, by dispensing with nature, contemporary modern liberal theorists have discarded the constraining and stabilizing instrument (which is at the same time the principal source of creativity) forged by political philosophers. They have substituted 'second nature'[32] – history, convention, tradition – in its place. Indeed, a distinctive strain in contemporary modern liberal political philosophy denies the necessity of any foundation.[33] The substitution of 'secondary' for 'primary' nature – the elevation of *nomos* into *physis* - makes contemporary modern liberalism particularly vulnerable to the cannons of advocates of old liberalism; the latter pit 'nature' (as they conceive it) against 'convention.' Besides, contemporary modern liberalism appears to be an explain-all theory. It is at once made to shatter racism and to justify, in the name of freedom of expression, the right to match through a predominantly Jewish town chanting Nazi cadences. It upholds atomized society, yet it holds fast to the notion of 'community'; it attempts to accommodate every imaginable lifestyle and to explain and evaluate virtually all social, legal, economic, and political relations in contractarian terms.[34] It will be suggested here that these perplexities originated with the founders of modern liberalism. But we have not yet located Ronald Dworkin.

(c) Ronald Dworkin

At first sight, Dworkin is very difficult to place. However, Dworkin's candor entirely obviates the difficulty. Dworkin avows that the idea of rights he defends is not of a different metaphysical character from that of the dominant political theory and that it is in fact 'parasitic on the dominant idea of utilitarianism, which is the idea of *a collective goal of the community as a whole'*.[35] The meaning of that phrase is crucial to placing Dworkin. Yet, that way of putting his thesis effectively obscures the historiographical import of the phrase 'collective goal of the community as a whole'. Once recognized, however, the ambiguity could be easily resolved.

Gierke[36] noted that when the theory of the state of nature triumphed and the unity of the people was referred to a contractual act, it became entirely impossible to escape from the circle of individualistic mode of thought. Bentham, who represented the presumably 'dominant idea of utilitarianism', was one of the principal political philosophers who shared the spoils of the triumph of the social contract theory. (It is commonplace knowledge that Bentham and the utilitarians rejected both the 'state of nature' and the 'social contract'). To Bentham, the community was a fictitious entity composed of the individual persons constituting its members. Secondly, those individuals were self-centred (though this did not necessarily mean that they were selfish) beings. In short, 'the collective goal of the community as a whole' does not imply a collectivist orientation. At best, it means individuals' 'disinterested interest in the survival and welfare of their fellows.'[37] Now, if the embarrassing ontological luxury called 'nature' is jettisoned, and we substitute in its place, as contemporary modern liberalism does, 'respectably empirical metaphysics' or 'the canons of reasonable empiricism'[38] then we will be left with only the concept of 'right' embedded in our political institutional history. Dworkin elsewhere called it 'naturalism'.[39] In short, Dworkin is intellectually situated in the period when the metaphysical trappings of modern liberalism - the state of nature and the social contract – had been discarded but before the Enlightenment assault on history and tradition and the ascendance of utilitarianism. Dworkin is thus rightly described as 'pre-Benthamite.'[40]

This leads to at least three conclusions. First, it means that Dworkin tacitly accepts the whole phalanx of assumptions about man and society made by modern liberal political philosophers. Second, it means that he rejects Bentham's rejection of 'natural rights' as 'nonsense upon stilts'. Third, it means that he substitutes the concept of 'individual rights' without nature for the concept of natural right formulated by post-renaissance modern liberal political philosophers. In short, Dworkin is faithful to the atomistic theory of society; although he is not averse to collective goals, he views any political theory that is not suitably individualistic as an anathema. Conceptually, in liberal history and tradition, only individuals have rights. So, Dworkin can at once regard individual 'rights as trumps', and talk about the collective goal of the community as a whole without necessarily having anything to do with so-called group entities. But the resuscitation of the concept of rights in an attenuated form imparts a measure of kinetic energy into Dworkin's rights-based political theory.

Yet, the measure of kinetic energy in Dworkin's rights theory is too phlegmatic. I will demonstrate this by referring to Dworkin's view on the judicial enforcement of fugitive slave laws. Dworkin says that judicial enforcement of fugitive slave laws could be put down to 'failure in jurisprudence;'[41] it is as if the judges who enforced the fugitive slave laws failed Dworkin's course in jurisprudence. If Dworkin is right then one can equally put down colonialism and imperialism with all the attendant dehumanization to 'failure in jurisprudence.' But to do this is to use 'failure in jurisprudence' as a counterpane to shield from view the iniquities perpetrated in the course of the centuries when modern liberalism was at its pinnacle. It is a core of Dworkin's rights-thesis that there is almost always a 'right answer' for every conceivable instance in which the question of right can present itself. And, the only test is whether the proffered answers cohere with the moral principles that have institutional support in our legal and political history.[42]

Academic lawyers steeped in the common law tradition have long learned the strategy of linking the question of the existence and extent of 'rights' with the judicial process. This practice manifests itself in Dworkin's ideal figure, Hercules or Hercules' interpretive judge, Hermes. Dworkin offers a conception of the judge who judges if, and only if, he treads Hercules' path, namely, to put the best construction on the institutional 'history he finds' rather than 'to invent a better history'.[43] The institutional history the ideal judge finds is itself a seamless web of rights, and the ideal judge rests answers about right that cohere with the moral principles embedded in that history. If ordinary judges fail to live up to Hercules' standard, we can throw up our arms and say that the god is not to blame.

Philosophers cannot do without deities anymore than theologians can do without the Deity. Yet it is a notorious fact that when mortals cast gods, they almost always invariably make them in their own images.

And, the way of such gods almost always invariably leads directly to a Panglossian abode. The problem is always that while a god's dwelling may be a good place in itself, it does not necessarily follow that it is the best possible world for all its inhabitants.[44] First, facts are stubborn things; they hardly yield to arguments. The historical fact of slavery, the social and political results of imperialism, the sociological fact of racism, and the economic bifurcation of society into two classes cannot be exceptions. They will not yield even before Hermes' gargantuan interpretive skills. Second, if the only yardstick for ascertaining fidelity to the underlying moral principles of our political institutions is our understanding, how shall we know when the understanding strays? And, when we do know, *ex post facto*, that the understanding had strayed (and assuming that the same political structures would have been devised anyway) is it not unreal to assume that the content of the political structures would not materially differ from the one thrown up by our political history? Third, the underlying moral principles of our political institutions are not the deliverance of 'pure' reason. Rather, they were fashioned by men of 'practical' reason specifically in response to concrete problems and issues of their own time and age.[45] They may not be suitable for the problems and challenges of a different time and age.

The institutional history from which Dworkin requires Herculean scholars to extract the materials for the best interpretive political theory knows no evil. As such it cannot do anything except good. Yet, while the political ideal of freedom and equality pulsates within 'the north', the same conviction is virtually nonexistent in 'the south'. Of course, 'the south' is diverse, but it is predominantly comprised of ex-colonial societies, and in the case of African societies, once wholly enslaved. There is little hint of the recognition of the damage done by 'the north' within living memory to the individual and/or the collective goals of these communities in Dworkin's theory. This is not surprising, for the institutional history on which Dworkin relies mutes the colonizing and imperial impulse of 'the north' that ensured that 'the south' lacks an essential component of liberal democratic institutions, namely, a liberal 'aristocracy'.

I use the term 'aristocracy' Humpty Dumpty-wise here to mean incipient or crystallized indigenous political actors, committed to modern liberal ethos and procedural democracy. This usage should not be confused with the ordinary meaning of the term. Later on, I will use the word in its ordinary sense. But, for the nonce, I am content with advancing the simple argument that while a requisite 'aristocracy' for the operation of liberal political infrastructures subsists in 'the north', colonialism ensured that it does not exist in 'the south'.

III

'ARISTOCRACIES': THE HUB OF LIBERAL POLITIES?

Contemporary modern liberal theorists take as given the existence of the liberal constitutional political society; they concentrate on its justification. Now, modern liberal constitutional polities are the direct offspring of the natural right-based philosophy of post-renaissance political theorists. As noted above, post-renaissance political philosophy represents a fundamental break from pre-modern political thought. Its fulcrum is the voluntaristic basis of government. The social-contract theory stood classical political philosophy on its head by denying that man was naturally a political animal. Instead, it postulated that man was a rational being which saw political society as a necessary evil – serving purely self-interested purposes – to curtail or remove the shortness, nastiness, and brutishness of the Hobbesian state of nature, or, in Locke's version, to preserve the natural right to life, liberty and estate.[46] This set the stage for, and put limits on, rationalism in law and politics. Specifically, it institutionalized what Isaiah Berlin[47] called 'the negative conception of liberty,' that is, freedom from intrusive governmental interference.

Modern liberal political philosophy, therefore, guarantees individual freedom and security by fixing for once the orbital tracks within which moves the relationship between the State and the individual. Considered in the abstract, the modern liberal polity is an institutional arrangement in which the natural right to life, liberty and estate is guaranteed. The concept of justice and the function of law in society derive from these background philosophical scaffolds; contemporary modern liberalism inherited these intellectual foundations of modern liberal political theory. Consequently, all rights-based theorists are voluntarists. Although historicists and utilitarians are wont to explain 'consent' in terms of interest or necessity,[48] they too assume that consent is the basis of political power.

It is almost superfluous to ask, 'what was the aim of the modern liberal political philosophers when they asserted the right to life, liberty and estate?' For, it is clear that the purpose was to enable individuals to perform the duty to promote their own 'happiness' without let or hindrance of governmental authorities. This appears to be the meeting point between 'right' and 'utility'. In other words, modern liberal political philosophy was hedonistic from the start. Whether modern hedonism entailed 'possessive individualism', as C.B. MacPherson contends,[49] or 'acquisitiveness' as Leo Strauss maintains,[50] the rejection of 'authority' for 'reason' and 'utility' was meant to do away with the hitherto prevalent (positive) conception of liberty – a conception that was basically Aristotlean.[51]

Since rights are purposeful things, a right that lacks the potential of fulfilling its rational purpose is sterile and worthless. Now, a 'right' may be bereft of such potentials right from the beginning in respect of some members of a political society. Or, a 'right' might be robbed of such potentials in respect of some members of society by changed or new circumstances. In either case, it smacks of 'analytical and moral dogmatism'[52] to be content with the assertion that, because that result was not envisaged or intentional, there is no obligation to take any or such steps as could remedy the deficiency. Yet, that we are not obligated to take any corrective measures is precisely the response of some doctrinaire and some not-so-ideological contemporary reinstatement of modern liberal political philosophy. Such modern liberal political theorists, who are content with quoting their 'own consciousness,'[53] give their theoretical turgidity suave expression by characterizing 'liberty' and the 'rule of law' as neutral in purpose.[54]

It is of the utmost importance to ascertain at what level and to what extent 'liberty' or the 'rule of law' is neutral in purpose. Is it at the level of the kind of political society in which we want to live? Or, is it at the level of the type of private life we want to pursue? The first relates to the idea of justice that the socioeconomic and political institutions should serve. There, neutrality is a chimera.[55] The second relates to the individual plans of life. It is in the latter sphere that liberalism can and ought to be neutral. Yet, since there is no reason to believe that any system will necessarily enhance the political attitudes that serve the purpose for which it was designed,[56] neutrality in the private sphere must be coupled with eternal vigilance at the public sphere. Moreover, it is well known that abstract political concepts and ideas are very often given circumscribed meanings.[57]

Historically, the feudal aristocracy or gentry first touted the idea of freedom. The feudal aristocracy's struggle with feudal monarchies led to the elevation into constitutional status of the liberties and privileges they wrung from monarchies. In fact, fragments of the feudal aristocracy were the prime movers of modern liberal political philosophy. It is not surprising that they favored aristocratic conception of freedom.[58] Rationalists and utilitarians subsequently seized upon the idea of freedom. While rationalists endeavored to put the concept of freedom to general use, utilitarians confined themselves to applying it to the situation of a specific socioeconomic class – the middle-class at the time. But there is scarce doubt that the aristocratic conception of liberty is the pantheon of modern liberal political philosophy. It was neither part of the intention of the original movers of modern liberal philosophy nor did they subsequently capitulate to the rationalists' resolve to use the concept to affirm 'the innate rights of man.'[59] In practical terms, it is perhaps only in France that it ever had sweeping consequences.

Modern liberalism thrives in the 'North'. It is difficult to resist the conclusion that this is due to its aristocratic foundations. For, it seems that liberalism is a shield that protects the rulers no less (and perhaps not greater) than the ruled, and democracy is a sword with which the people fell and replace one aristocratic personnel with another. Trouble arises only when the people slacken its vigilance or the incumbent aristocracy attempts a violent change of the rules of the game. That happened in Nazi Germany. In sharp contrast, the aristocracy in the 'south', particularly ex-colonial African political entities, have been undermined, emasculated and mostly subdued and completely disintegrated by colonialism and imperialism. For instance, long after the abolition of slavery, which marked the beginning of direct colonialism,[60] Britain excluded the 'colonial intelligentsia'[61] from the seats of power in anglophonic African polities. Instead, Britain nurtured a band of traditional rulers who readily danced to the tunes dictated by colonialists. Consequently, the traditional institutions were fossilized, but the traditional respect for them was undermined,[62] while the traditional constraints on power disappeared and the moral responsibilities they entailed were thrown overboard. Aside from 'ideological political beliefs about the reordering of economic activity', the crop of educated men and women that later emerged were neither inducted into nor did they develop profound interest in the philosophical basis of law and politics; instead they were oriented to mere commerce.[63] And so, the bold political experiments that some of them embarked upon immediately after attaining political independence were doomed from the start. In any event, the only colonial institution that survived political independence - the military[64] - quickly disbanded post-colonial constitutional governments. Military juntas notoriously rule by guns and decrees; they make pretensions to neither liberal nor democratic values. Hence, the lack of indigenous aristocracy attuned to liberal democratic values stultifies attempts to establish any semblance of liberal constitutional political institutions in these countries. It is now time to look closely at the theoretical underpinning and the shortcoming of modern liberalism vis-à-vis 'the south' and 'visible' minorities.

IV

MODERN LIBERALISM: THEORY, CONTEXT, AND CONSTRAINTS

From the beginning, the aim of political philosophy was to validate some 'ideal' sociopolitical and economic institutional structures. Contemporary modern liberalism is not an exception; its primary focus is the formulation of 'the principles of justice for the basic structure'[65] of liberal democratic polities. It hardly poses the question: what are the sociopolitical and economic iniquities created by or which have arisen since the advent of modern liberalism?[66] As a result, the 'resurrection of ethics'[67] by contemporary modern liberal theorists has been largely confined to proffering cultural interpretations of modern natural rights theories.

Historically, 'natural rights theories were developed by conservative thinkers as a defence of property, competition and other related values'.[68] Philosophically, natural rights theories were devices for safeguarding the right to life, liberty, and estate from the grabbing hands of princes and priests. Politically, natural rights theories enabled thinkers to loosen 'the people' – who they saw 'as a relatively homogenous entity so that the problem of freedom turned, as with the classical political philosophers, on the relation between the people and government'[69] – from the mooring of pretenders to absolutist political powers.

However, the first in the series of modern political revolutions culminated in 'the perpetuation of collective leadership of the nation in the form of a propertied aristocracy'.[70] The ascendance of a propertied aristocracy greatly shaped the ends of politics and the policy furthered by the law.[71] In the aftermath of that epoch-making revolution,[72] 'the primary goal of law and politics was the preservation and advantage of propertied interests'.[73] The obsession with propertied interests, the 'castle of unreason' as J.S. Mill[74] uncharitably called it, led imperceptibly to the erosion of what D.H. Lawrence termed 'the higher emotion', that is, 'love in all its manifestations, genuine desire, tender love, love of our fellow men, and love of God.'[75] But we need not dilate on politics and the psyche here. Rather, our immediate concern is to look closely at the theoretical foundations and limitations of modern liberalism.

(a) The State of Nature: Fact, Fiction or Hypothesis?

The pioneer social contract theorists, Hobbes and Locke, regarded the state of nature as a historical fact.[76] David Hume was the first modern philosopher to deny the historical character of the state of nature; deep historical researches led Hume to that irresistible conclusion. Believing, perhaps, that the persuasiveness of Locke's political theory depended entirely on the supposed historicity of the state of nature, Hume declared, in the early pages of his *Enquiry Concerning Human Understanding*, that it would not be long before Locke's name would be entirely forgotten.[77]

The rationalist social contract theorists, notably Rousseau and Kant, forestalled Hume's prophecy. They forthrightly acknowledged that the 'state of nature' and, indeed, the 'social contract' were hypothetical or logical presuppositions, not historical or moral facts.[78] Unlike Rousseau, 'the harbinger of the Romantic Movement,'[79] who was not particularly interested in the individual of the social contract construct, Kant tore that individual from the hypothetical state of nature, and planted it as a sovereign in a noumenal universe. In the noumenal universe, the individual was unconstrained by the plurality of ends in the phenomenal world, unfettered by the tie of social duties, and beyond the reach of the trappings of conventional morality and traditional restraints. In short, the noumenal self was in a state of natural liberty and, with the aid of reason, free to construct principles of justice untrammeled by any antecedently-given order. As Sandel[80] puts it,

> freed from the dictates of nature and the sanction of social roles, the deontological subject is installed as sovereign, cast as the author of the only moral meanings there are. As inhabitants of a world without telos, we are free to construct principles of justice unconstrained by an order of value antecedently given.

With that incomparable rigorous rationalism, Kant thus defended a modern liberal conception of the state. Nevertheless, (as many of Kant's critics[81] have repeatedly pointed out) the moral outlook he idealized closely resembled the socioeconomic and political order that was emerging in late eighteenth century Germany, from the political structures of 'old Europe.'[82]

It is well known that Kant's rationalism met a match in Hegel. Although Hegel rejected outright the social contract doctrine, he did resort to 'a crypto-state of nature'[83] that was not dissimilar to the state of nature of the social contract theorists. Hegel dipped political philosophy in a historical consciousness that is incomparably deeper than anything imagined before or ever since. Instead of deducing principles of political right from the terms of a social contract, real or imagined, or from the consciousness of a Kantian noumenal being, Hegel followed the trail of the spirit of freedom as it had manifested itself in 'world history' – which he divided into four epochs – the Oriental, the Greek, the Roman, and the Germanic. Hegel notably and neatly excised from 'world history' what he called 'Africa proper'.[84]

As a moral philosopher, Hegel saw plainly that 'freedom' is ethical in character and that it could be best assured by a political structure that fastens on its normative nature. Now, Hegel held not only that ethical freedom peaked in the Germanic epoch of world-history but also that traditional Germanic political institutional structure was not inherently antagonistic to it.[85] And so, he enunciated what Carl J. Friedrich called 'monarchical liberalism.'[86]

Nonetheless, Hegel depicted the state as 'the actuality of the ethical Idea', 'absolutely rational', 'an end in itself'. Consequently, while the individual had the right to be subjectively free within the State, the State 'has supreme right against the individual whose supreme duty is to be a member of the State.' That formulation apparently makes Hegel's state indistinguishable from a Hobbesian sovereign. Until recently this apparent ambivalent character of Hegel's monarchical liberalism provoked, particularly in English-speaking countries, the allegation that his theory of the state 'put the stamp of philosophical respectability on doctrines which are necessary for the emergence of a totalitarian State.'[87] Be that as it may, the totalitarian state has been an exception; the rule has been the liberal polity in which the modern conception of right was kept largely intact. After Hegel, a century elapsed before the notions of a 'state of nature' and of 'social contract' featured prominently in influential political philosophical treatise. Before that happened, utilitarianism reigned supreme. This brings us to a discussion of 'right' vis-à-vis utilitarianism and democracy.

(b) Right, Utilitarianism, and Democracy

It conduces to clarity to distinguish three forms of right. The first is purely political; it is the concept of a right to rule. The second is sociological; it is the concept of the right to rule that prevailed in Europe generally and on the English Channel up until the nineteenth century. It was based on an 'aristocratic tradition grounded in privileges of birth.'[88] The third is ethical; it is the concept of the right of the individual to life, liberty, and estate. Well into the eighteenth century, philosophers used the third form of right primarily for conservative political purposes.

In the eighteenth century, rationalists radicalized the right to life, liberty, and estate. As a result, that concept of right became a powerful tool in the hands of demagogues. The attempt to put the radicalized form of the third concept of right into practice led to excesses, and made observers of the French Revolution apprehensive of natural rights theories. 'Natural rights' became particularly dreadful. It provoked, among others, not only Edmund Burke's anti-rationalist *Reflections on the Revolution in France*, but also Bentham's ire. Bentham famously dismissed 'natural rights' as 'nonsense upon stilts'. Although unlike Burke, Bentham eventually rejected the concept of the right to rule prevalent in his days, he was not initially averse to it. However, Bentham never doubted the existence of the political concept of a right to rule; he would not have been a political philosopher if he did.

All major political thinkers proceed upon the assumption that their theories capture and reflect the aspirations of 'the people' as a whole. It is well known that Bentham was the architect of 'secular utilitarianism'.[89] Now, Bentham's 'vision of a utilitarian society embodied the idea of a near-unanimity of wills founded upon a near-homogeneity of individual personalities'.[90] Yet, in its essence, Bentham's utilitarianism was neither more nor less than the simmering political ideas of his time.[91] Shorn of its metaphysical foundations, the idea of freedom and equality became a tool with which to push ahead the political interests of the middle class of the time, coupled with a megalomaniac belief that the middle class alone would, thenceforth, superintend the affairs of the State.[92]

As a political intellectual movement, utilitarianism did not entail democracy. Until well into the nineteenth century, learned opinion held Athenian democracy responsible for the decay and eventual demise of the intellectual home of the north, Athens.[93] As a result, distrust of, aversion to, or downright hatred of, democracy as a form of government by political theorists of diverse moral persuasions pervaded political thought.[94] Bentham and the utilitarians were no exception; they advocated democratic parliamentary institutions only for the purpose of facilitating the political reforms they wished effected.[95]

Next to Bentham, J.S. Mill is a tall figure in the annals of utilitarianism. Like so many great works, Mill's *On Liberty*, was a reaction to the practical political problems of the time. Mill saw the morality and the actions of political reformists of his time as 'really liberticide.' To stem the tide of 'liberticide' Mill asserted what he modestly called 'one very simple principle', namely, 'that the sole end for which mankind are warranted individually or collectively, in interfering with the liberty of action of *any* of their number is self-protection'. Paternalism won't do:

> The only purpose for which power can be rightfully exercised over any member of a civilized community, against his will, is to prevent harm to others. His own good, either physical or moral, is not a sufficient warrant.[96]

Of course, Mill was a modern liberal, and although his own brand is in many respects different from Bentham's, he maintained utilitarian individualism. Unlike Bentham, however, Mill's commitment was not really happiness in the utilitarian sense, but in the sense of respect for the moral personality, for the capacity to choose.[97] Further, because he believed that the doctrine of natural law had spent all its creative and constructive forces, Mill was averse to and did not subscribe to any species of natural law theory[98]:

> ... whatever power of liberalising men's minds may once have belonged to the doctrine of Natural Law, that power is now exhausted; the doctrine has done all it can in that direction, and its remaining influence serves only to make men greater bigots, not indeed to the peculiar vices of any given system, but to whatever vices have existed from the beginning in them all ...

Mill equally disdained democracy, for he stated, in no unmistakable terms, his distrust of, or, more accurately, ambivalence about what conservative liberals in the latter part of the nineteenth century perceived as an immoderate modern democratic impulse. According to Mill,

> No government by a democracy or a numerous aristocracy, either in its political acts or in the opinions, qualities, and tone of mind which it fosters, ever did or could rise above mediocrity except in so far as the sovereign many have let themselves be guided ... by the counsels and influence of a more highly gifted and instructed one or few ...[99]

This is a modern liberal's version of old liberalism. As Isaiah Berlin[100] has pointed out, there is no necessary connection between liberty (even in its negative conception) and democracy. In the sight of many learned men democracy has always been what Adam Smith, echoing Aristotle, conceived it to be, namely, 'degenerate aristocracy'.[101]

As an intellectual movement, utilitarianism departed radically from traditional political philosophy. Instead of busying themselves with metaphysical questions, utilitarians shifted attention to and concentrated on epistemological points. Specifically, instead of asking the typical ethical question, 'what is right?' they posed the epistemological question, 'how do we know what is right?' Bentham's answer to the latter question was that the rightness or wrongness of any act depended solely on whether it conformed to the principle of utility. And, 'an action may be said to be conformable with the principle of utility when the tendency it has to augment the happiness of the community is greater than any it has to diminish it.'[102] Thus the standard of justice is 'the greatest happiness of the greatest number.' In Bentham's intellectual universe, there was no independent basis for 'right' except 'utility'; 'right' stands or falls as the principle of utility dictates.

Utilitarianism was insidiously malignant, for, the 'greatest happiness of the greatest number' perforce excluded the happiness of some numbers. As the ascending middle energetic class displaced or aligned themselves with the feudal fragments of yesteryears, utilitarianism waxed strong. As it waxed strong the marginalized number swelled, and the cancerous element in the theory festered. The result was a degeneration of the theory, moral suffocation, political suppression, and social tyranny.[103] In short, Benthamite utilitarianism debut as a lamb but turned into a lion bent on preserving the strength of the state much to the detriment of the individual. It was the potential eclipse of moral personality under Benthamite utilitarianism that galvanized Mill's revolt. *On Liberty* was a valiant attempt 'to rescue from among the ruins of natural rights theory such valuable materials as had been built in among rubbish, and given them the new and workmanlike shape which fitted them for a better edifice.'[104] In short, Mill made 'right' an implicit premise of political philosophy. Until the explicit resuscitation of rights-based political theory in the nineteen seventies, utilitarianism, with its distrust of the concept of right, had been the dominant theoretical approach. But contemporary modern liberalism claims that rights-based theories are fundamentally different from utilitarianism.

(c) Right-based Theories and Utilitarianism

Of late utilitarianism has fallen into disrepute. Rights-based political theories are not only antiutilitarian, but also professedly nonutilitarian.[105] Utilitarianism has been charged with the abominable crime of ignoring the distinctness of separate individuals, of conflating all persons into one and combining the desires of all persons into one coherent system of desire.[106] Contemporary modern liberalism opposes this and dichotomizes utilitarianism and rights-based (deontological) theories. But are contemporary rights-based liberal theories as different from utilitarianism as they are made to appear?

First, it needs be emphasized, following Sandel,[107] that deontological political philosophy is above all a theory about justice, and particularly about the primacy of justice among political ideals. Now, the primacy of justice among political ideals seems to be generally assented to. Disagreement centers round the design of the institutional devices that would accord justice a pride of place and the conception of justice that political institutions should serve. Rights-based liberal theories work with the unarticulated major premise of the modern form of the right to rule and the constraints on that right by the right to life, liberty, and estate. Rights-based theorists are, therefore, enamoured to conceive justice in procedural terms only: the elaboration of principles and rules that would be faithful to an already settled conception of justice. Hence, contemporary rights-based liberal political theory of all stripes is procedural and/or interpretive. Rawls' theory of justice, which forms the starting point of contemporary modern liberal attempt at resurrecting ethics, is basically procedural. It assumes that the end of political society is the promotion of a particular ideal of freedom and equality. Thus, Rawls' 'original position' is 'characterized so as to lead to a certain conception of justice,' that is, one which would guarantee the particular political ideal underwritten by 'our considered convictions of justice.' [108] Unlike their predecessors who theorized at a time when democracy was not an item on the political agenda, the existing political systems are democratic. And, contemporary modern liberal theorists assume that liberal values will continue to be protected by democratic political institutions. Hence, the tacit association of liberalism with democracy. We should note, parenthetically, that there is no necessary connection between 'liberalism' and 'democracy'.[109]

Second, (and, again, following Sandel) Kant's deontological break with the social contract construct, and the consequential foundation of rights on 'reason', for all its logic fails to give an account of the circumstances of justice.[110] It fails to give an account of the circumstances of justice not so much because it has none of its own (as Sandel implied), but because it is hamstrung or precluded by the nature of its method from enunciating such circumstances. If its circumstances of justice were enunciated it would be seen that its precepts are contingent rather than necessary, that is, they were not the products of a disembodied but biased (not in a pejorative sense) and interested reason. Specifically, it favors a conception of justice to which a child living at the time Locke's political theory was at its zenith would have readily subscribed; Locke supplied the content for Kant's abstract exposition. The link between the Englishman and the German underscores the historiographical continuity of modern natural rights theories. As we shall see presently, that historiography conceals the dynamic attribute of modern liberalism.

Third, the earliest time to which authentic history extends was a state of warfare between 'states' or peoples.[111] And, wherever we first catch a glimpse of complex sociopolitical economic order we see a world with 'an already developed hideous inequality'.[112] No pre-modern complex political society was an exception, and we know that political philosophy first arose in complex societies. From the beginning political philosophy rested on the assumption that there could be no complex but classless sociopolitical economic system. Although modern political thought seems to have discarded the 'homo hierarchicus,'[113] the assumption that any complex political society presupposes differentiated sociopolitical and economic classes is imbricated in modern political thought;[114] comparative analysis of contemporary complex political societies confirms it.[115] It is the metaphysics of political conservatism.

C.S. Lewis once remarked that 'it is usually theologians, philosophers and politicians who become historicists.'[116] The historicist path leads a philosopher 'to adjust his innovations as much as possible to the ancient fabric'.[117] We have repeatedly pointed out that Locke's political theory stands at the head of modern liberal political thought. Whether or not Locke's philosophical treatise was a preface rather than a postscript to the Glorious Revolution in 1688 or meant to educate a new king,[118] neither the theory it expounded nor the revolution it rationalized was intended to rupture the extant sociopolitical and economic structure. As Edmund Burke puts it, in his appeal to the Old Whigs, what transpired in 1688 was not a *complete* revolution. Of course, Burke, the chaperon of Whig oligarchy rather than Locke, the revolutionary Whig political theorist, is the patron of modern political conservatism.

The thread of modern political conservatism can be traced briefly. It was Hume's empiricism that roused Immanuel Kant from his 'dogmatic slumber'. Likewise it was Hume who opened Bentham's eyes. Now, Hume himself did say that his views of things were more conformable to revolutionary Whig principles, and his representation of persons conformable to Tory prejudices.[119] Hume had ransacked the whole of Europe and found that the cause of the frequent disorders in ancient governments, namely, the extreme love of liberty and, particularly, 'the great difficulty of establishing any aristocracy' had been removed. 'At present', Hume wrote, 'there is not a republic in Europe that is not remarkable for justice, lenity and stability, equal to, or even beyond … the most celebrated in antiquity. Almost all of them are well-tempered Aristocracies.'[120] The unity of the ruling aristocracies having been established, nothing remained but to nurture the existing sociopolitical structures. And, nurture it they did.[121] As Alfred Cobban[122] points out, Hume had had no particular desire to reform anything; rather, he showed that there was no incompatibility between devotion to the pursuit of one's socioeconomic interests and a completely conservative political outlook.

Political theorists who came after Hume, including the utilitarians, imbibed this neo-classical, 'new' Whig realism. (Incidentally, Rawls finds that Hume did not differ from Locke).[123] Yet, Locke had been a reformer. But, like many a reformer, Locke had taken care 'to prevent any future reformation'[124] by anchoring his conclusions on nature. When Locke's successors frankly discarded 'the state of nature' and 'the social contract', they realized and openly acknowledged (as the ancients had done before them) 'the indispensability of tradition'[125] for political philosophy. With the post-Enlightenment rejection of rationalistic interpretation of modern natural rights thesis and the explicit substitution of tradition, the historical premise boldly came to the surface. Consequently, political thinkers increasingly grounded themselves on history – a trend that culminated in descriptive theories of law and politics to which we alluded at the beginning of this chapter. In short, 'liberty,' 'freedom', 'equality,' etc, had restrictive meaning within the framework of even revolutionary modern liberal political thinkers.

When the rights-based liberal political philosophers of our own time are professedly antiutilitarian, and when they charge utilitarians with conflating the diverse desires and ends of plural individuals, it is appropriate to ask: which or whose diverse desires did the utilitarians aggregate? The answer, I suggest, is that the utilitarians combined the desires of the plural members of the same sociopolitical and economic class: the middle class of the late eighteenth and early nineteenth centuries. This gave them 'the greatest number.' The promotion of the 'greatest happiness of the greatest number' was the utilitarian abacus' answer to the question, 'what is the end of government?' However that may be, and this is the crux of the matter, utilitarians not only equated the ends and desires of that 'greatest number' with the desires and ends of all, but they also assumed that 'the greatest number' of the late eighteenth and early nineteenth centuries would remain unchanged. As

Mill's critics have been quick to point out, utilitarians committed the 'fallacy of composition.'[126]

This somewhat static conception of the 'greatest number' and the equation of the convergent desires of individual members of the same sociopolitical and economic class with the desires of all, coupled with the deployment of political institutions in its service inevitably resulted in the suppression and loss of freedom by members of the subsequent 'greatest number'. In rejecting philosophical contractarianism it was as if historicists and utilitarians dynamited the bridge after the river had been crossed.

Like its theological antecessors, modern individualism rests on equality, and equality was as much the basis of pre-modern natural law[127] thought as it was the theoretical foundation of modern liberalism. As already noted, however, from a historical point of view, 'aristocracy' has always been the mainspring of the practice of freedom. Modern liberal polities that have always been 'socially, economically, politically and mentally an aristocratic country'[128] tempered democracy with the aristocratic tradition. The ethic of care of the aristocratic tradition partly paved the way for the welfare state, but afterwards they became least perturbed by sociopolitical and economic inequities. In contrast, modern liberal polities that were born equal rather than being made equal (to use Tocqueville's words) were not put to the test until gaping sociopolitical and economic inequities arose.

To condone manifestly appalling social and economic conditions of theoretically equal individuals requires a great deal of indoctrination, euphemistically called 'education'. And, what could better salve the conscience than the assurance that the basic structure of existing political systems rests more or less on immutable or rational foundation? This explains at one and the same time the unpopularity of utilitarianism (with its formal denial of 'natural right') and the interpretive retreat by contemporary modern liberal political philosophers (with their emphasis on tradition and 'our shared understandings'). It also explains the flagrant revival and popularity in contemporary times of old liberalism with its whitewashed and thinly disguised notion of the necessarily hierarchical character of political society.[129]

The socioeconomic ramifications of a political theory are helpful measure of its relevance to concrete problems. But it cannot be over-emphasized that the postulates of any political theory, however novel or great, are dictated by the problems it was fashioned to combat or the circumstances to which it was reacting. Modern natural rights theories arose as a reaction to the pretence to absolute powers by princes and priests. To preserve recognized principles of right, modern liberal political theorists traced the origins (and limits) of government; they asserted the rights of the 'individual' *against* the 'state'. Rights limit governmental powers: the individual has the right to life, liberty, and estate untrammeled by restrictions except to the extent necessary to assure the same to others. The utilitarian retorts: the purpose of political power (government) is the promotion of the greatest happiness of the greatest number unconstrained by individual rights except to the extent that they conduce to the principle of utility.

Like any other dichotomy, the opposition between 'rights' and 'utility' should be taken with more than a pinch of salt. The utilitarian achieved through a practical method what Locke and Kant did through the metaphysical and logical methods respectively. For the ends and desires of Kant's noumenal being correspond with the ends and desires of the individual in Locke's 'state of nature'. And, it was the positive world outlook projected by the creature in the noumenal universe that shaped and determined the ends of society that utilitarianism pursued. It is, therefore, a case of the pot calling the kettle black when the deontological writer indicts the utilitarian for dealing with only 'first order desires' and for ignoring man's 'capacity for reflective self-evaluation that is manifested in the formation of 'second-order desires'.[130] The point here is that there is an elective affinity between Locke's or Kant's individual and utilitarianism. Put differently, the Kantian self can not exercise the capacity for reflective self-evaluation unconstrained by the sociopolitical milieu in which it was conceived, born, and reared. This makes it difficult for neo-Lockean and neo-Kantian rights-based theorists to come into grips with the concrete sociopolitical and economic problems of a different world – an industrialized and politically democratic world in which there is not simply minorities but very visible minorities, and an impoverished 'south'.

When Kant reconstructed the modern natural rights thesis he modeled his thought after the logic of the world captured by Newtonian physics. Yet Kant could not and did not round off a Newtonian moral universe,[131] for, once it is apparently denuded by its own method of the Lockean substance, Kant's logical reconstruction of modern natural rights gives 'the impression of being oddly without content, as if hanging in the air.'[132] One is reminded of Kelsen's 'pure theory of law'[133] which Harold Laski[134] roundly declared as an exercise in logic, not life. Since Kant's liberal idealism was immersed in 'logicism', any liberal political theory that takes its source from Kant's logical reconstruction of the modern natural rights thesis will be infected with its atavistic defects. Indeed, for Rawls, 'the parties in the original position are *theoretically* defined individuals.'[135] Moreover, although Kant rejects 'all prerogatives of birth and class, and traces all hereditary privilege to some violent conquest in the past and calls for equality of opportunity for the development and application of ability',[136] he 'expressly attacks the *idea* of the 'welfare state''.[137]

Kant's understanding[138] of the 'welfare state' was fundamentally different from its present meaning, for he wrote in an age in which the 'welfare state' was synonymous with the paternalistic political order favoured by the philosophical position against which he and other modern liberal political theorists reacted. Nevertheless, the anti-welfarist foundation of Kant's liberal idealism explains why recrudescences of Kant's liberal political theory are basically anti-welfarist. Similarly, lucubrations of Locke's political theory cannot but be anti- and non-welfarist. Both lack the substratum upon which welfarist programs can rest. Indeed, the modern welfare state rests on neo-Hegellian political ideal.[139] It is because neo-Lockean or neo-Kantian political theory is steeped neck-deep in the logic of its own premises that objections to its conclusions would not bite.

It may well be true, as Rawls asserts,[140] that political philosophy 'must be free to use contingent assumptions and general facts as it pleases.' It is equally true, however, that once this is done, political philosophers are no longer at liberty; rather, they think only as they could.[141] Nor are they likely to start from contingent assumptions and general facts that they find unappealing or unfamiliar.[142] This aesthetics ensures the coherence of the resultant sociological dream, but it does not suffice to guarantee the eternal justice of the social, economic, and political practices it underwrites. John Austin noted that Locke had expressed the hope that when the jar of the controversy that attended the results and conclusions reached by the modern adepts in political philosophy would have subsided, a body of principles that the multitude would trust would emerge. He added that the result of such a 'mark of trustworthiness' would be that their successors would be 'debarred the opportunity of examining the evidence [them]selves.'[143] A corollary of this, as Tocqueville found out in antebellum America – a period recently described by one scholar as a kind of pre-democratic hell for visible minorities and their sympathizers[144] - would be a hallowed measure of homogeneity that would foreclose differences of opinion. Consequently, any demand for demonstration of the truth of their first principles could be met with Aristotle's[145] retort that such demands betray lack of education. Contemporary modern liberalism bids us submit to the 'dominant regimes of truth'[146] by appealing to the logic of its own theoretical premises! The dominant regimes of truth themselves wallow in 'congealed history'[147] that, in turn, rests ultimately on 'the glory myth.'[148]

At the beginning of the modern period, the adepts in political philosophy closely observed the behavioral patterns of men in their own immediate circle in their own immediate society. They found that competition, self-centeredness, and acquisitiveness characterized men's actions. They then concluded that that was as much natural as the movement of the earth. Hence, they formulated first principles of political justice that captured the observational data. They did not stop there. They decreed that thenceforth everyone should behave conformably with the rules logically deduced from the principles dictated by the established construct.

It is precisely because Kant's liberal idealism encapsulates the principles of the modern natural rights theories that accounts for the apparent appositeness of neo-Kantian rights-based approach. But it is well to reiterate that the individual of the modern natural rights theorists was what Rousseau derisively called the 'bourgeoisie.' This ideological characterization sanctions the solecism that Locke expounded, and Kant rationalized, the bourgeois view of life.[149] Whatever may be said for or against that characterization, the Lockean person occupied the Kantian noumenal world. The same individual was the sovereign in Adam Smith's economic system in which the economic onslaughts of the individual move untrammeled in a market patronized by equally egocentric individuals. Economic liberty was a crucial aspect of the right to life, liberty, and estate. As such, it was not open to the State to fetter it; rather, the duty of the state was to ensure its fulfillment. Thus, just as Locke wrestled political philosophy from the stranglehold of princes and priests, Smith emancipated political economics from politics and religion.[150] Unlike his successors, however, Smith did not theorize with the construct known as the 'economic man'.[151] If he had any notion of the 'economic man', Smith's catholicity prevented him from sending such a creature 'into the streets like a man of flesh and blood to make laws for his fellow men'.[152] Moreover, in the eighteenth century speculative reasoning led to the conclusion that in the pursuit of one's own private interests, the individual would of necessity, indirectly and effectively, promote the public interest. There was thus a considerable measure of agreement on the end of political society: the pursuit of individual interests.

As already noted, historicists and utilitarians rejected the substratum for this agreement – the state of nature and the social contract. As Bentham emphatically puts it, 'the indestructible prerogatives of mankind need not be supported on the sandy foundation of a fiction.'[153] Again, as we have seen, Bentham took the agreement as to the end of political society as clay and malled it into the now familiar idea of the promotion of the 'greatest happiness of the greatest number'. As already noted, like most other great thinkers, Bentham did not transcend the age and time for which he wrote. To him, 'the community was a fictitious body, composed of the individual persons who are considered as constituting as it were its members'. It followed that the interest of the community was merely 'the sum of the interests of the several members who compose it.'[154] Add to this the identification, by theorists of the Enlightenment, of the majority with the 'community' such that 'the majority was the community',[155] and you get Tocqueville's 'tyranny of the majority', or what Acton called 'the supremacy of numbers'. What is more, 'the community' was equated with the 'state', and both in theory and practice, 'the majority' was identified with the 'state'. This culminated in the doctrine of 'popular sovereignty',[156] - a legerdemain that obscured the fusion of the negative with the positive conception of liberty. Thus did modern political philosophy engender liberal political institutional practices that shade imperceptibly into a majoritarian construct.

At this juncture, let us step back from the concession that Locke and Kant were *tout court* spokesmen for a particular economic view of life. It is one thing to historicize or ideologize Locke and Kant, it is quite another to overlook their modernity. Specifically, if it is misleading to see Locke as a historicist, it is doubly so to see Kant as a mere empiricist who rationalized the worldview of the denizens of Locke's state of nature. We noted earlier that, from its inception, political philosophy presupposed the existence of differentiated sociopolitical and economic classes. While old liberalism posits naturally fixed sociopolitical and economic classes, Hume-inspired political conservatism, reinforced by the reaction to the French Revolution, posits historically determined sociopolitical and economic classes. One of the fundamental differences between old liberalism and Hume-inspired political conservatism on the one hand, and the social contract doctrine on the other, is that the latter denies the fixity of sociopolitical and economic classes. In other words, if we discount the undeniably conservative origins of modern natural rights theory, we might discern its dynamic quality. Unfortunately, the historicist outlook that emerged in the eighteenth century and which was accentuated by the reaction to the French Revolution quickly overshadowed social contract theory. The historicist orientation cascaded into the analytic or general theoretic mould in the nineteenth century. Coupled with the anti-

Enlightenment orientation of post-Revolutionary political thinkers of all stripes,[157] political philosophy has stifled the dynamic quality of philosophical contractarianism. The eclipse of the Enlightenment was the demise of the reformatory power of modern liberalism.

The Archimedian points of modern liberalism are the idea of free and equal individuals, and the negative conception of liberty. The obsession with highly pulverized society and the egocentrism embedded in its individualism are its Achilles heels. It is here that a spectator might suggest to participants in 'the conversation of the West'[158] that it might be worthwhile eavesdropping at other political cultural conversations.[159] Pre-modern political cultures generally recognize a duty of care for all members of the commonwealth.[160] Indeed, modern liberal welfare programs would be inconceivable but for sediments of such moral outlook embedded in the political conversation and culture of the West. Its explicit integration into contemporary liberal conversation of justice will facilitate a synthesis rather than a symbiotic development of rights. It would enable us to see that 'public assistance ... is not mere charity, but a means to promote the general welfare, and secure the blessings of liberty to ourselves and our posterity.'[161] As Sandra Harding puts it, 'justice, the goal of the rights orientation need not be uncaring, and caring need not be unfair; rather they are complementary.'[162]

As perceived by some contemporary advocates of modern liberalism, the most pressing political problem is the burgeoning power of the society as personified in the state vis-à-vis the individual. It is not unknown, however, that social and economic malaise frequently masquerades as political problems. Since politics has been for long the handmaiden of economics, a formal approach to what is at bottom social and economic problems will leave the problems themselves untouched. Modern liberal political philosophy introduced and limited rationalism into law and politics; it articulated sound philosophical principles for new local practices. But the Crusoean cast of its premises remolded morality so much so that individual misfortune was not viewed with concern. On the contrary, poverty began to be seen as a mark of low or lack of intelligence. Aided and abetted by biological theory, men started talking seriously about the betterment of the race by selective breeding – eugenics. That was just only a step short of Nazi genocide. Political upheavals orchestrated by 'lower' sociopolitical and economic classes, and spearheaded by 'intellectuals,'[163] initially met stiff opposition and ruthless repression.[164] Ultimately, however, the liberal conscience awoke from its dogmatic slumber; hence the modern welfare state.

For some time, normalcy was restored, and some liberal scholars enthusiastically proclaimed the 'end of ideology'.[165] Apparently, the modern welfare state can no longer sustain the weight it was designed to bear without at one and the same time trampling on the *perfect* rights of those who have and the *imperfect* rights[166] of the beneficiaries of the eleemosynary programs of the welfare state. It is within this context, and against the background of the partition of society into two opposing sociopolitical and economic classes – the owners of capital and the owners of labor - that contemporary rights-based theorists like Rawls, Nozick, and Dworkin – despite the differences between and among them – speak for modern liberalism. We are not oblivious of the hazards of ideological characterization of political philosophers. But, it is not inaccurate to say that Nozick raises his pen for the owners of capital only. Rawls is a modern welfarist, and so he speaks to both capital and labor while Dworkin recalls the empirical metaphysical concept of 'natural' rights and insists on giving it an egalitarian interpretation. In short, we are thrust with the conceptual problems that accumulated over more than two hundred years since the birth of modern liberalism.

Contemporary advocates of old liberalism believe that the cause of these problems was the Enlightenment's goal to liberate individuals from the thralls of tradition and history. They perceive the magnitude of the damage done by contractarian subversion of what we earlier called 'the metaphysics of political conservatism'. They asseverate that the denial of the fixity of sociopolitical and economic classes or the attempt to dispense with tradition and history was a promise of 'universal emancipation'[167] that the Enlightenment failed to deliver; and that the remedy is to return to the republican or communitarian ideal of old liberalism. In my view, the real culprit is *conventional* modern liberalism that seems to uphold 'pleasure without happiness.'[168] The successive novelists of modern liberal political philosophy (to use Dworkin's literary analogy[169]) have been enamoured with the furtherance and preservation of the life and liberty of estate to the prejudice of the other two constants of the natural rights theory.. The other pillars of modern liberal political philosophy have fallen into decrepitude through neglect thus impoverishing modern liberalism. As one commentator succinctly puts it, 'the nucleus of eighteenth and nineteenth centuries civilization in Europe and America has been largely disintegrated by discontinuations of its sociopolitical and intellectual humanized traditions.'[170] Libertarians allege that contemporary egalitarian liberal theorists like Dworkin and Rawls corrode rather than fortify modern liberal political philosophy.[171] Yet, neither libertarians nor egalitarians transcend the precepts of the founders of modern liberal political philosophy. Whether we call neo-Kantian rights-based theories 'deontology with a human face',[172] or 'naturalism',[173] and J.S. Mill's version of modern liberalism 'utilitarianism with a human face',[174] they are all intellectually situated in the eighteenth century – a century which modern historians say was the most classical-minded of all modern centuries.[175]

The precepts of the modern natural rights theorists were their own conclusions. Is it philosophy to make those conclusions our own premises, or, to make them our own conclusions? In either case, we would end up making this world look pretty much like Alice's strange country where it takes all the running one could do in order to keep in the same place. It is hard to explain how a twentieth-century modern liberal theorist like John Rawls started out on a pilgrimage with persons behind an imaginary veil of ignorance, and yet arrived at the twentieth century; the journey ending, as it were, at its starting point. The smell of what Etienne Gilson calls 'mathematicism' and 'logicism' permeates the whole stage. As Michael Sandel implies, there is only one single (and one should hasten to add) male Teutonic figure in the deontological universe. This is the new 'Zeus'. Like the Olympian of old, it would not tolerate any Prometheus. Hence, the post-modern 'hermeneutics of suspicion' which recommends 'perpetual watchfulness over the purveyors of schemes' for 'universal emancipation and enlightenment'.[176] The first task for contemporary modern liberalism is to find the ways and means to make the Crusoe in the noumenal universe take aboard fellow creatures.

Contemporary modern liberalism solves that problem by avoiding it. It simply denies that there is a problem for solution. In Dworkin's view, all we need do is for our political institutions to accord everyone 'equal respect and concern.' In Rawls' account, we only need to formulate principles that would not, at least, exarcebate the sociopolitical and economic position of the worst off. In Nozick's views, we only need to return to the so-called nightwatchman state of the nineteenth century. Closing his eyes to the fact that 'economics is a science which is above morality, a science where ethical good may even be an economic evil,'[177] Posner attacks with high intellectual vigor and a virulent pen what he calls 'conventionalism' in legal theory. Like his brilliant colleagues at Chicago,[178] Posner wants to see 'law's empire' invaded by 'wealth maximization', which is, in his own words, and in spite of initial protests to the contrary, 'practical utilitarianism.'[179] Fredrick Hayek's retort is that 'the only common values of an open and free society are not concrete objects to be achieved, but only those common abstract rules of conduct that secured the constant maintenance of an equally abstract order which merely assured to the individual ends but gave him no claims to particular things'.[180] What would Sir Edward Coke, who Hayek himself described as 'the great fountain of Whig principles'[181] in pre-revolutionary England or John Locke, the Whig political theorist who exerted as much influence in post-revolutionary England as he did in revolutionary America, say about Hayek's self-sustaining 'abstract order'?

The broad difference between a libertarian like Nozick, a neo-classical libertarian like Hayek, and liberal welfarist like Rawls or Dworkin's egalitarian liberalism on the one hand, and, on the other, old liberals like Strauss, MacIntyre, and communitarians generally, approximates to Isaiah Berlin's distinction between 'negative' and 'positive' conceptions of liberty. J.S. Mill is a Janus-headed liberal. Like Rousseau, both old and modern liberals can press Mill into service. As a modern, and because he was firmly convinced that the peoples of Western Europe (except the Irish) were already civilized, Mill recognized and insisted on the distinction between the 'private' and the 'public' spheres. In this regard, Mill differed from old liberalism. So Mill defended 'negative' liberty. Since economic pursuits fell within the private sphere, Mill professed, by and large, laissez faire political economy. However, the streak of old liberalism in Mill compelled him to cast his lot for pre-modern political theory, that is, rule (or, as he puts it, guidance) 'by a more highly gifted and instructed one or few.'[182] In other words, under the banner of utilitarianism, Mill smuggled into the private sphere modern liberalism, and in the public sphere he incorporated old liberalism. Nonetheless, because Mill was a modern, the scope for authoritarianism in the public sphere was greatly reduced. No matter how difficult it might be to draw the line between the private and public spheres, Mill here also differed from old liberalism. Mill's Janus-headed stature explains the seemingly confounding principles he enunciated in *On Liberty.*[183]

The leading proponent of economic analysis of law, Richard Posner, fastens his horse to the chariot of Adam Smith and Fredrick Hayek. We have already described Hayek as a neo-classical libertarian. In order to classify Posner we need to characterize Smith. Although Smith rejected the social contract theory, he was neither a historicist nor a utilitarian. Rather, he deployed the historiographical hypothesis called 'stadial' or 'conjectural' history that furnished 'the four-stage theory of development of societies.'[184] Smith postulated that every society passes through four ages: Hunting, Pastoral, Agricultural, and Commercial. England was in the Commercial (final?) stage in Smith's time. In short,

Smith wrote for a pre-industrial society. Although he was skeptical about merchants qua merchants,[185] Smith discerned that individual freedom is the 'rational moral basis of liberal society,'[186] and he almost single-handedly formulated the principles of a market economy. In short, as a political *economist,* Smith was a thorough modern, but as a political *philosopher*, he was a neo-classical libertarian.[187] It seems, therefore, that Posner uses Smith and Hayek as a peg on which to hang 'wealth maximization' and implicitly accepts the neo-classical libertarian assumptions of the latter: economics and neo-classical libertarianism go hand in hand. And, without a veneer of traditional morality, neo-classical libertarianism culminates in Nozickian callousness and Posnerian 'outrageous pragmatism.'[188]

Since the classical economists – Smith, Mill, Ricardo – to mention a few, and modern economists like Hayek, and now Posner were applying modern liberalism in the economic field, and since (ideologically) Locke crystallized and Kant rationalized the same economic view, contemporary advocates of modern liberalism converge in defending the abstract form assumed by modern sociopolitical and economic order. Yet, that idealism rests on ethics, for the foundation of the wealth of nations is 'individual human freedom'.[189] They disagree profoundly on whether (and if so, to what extent) public power should and could be allowed to tinker with the established institutional structures and practices for the purpose of effecting 'social' and 'economic' justice. Rawls would permit governmental interference provided it would not lead to killing the goose that lays the golden eggs. Dworkin would say that 'efficiency' could sit at the boardroom – stay where it belongs - but that it has nothing to do with rights. The questions of 'social' and 'economic' justice hardly enter into Nozick's brand of modern liberalism. This is also true about 'wealth maximizers' and, to a very large extent, devotees of the 'free society'. Thus, long after the movement of peoples, the industrial revolution, technological advancement, and two world wars have radically altered the contours of modern liberal constitutional polities, the tenets of the market impedes the political thought of many contemporary modern liberal theorists. It is a sad commentary that economics drives a wedge between modern liberalism and equity and humanity.[190] The abstract form assumed by the existing sociopolitical and economic order is the metaphysics of contemporary modern liberal theorists.

Why is philosophy, adversity's sweet milk as Shakespeare called it, so insipid? It is because of the working but unarticulated belief that the abstract form assumed by modern sociopolitical and economic institutional structures are immutable. This belief might be false. To put it starkly, contemporary modern liberal theorists have substituted one hypothesis with another presupposition. There is, perhaps, 'no society, history or civilization as such which affords a transcendent universal.'[191] At any rate, 'in social evolution nothing is inevitable but thinking makes it so.'[192]

Neo-classical libertarians are wont to emphasize the impossibility of reaching consensus on values. For instance, in *The Road to Serfdom*, Hayek was not shocked at the fact that those with higher education are unable 'to agree on a particular hierarchy of values.' Instead, Hayek saw it as a thing to be lauded. He inveighed against the majority of the people, who, according to Hayek, occupy 'the regions of lower moral and intellectual standards', among whom only could be found a 'high degree of uniformity and similarity of outlook'. Yet it did not seem to have occurred to Hayek that, but for a high degree of uniformity and similarity of outlook of Locke, Hume, Smith, and others, the modern world may not have known individual human freedom and all that it entails. Again, Hayek professes that 'we have learned that knowledge cannot create new ethical values,' and 'that no amount of learning will lead people to hold the same views on moral issues'. The latter part of this claim may well be empirically true, for learning is apt to dichotomize humanity and polarize society. In particular, learning tends to make the learned impervious to the likelihood that talent, intelligence, genius (or what not) is neither a property of a 'race', 'class' or gender nor (without going to the other extreme that it is morally irrelevant) is it, strictly speaking, a matter of desert. But the first part of the claim may not be true at all, for the ethical basis of liberal society, individual human freedom, enunciated by modern liberal political philosophers was fostered by learning. It was when, forgetting that statistics and economics did not deal with values *qua* values, and when ethical questions were considered settled[193] such that liberal scholars believed that 'the man of the future is the man of statistics and the master of economics,'[194] that modern liberalism came to be overseen by statisticians and (pure) economists. As a result, mathematics replaced ethics, and statistical aggregates replaced the individual human personality. However, the early economists were not simply infatuated with numbers. Rather, they were practical men who discerned the invigorating quality of the competitive spirit on the human condition.[195] It is therefore not surprising that, to them, any form of governmental interference that could hinder competition was anathema; that was the kernel of the economic dogma of laissez-faire. The economic dogma of laissez-faire invaded law and politics in the nineteenth century; it found its clearest expression in legal treatise in Dicey's *Introduction to the Study of the Law of the Constitution*, and in judicial decision in *Lockner v. U.S.*[196]

Contemporary modern liberalism blinds itself to the moral challenges of its own day. And, the division of political theorists into two broad camps - the left and the right - has had and continues to have the peccant effect of provoking heterodoxy from either camp. As Neil MacCormick puts it,[197]

> the great heresy of the political right wing is to pretend that there are no liberties which compete with economic fairness, and the more that heresy is pressed ... the more it generates a counter-heresy of the left: that a concern for liberty in any aspect is merely a manifestation of bourgeois ideology fit to be swept away with all else therein.

But, of course, just as 'we walk right foot, left foot, not right foot, wrong foot',[198] we know that 'there are sins on the right as well as on the left.'[199]

The individual ought to be free to choose his ends, and be at liberty to pursue those ends to the utmost limits. Likewise, the 'state' should be free to determine its own ends, and be free to strive to accomplish the set goals. However, neither the individual nor the State can be absolutely free for 'freedom itself is never free;'[200] it is always freedom *within* and *under* the *Law*. The manifestation of individual aspirations and ends can only be accomplished in society, and the society is a conglomeration of individuals. Nonetheless, as Aristotle[201] pointed out long ago, human beings living in society are not a herd of cattle that happens to share pasture. In other words, law, right, and equity should constrain both the individual and the State. But, in our own time,

> Those who attempt to discuss values as values typically follow ancient tradition, formed in pre-liberal society; they hardly come to grips with the problems of modern democracy. The value theorists shirk the responsibility of understanding the economic order, in theory or as it works in reality and rarely indeed seriously try to understand both systems of organization ... lucubration about values in the abstract, building on ancient tradition sheds little light on current problems arising out of freedom, [and] tends more to promote controversy than to establish agreement among the disputants themselves.[202]

The State is not synonymous with society:

> A society is a community of human beings who seek to fulfil the general purposes of human life in all its aspects. A state is an association of the

> same beings in legal form for the specific purpose of regulating life, in the sphere of external action, by rules designed to secure the minimum friction between its members and the maximum of their development.[203]

The dichotomy created and maintained by contemporary modern liberal theorists between neo-Kantian and neo-Lockean political theories on the one hand, and utilitarianism on the other, is less important than the correlation between them. What is more, the distinction is sustained at the grave price of sweeping large chunks of the moral problems of our own time under the carpet. While utilitarianism and rights-based theories are not identical the affinity between them is so strong that they cannot be kept in watertight compartments. Besides, the world has not stood still since the birth of modern liberalism. As Kai Nielson reminds us, through conquest, domination and exploitation, people have been made worse off than they were before those relations were brought into place.[204] The 'liberal idea' has been transformed into liberal ideology: the word 'liberal' has been suffixed and become 'liberalism', and an ideal of freedom has become the idea of freedom itself. The upshot is a form of cultural intellectualism that purveys what can elevate any people as the unique possession of a 'superior people.'[205] From the point of view of 'the south', contemporary modern liberalism is really liberalicide. As it reposes in cultural theories of law and politics, contemporary modern liberalism leaves no room for comparative capacity to doubt and the attendant enlargement of intellectual horizon. It was the happy conjunction of such factors in an earlier age that enabled scholars in 'England's cultural provinces' to see and articulate non-ideological ways in which things could be different than they were at the homeland of modern liberal philosophy itself.[206] It is one of the paradoxes of intellectual history that the most outstanding scholar from 'the Athens of the north' – Adam Smith – and the American 'founding fathers' are almost always portrayed as ideological epigones by contemporary political scholars of diverse moral persuasions.[207]

(d) Equality, Race, and Liberalism

We saw above that equality is the theoretical foundation of modern liberal political philosophy. Now, the principal architects of modern liberal political philosophy constructed it for a particular society – the so-called civilized societies; it was utilized to brutalize the supposedly uncivilized and barbarous societies. Ironically, and *pace* contemporary modern liberalism and postmodernism, the same philosophical thought is a potential liberator of the whole of mankind. David Hume, for instance, was a self-confessed racist.[208] Like the juggernauts of Greco-Roman societies, neither Locke[209] nor Adam Smith was perturbed with the institution of modern slavery. Like many eighteenth century neo-classical scholars, Smith had no doubts that the spirit of Christianity was not opposed to slavery. In Smith's intellectual universe slavery was a permanent feature on the political terrain: 'the institution of slavery which has taken place in the beginning of every society,' Smith wrote, 'has hardly any possibility of being abolished.'[210] In Smith's theory of moral sentiments, then, the only moral sentiments Blacks could have would be that of slaves to slaves and slave masters. And, in his economic system, therefore, Blacks were no more than items of commerce. Although Immanuel Kant believed that he was philosophizing for all rational beings, he did not consider Africans as such rational creatures.[211] North American Whigs, men whose colonial experience enabled them to combine the interests of Tories with the opinions of Radicals,[212] were as racial minded as their brethren across the channels.[213] J.S. Mill was certain that Africans, Asians, and the Irish were uncivilized and barbarous. He, therefore, expressly excluded them from the purview of his 'very simple principle'; instead, he put them under 'benevolent despotism'. A.E. Freeman asserted that Darwin had left Blacks unfinished, and wanted Negroes in America slaughtered by Irish-Americans who would, in turn, be hanged for their crime.[214] Although there is no necessary connection between empiricism and racism,[215] Locke's epistemological theory has been deployed to reinforce and foster 'scientific' racism. It cannot be gainsaid that slavery, racism and racial prejudice as well as imperialism and colonialism mortified 'colored' peoples:[216] 'regardless of class, all white men were made honourable by slavery's disgrace of all black people.'[217]

The path of civilization is littered with the corpses of intellectual beliefs that were once thought to be irrefutable. 'The entire history of social improvement', writes J.S. Mill, 'has been a series of transitions by which one custom or institution after another, from being a supposed primary necessity of social existence, has passed into the rank of a universally stigmatised injustice and tyranny'.[218] And, Michael Polanyi[219] has pointed out that 'in the clash of intellectual passions each side must inevitably attack the opponent's person.' The fathers of modern liberal political philosophy were 'metaphysicians.' Whether he was catapulted into the state of nature as did Hobbes and Locke or depicted as a social atom as in Hume's empiricism or Adam Smith's economic system or erected in the noumenal universe as did Immanuel

Kant, the man they dealt with was not a universal man. Rather, it was an abstraction from a modern European moral, psychological, economic, and political person. It is that *persona* that determined the principle that rights-based theorists have recently resuscitated. It is that *persona* that determined the policy that utilitarianism prosecuted. It is that same *persona* that would opt for 'wealth maximization' either as the sole component of or a surrogate for value. The depiction of man in, and the particular report of, the supposed original state of mankind and world history brought by philosophers of the seventeenth and eighteenth centuries is one myth that looms large in the horizon. The time is long past for new playwrights.

One of the enduring legacies bequeathed to the modern world by Natural Law philosophy is the fundamental idea of the identity of the human race – an idea that is irrepressibly represented in the biblical poetic depiction of man as the image of God. In all historical epochs – Egyptian,[220] Babylonian, Greco-Roman and pre-modern – slavery was initiated by sheer might,[221] and then enforced and perpetuated by positive law. It was subsequently widely practiced and made an integral part of creation itself by theologians and an indispensable socioeconomic, political, and legal institution by philosophers and statesmen. When, in the sixteenth century of the Christian era, the unlicensed violence of European seafarers combined with the unsuspecting but nonetheless base venality of some African personalities,[222] the resultant infernal inhumanity of man to man lasted nearly four hundred years.[223] Through morbid distortion of cultural, literary, anthropological and historical evidence,[224] fuelled by one master passion over another, racism[225] became ingrained in European political thought and society.[226] This is also true about Near and Far Eastern society.[227] For the first time in modern history, the Nazi enactment of an ancient evil practice brought the horrendous implications of racism to the occidental world. It receded after the Second World War. But,

> today…the racist movement is attempting a very subtle come back. Stressing the problem of the standardization and leveling which modern life imposes on many people, it extols the right to be different, but this is only in order to go on immediately to extol inequality and even the barbaric societies of Antiquity.[228]

Put starkly, the second task for contemporary modern liberalism is: how to make the Crusoe in the noumenal universe take in not just fellow creatures but non-Teutonic humanity. The third task follows on the heels of the second. It is: how to make that Crusoe take in not just non-Teutonic humanity but 'colored' humanity. The attempt to provide answers to these questions by some contemporary political philosophers terminates in the concession that it *might* be that principles of political justice are local or culture-bound. In that case the best we can *do* is to jealously guard our political ideals and energetically protect the localities over which our political ideals hold sway. Instead of laying bare the wrongs wrought by past and continuing ethnocentric uses of reason, contemporary modern liberalism barely acknowledges the existence of 'the south' and presence of 'visible' minorities. Rather, it expresses preference for the culture of its own immediate society, and takes refuge in 'epistemic abstinence.'[229] It largely shuts its eyes to the sociopolitical and economic plights of minorities in liberal polities, and the teeming impoverished souls in the Third World. This is tantamount to abandoning the task of finding rational solutions to practical problems.[230]

Malthusians hypothesize that the ship of the world would sink if steps were taken to correct world economic imbalance. Nozick would have us believe that taxation is at par with forced labor. Rawls speaks of principles that would at least not sink further the 'worst off'. Unlike Rawls, the liberal theorists of the seventeenth and eighteenth centuries did not seek to perpetuate the sociopolitical institutional practices of their time; rather, they sought to reform them. Hence they fashioned the right to life, liberty and estate. To arrive at principles which would merely confirm the justice of the basic structure of the existing sociopolitical and economic institutional practices it was necessary that Rawls deconstruct (and then reconstruct) Kant's deontological reconstruction of modern natural rights thesis. Dworkin reposes in the distinction between 'concept' and 'conception' – a distinction that enables contemporary modern liberal theorists generally, and Dworkin particularly, to be at one and the same time cultural Platonists and practising Aristotleans – and he dichotomizes 'personal' and 'external' preferences. Yet, Dworkin fails to see that all the competing brands of contemporary modern liberalism are so many different interpretations of a particular conception of the concepts of equality and freedom. In spite of its contemporary purveyors, modern liberalism reeks with its originators' 'external preferences', especially racism.[231] It is difficult to see how a political culture and intellectual tradition whose concept of man was the so-called 'man pre-eminently so called,'[232] could have fostered national sociopolitical and economic institutional *practices* or planetary order that could accord 'equal respect and concern' to those who were presumptuously excluded from its orbit or be made to bend over backwards to achieve the same feat.[233]

Are contemporary modern liberals not troubled by the fact that the liberal democratic polities which possess freedom, wealth and power did so partly by subjugating and partly by exploiting and raping 'colored' peoples? Or, is it that the 'relatively leisured intellectuals, inhabiting a stable and prosperous part of the world' are so enchanted by their continual ability 'to say new and interesting things about'[234] the self-portrait of their immediate societies that they are enamoured to gloss over the appalling sociopolitical and economic conditions of many individuals at home and abroad? It may well be that 'no elite on earth has been without its victims.'[235] But that merely affirms a historical, not a rational fact. It is, of course, true that the elite produce political theories. However, unless philosophy is inherently ethnocentric, and even if it is a 'principle of human [masculine] nature to hate those whom one has injured,'[236] it will always be possible to recognize the individuality, the humanity, of others. As well, unless the modern world is a reincarnation of the Roman world which regarded plebeians as well as 'the rest of the world simply as an udder to be milked dry,'[237] it will always be possible to regard each and every individual and state as objects in their own right rather than as 'something to be made use of or exploited.'[238] The ethics of contemporary modern liberalism is determined less by history and tradition than by historicism and traditionalism. The newly established orthodoxy has dug a new and deeper 'graveyard of creativity.'[239]

In contradistinction from the liberal idea, liberalism requires only rhetoricians[240] while utilitarianism requires only technicians. Rhetoricians and technicians are neither trained to ask nor do they have the competence for answering moral questions. Specifically, both rights-based theories and utilitarianism postulate the same conception of equality and freedom. The institutionalized conception of equality and freedom did not include several classes of individuals in society: it excluded women, children, the majority of people who occupy 'the regions of lower moral and intellectual standard,'[241] and the whole of the Third World. The liberal idea, on the other hand, requires architects, that is, philosophers. Logic and rhetoric are the midwives, so to speak, which deliver philosophical pregnancy. When the same hand performs the roles of philosopher and logician or rhetorician the result is often stupendous. But when there are only logicians and rhetoricians, when the tools of the trade are taken for the trade itself, the trade atrophies. In vain do intellectual historians test the precepts of the founders of modern political philosophy for consistency. The fact is that 'the greatest thinkers are not strictly speaking consistent,' and perhaps 'would not be great if they were,' for, being pioneers, they were not constrained by the rules invented by their successors 'for the purpose of avoiding new ideas and hard problems.'[242] At all times, 'we have to get our food first before using logic to digest it,'[243] and rhetoric to pass it around.

I have suggested that there are only rhetoricians and technicians, that there are no architects or philosophers. Why is this so? The answer is simple. Fashions in intellectual discourse, like fashions in everyday life, move from the top downwards, but ideas arise from below and move upwards, and are then made fashionable after being entrenched. In the contemporary market-place of political philosophy, the dealers are neither those who, like Marx and others in the nineteenth century, are evaluating the actions of men at the top. Nor, are they those who, like Locke in the seventeenth century, are explaining or rationalizing the actions of 'revolutionary' men or like Kant and others in the eighteenth century, scholars exploring the logical implications of moral postulates. Rather, they are conventionalists like Hume who are analyzing, unifying, and explicating the practices of those already at the top.

Even so, rhetoricians and logicians, when they push aside their calling are by no means incompetent to philosophize. In a rare display of candor, one of the outstanding liberal scholars of the twentieth-century, J.M. Keynes (who was certainly not an economist for the underdog) penned the following lines:[244]

> When the accumulation of wealth is no longer of high social importance, there will be great changes in the code of morals. We shall be able to rid ourselves of many of the pseudo-moral principles which have hag-ridden us for two hundred years, by which we have exalted some of the most distasteful of human qualities into the position of the highest virtues. We shall be able to afford to dare to assess the money-motive at its true value ...All kinds of social customs and economic practices affecting the distribution of wealth and of economic rewards and penalties, which we now maintain at all costs, however distasteful and unjust they may be in themselves, because they are tremendously useful in promoting the accumulation of capital, we shall then be free, at last, to discard ... We shall once more value ends above means and prefer the good to the useful.

But, the rhetorician took the better part of the philosopher, for Lord Keynes immediately added:

> But ... the time for all this is not yet... we must pretend to ourselves and to everyone that fair is foul and foul is fair; for foul is useful and fair is not. Avarice and usury and precaution must be our gods for a little longer still.

If judged by the volume of literature that it has produced so far, contemporary modern liberalism is very rich indeed. But, as Shakespeare[245] says, words are least in themselves. Francis Bacon once wrote that it is futile to attempt 'to go beyond Aristotle by the light of Aristotle'. The founders of modern liberal political philosophy, who certainly did not include Bacon himself,[246] took that precept seriously, and so they badgered pre-modern political philosophy. And, while among several competing interpretations of a particular conception of a concept one may be superior to the others, it does not *ipso facto* mean that it meets head-on the moral challenges of the day. Nor should any theorist delude himself that his is the best, the last and ultimate truth,[247] for there is always the possibility of paradigm shift.[248] The fourth challenge for contemporary modern liberalism is how to refurbish the concept of freedom and equality without jettisoning our own 'ancient fabric.'

V

LIBERALISM, DEMOCRACY, AND SCHOLASTICISM

'O admirable Lysias! If only he would write that a poor man must be accepted before a rich one, and an old man before a young one, and so on, how that would hit the case for me and so many of us! There you will have urbane arguments, and utterances for the public welfare!'[249] Socrates uttered these words to his interlocutor (Phaedrus) after the latter had recited Lysias poem supporting the proposition that the non-lover was to be preferred to the lover. After some coyness, Socrates proceeded to show, in his characteristic manner, why the lover was to be preferred to the non-lover. By implication, Socrates showed that the old was preferable than the new or the poor man than the rich man. Needless to say, these are all figures of speech.

The most cursory look at the works of contemporary advocates of old liberalism will show that they conceptualize 'liberal democracy' as the political philosophy of aristocratic personalities. They are skeptical, to put it mildly, of 'liberal democracy' when it is construed as the political philosophy of democratic individuals.[250] We noted earlier that although the founders of modern liberal political philosophy would not have opted for democracy as a form of government, subsequent institutional developments have yoked modern liberalism with democracy. The question I want to ask, and quickly dispose of, is whether the contemporary modern liberal theorists' love for democracy is a pure or a utilitarian one.

The answer, I suggest, is that contemporary modern liberal theorists are paramours of democracy. Put differently, their love for democracy is not a pure but a utilitarian love. They serenade democracy not so much because they think that democracy is beautiful, but because they think that it is useful. In their scheme of things, democracy is not an end in itself. Rather, democracy is 'essentially a means, a utilitarian device for safeguarding internal peace and individual freedom.'[251] This utilitarian justification of democracy has deepened the coupling of modern liberalism and democracy. As was the case in classical antiquity, the coupling of liberalism with a form of government has turned the practice of freedom from a 'convergent' into a 'divergent' problem.[252] Predictably, it has also provoked uneasiness with democracy.[253] Moreover, having ceded the reformatory power of modern liberal political philosophy and embraced instead the abstract form assumed by the established sociopolitical and economic institutional practices, contemporary rights-based philosophers can only see and identify with the type of freedom and equality thrown up by the legal and political history with which they operate. This explains the paradox that contemporary modern liberalism rests 'upon a rightwing Hegelian view of social and legal history' as well as its concealed intellectual 'discomfort with democracy.'[254]

Contemporary old liberals decry modern liberalism, and they portray themselves as friends of the so-called lower sociopolitical class. The louder they shrill the more strident sounds the supposed enemies of this class; the more offensive contemporary old liberals become, the more defensive contemporary modern liberals turn. I hope to have shown, *sub silentio*, that old liberalism and Hume-inspired conservatism are not really friends of lower sociopolitical and economic classes. They love that class in the same sense that wolves love lambs, or, changing metaphors, masters love servants or slave-owners love slaves. As we have seen, the metaphysics of political conservatism is fatalistic; it presupposes not only that there are 'high' and 'low' but also that the 'high' and the 'low' are naturally and permanently so. But the 'respectably empirical metaphysics' which commits contemporary modern liberalism to the political institutional history of the last two hundred years or so constrains its ability to relieve the conditions of disadvantaged individuals within liberal polities, and to extend a hand to lift up 'the south.'

This is the crux of this chapter. The cloud of dust raised by the clash between contemporary advocates of 'old' and 'modern' liberalism is so thick that it obscures the fact that the really old but poor man and the young sprite but rich man – freedom and equality – are no longer in the foreground. Contemporary modern liberals are too earthbound. They scuttle into the caves dug by the founding fathers of modern liberalism. They peep from these holes. They are so pleased with the glimpses of freedom and equality they see that, like the lotus-eaters, they have lost all memory of, and desire to return to, the metaphysical base of political liberalism. The result is that they offer us traditional though 'modern' wisdom.

Contemporary advocates of old liberalism have the wings of an eagle, but lack the power of its sight. They consult the socratics. Unlike Socrates, however, they do not consult 'reason to see whether it chimes in,'[255] or, rather, they assume that reason chimed in long ago. They bring a scholastic disposition into political philosophy. They do not ask the immortal question, 'what is freedom and equality?' Rather, they ask the scholastic question, 'which conception of or books about freedom and equality should we believe, the ancients or the moderns?' They answer with a chorus, 'the ancients!' or, in hagiographical terms, 'the Founding Fathers'.[256] They forget that, like Ulysses, philosophy is hardly ever quiescent. Further, they overlook the irreproachable dictum that 'philosophy suffers no persuasion.'[257] In the end, they also offer us traditional albeit 'ancient' wisdom.

The 'ancients' steeped political philosophy in the life of the polis. In spite of all talks about the state of nature, Hobbes, Locke, and Rousseau took their flights from the phenomenal world. The crypto-historical state of nature outlined by the German Aristotle, Hegel, prevented him from being an Aristotlean, and the German Plato, Immanuel Kant, though platonic was not himself a Platonist; and Karl Marx boasted that he stood Hegel on his head! They all produced great books. The scholastic character of contemporary political philosophy that continually slabs gray on gray has turned political philosophy into morbid anatomy. This is one of the reasons why contemporary political philosophers hardly produce great books, for, like great fictions, 'great books are not distilled out of books, but out of life.'[258]

Confronted with the anarchy of English civil war, Thomas Hobbes seemingly introduced political absolutism with its concomitant passive obedience into the English-speaking world. John Locke, who moved in a political class that had a distinctive distaste for absolutism,[259] substituted limited government, only for absolutism to be restored by historicists/utilitarians. Ironically, absolutism reached its apotheosis in the logicism of Kant.[260] But it is well to remember that Kant's being emerged from the earth and was weaned in this world before it resorted to the recluse of the noumenal universe; it has resided therein ever since. It designed the 'is.' It is thus unaware of the present state of things here. It is high time it descended from the sky such that the foundation could be lowered once more. If Kant were to think in the present century, he would not regard himself a foe of established sociopolitical and economic institutions anymore than he regarded himself an enemy of the Prussian monarchy. But Kant would almost certainly do what he did when he first philosophized: he would reject all prerogatives of birth and class, trace all economic privilege to domination, conquest or exploitation in the past, and call for equality of opportunity for the development and application of ability.[261] He would still be averse to the paternalistic state.

In the final analysis we have to return to John Locke. 'The philosopher', wrote William James, 'must be a conservative'.[262] Of course, there are different kinds of conservative philosophers. Here, conservatism means ethical conservatism. This kind of conservative philosopher is neither the political theorist who constructs 'an ideology or a self-image'[263] of a tradition thereby shrugging off philosophy altogether. Nor is he or she a theorist who turns the internal point of view into philosophy. Realizing that 'the present is the only place in which men can dwell' such that 'it is unwise to shake its foundation,'[264] such a theorist would regard existing democratic political institutions as the 'ancient fabric,' but would jettison thralldom to the curious hybrid called 'empirical metaphysics'. In short, such a philosopher would not be a partisan of a particular constellation of political and economic interests. Rather, he or she would be a 'pure' philosopher, that is, one who 'never becomes one of the parties to the fray.'[265]

Locke's radical (not in the socialist sense) political principles were neither antithetical nor merely conservatory of seventeenth century sociopolitical institutional practices. In fact, Locke's imagination captured a state of nature in which the 'capacity to discover the moral law'[266] unclouded by passion, was intact. In contrast, historicists/utilitarians conceive the office of reason as that of servant to the passions, and they passionately recommend and concentrate on the propagation of *opinion* attuned to established sociopolitical and economic institutional practices.

If we succumb to the temptation to localize political philosophy, 'the ancients' would be seen as having elaborated a form of 'local knowledge.'[267] Likewise, we might say that 'the moderns' were not averse to singing ethnocentric songs, only that they insisted on rehearsing the most recently composed lyrics. That is, if 'the ancients' transcribed Greek coral songs into philosophical verses and the moderns did the same for what postmodernist liberals cavalierly misname 'Western eccentricity' then both old and modern liberal political philosophers represented what was essentially local as universal knowledge. That way of looking at the history of political philosophy has obvious interpretive, rhetorical, or epistemological advantages. But the nature of the art or science (take your pick) they practiced would elude us unless we concede that there might be more to political philosophy than the local practices – the spatio-temporal or cultural matrix – that produced it, and the text in which it is embodied. Specifically, if we imagine that political philosophers were precisely what some sociologists, anthropologists, and historians of ideas deny, namely, 'pure rationalists constructing a pure understanding in the sky,'[268] then we might be able to recover the primeval meaning of philosophy.

Originally, philosophy meant the quest for human understanding of phenomena, natural or moral. Methodologically, it entailed careful consideration of received opinions on and relentless analysis of the subject of inquiry free from presuppositions, prejudice, and scribal authority. The men of the Enlightenment recovered and practiced political philosophy the ancient style.[269] It was this that culminated in the rediscovery of the idea of individual freedom and equality – an idea that had been long paralyzed by the dogmatic political thought and theories fathered by the prodigious intellectual product of the socratics. Yet, in attacking modern liberalism, contemporary advocates of old liberalism identify with, and fondly invoke the authority of, the ancients who they portray as 'a galaxy of anti-democratic thinkers' committed 'to the proposition that all men are not created equal.'[270] But it is as much a mistake to associate 'freedom and equality' with a particular form of government as it is to insist that one's intellectual forebears found the final answers to the complex theoretical and practical problems involved in their interaction.

The 'interpretive turn'[271] in contemporary modern liberalism has mutilated the modern liberal song into subjective stanzas. Now, aside from the crucial fact that an 'interpretive enterprise can only articulate a paradigm, not correct it,'[272] it is one thing to deflate 'the conversation *of* mankind'[273] into a conversation *with* mankind, it is another for 'solidarity' with our conceptual self to displace the latter. Like an image, the conceptual self holds its devotees' understanding captive. As well, it is one thing for disinterested interest in the pursuit of truth within a paradigm to replace the noble dream of 'objectivity', it is quite another for the paradigmatic pursuit of truth to be replaced by loyalty of disparate intellectual tribal bands to an ideational self. Surely, such solidarity fosters cultural intellectualism and deadens the 'critical judgment.'[274] Must the dialogue metamorphose into monologues?

It is not helpful to proceed upon the assumption that what is important is not a particular set of rights that Locke and others thought essential,[275] for that is tantamount to saying that Locke's method cannot be put to new and fruitful use. Specifically, the proposal to abandon the ahistorical orientation of 'the moderns,' and instead to rivet political philosophy on our ethnos[276] would merely strengthen the belief that political philosophy is inevitably ethnocentric. As well, the question of right would continue to require the parties to wage agonizing battles in which the winner takes all while the worsted go home empty handed. Moreover, no matter how robust the new ethnocentric twig is made to be it will be just another form of ethnocentrism that will still enable Achaeans to dishonor 'strangers' in the corridors as in the days of Odysseus. There is, at least in so far as our planet is concerned, no more frontiers to be conquered, but there is, on our own planet, abundant psychological and intellectual frontiers to be explored.

Why is it difficult for contemporary modern liberalism to reform and weave into its own lattice a reconstituted right to life, liberty, and estate? The answer is not far to seek. Every intellectual age tends to have its imperial science. Economics is the imperial discipline of the human sciences in the twentieth century,[277] and its Leviathan ambitions have displaced ethics. The result is that, today, 'sophistication about history and politics avails little without sophistication about economics.'[278] In other words, economics shelters 'reason' but at the enormous price of castrating ethics; economics curtails rationalism in law and politics, and stifles all reformatory measures except those sanctioned directly or indirectly by its own precepts:

> Ethics seems dethroned and the emergence of the free human personality... has been rejected as an idea appropriate to 'the age of expansion' from sixteenth to the nineteenth centuries but inappropriate to our own. Economics reigns, having driven out ethics and notions of 'solidarity' or 'social utility' have expelled ... the old notion of the intrinsic value of human personality.[279]

To adapt Ernest Barker's words, the rights-based theorists of our own time should take the minted coin of the natural rights theorists in the form which it had attained after three centuries of circulation, reevaluate it, melt it down and stamp it with a new dye. Unless modern liberalism (which focuses on individual freedom) is against modern democracy (which focuses on equality) and vice versa, contemporary modern liberal political philosophy should break out of its self-imposed constraints. Modern liberalism should 'look beyond the smoke of its own chimneys' and endeavor to transform the sociopolitical and economic practices of our time. Each cannon shot hauled by a neo-Lockean or neo-Kantian against the utilitarian or the wealth-maximizing camp weakens its own foundation and vice versa. Each attacks its own theory under a different sobriquet. The present landscape is a replica of Mount Olympus – an assembly of jealous and contesting gods that take for granted the mythic order established and presided over by 'Zeus', and who are only marginally concerned with the wellbeing of ordinary mortals.

Contemporary advocates of modern liberalism have been asking the type of questions logicians and rhetoricians are particularly adept in tackling, namely, how to conserve the abstract form assumed by modern liberal constitutional sociopolitical and economic institutional practices. Flush out racism from the sinews of modern liberalism, and it would be impossible to utilize the freedom of expression to sanction matching through a predominantly Jewish town chanting Nazi cadences. Likewise, the so-called 'reverse discrimination' cases would be exposed for what they are – pure sophism. For, modern liberalism would then be recriminating with itself, and not discriminating, directly or indirectly, against anyone. Nor will there be the need to enlist the services of Hercules in order to uphold 'affirmative action' if actual sociopolitical institutional practices afford everyone equal opportunity for the development and application of ability. Of course, by the time these and more may have been done we would have a new concept of freedom and equality. That is a task for philosophy, not logic, rhetoric, or interpretation. It is a task that cannot be undertaken without first breaking lose from the precepts of seventeenth and eighteenth centuries political thought. As it has been well put, 'each age requires a philosophy of its own, and while it may learn from its predecessors, it can never take over its philosophy entire.'[280] To reformulate the concept of the right to life, liberty and estate, 'we must make for the open sea of fresh, unprejudiced, far-seeing thought ... remembering that, if they are in themselves the oldest objects of human action and human thought, the answers they ask for from us today are new.'[281] It is only if we are prepared to do this, if, that is, we are 'ready to look at life critically and analytically with no holds barred'[282] that we can hope to recover the core of liberal political philosophy. That core is 'the concept of the worth of persons within society as an end in itself, joined to the determination to shape social and political institutions to promote'[283] it.

The industrialized polities have so mastered the intricacies of political economy that they reflexively oscillate from principles appropriate for generating and strengthening domestic industrial growth to those suitable for operating at the international plane. Recognizing that there is nothing inherently conspiratorial in cooperation between business and government, they deploy skillful panoply of social, economic, and political measures to nurture industries capable of holding their own. At the international level, they extol the age-old virtue of commerce: free trade. The result is that the industrialized nations wield the price mechanism like a sledgehammer; they use it as an instrument for keeping the head of emergent states or 'the south' perpetually pinned down to the pillows, as the Japanese would put it. Indeed, the giant nations run 'the world economy as a zero-sum game.'[284] And, laissez faire exclusion ensures the continued and effective segregation of very visible minorities within many a liberal polity.[285]

Any political theory that stratifies, overtly or covertly, mankind or that arranges society hierarchically such that men and women are shunted into predetermined tracks and roles is not good enough. As David Spitz succinctly puts it, 'utopias of whatever kind are always rooted in a rigid authoritarian mold ... [they] are static societies, and men within them, frozen into higher and lower orders...' [286] It is what breeds 'sedition' in the minds of men and women. Aristotle[287] recognized this when he wrote:

> There are some who stir up sedition because their minds are filled by a passion for equality, which arises from their thinking that they have the worst of the bargain in spite of being the equals of those who have got the advantage. There are others who do it because their minds are filled with a passion for inequality (i.e. superiority), which arises from their conceiving that they get no advantage over others (but only an equal amount, or even a smaller amount) although they are really more than equal to others... Thus inferiors become revolutionaries in order to be equals, and equals in order to be superiors.

St. Augustine[288] said the same thing in a theological context:

> Remove justice and what are kingdoms but gangs of criminals on a large scale? What are criminal gangs but petty kingdom? A gang is a group of men under the command of a leader, bound by a compact of association, in which the plunder is divided according to an agreed convention. If this villainy wins so many recruits from the ranks of the demoralized that it

> acquires territory, establishes a base, captures cities and subdues peoples, it then openly arrogates to itself the title of kingdom, which is conferred on it in the eyes of the world, not by the renouncing of aggression but by the attainment of impunity. For it was a witty and truthful rejoinder which was given by a captured pirate to Alexander the Great. The king asked the fellow, 'What is your idea, in infesting the sea?' And the pirate answered, with uninhibited insolence, 'The same as yours, in infesting the earth! But because I do it with a tiny craft, I'm called a pirate: because you have a mighty navy, you're called an emperor'.

In this *Amarna* age of the modern world, the 'good professors' teaching the 'good students' in the 'good universities'[289] are afflicted by an old syndrome, namely, the scholastic 'assurance that reason and morality… had discovered the final answers to the mysteries of the universe' such that 'the teacher's responsibility to his students was to explain those answers and develop an appropriate humility before the altar of unalterable truth.'[290] It is puzzling that the civilization that has already mapped human genetic makeup has not been able to 'domesticate justice,'[291] such that after two thousand years, the theory of justice is still in a 'parlous state.'[292]

J.S. Mill's 'benevolent despot' bequeathed to 'the south' a nimbus of liberty shrouded in imperialism, and all too quickly eclipsed by colonialism. Those who look back to 'the ancients' are committed more to 'memorizing the politics of ancient history'[293] than in what 'the ancients' taught the world how to do. They deprecate and depreciate the lofty achievements of modern liberalism; they pour scorn on what they call the 'modern project.' But all they see in their crystal ball is a world in which (to use Shakespeare's words) men are cut like grandsires in alabaster: a state of natural inequality. Those who look back to 'the moderns' are wedded to the curious hybrid called 'empirical metaphysics.' They remain immobile in and are committed to rationalizing the conventional world. Yet, no matter how hard we strive to systematize an historically determined sociopolitical and economic structure by the time-honored method of rational reconstruction, the resultant ideals are no more than analytic judgments which go behind but not beyond the historical experience that supplied the furniture in its intellectual universe. Contemporary political theorists have set up the concepts embedded in particular forms of life as the structures of life itself. And so they draw the curtain on any attempt to transcend the limits of certain cultural experience. If political philosophy is committed at all, it is neither to the past or the present nor the future; rather, it is committed to the singular and endless pursuit of wisdom. This makes the function of moral philosophy that of synthesizing and constantly re-kneading values, including political values. Unfortunately, all that we hear is the old story of Tweedledee and Tweedledum: both old and modern liberal approaches terminate at the same point. Political philosophy has narrowed its interests 'to the discussion of problems of meaning,'[294] the study of political history, the explication of the political thought of 'the ancients' or 'the moderns'. It is the tragedy of living backwards. It is a double tragedy for 'the south,' for whether we look back to Europe or America, 'the south' generally, and Africa particularly, would be seen as an underdog.

We should be slow to impugn a political philosopher for failing to be ahead of his or her time. The philosophers' philosopher may well have been an authoritarian, and the ancient master of those who know may well have believed that slavery is the natural lot of some individuals. Hobbes may have shown us (in Rousseau's words) the human species divided into so many herds of cattle, each with its cattleherd, who fattens them for the singular purpose of devouring them. Locke may well have been (in Acton's phrase) 'a philosopher of government by the gentry'. Hume, Kant, (and Marx, Engels, and their disciples[295]) may well be racists. Adam Smith may be the modern master of those who know, but who 'converted the Chair of moral philosophy into a professorship for trade and finance.'[296] Bentham and the utilitarians may have been spokesmen for merchants and entrepreneurs. As well, Hegel may be the 'missing link' between old and modern totalitarianism. And, Karl Marx may well be 'the Red Prussian' who saw the industrial workers of the nineteenth century as 'the material weapon of philosophy.'[297] In short, while there may be more than one excuse for being 'ancients' or 'moderns' there is no reason whatsoever for being ancients or moderns in an age in which the light of human reason shines brighter than it has ever shone before. Or does it? It is said that the history of political philosophy must be Whig as to subject-matter but Tory as to truth.[298] That may well be so, as far as intellectual history goes. Nonetheless, there is something wrong about an intellectual orientation that sees the individual and society only through the lenses of these modern cultural intellectual reincarnations of the Socratics.

Notes

[1] Joseph Glanvill, *The Vanity of Dogmatizing: The Three Versions (1676)*, ed. S. Medcalf (Sussex: Harvester Press, 1970) III, 28.

[2] J. Rawls, *A Theory of Justice* (Cambridge, Mass: Harvard Univ. Press, 1971); J. Rawls, *Political Liberalism* (New York: Columbia Univ. Press, 1993)
[3] R. Dworkin, *Taking Rights Seriously* (Cambridge, Mass: Harvard Univ. Press, 1977), *A Matter of Principle* (Cambridge, Mass: Harvard Univ. Press, 1985); *Law's Empire* (Cambridge, Mass: Harvard Univ. Press, 1986); *Freedoms' Law: The Moral Reading of the American Constitution* (Cambridge, Mass.: Harvard Univ. Press, 1996)
[4] R. Nozick, *Anarchy, State and Utopia* (Oxford: Oxford Univ. Press, 1974)
[5] M.J. Sandel ed. *Liberalism and Its Critics*, (New York: New York Univ. Press, 1984). A broad division into the 'resistance' and 'revision' camps exists within the triumphant rights-based theorists. See, N.E. Simmonds, *The Decline of Juridical Reason: Doctrine and Theory in the Legal Order* (Manchester: Manchester Univ. Press, 1984) at 121ff. Stephen Macedo described the division as a split between adherents of libertarian and egalitarian (modern) liberalism: *The New Right v The Constitution* (Washington: Cato Institute, 1986) at 53 n.112.
[6] M.J. Sandel, *Liberalism and The Limits of Justice* (Cambridge Univ. Press, 1982); *Democracy's Discontent: America in Search of a Public Philosophy* (Cambridge, Mass.: Belknap Press, 1997).
[7] A. MacIntyre, *After Virtue* (Notre Dame: Univ. of Notre Dame Press, 1981); *Whose Reason? Whose Justice?* (Notre Dame: Univ. of Notre Dame Press, 1988)
[8] Leo Strauss, *Natural Right and History* (Chicago & London: Univ. of Chicago Press, 1953). And see, Allan Bloom, *The Closing of the American Mind* (New York: Simon & Schuster, 1987); Thomas L. Pangle, *The Spirit of Modern Republicanism: The Moral Vision of the American Founders and the Philosophy of Locke* (Chicago: Univ. of Chicago Press, 1988)
[9] Ecclesiastes 2:17
[10] I. Kant, 'On the Proverb: That May be True in Theory, But is of No Practical Use', (1793) in, *Perpetual Peace and Other Essays*, trans. T. Humphrey (Indianapolis: Hackett Publishing Co., 1983) at 73.
[11] See, e.g. J. Rawls, *A Theory of Justice*, supra note 2 at 587.
[12] Stanley Fish, *Doing What Comes Naturally: Change, Rhetoric, and the Practice of Theory in Literary and Legal Studies* (Duke Univ. Press, 1989) at 435.
[13] It is, therefore, based on omnibus sources. Nonetheless, I would like to mention Leo H. Craig, *The War Lover: A Study of Plato's Republic* (Toronto: Univ. of Toronto Press, 1994); Richard Tarnas, *The Passion of the Western Mind* (New York: Ballantine Books, 1991); Eric A. Havelock, *The Liberal Temper in Greek Politics* (New Haven: Yale Univ. Press, 1964); Eric A. Havelock, *The Greek Concept of Justice From Its Shadow in Homer to Its Substance in Plato* (Cambridge, Mass.: Harvard Univ. Press 1978); H.B. Parkes, *Gods and Men: The Origin of Western Culture* (New York: Alfred A. Knopf, 1959); Jacqueline de Romilly, *Thucydides and Athenian Imperialism* trans. Phillip Thody (Oxford: Basil Blackwell, 1963)

[14] On the sophists, see, generally, Harold Barrett, *The Sophists: Rhetoric, Democracy and Plato's Idea of Sophistry* (Novato, California: Chandler & Sharp Publishers, 1987) ; H.D.Rankin, *Sophists, Socratics and Cynics* (London & Totowa, New Jersey, 1983); G. B. Kerfeld, *The Sophistic Movement* (Cambridge: Cambridge Univ. Press, 1981); W.K.C. Guthrie, *The Sophists* (Cambridge: Cambridge Univ. Press, 1971); Werner Jaeger, *Paideia: The Ideals of Greek Culture*, trans. Gilbert Highet Vol. I (New York: Oxford Univ. Press, 1945) at 286-331.

[15] Jeffrey A.Standen, 'Critical Legal Studies as an Anti-Positivist Phenomenon' [Note], *Virginia L.. Rev.* 73 (1986) 983 at 985.

[16] Thomas Hobbes, *Leviathan*, ed. W.G. Pogson-Smith (Oxford: Clarendon Press 1909); John Locke, *Two Treatises of Government* ed. P. Laslett rev. ed. (New York: New American Library, 1965); Jean-Jacques Rousseau, *The Social Contract*, ed. M. Cranston (Penguin 1968)

[17] Martyn P. Thompson, 'Significant Silences in Locke's Two Treatises of Government: Constitutional History, Contract and Law', *Historical Journal* 31 (1987) 275 at 281.

[18] Andreas Pickel, 'Never Ask Who Should Rule: Karl Popper and Political Theory', *Can. J. of Political Sc.* 22 (1989) 83.

[19] Thomas L. Pangle, ed. *The Roots of Political Philosophy: Ten Forgotten Socratic Dialogues* (Ithaca & London: Cornell Univ. Press, 1987)

[20] Michael S. Moore, 'The Interpretive Turn in Modern Theory: A Turn for the Worse?', *Stanford L.Rev.* 41 (1989). Cf. Stephen M. Feldman, 'The New Metaphysics: The Interpretive Turn in Jurisprudence', *Iowa L.R.* 76 (1991), and, 'Republican Revival/Interpretive Turn,' *Wisconsin L.R.* (1992) 679; David Johnston, *The Idea of a Liberal Theory: A Critique and Reconstruction* (Princeton, N.J.: Princeton Univ. Press, 1994)

[21] John Locke, supra note 16, *Second Essay*, Ss. 124, 36, 50. (Emphases original).

[22] The two principles are: '(1) Each person is to have an equal right to the most extensive basic liberty compatible with a similar liberty for others, (2) Social and economic inequalities are to be arranged so that they are both (a) reasonably expected to be to everyone's advantage, and (b) attached to positions and offices open to all.': J. Rawls, *A Theory of Justice*, supra note 2 at 60. The final statement of the two principles, and their lexical ordering, are at p. 302. In his 'second treatise', *Political Liberalism*, Rawls worded/structured the principles differently, but they are substantively the same.

[23] R. Tur, 'Paternalism and the Criminal Law', *Journal of Applied Philosophy* 2 (1985) 173.

[24] Rawls, *A Theory of Justice*, supra note 2 at 12 states categorically that 'the original position of equality corresponds to the state of nature in the traditional theory of the social contract.'

[25] Margaret C. Jacob, *Scientific Culture and the Making of the Industrial West* (N.Y.: Oxford Univ. Press, 1997) at 47; Stephen Toulmin, *Cosmopolis: The Hidden Agenda of Modernity* (1990) (Chicago: Univ. of Chicago Press, 1992)

[26] It is, therefore, not surprising that, 'despite the radicalness of [Descartes'] methodological thinking, he excluded morality from the total reconstruction of all truths by reason… he did not in fact elaborate his definitive morality and … its principles, as far as we can judge … contain hardly anything new': Hans Georg Gadamer, *Truth and Method* (New York: Seabury Press, 1975) at 248.

[27] Q. Skinner, 'The Ideological Context of Hobbes's Political Thought' *The Historical Journal* 9 (1966) 286.

[28] 'Locke had been one of those who had borne a hand in building the new England… from his vantage ground, he studied with observant eyes the wiles and manoevres of his fellow mortals': Paul Hazard, *The European Mind 1680-1715* (London: Hollis & Carter, 1953) at 240.

[29] Robert Nozick, supra note 4 at ix-xii. Cf.: Robert Nozick, "The Zigzag of Politics', in *The Examined Life: Philosophical Meditations* (New York: Touchstone, 1989) at 286-296.

[30] S. Stromholm, *A Short History of Legal Thinking in the West* (Stockholm: Norstedts, 1985) at 214.

[31] P. Milton, 'H.L.A. Hart: Jurisprudence and Linguistic Philosophy', [Book Review] *Modern L.R.* 47 (1984) 751; Lloyd L. Weinreb, *Natural Law and Justice* (Cambridge, Mass.: Harvard Univ. Press, 1987) Chapter 4.

[32] On 'second nature', see, D.R. Kelley, '"Second Nature": The Idea of Custom in European Law, Society, and Culture', in *The Transmission of Culture in Early Modern Europe* ed. Anthony Grafton & Ann Blair (Philadelphia: Univ. of Philadelphia Press, 1990); D.R. Kelley, 'The Old Cultural History,' *Hist. of the Human Sciences* 9 (1996) 101.

[33] See, particularly, Richard Rorty, *Philosophy and the Mirror of Nature* (Princeton, N.J.: Princeton Univ. Press, 1979). See, further, Don Herzog, *Without Foundations: Justification in Political Theory* (Ithaca & London: Cornell Univ. Press, 1985)

[34] But see, J. Waldron, 'When Justice Replaces Affection: The Need for Rights' *Harvard Journal of Law and Pub. Policy* 11 (1988) 624; Will Kymlicka, *Liberalism, Community, and Culture* (Oxford: Clarendon Press, 1989); Stephen Macedo, *Liberal Virtues: Citizenship, Virtue and Community in Liberal Constitutionalism* (Oxford: Clarendon Press, 1990). On contractarianism as an evaluative device, see Kim Lane Schepelle and Jeremy Waldron, 'Contractarian Methods in Political and Legal Evaluation,' *Yale J. of Law & Humanities* 3 (1991) 195.

[35] R. Dworkin, *Taking Rights Seriously*, supra note 3 at xi. (Emphasis added)

[36] Otto Gierke, *Natural Law and the Theory of Society* trans. Ernest Barker, (Cambridge: Cambridge Univ. Press, 1933) at 46.

[37] The phrase is from H.L.A. Hart, *The Concept of Law* (Oxford: Clarendon Press, 1961) at 191.

[38] Dworkin, *Taking Rights Seriously*, supra note 3 at xi; J. Rawls, 'The Basic Structure as Subject', *American Philosophical Quarterly* 14 (1977) 159 at 165.
[39] Dworkin, '"Natural Law" Revisited' *Univ. of Florida Law Rev.* 34 (1982) 165.
[40] N. MacCormick, *Legal Right and Social Democracy* (Oxford: Clarendon Press, 1982) at 128.
[41] R. Dworkin, 'The Law of the Slave Catchers' [Book Review] *Times Literary Supplement*, December 5, 1975. Cf: H.L.A. Hart, 'Law in the Perspective of Philosophy 1776-1976' *New York Univ. L. Rev.* 51 (1976) 538.
[42] R. Dworkin, 'No Right Answer?' in, *Law, Morality and Society: Essays in Honour of H.L.A. Hart,* ed. P.M. Hacker & J. Raz (1977) 58-84; *Taking Rights Seriously,* supra note 3 at 101-5; *Law's Empire*, supra note 3 at 266-75; *Freedoms' Law: The Moral Reading of the American Constitution*, supra note 3 at 10-11.
The cultural historical nature of institutional rights perhaps betrays the fact that Dworkin is after all a cultural relativist. See, Michael Freeman, 'The Philosophical Foundations of Human Rights' *Human Rights Quarterly* 16 (1994) 491 at 500; Heidi M. Hurd, 'Relativistic Jurisprudence: Skepticism Founded on Confusion', *South California L.R.* 161 (1988) 1417 at 1459.
[43] R. Dworkin, 'How Law is Like Literature', in *A Matter of Principle*, supra note 3 at 160.
[44] Hart adverted to this point in *The Concept of Law*, supra note 37 at 195-7.
[45] Alfred Cobban succinctly articulates this point: 'Mill lived in an age when new social problems called for measures of State action which conflicted with established ideals of individual liberty; his thought derives its value from the fact that he devoted himself to the task of attempting to reconcile the two demands. Bentham's lifework was to establish a theoretical basis for the legislative and administrative reforms that were urgently needed in his day. Burke, faced in Great Britain, America, Ireland, France with a challenge to the existing bases of political allegiance, attempted to provide an alternative to the new democratic principle of the sovereignty of the people. Rousseau, conscious of the moral collapse of divine-right monarchy, offered a new justification for political authority. Montesquieu, earlier, had seen the defects of absolutism, and established the case for the limitation of all power by law. Locke provided a political theory for a generation which wanted both to legitimize and restrict revolution. Hobbes and Spinoza, in an age of civil wars, maintained that sovereignty was all or nothing. And so we might continue, till we reached in the end – or rather the beginning – Plato and Aristotle, attempting to prescribe remedies for the diseases of the city-state': *In Search of Humanity* (New York: G. Braziller, 1962) at 212.
[46] See above. Otto Gierke, supra note 36 at 101-105.
[47] Isaiah Berlin, 'Two Concepts of Liberty', rep. *Liberalism and Its Critics*, ed. M. Sandel, supra note 5, 15-36
[48] See, e.g. David Hume, 'Of the Original Contract', in, *Philosophical Works*, eds. T.H. Green & T.H.Grose, Vol. III at 443-460.

[49] C.B., MacPherson, *The Political Theory of Possessive Individualism: Hobbes to Locke* (Oxford: Oxford Univ. Press, 1962)
[50] Leo Strauss, supra note 8 at 242-251.
[51] Stephen A. Siegel, 'The Aristotlean Basis of English Law 1450-1800', *New York Univ. L. Rev.* 56 (1981) 18; J.R. Pole, 'An Anatomy of the American Whig' [Book Review] *The Historical Journal* 9 (1966) 229.
[52]Marke DeWolfe Howe, 'The Positivism of Mr. Justice Holmes' *Harvard L.R.* 64 (1951) 529 at 538.
[53] Roberto M. Unger, *What Should Legal Analysis Become?* (London: Verso 1996) at 176
[54] See, e.g., R. Nozick, supra note 4; F.A. Hayek, *The Road to Serfdom* (Chicago: Univ. of Chicago Press 1944). Michael Oakeshott persuasively shows that such positions arise from a well-meaning determination to preserve traditional political freedom. But as it maintains a head-in-the-sand position its insidious effect is that it detracts and saps the strength from the very tradition that the doctrinal formulation is designed to strengthen. See, Michael Oakeshott, 'Rationalism in Politics', in *Rationalism in Politics* (London: Methuen 1962) at 21-22.
[55] R. Maceboy, 'The Public Morality of the Rule of Law: A Critique of Ronald Dworkin', *Harvard Journal of Law & Pub. Policy* 8 (1985) 79; Stephen Macedo, *The New Right v. The Constitution,* supra note 5 at 53; Stephen Macedo, *Liberal Virtues: Citizenship, Virtue and Community in Liberal Constitutionalism* (Oxford: Clarendon Press 1990); David Johnston, *The Idea of a Liberal Theory,* supra note 20 at 25. Cf: Robin L. West, 'Liberalism Rediscovered: A Pragmatic Definition of the Liberal Vision', *Univ. of Pitt. L.R.* 46 (1985) 673.
[56] F.A. Hayek, *The Road to Serfdom,* supra note 54 at 136. This has been constantly parodied in literature. See, e.g., George Orwell, *Animal Farm*; William Golding, *Lord of the Flies.*
[57] K. Mannheim, *Ideology and Utopia* (New York: Harcourt Brace & World 1968) at 3: 'it is not men in general who think or even isolated individuals who do the thinking, but men in certain groups who have developed a particular style of characterising their common position'. Hence, 'in studying a political doctrine, we must consider the bias, and even the class bias, of its originator': Leo Strauss, *Natural Right and History,* supra note 8 at 143.
[58] A.D. Kriegel, 'Liberty and Whiggery in Early 19th Century England', *Journal of Modern History* 52 (1980) 253.
[59] A.V. Dicey, *Law and Public Opinion in 19th Century England* (London: MacMillan Press 1963) at 82. 'The Revolution of 1689 was conducted under the guidance of Whig lawyers … their intention was to re-affirm … not the innate rights of man but the inherited and immemorial liberties of Englishmen'. 'The Revolution of 1688 struck the first real blow at Continental despotism … For the divine right of Kings it established … the divine right of freeholders; and their domination extended for seventy years, under the authority of John Locke, the philosopher of government by the gentry. Even Hume did not

enlarge the bounds of his ideas': Lord Acton, 'The History of Freedom in Christianity', in Acton, *Essays in the Liberal Interpretation of History* ed. W.H. McNeill (Chicago and London: Univ. of Chicago Press 1967) at 293. This may also be true of old liberalism. 'In many details, the ethical doctrines of Plato and Aristotle were founded on the aristocratic morality of early Greece... The class limitations of the old ideals were removed when they were sublimated and universalized by philosophy: while their permanent truth and their indestructible ideality were confirmed and strengthened by that process... in many respects Aristotle, like the Greeks of all ages, has his gaze fixed on Homer's characters, and he develops his ideals after the heroic patterns ..." W. Jaeger, *Paiedia: The Greek Ideal of Culture*, supra note 14, I at 11.

[60] Of course, colonialism is a euphemism for a 'forthright determination to exploit the colonies for the benefit of the colonial power.'

[61] Phillip S. Zachernuk, 'Of Origins and Colonial Order: Southern Nigerian Historians and the 'Hamitic Hypothesis' c.1870-1970', *Journal of African History* 35 (1994) 427: 'By 'colonial intelligentsia' I mean those [indigenous] members of the western-educated community who addressed the problem of [their countries] as a colonial entity.'

[62] L.C.B. Gower, *Independent Africa* (Cambridge, Mass: Harvard Univ. Press 1967) at 3; O. Awolowo, *The Problems of Africa* (Ibadan: Macmillan Press 1977), *passim*.

[63] Robert W. July, *The Origins of Modern African Thought: Its Development in West Africa during the Nineteenth and Twentieth Centuries* (New York: Frederick A. Praeger, 1967). The phrase, 'ideological political beliefs about the reordering of economic activity', is from Edward Shils, *Tradition* (London & Boston: Faber and Faber, 1981) at 136.

[64] Lord Hailsham, *Hamlyn Revisited: The British Legal System Today* (London: Sweet & Maxwell, 1983) at 16. The other two are the Church and modern Parliamentary institutions.

[65] John Rawls, *A Theory of Justice*, supra note 2 at 11.

[66] Steven Kantz, *Liberalism and Community* (Ithaca & London: Cornell Univ. Press 1995); Kirstie M. McClure, *Judging Rights: Lockean Polities and the Limits of Consent* (Ithaca & London: Cornell Univ. Press 1996).

[67] Mary Warnock, 'The Resurrection of Ethics', in, *Women of Ideas*, ed. Anita Avramides (London: Duckworth, 1995) at 9.

[68] R. Tuck, *Natural Rights Theories: Their Origin and Development* (Cambridge: Cambridge Univ. Press 1979) at 22.

[69] David Spitz, 'Freedom and Individuality: Mill's Liberty in Retrospect', *Nomos IV (Liberty)* 1962) 176 at 220.

[70] A.D. Kriegel, supra note 58. Burke captured the conservative spirit of Whig political theory in this words: 'It seems to me a preposterous way of reasoning and a perfect confusion of ideas to take the theories which learned and speculative men have made from that government and then supposing it made on those theories, which were made from it, to accuse the government as not

corresponding with them' quoted J.G.A. Pocock, 'Burke and the Ancient Constitution – A Problem in the History of Ideas', *Historical Journal* 3 (1960) 124 at 140.

[71] D. Hay, 'Property, Authority and The Criminal Law', in, *Albion's Fatal Tree,* ed. D. Hay et al (New York: Pantheon Books, 1975); E.P. Thompson, *Whigs and Hunters: The Origin of the Black Act* (London: Penguin Books, 1975) -

[72] See, Basil Williams, *The Whig Supremacy 1714-1760* 2nd ed. (Oxford: Clarendon Press, 1962). On the meaning of 'revolution' in seventeenth century England, see, Vernon F. Snow, 'The Concept of Revolution in Seventeenth Century England', *Historical Journal* 5 (1962) 167.

[73] N. Wood, *The Politics of Locke's Philosophy* (Berkeley: Univ. of California Press, 1983) at 11; Christopher Dawson, 'The Historic Origins of Liberalism', in *The Image of Man,* ed. M.A. Fitzimons et al (New York: Books for Libraries Press, 1971 rep.,) at 110.

[74] J.S. Mill, 'Austin on Jurisprudence', in *Collected Works of John Stuart Mill,* ed. John M. Robson (Toronto: Univ. of Toronto Press, 1984) Vol. XXI at 168

[75] D.H. Lawrence, 'A Propos of Lady Chatterley's Lover', in *Lady Chatterley's Lover* (1928) at 336.

[76] Richard Ashcraft, 'Locke's State of Nature: Historical Fact or Moral Fiction?' *Am. Pol. Sc. Rev.* 62 (1968) 898; Hans Aarsleff, 'The State of Nature and the Nature of Man in Locke', in, *John Locke, Problems and Perspectives: A Collection of New Essays* ed. John W. Yolton (Cambridge: Cambridge Univ. Press 1969) 99; Forrest McDonald, *Novus Ordo Seclorum: The Intellectual Origins of the Constitution* (Lawrence, Kansas: Univ. of Kansas Press, 1985) at 62.

[77] David Hume, *An Enquiry Concerning Human Understanding* ed. Eric Steinberg (Indianapolis: Hackett Publishing, 1977) at 3.

[78] See, e.g., Jean Jacques Rousseau, *A Discourse Upon the Origin and Foundation of the Inequality among Mankind* (1761) (New York: Burt Franklin 1971 rep.) at 10; Immanuel Kant, 'Perpetual Peace', in, *Perpetual Peace and Other Essays* trans. T. Humphrey (Indianapolis: Hackett Publishing, 1983); P. Riley, 'On Kant as the most adequate of the Social Contract Theorists' *Political Theory* 1 (1973) 450. (Both Rawls and Nozick emphasized that the state of nature is an explanatory model, not a historical fact: Rawls, *A Theory of Justice*, supra note 2 at 12; Nozick, supra note 4 at 6-9).

[79] D.D. Raphael, 'Enlightenment and Revolution' in *Enlightenment, Rights, and Revolution: Essays in Legal and Social Philosophy* ed. N. MacCormick and Zenon Bankowski (Aberdeen: Univ. Press, 1989) 3 at 15; Irving Babbitt, *Rousseau and Romanticism* (1919) (N.Y.: World Publishing Co. 1955).

[80] M.J. Sandel, *Liberalism and the Limits of Justice*, supra note 6 at 177; *Democracy's Discontent*, supra note 6 at 12.

[81] See, e.g. H. Reichenbach, *The Rise of Scientific Philosophy* (Berkely: Univ. of California Press, 1951) at 61; A. MacIntyre, 'Contexts of Interpretation (Reflections on Hans-Georg Gadamer's Truth and Method), *Boston Univ.*

Journal 24 (1976) 41, 43; S. Toulmin, *Human Understanding* (Oxford: Clarendon Press, 1972) Vol. I at 444. Of course, Kant's constructivist morality was not unconcerned with happiness, but his primary concern was not happiness in the utilitarian sense: Etienne Gilson, *The Unity of Philosophical Experience* (New York: Charles Scribner's, 1965) at 235.

[82] Dietrich Gerhard, *Old Europe: A Study in Continuity, 1000-1800* (New York: Academic Press 1981)

[83] Steven B. Smith, *Hegel's Critique of Liberalism: Rights in Context* (Chicago & London: Univ. of Chicago Press, 1989) at 115.

[84] G.W.F. Hegel, *The Philosophy of Right and the Philosophy of History* 46 Great Books of the Western World, Encyclopedia Britannica, Inc. 1952).

[85] See, e.g. G.W.F. Hegel, *The Philosophy of Right*, Ss.305-308.

[86] Carl J. Friedrich, 'The Political Thought of Neo-liberalism' *Am. Pol. Sc. Rev.* 49 (1955) 509 at 513 n.15..

[87] R.S. Peters, 'Hegel and the Nation-State', in *Political Ideas* ed. David Thomson (Pelican Books, 1966) at 133.

[88] Ronald D. Rotunda, *The Politics of Language* (Iowa City: Univ. of Iowa Press, 1986) at 21.

[89] James E. Crimmins, *Secular Utilitarianism* (Oxford: Clarendon Press 1990)

[90] Douglas G. Long, *Bentham on Liberty* (Toronto: Univ. of Toronto Press, 1977) at 118.

[91] J. Bentham, *A Fragment on Government* ed. F.A. Montague [Editor's Introduction] at 35.

[92] David Nicholls, 'The English Middle Class and the Ideological Significance of Radicalism, 1760-1886', *Journal of British Studies* 24 (1985) 415; Isaac Krammick, 'Eighteenth Century Science and Radical Social Theory: The Case of Joseph Priestley's Scientific Liberty', *Journal of British Studies* 25 (1985) 1. Cf: Margaret Canovan, 'Paternalistic Liberalism: Joseph Priestley on Rank and Equality', *Enlightenment and Dissent* 1 (1983) 23.

[93] See, e.g., Russell Kirk, *The Roots of American Order* (LaSalle, Illinois, Open Court, 1974) at 69-71.

[94] See, inter alia, Jennifer T. Roberts, *Athens on Trial: The Anti-democratic Tradition in Western Thought* (Princeton, N.J.: Princeton Univ. Press, 1994); A.H.M. Jones, 'The Athenian Democracy and Its Critics' *Cambridge Historical Journal* 11 (1953) 1; D. Spitz, *Patterns of Anti-Democratic Thought* (1949); Kyriacos Demetriou, 'In Defence of the British Constitution: Theoretical Implications of the Debate Over Athenian Democracy in Britain, 1770-1850' *Hist. of Political Thought* 17 (1996) 280; David Held, *Models of Democracy* (Stanford: Stanford Univ. Press, 1987) at 33: 'until the early eighteenth century almost no one who recorded their views at length thought democracy a desirable way of organizing political life.'

[95] W.S. Holdsworth, 'Gibbon, Blackstone and Bentham' *Law Quarterly Rev.* 52 (1936) 46 at 57; J.R. Dinwiddy, 'Bentham's Transition to Radicalism', *Journal of the History of Ideas* 36 (1975) 683; James E. Crimmins, *Secular Utilitarianism*, supra; James E. Crimmins, 'Bentham's Political Radicalism Re-

examined', *Journal of the History of Ideas* 55 (1994) 259; H.O. Pappe, 'The English Utilitarians and Athenian Democracy', in *Classical Influences on Western Thought A.D. 1650-1870* (Proceedings of an International Conference Held at King's College, Cambridge, 1977), R.R. Bolgar, ed. (Cambridge: Univ. Press, 1978) 295 at 296; L.T. Hobhouse, *Liberalism* (1911) (Oxford: Univ. Press, 1964) at 42; E. Halevy, *The Growth of Philosophic Radicalism* (London: Faber & Faber, 1928) at 254-64.

[96] J.S. Mill, *On Liberty*, ed. G. Himmelfarb (New York: Penguin Books, 1985) at 68. (Emphasis added). 'Harm' is profoundly disciplinary, not literally utilitarian or communitarian. See, Jeremy Waldron, 'Homelessness and Community,' *Univ. of Toronto Law Journal* 50 (2000) 371.

[97] D. Spitz, supra note 69 at 206.

[98] J.S. Mill, 'Austin on Jurisprudence', supra note 74 at 188. As Mill saw it, pre-Austinian legal philosophy based, as it was, on natural law doctrine, was little more than an 'incondite mass of barbarian conceits, obsolete technicalities, and contrivances which had lost their meaning, bound together by sophistical ingenuity into a semblance of legal science, and help up triumphantly to the admiration and applause of mankind', at 168.

[99] J. S. Mill, *On Liberty*, supra note 96 at 131, 135. On Mill's consistent view on democracy, see, J.H. Burns, 'J.S. Mill and Democracy, 1829-61' *Political Studies* 5 (1957) 158-175, 280-294.

[100] Isaiah Berlin, supra note 47.

[101] Adam Smith, *Lectures on Jurisprudence*, ed. R.L. Meek, *et al.* (Oxford: Clarendon Press, 1978) at 320.

[102] J. Bentham, *An Introduction to the Principles of Morals and Legislation* ed. J.H. Burns and H.L.A. Hart (London: Athlone Press 1970) at 12-13.

[103] See, generally, R.J. Goldstein, *Political Repression in 19th Century Europe* (London: Croom Helm, 1983)

[104] J.S. Mill, 'Austin on Jurisprudence', supra note 74 at 168.

[105] D.A.J. Richards, 'Human Rights and The Moral Foundations of the Substantive Criminal Law' *Georgia Law Rev.* 13 (1979) 1395 at 1410.

[106] R. Dworkin, *Taking Rights Seriously*, supra note 3; J. Rawls, *A Theory of Justice*, supra note 2 at 22-27; R. Nozick, supra note 4.

[107] M.J. Sandel, *Liberalism and the Limits of Justice*, supra note 6 at 1.

[108] J. Rawls, *A Theory of Justice*, supra note 2 at 12, 13; J. Rawls, *Political Liberalism* supra note 2 at 44-5: 'in political philosophy the work of abstraction is set in motion by deep political conflicts ... We turn to political philosophy when *our shared political understandings* ... break down, and equally when we are torn within ourselves... No political conception of justice could have weight with us unless it helped to put in order *our considered convictions of justice* at all levels of generality, from the most general to the most particular. To help us do this is one role of the original position'' (Emphasis added).

For particularly keen elaboration of the necessity for shifting, and what happens if the location of culture is shifted from the oracular stability of liberal vision to the 'occult instability of critical theory,' see, particularly, Homi K.

Bhabha, *The Location of Culture* (London & New York: Routledge, 1994); James Tully, *Strange Multiplicity: Constitutionalism in an Age of Diversity* (Cambridge: Cambridge Univ. Press, 1995); V.Y. Mudimbe & Kwame A. Appiah, 'The Impact of African Studies on Philosophy,' in, *Africa and the Disciplines: The Contributions of Research in Africa to the Social Sciences and Humanities* ed. Robert H. Bate *et al* (Chicago & London: Univ. of Chic. Press, 1993) 113.

[109]See, *inter alia*, Richard Flathman, 'Liberalism and the Suspect Enterprise of Political Institutionalization: The Case of the Rule of Law,' *Nomos: The Rule of Law* XXXVI (1994) 297; Forrest McDonald, *Novus Ordo Seclorum: The Intellectual Origins of the Constitution*, supra note 76; Jonathan R. Macey and Geoffrey P. Miller, 'The End of History and the New World Order: The Triumph of Capitalism and the Competition Between Liberalism and Democracy', *Cornell International L.J.* 25 (1992) 277; Francis Fukuyama, *The End of History and the Last Man* (New York: Free Press, 1992) at 42.

[110] M.J. Sandel, supra note 107.

[111] Max Hamburger, *The Awakening of Western Legal Thought* (1942) trans. Bernard Miall (Westport, Connecticut: Greenwood Press, 1970 rep.) at 148: "At the beginning of normal relations between foreign tribes and states we find – war! … the predominant factor [in antiquity] was always the tendency of the stronger state to enforce its will upon the weaker. Such was the origin of the empire of imperialistic Hellas, the world-empire of Alexander the Great, and the Roman Empire'. See further, J.L. Myres, *The Dawn of History* (London: William & Norgate, 1915)

[112] C. Kingsley, *Lectures Delivered in America in 1874* (Philadelphia: Jos H. Coates, 1875) at 131.

[113] On 'homo hierarchicus', see Louis Dumont, *Homo Hierarchicus: The Caste System and Its Implications* trans. M. Sainsburg, L.Dumont and Basia Gulati (Chicago: Univ. of Chicago Press, 1980)

[114] E.D. Genovese, 'Critical Legal Studies as Radical Politics and World View' [Book Review] *Yale Journal of Law and Humanities* 3 (1991) 131.

[115] See, B. Moore, Jr. *Authority and Inequality under Capitalism and Socialism* (Oxford: Clarendon Press, 1987)

[116] C.S. Lewis, 'Historicism', in, *God, History and Historians* ed. C.T. MacIntire (New York: Oxford Univ. Press 1977). For a recent affirmation of the affinities among theology, philosophy, and historicism, see, Thomas A. Howard, *Religion and the Rise of Historicism: W.M.L. de Wette, Jacob Burchkhardt and the Theological Origins of Nineteenth Century Historical Consciousness* (Cambridge: Cambridge Univ. Press, 2000)

[117] David Hume, Philosophical Works, Vol. II Essay XVI. See also Adam Smith, *Theory of Moral Sentiments*, at 233.

[118] Peter Laslett, 'The English Revolution and Locke's Two Treatise of Government', *The Cambridge Historical Journal* 12 (1956) 41; M. Oakeshott, in, *Liberalism and Its Critics*, ed. M. Sandel, supra note 6; James Farr & Clayton Roberts, 'John Locke on the Glorious Revolution: A Rediscovered

Document' *Historical Journal* 28 (1985) 385; Richard Tuck, *Natural Rights Theories*, supra note 68 at 170; J.R. Milton, 'Dating Locke's Second Treatise' *Hist. of Political Thought* 16 (1995) 356; J.G.A. Pocock, 'The Fourth English Civil War: Dissolution, Desertion, and Alternative Histories in the Glorious Revolution,' in, *The Revolution of 1688-89: Changing Perspectives* ed. Lois G. Schwoerer (Cambridge: Cambridge Univ. Press, 1992) 52-64 at 60-1: 'we are now sure that Locke wrote his Second Treatise somewhere between 1680 and 1683'; Charles D. Tarlton, '"The Rulers Now on Earth": Locke's Two Treatises and Revolution of 1688.' *Historical Journal* 28 (1985) 279.

[119]F.A. Hayek, *The Constitution of Liberty* (London: Routledge & Kegal Paul 1960) at 467 n.81; Ernest C. Mossner, 'Was Hume a Tory Historian? Facts and Reconsiderations' *Journal of the History of Ideas* 2 (1941) 225.

[120] David Hume, *Philosophical Works*, Vol. III. Essay XI: 'On the Populousness of Ancient Nations', 381 at 409.

[121] See, generally, Basil Williams, supra note 72 ; B. Inglis, *Poverty and the Industrial Revolution* (London: Hodder & Stoughton, 1971)

[122] Alfred Cobban, supra note 45 at 137.

[123] J. Rawls, *A Theory of Justice*, supra note 2 at 33. See also, Acton, 'The History of Freedom in Christianity' supra note 59.

[124] Edward Gibbon, *The Decline and Fall of the Roman Empire* Vol. V, Chapter 44 at 287: 'the first task of all reformers is to prevent any future reformation.'

[125] Hans Georg Gadamer, *Truth and Method*, supra note 26 at 249.

[126] See, e.g. J.P. Day, 'J.S. Mill', in, *A Critical History of Western Philosophy* ed. O.J. O'Connor (New York: Free Press 1964) at 363.

[127] Louis Dumont, 'A Modified View of our Origins: The Christian Beginnings of Modern Individualism' *Religion* 12 (1982) 1; A.P. d'Entreves, *Natural Law* (New York: Harper & Row 1965) at 21-22; Ernest Baker, in Gierke, supra note 36 at XXXV-L. Ernest Baker, 'Some Foreign Influences in Greek Thought,' *Greece and Rome* 5 (1935-6) 2. Cf. Leo Strauss, *Natural Right and History*, supra note 8 at 134-5.

[128] Francois Bedarida, *A Social History of England 1851-1975* trans. A.S. Forster (London & New York: Methuen, 1979) at 41, 257; Walter Berns, *Taking the Constitution Seriously* (New York: Simon and Schuster, 1987); Maimon Schwarzchild, 'Class, National Character and The Bar Reforms in Britain: Will There Always be an England?' 9 *Connecticut J. of International Law* 185. When Sir Winston Churchill, perhaps the most outstanding English statesman of the twentieth century, read Plato's *Republic*, he immediately conceived a political society modeled after the same: Winston Churchill, *My Early Life* (New York: Manor Books, Inc. 1972)

[129] See, particularly, Richard J. Herrnstein and Charles Murray, *The Bell Curve: Intelligence and Class Structure in American Life* (New York: Free Press, 1994). Of course, the theory has an ancient lineage: 'Plato thought it necessary for the first generation of his new society (in the perfect state) to be brought up with help of a "mighty-lie". The children were to be taught to believe that they

had all lain dreaming for a long time under the earth, where they had been molded and formed by the masterhand of Nature. It was impossible to go against the past, and work against the work of gods! And so it had to be an unbreakable law of nature that he who is born to be philosopher has gold in his body, the fighter has only silver, and the workman iron and bronze. As it is impossible to blend these metals, according to Plato, so there could never be any confusion between the classes; the belief in the *aeterna veritas* of this arrangement was the basis of the new education and the new state …'. F. Nietzsche, *The Use and Abuse of History*, 2nd rev. ed. trans. Adrian Collins (New York: Bobbs-Merrill, 1957) at 67-8. Nietzsche, of course, opposed his own 'mighty truth' to Plato's 'mighty lie'.

[130] H. Frankfurt, 'Freedom of the Will and the Concept of a Person', *Journal of Philosophy* 60 (1971) 5.

[131] Kant 'had conceived his whole doctrine in such a way as to satisfy two postulates: the physics of Newton is possible, moral duty is possible. A philosophy thus conceived usually succeeds in carrying out its program, but as it is entirely governed by its postulates as by external requirements, its component elements necessarily remain more or less unrelated. In spite of his efforts to multiply the internal connections between the several parts of his doctrine, Kant never succeeded in giving it an organic unity': E. Gilson, *The Unity of Philosophical Experience*, supra note 81 at 236.

[132] G.J. Warnock, 'Kant', in *A Critical History of Western Philosophy*, supra note 126, 296 at 308.

[133] Hans Kelsen, 'The Pure Theory of Law,' *Law Quarterly Rev*. 50 (1934) 474.

[134] H. Laski, 'The Crisis in the Theory of the State', in *LAW: A Century of Progress 1835-1935* (New York: New York Univ. Press, 1937). Hans Kelsen described Kant's 'categorical imperative' as a meaningless tautology: Hans Kelsen, *General Theory of Law and State* (Cambridge, Mass: Harvard Univ. Press 1946) at 10. See also, Mortimer J. Adler, *Ten Philosophical Mistakes* (New York: MacMillan Publishing, 1985) at 122.

[135] J. Rawls, *A Theory of Justice*, supra note 2 at 147. (Emphasis added). Rawls thus opened himself to the same charge against Kant, namely, 'that he had to make substantive assumptions about moral attitudes and desires before his theory could yield recognizable moral principles': T. Morawetz, 'Efficiency, Morality and Rights: The Significance of 'Cleaning Up'' *Harvard Journal of Law and Pub. Policy* (1987) 431 at 443. This criticism of Kant is as old as Hegel. See, Steven B. Smith, *Hegel's Critique of Liberalism*, supra note 83 at 73-75; G.W.F. Hegel, *The Philosophy of Right*, supra note 84, s.135.

For the view that the criticism is itself empty, see, P. Riley, *Will and Political Legitimacy: A Critical Exposition of Social Contract Theory in Hobbes, Locke, Rousseau, Kant, and Hegel* (Cambridge, Mass.: Harvard Univ. Press, 1982) at 146 et seq; P. Riley, '"The Elements" of Kant's Practical Philosophy: The 'Groundwork' after 200 Years, 1795-1985', *Political Theory* 14 (1986) 552; Ping-Cheun Lo, 'A Critical Reevaluation of the Alleged 'Empty Formalism' in Kantian Ethics,' *Ethics* 91 (1981) 181; Sally S. Sedgwick, 'On the Relation of

Pure Reason to Content: A Reply to Hegel's Critique of Formalism in Kant's Ethics', *Philosophy and Phenomenological Research* 49 (1988) 59.
136 Will Durant, *The Story of Philosophy: The Lives and Opinions of the Great Philosophers* (New York: Simon and Schuster, 1926) at 311.
137 A. Cobban, *In Search of Humanity*, supra note 45 at 212. (Emphasis added).
138 See, e.g. Kant, 'On the Proverb: That May be True in Theory, But is of No Practical Use', in supra note 10 at 72; Mary Gregor, 'Kant on Welfare Legislation,' in, *Poverty, Justice, and the Law: New Essays on Needs, Rights, and Obligations* ed. George R. Lucas, Jr. (Univ. Press of America, 1986) 49.
139 See, inter alia, Adam B. Ulam, *Philosophical Foundations of English Socialism* (Cambridge, Mass: Harvard Univ. Press, 1951) at 150; G. Himmerfarb, *Poverty and Compassion: The Moral Imagination of the Late Victorians* (New York: Alfred Knopf, 1991)
140 J. Rawls, *A Theory of Justice*, supra note 2 at 51.
141 E. Gilson, *The Unity of Philosophical Experience*, supra note 80 at 302.
142 A. Cobban, *In Search of Humanity*, supra note 45 at 235.
143 J. Austin, *The Province of Jurisprudence Determined and The Uses of the Study of Jurisprudence* (with introduction by H.L.A. Hart (London: Weidenfeld & Nicolson, 1954) at 79. The 'four-stage sequence' and 'the morality of principles' described by Rawls, *Theory of Justice, supra note 2* at 195-200, 472-9 would have precisely the same soporific intellectual effect. Surprisingly, the point was explicitly made in Plato, *The Republic*, III, 415d.
144 Daniel Lazare, *The Frozen Republic: How the Constitution is Paralyzing Democracy* (New York: Harcourt, Brace, 1996) at 306.
145 Aristotle, *Metaphysics* 1006A5-10.
146 Amina Mama, *Beyond the Masks: Race, Gender and Subjectivity* (London & New York: Routledge 1995) at 65.
147 George A. Kelley, 'Veils: The Poetics of John Rawls,' *Journal of the History of Ideas* 57 (1996) 343 at 360.
148 Annette Teffeteller, 'The Glory Myth', in *The Spoils of War* ed. Jurgen Kleist & Bruce A. Butterfield (New York: Peter Lang Publishing 1997) 139; Robin West, 'Progressive and Conservative Constitutionalism,' *Michigan L. Rev*. 88 (1990) 641.
149 See, e.g. Maurice Cranston, 'John Locke and Government by Consent', in *Political Ideas* ed. David Thomson (Pelican Books 1966) at 67; N. Wood, *The Politics of Locke's Philosophy*, supra note 73.
150 Peter Minowitz, *Profits, Priests and Princes: Adam Smith's Emancipation of Economics from Politics and Religion* (Stanford: Stanford Univ. Press, 1993)
151 D. Winch, *Adam Smith's Politics: An Essay in Historiographical Revision* (Cambridge: Cambridge Univ. Press 1978) at 167.
152 Guido De Ruggiero, *The History of European Liberalism* trans. R.G. Collingwood (1959), cited, Ronald D. Rotunda, *The Politics of Language*, supra note 87 at 23.
153 J. Bentham, *A Fragment on Government*, supra note 91 at 154.

[154] J. Bentham, *An Introduction to the Principles of Morals and Legislation*, supra note 102, S.4.
[155] Otto Gierke, *Natural Law and the Theory of Society*, supra note 36 at 49.
[156] Ibid. at 128-135; A. Cobban, supra note 45. Instead of grounding law on either ancient custom or the logic of a social contract, American proponents of 'popular sovereignty' followed the lead of Montesquieau and Rousseau by replacing the idea of fundamental law with the idea of the public will as the legitimating principle of the republic: James T. Kloppenberg, 'The Virtues of Liberalism: Christianity, Republicanism and Ethics in early American Political Discourse', *Journal of American History* 7 (1987) 9 at 25.
[157] Judith N. Shklar, *After Utopia* (Princeton, N.J.: Princeton Univ. Press, 1957)
[158] R. Rorty, *Philosophy and the Mirror of Nature*, supra note 33 at 394.
[159] Plato, *Laws* 951e-952a. Cf. Allan Bloom, *The Closing of the American Mind*, supra note 8 at 38, 203.
[160] Cf. Makau wa Mutua, 'The Banjul Charter and the African Cultural Fingerprint: An Evaluation of the Language of Duties', *Virginia J. of International Law* 35 (1995) 339; T.O. Elias, *The Nature of African Customary Law* (Manchester Univ. Press 1956); Kwame Gyekye, *An Essay on African Philosophical Thought: The Akan Conceptual Scheme* rev. ed. (Philadelphia: Temple Univ. Press, 1989) at 208-210.
[161] *Goldberg v. Kelley* 397 U.S. 254, 265.
[162] Sandra Harding, 'The Curious Coincidence of Feminine and African Moralities: Challenges for Feminist Theory', in, *Women and Moral Theory*, ed. Kittay & Meyers (Ottawa: Rowmans & Littlefield, 1987) at 297.
[163] I use 'intellectual' here in contradistinction from 'scholar' in the same sense that Daniel Bell used these phrases in the following passage: 'The differences between the intellectual and the scholar ... are important to understand. The scholar has a bounded field of knowledge, a tradition, and seeks to find his place in it, adding to the accumulated, tested knowledge of the past as to a mosaic. The scholar, qua scholar, is less involved with *his* 'self'. The intellectual begins with *his* experience, his individual perceptions of the world, *his* privileges and deprivations, and judges the world by these sensibilities. Since his own status is of high value, his judgments of the society reflect the treatment accorded him. In a business civilization, the intellectual felt that the wrong values were being honoured, and rejected the society. Thus there was a 'built-in' compulsion for the free-floating intellectual to become political. The ideologies, therefore, which emerged from the nineteenth century had the force of the intellectuals behind them ...' Daniel Bell, *The End of Ideology: On the Exhaustion of Political Ideas in the Fifties* (1960) (Cambridge, Mass.: Harvard Univ. Press, 1988) at 402. (Emphasis in the original).
[164] See, generally, R.J. Goldstein, *Political Repression in 19th Century Europe* (London: Croom Helm, 1983)
[165] See, particularly, D. Bell, supra note 163. On the political context and ideology of the 'end of ideology' school of thought, see, *inter alia*, William

Buxton, *Talcott Parsons and the Capitalist Nation-State: Political Sociology as a Strategic Vocation* (Toronto: Univ. of Toronto Press, 1985) at 218 *et seq*; Robin Blackburne ed. *Ideology in Social Sciences: Readings in Critical Social Theory* (New York: Vintage Books, 1973); Fredric Jameson, *The Ideologies of Theory Essays 1971-1986* (Minneapolis: Univ. of Minnesota Press, 1988); Clifford Geertz, 'Anti-Anti-Relativism', in *Relativism: Interpretation and Confrontation* ed. Michael Krauz (Notre Dame Univ. Press, 1989); Stephen Macedo, *Liberal Virtues*, supra note 55 at 36-7; John A. Hall, *Liberalism: Politics, Ideology, and the Market* (Chapel Hill, Univ. of North Carolina Press, 1988) at 166-8.

[166] On the distinction between 'perfect' and 'imperfect' rights, see, e.g. Adam Smith, *Lectures on Jurisprudence*, supra note 101 at 9: '... perfect rights are those which we have a title to demand and if refused to compel an other to perform. ... imperfect rights are those duties which ought to be performed to us by others but which we have no title to compel them to perform; they having it intirely in their power to perform them or not...'

[167] Steven B. Smith, *Hegel's Critique of Liberalism*, supra note 83 at 243.

[168] Jean Jacque Rousseau, *Discourse Upon the Origin and Foundation of the Inequality among Mankind* supra note 78 at 181.

[169] R. Dworkin, *Law's Empire*, supra note 3 at 228.

[170] Edward W. Strong, 'Civilizations in Historical Perspective', *University of California Publications in Philosophy* 23 (1942) 103 at 128. In contemporary times, 'liberalism does not mean the emancipation of the working man, [visible] and ethnic minorities but rather their streamlined suppression in the name of the free market...' Arthur Mitzman, 'On the Historicity of High Culture' [Book Review] *Journal of the History of Ideas* 55 (1994) 159 at 172.

[171] See, e.g. R. Maceboy, supra note 55.

[172] M.J. Sandel, *Liberalism and the Limits Justice*, supra note 6 at 13.

[173] R. Dworkin, 'Natural Law' Revisited', supra note 39.

[174] P. Milton, 'H.L.A. Hart: Jurisprudence and Linguistic Philosophy,' supra note 31.

[175] See, *inter alia*, James W. Johnson, *The Formation of English Neo-classical Thought* (Princeton, 1967); Philip Ayres, *Classical Culture and the Idea of Rome in 18th Century England* (Cambridge: Cambridge Univ. Press, 1997); Meyer Reinbold, *Classica Americana: The Greek and Roman Heritage in the United States* (Detroit: Wayne State Univ. 1984); Richard M. Gummere, *The American Colonial Mind and The Classical Tradition: Essays in Comparative Culture* (Cambridge, Mass.: Harvard Univ. Press, 1963); H. Trevor Colbourn, *The Lamp of Experience: Whig History and the Intellectual Origin of the American Revolution* (Chapel Hill: Univ. of North Carolina Press, 1965).

[176] Steven B. Smith, supra note 83 at 243.

[177] T.W. Arnold, *The Symbols of Government* (New Haven: Yale Univ. Press 1935) at 72.

[178] See, Edward W. Kitch, '"The Fire of Truth": A Remembrance of Law and Economics at Chicago, 1932-1970' *Journal of Law and Economics* 26 (1983)

163 (various discussants); Paul A. Samuelson, 'Economics in a Golden Age: A Personal Memoir,' in, *The Twentieth Century Sciences: Studies in the Biography of Ideas*, ed. Gerald Holton (New York: W.W. Norton, 1972) 155-170. For a comprehensive history of the law and economics movement, see, Neil Duxbury, *Patterns of American Jurisprudence* (Oxford: Clarendon Press, 1995) Chap. 5. See also, *Law and History Review* 15 (1997) 275-338. For an extended intellectual history of 'law and economics', see, Hearth Pearson, *Origins of Law and Economics: The Economists' New Science of Law, 1830-1930* (Cambridge: Univ. Press, 1997)

[179] Richard A. Posner, 'Conventionalism: The Key to Law as an Autonomous Discipline?' *University of Toronto Law Journal* 38 (1988) 333.

[180] F.A. Hayek, *Law, Legislation and Liberty* Vol. 3 at 164.

[181] F.A. Hayek, *The Constitution of Liberty* at 168.

[182] J.S. Mill, *On Liberty*, supra note 96.

[183] Cf. Paul Smart, 'Some Will Be More Equal Than Others': J. S. Mill on Democracy, Freedom and Meritocracy' *Archiv fur Rechts und Sozialphilosophie* 75 (1990) 308. But see, J.H. Burns, supra note 99.

[184] '"Stadial history", ... describes a natural trajectory or spiral of development in which societies undergo change through successive stages based on different forms of subsistence': Karen O'Brien, *Narratives of Enlightenment: Cosmopolitan History from Voltaire to Gibbon* (Cambridge: Cambridge Univ. Press 1997) at 133; P. Stein, 'The Four Stage Theory of the Development of Societies', in *The Character and Influence of the Roman Civil Law: Historical Essays* (Hambledon Press, 1988) at 395-409; P. Stein, *Legal Evolution: The Story of an Idea* (Cambridge: Cambridge Univ. Press, 1980)

[185] Adam Smith, *An Inquiry into the Nature and Causes of The Wealth of Nations* , ed. E. Cannan, (New York: Modern Library, with an introduction by Max Lerner, 1937) at 249-250.

[186] Allan Bloom, *The Closing of the American Mind*, supra note 8 at 210.

[187] This picture of Smith's intellectual allegiance was derived mainly from his *Lectures on Jurisprudence*, supra note101. As the title of his classic treatise on political economy suggests, the focus of Smith's inquiry was the political household, that is, the State, rather than the individual, firm, or corporation.

[188] James Ryerson, 'The Outrageous Pragmatism of Judge Richard Posner,' *Lingua Franca* 10, No. 4, May-June 2000, 26-34; Lester J. Mazor, 'The Polarization of American Legal Theory,' *Archives for Phil. Of Law and Social Philosophy*, Supplement I Part 2 (1982) 339 at 342.

[189] The phrase is from Arthur A. Leff, 'Economic Analysis of Law: Some Realism about Nominalism', *Virginia L. Rev.* 60 (1974) 451 at 477.

[190] 'What is ignored is that the market system is not a neutral mechanism... the market economy creates the market society and thereby a set of institutions and values which are anything but neutral...Economists become without quite being aware of it, rationalizers of the *status quo*. Their theories deal with efficiency and equity and humanity get neglected': M.H. Watkins, 'Economics and Mystification', *Journal of Canadian Studies* 4 (1969) 55 at 56. Discontent

with democracy, especially by the political right, arises principally from the felt necessity to distinguish and separate capitalism and liberalism on the one hand, and liberalism and democracy on the other. For instance, neo-conservatives like Irving Kristol, who rebukes democrats for focusing on 'equality' and libertarians for their fascination with the 'free society', and who justly laments the unwillingness of a lot of intellectuals to say or even appear to say 'a few kind words for capitalism' nevertheless pointed out that '... efficiency is a means, not an end in itself. Capitalist efficiency may ... be regarded as a most useful precondition for a good life in a good society. But one has to go beyond ... capitalism itself, to discover the other elements that are wanted...': Irving Kristol, *Two Cheers for Capitalism* (New York: Basic Books, 1978) at 43, 140.

Dworkin quite frankly avows that his theory is neither a reformist creed nor a banner for revolution: *Taking Rights Seriously*, supra note 3 at 312. Dworkin's mission is to *rehabilitate* an old idea: 'Law's Ambitions for Itself', *Virginia L.Rev.* 71 (1985) 173. Dworkin's greatest achievement is that he has shown that 'economics' cannot be the emperor in 'law's empire'. See, particularly, 'Is Wealth a Value?' in, *A Matter of Principle*, supra note 3. But to remain wedded, as Dworkin is, to 'empirical metaphysics' is to be cut in the strait-jacket of the 'philosophy of history' which, as Leo Strauss, *Natural Right and History*, supra note 8 at 320 points out, deals only with completed, past action.

[191] E.W. Strong, 'Civilizations in Historical Perspective', supra note 170 at 117. Cf. Allan Bloom, *The Closing of the American Mind*, supra note 8 at 203: 'If there are many cultures unsolicited by one perfect or complete culture in which man is man simply – without prefix ... then the very word "man' is a paradox.'

Hegel dropped a bombshell when he wrote that 'whatever happens, every individual is a child of his time; so philosophy too is its own time apprehended in thoughts. It is just as absurd to fancy that a philosophy can transcend its contemporary world as it is to fancy that an individual can overleap his own age [or] leap over Rhodes." G.W.F. Hegel, *The Philosophy of Right* supra note (Preface). Yet, Hegel purchased finality for his own system by designating his 'contemporary world' - the Germanic world - as the final stage of world history.

[192] F.A. Hayek, *The Road to Serfdom*, supra note 54 at 48.

[193] Due largely to the work of Adam Smith in the latter part of the eighteenth century, modern liberal political theory was transformed and formalized into the doctrines of a new political economy: Pierre Manent, *An Intellectual History of Liberalism* trans. Rebecca Balinsky (Princeton: Princeton Univ. Press, 1994) at 46.

[194] O.W. Holmes, Jr. 'The Path of the Law' *Harvard L.Rev.* 10 (1897) 457 at 469.

[195] J.K. Gailbraith, *American Capitalism: The Concept of Countervailing Power* (1980 ed.) at 15. A.N. Whitehead, *Adventures of Ideas* (New York: Free Press, 1967) at 94: 'The older political economy reigned supreme for about a hundred years from the time of Adam Smith, because in its main assumptions it

did apply to the general circumstances of life as led, then and for innumerable centuries in the past.'

[196] A.V. Dicey, *The Law of the Constitution* (1885). Dicey himself was a son of a commercial gentry, and his analysis of English legal and political history yielded ideologically slanted, politically conservative, principles. Specifically, like many of his 'liberal unionist' confreres, Dicey 'never wholly reconciled himself with the movement toward democracy in nineteenth century Britain': P.S. Atiyah, *The Rise and Fall of the Freedom of Contract* (Oxford: Clarendon Press, 1979) at 583. Or, more accurately, Dicey aligned himself with the intellectual forces of 'conservative democracy' in late nineteenth and early twentieth century Britain. See, *inter alia*, T.H. Ford, *Albert Venn Dicey: The Man and His Times* (Chichester: Barry Rose Publishers 1985); Bernard J. Hibbits, 'The Politics of Principle: Albert Venn Dicey and the Rule of Law' *Anglo-American L. Rev.* 23 (1994) 18; David Sugarman, 'The Legal Boundaries of Liberty: Dicey, Liberalism and Legal Science' [Book Review] *Modern L. R.* (1983); Julia Stapleton, 'Dicey and His Legacy' *Hist. of Political Thought* 16 (1995) 234. On 'liberal unionism', see, John Roach, 'Liberalism and the Victorian Intelligentsia' *Cambridge Hist. Journal* 13 (1957) 58; Gordon L. Goodman, 'Liberal Unionism: The Revolt of the Whigs' *Victorian Studies* (1959) 173. On the meaning of *'laissez-faire'* see, Jacob Viner, 'The Intellectual History of Laissez-Faire' *Journal of Law and Economics* 3 (1960) 45.

[197] N. MacCormick, *Legal Right and Social Democracy*, supra note 39 at 43. Philosophers who see 'no blot of villainy in the beloved oppressed nor grant the faintest glimmer of humanity to the hated oppressor' are as much 'partisans, patriots and party liners' as those who stabilize a cultural experience by attempting and proffering a single coherent account of a multifaceted tradition. The quotations are from Chinua Achebe, *Anthills of the Savannah* (1987) at 100.

[198] R. Buckminster Fuller, *Critical Path* (New York: St. Martin's Press 1981) at x.

[199] F. Bacon, *An Advertisement Touching the Controversies of the Church of England*, in, *An Introductory Sketch to the Martin Marprelate Controversy, 1588-1590*, ed. Edward Arber (London: Southgate 1879) The English Scholars Library of Old and Modern Works, No. 8) at 166.

[200] D.L. Bazelon, 'Civil Liberties – Protecting Old Values in the New Century', *New York Univ. L. Rev.* 51 (1976) 505.

[201] Aristotle, *Nicomachean Ethics*, 1170b11-12.

[202] F.H. Knight, ':Political Responsibility in a Democracy', *Nomos: Responsibility* III (1960) 171 at 183-4.

[203] Ernest Baker, Otto Gierke, *Natural Law and the Theory of Society*, supra note 36 [Translator's Introduction] at LXX.

[204] K. Nielsen, 'Global Justice, Capitalism and The Third World', *Journal of Applied Philosophy* 2 (1984) 175 at 182. Cf: Stephen M. Schwebel, *Justice in*

International Law: Selected Writings of Judge Stephen M. Schwebel (Grotius Publication, Cambridge Univ. Press 1994)

[205] B. Parekh, 'Superior People: The Narrowness of Liberalism from Mill to Rawls,' *Times Literary Supplement*, February 25th, 1994, pp. 11-13.

[206] John Clive and Bernard Bailyn, 'England's Cultural Provinces: Scotland and America,' *William and Mary Quarterly* (3rd Series) 11 (1954) 200; Hugh Trevor-Roper, 'The Scottish Enlightenment,' *Studies in Voltaire and the Eighteenth Century* 58 (1971) 1635, and *Blackwood's Magazine* 327 (1977) 371.

[207] But see, I. Bernard Cohen, *Science and the Founding Fathers: Science in the Political Thought of Jefferson, Franklin, Adams, and Madison* (New York: W.W. Norton, 1991); Roger L. Emerson, 'Conjectural History and Scottish Philosophers,' *Historical Papers* (1984); H.M. Hopfl, 'From Savage to Scotman: Conjectural History in the Scottish Enlightenment,' *J. of British Studies* 17 (1978) 19; Allan Bloom, *The Closing of the American Mind*, supra note 8; Joyce Appleby, 'Republicanism in Old and New Contexts', *William and Mary* Quarterly (3rd Series) 43 (1986) 20; J.R. Pole, 'Slavery and Revolution: The Conscience of the Rich', *Historical Journal* 20 (1977) 503.

[208] See, David Hume, *The Philosophical Works*, ed. T.H. Green & T.H. Grose (Scientia Verlag, 1964 rep.) at 252fn; Richard H. Popkin, 'Hume's Racism', *Philosophical Forum* 2 (1978) 211; John Immerwah, 'Hume's Revised Racism', *Journal of the History of Ideas* 53 (1992) 481; Richard H. Popkin, 'The Philosophical Basis of 18th Century Racism', in *Studies in 18th Century Culture* 3 (1974) 245.

[209] Jennifer Welchman, 'Locke on Slavery and Inalienable Rights,' *Canadian Journal of Philosophy* 25 (1995) 67; Charles W. Mills, *Blackness Visible: Essays in Philosophy and Race* (Ithaca & London: Cornell Univ. Press, 1998) at 4: '... nothing at all is formally said in the Second Treatise of Government about justifying black subordination: blacks are just outside the scope of these principles.'

[210] Adam Smith, *Lectures on Jurisprudence*, supra note 101, ii, 117. He added at p. 181: 'it is indeed almost impossible that it [slavery] should ever be totally or generally abolished. In a republican government it will scarcely ever happen that it should be abolished ...' John Millar noted that '...it does not seem to have been the intention of Christianity to alter the civil rights of mankind, or to abolish those distinctions of rank which were already established. There is no precept of the gospel by which the authority of the master is in any respect restrained or limited; but, on the contrary, there are several passages from which it may be inferred that slaves, even after they had embraced the Christian religion, were not absolved from any part of the duties formerly incumbent upon them. We accordingly find that slavery remained all over Europe for several centuries after Christianity became the established religion...': John Millar, *The Origin of the Distinction of Ranks* (1806 ed.) (with a new Introduction by John Valdimir Price) (Thoemmes: Bristol, 1990) at 272-3. Lord Acton wrote that 'the sort of civil liberty which came with Christianity into the

world, and was one of her postulates, did not require the abolition of slavery. If men were being free by virtue of their being formed after the image of God, the proportion in which they realised that image would be the measure of their freedom. Accordingly, St. Paul prescribed to the Christian slave to remain content with his condition: l Cor. Vii 21. The opposite interpretation, common among Protestant commentators, is inconsistent with verses 20 and 24, and with the tradition of the Greek Fathers': 'Political Causes of the American Revolution', in, *Essays in the Liberal Interpretation of History* ed. W.H. McNeill (Chicago and London: Univ. of Chicago Press, 1967) at 90-94.

Although the Scottish Enlightenment, to which Adam Smith and John Millar belonged, condemned slavery as uneconomic or ruinous, it did not see slavery as a moral evil that needed to be attacked as such and extirpated: C. Duncan Rice, 'Controversies Over Slavery in 18th and 19th Centuries Scotland,' in *Antislavery Reconsidered: New Perspectives on the Abolitionists* ed. Lewis Parry & Michael Fellman (Baton Rouge & London: Louisiana State Univ. Press, 1979) 24-45; C. Duncan Rice, 'Archibald Dalzel, the Scottish Intelligentsia, and the Problem of Slavery,' *Scottish Hist. Rev.* 62 (1983) 121.

[211] Immanuel Kant, *Observations on the Feeling of the Beautiful and Sublime*, trans. J.T. Goldthwait, (Berkeley: Univ. of California Press, 1960). At p.110 Kant states: "The Negroes of Africa have *by nature* (emphasis added) no feeling that rises above the trifling. Mr. Hume challenges anyone to cite a single example in which a Negro has shown talents, and asserts that among the hundreds of thousands of blacks who are transported elsewhere from their countries, although many of them have even been set free, still not a single one was ever found who presented anything great in art or science or any other praiseworthy quality, even though among the whites some continually rise aloft from the lowest rabble, and through superior gifts earn respect in the world. So fundamental is the difference between these two races of man, and it appears to be as great in regard to mental capacities as in colour...' While discussing the condition of women, Kant recounts (p.113) that one 'Father Labat reports that a Negro carpenter, who he reproached for haughty treatment toward his wives, answered 'You whites are indeed fools, for first you make great concessions to your wives and afterward you complain when they drive you mad'. Kant's quintessentially *ad hominem* comment is: 'And it might be that there were something in this which perhaps deserved to be considered; but in short this fellow was quite black from head to foot, a clear proof that what he said was stupid'. Like many a German thinker, Kant never missed any opportunity to hurl invectives at Blacks. See, e.g. Kant, 'On the Different Races of Man (1775), in, Earl W. Count, *This is Race* (New York: Henry Schuman, 1950); E.C. Eze, 'The Color of Reason: The Idea of "Race" in Kant's Anthropology', in, *Anthropology and The German Enlightenment: Perspectives on Humanity*, ed. Katherine M. Faull (Lewisburg: Bucknell Univ. Press, 1995) 200-241; Beverly Harris-Schan, *Black Images in Eighteenth Century German Literature* (Stuttgert, 1981).

Hume's supposedly heuristic statement reverberated in colonial America. See note 213 below. But neither Hume nor Kant noted that the opportunity for private or public education was not available to even 'free' Negroes. See, inter alia, K.L. Little, *Negroes in Britain* (London: Keagan Paul, 1948); I. Berlin, *Slaves Without Masters: The Free Negro in the Antebellum South* (1974) (Oxford: Univ. Press, 1981) at 76-78; E. Genovese, *Roll, Jordan Roll: The World the Slaves Made* (New York: Pantheon Books 1976) at 561-66; Doris Y. Wilkinson, 'The 1850 Harvard Medical School Dispute and the Admission of African American Students,' *Harvard Library Bulletin* 3 (1992) (New Series) (No. 3) 13-27.

212 J.R. Pole, 'An Anatomy of the American Whig', [Book Review], *The Historical Journal* 9 (1966) 229 at 233; John C. Greene, 'The American Debate on the Negro's Place in Nature 1780-1815', *Journal of the History of Ideas* 15 (1954) 384.

213 W.D.Jordan, *White Over Black* (Chapel Hill: Univ. of Carolina Press, 1968); P. Curtin, *The Image of Africa: British Ideas and Action 1780-1850* (Madison: Univ. of Wisconsin Press 1964)

214 Eileen P. Sullivan, 'Liberalism and Imperialism: J.S. Mill's Defense of the British Empire', *Journal of the History of Ideas* 44 (1983) 599; C.J.W. Parker, 'The Failure of Liberal Racism: The Racial Ideas of E.A. Freeman', *Historical Journal* 24 (1981) 825 at 843. Like the bulk of the society, 'liberals' took Negro 'inferiority' for granted: See, *inter alia*, Christopher Harvie, *The Lights of Liberalism: University Liberals and the Challenge of Democracy, 1860-86* (London: Allen Lane l1976) at 106; Dinosh D'Souza, *The End of Racism* (New York: Free Press, 1995) at 120.

215 See, particularly, Geoffrey Sampson, *Liberty and Language* (Oxford: Oxford Univ. Press, 1979) Chapter 5.

216 O. Awolowo, *The Problems of Africa: The Need for Ideological Re-Appraisal* (Ibadan: MacMillan Education Ltd. 1977); W. Rodney, *How Europe Underdeveloped Africa* (Howard Univ. Press, 1974); B. Davidson, *Black Mother: Africa, the Years of the Slave Trade* (Boston: Little Brown, 1961). The optative approach of many African scholars to political ideologies almost invariably result in a rejection of individualism and liberalism. See, inter alia, O. Awolowo, supra; Chinweizu, *The West and the Rest of Us* (New York: Random House 1975). Or, recommending a one-party state: K. Busia, *Africa in Search of Democracy* (Oxford Univ. Press 1967). T.O. Elias, *The Nature of African Customary Law*, supra at 82 et seq. debunked the notion that the individual was invariably submerged in the African community. It has also been pointed out recently that socialism and/or communism is 'elementally alien to the African and *no version of this concept, however modified, would be endorsed by the unlettered majority.*': E.A. Ayandele, *African Historical Studies* (London: Frank Cass & Co. 1979) at 291. (Emphasis added). Indeed, 'conditions in tropical Africa are ... downright hostile to socialism ...': R. Sandbrook, 'Liberal Democracy in Africa: A Socialist-Revisionist Perspective,' *Canadian Journal of African Studies* 22 (1988) 246 at 250. But, when formal

western-type democracy is tried and it rapidly fails, foreign observers do one of two things: they either mourn the death of democracy or see it as evidence that Africans are incapable of ruling themselves. See, e.g. Walter Berns, *Taking the Constitution Seriously* (New York: Simon & Schuster, 1987); Lord Hailsham, *Hamlyn Revisited: The British Legal System Today* (London: Stevens & Sons, 1983). Cf. R. Neibuhr, *The Democratic Experience* (London: Pall Mall Press 1969); Fred M. Hayward, ed. *Elections in Independent Africa (London: Westview Press, 1987)*

[217] Robert P. Weiss, 'Humanitarianism, Labour Exploitation or Social Control? A Critical Survey of Theory and Research on the Origin and Development of Prisons', *Social History* 12 (1987) 331 at 343.

[218] J.S. Mill, *Utilitarianism*, ed. Oskar Piest (Liberal of Arts Library, 1977) at 178.

[219] Michael Polanyi, *Personal Knowledge: Towards a Post-Critical Philosophy* (New York: Harper Tochbooks, 1964) at 152.

[220] The institution of slavery was neither documented in Egypt until after the incursion of the Hyksos into Egypt in the eighteenth century before the Christian era nor was it 'racial' when it was documented. See, A.M. Bakir, 'Slavery in Pharaonic Egypt', *Annales Service des Antiquites de L'Egypte* 45 (1947) 135; William C. Hayes, *A Papyrus of the Late Middle Kingdom in the Brooklyn Museum* (1955) at 90; Emil G. Kraeling, *The Brooklyn Museum Aramaic Papyri: New Documents of the Fifth Century B.C. from the Jewish Colony at Elephantine* (New Haven: Yale Univ. Press, 1954); John Van Seters, *The Hyksos (A New Investigation)* (New Haven: Yale Univ. Press 1966) at 110.

[221] Isaac Mendelsohn, *Slavery in the Ancient Near East* (New York: Oxford Univ. Press 1948)

[222] Slavery became so ingrained on the African continent that even when, in the nineteenth century, a British cedilla marked down slavery for destruction, recalcitrant African personalities declared that they could 'no more give up slave-hunting than a cat can be stopped from mousing': Lawrence James, *The Savage Wars: British Campaigns in Africa, 1870-1920* (London: Robert Hale, 1985) at 129. See, further, Paul E. Lovejoy, *Slow Death for Slavery: The Course of Abolition in Northern Nigeria, 1897-1936* (Cambridge: Cambridge Univ. Press, 1993); G. Ugo Nwokeji, 'The Slave Emancipation Problematic: Igbo Society and the Colonial Equation,' *Comp. Studies in Society & History* 40 (1998) 318.

[223] European exploits on the African continent was initiated in 1442 by Prince Henry of Portugal, ostensibly in the zeal to spread Christianity, but in actual fact in pursuit of imperialistic ethos. See, Azurara, *Chronicle of the Discovery and Conquest of Guinea*, trans. C. Beazley and E., Prestage (London: Hakluyt Society, 1896) 2 Vols; C. Beazley, 'Prince Henry of Portugal and The African Crusade of the 15th Century', *American Historical Review* 16 (1910-11) 11; J.W. Blake, trans. & ed. *Europeans in West Africa 1450-1560* Vol. I (London, 1942)

The exploits of men from the Arabian peninsular, whose Muslim dynasties in Africa regarded slavery as a 'capital matter' is another harrowing tale. See, *inter alia*, Yusuf Fadl Hasan, *The Arabs and The Sudan: From the Seventh to the Early Sixteenth Century*) (Edinburgh Univ. Press 1967); Reginald Coupland, *East Africa and Its Invaders: From the Earliest Times to the Death of Seyyid Said in 1856* (Oxford: Clarendon Press, 1938); John R. Willis ed. *Slaves & Slavery in Muslim Africa* 2 Vols. (London: Frank Cass, 1985); I.B. Kake, 'The Slave Trade and the Population Drain from Black Africa to North Africa and the Middle East', in, *The African Slave Trade From the 15th to the 19th Centuries* (Unesco, 1979) 165-182; J.B. Condliffe, *The Commerce of Nations* (New York: W.W. Norton & Co. 1950); Frederick Cooper, *Plantation Slavery on the East Coast of Africa* (New Haven & London: Yale Univ. Press, 1977); Janet E. Ewald, *Soldiers, Traders, and Slaves: State Formation and Economic Transformation in the Greater Nile Valley, 1700-1885* (Madison: Univ. of Wisconsin Press, 1990)

Africans were sold into slavery as far away as China: see, Chang Hsing-lang, 'The Importation of Negro Slaves into China under the T'ang dynasty (A.D. 618-907),' *Bulletin of the Catholic Univ. of Peking* 7 (1930) 37-59, cited, C. Martin Wilbur, *Slavery in China During the Former Han Dynasty 206 B.C. – A.D. 25* (Chicago, 1943) Anthropological Series, Vol. 34. On the volume of the slave trade, see, Charles Issawi ed. *The Economic History of Iran, 1800-1914* (Chicago: Univ. of Chicago Press, 1971) at 124-126; Ralph A. Austen, 'The Trans-Saharan Slave Trade: A Tentative Census,' in, *The Uncommon Market: Essays in the Economic History of the Atlantic Slave Trade* ed. Henry A. Geney & Jan S. Hogenborn (New York: Academic Press, 1979) 36-76. Of course, while the slave trade was on, European philosophers from the countries most involved in it were spinning theories justifying slavery. See, R. Tuck, *Natural Rights Theories: Their Origins and Development* (Cambridge Univ. Press, 1979) at 50-7; Alan Watson, 'Seventeenth Century Jurists, Roman Law, and the Law of Slavery,' *Chic.-Kent L. Rev.* 68 (1993) 1343 at 1354.

[224] See, generally, Martin Bernal, *Black Athena: The Afroasiatic Roots of Classical Civilization (The Fabrication of Ancient Greece 1785-1985)*, Vol. I (London: Free Association Books, 1987); Jan Best, 'Racism in Classical Archaeology,' *Talanta* 24 (1992) 7; St. Clair Drake, *Black Folk Here and There (An Essay in History and Anthropology*) 2 vols. (Los Angeles, 1990); Lt. Francis Wilford, 'On Egypt and Other Countries Adjacent to the Cali River or Nile of Ethiopia From the Ancient Books of the Hindus', *Asiatic Researches* III (1799) 295; A.W. Kinglake, *Eothen* (London: Longmans, Burne and Green, 1852); Alexander Winchell, 'Our Remote Ancestry', *North American Review* 139 (1884) 246; J.E. Casely Hayford, *Ethiopia Unbound*, 2nd ed. (London: Frank Cass, 1969)

Hellenists reacted negatively to the pith and substance of Bernal's book. See, particularly, Mary R. Leftkowitz, *Not Out of Africa* (New York: 1994), *Black Athena Revisited* ed. Mary R. Leftkowitz and Gary Maclean Rogers (Chapel Hill & London: Univ. of North Carolina Press, 1996); John Ray, 'Before the

Pharaohs: The Escavation of Egyptian Pre-history,' *Times Literary Supplement* (October 1993) 27; Norman Levitt, *Promethus Bedevilled: Science and The Contradictions of Contemporary Culture* (New Brunswick, N.J: Rutgers Univ. Press, 199) Chapter 7. But see, Jacques Berlinerblau, *Heresy in the University: The Black Athena Controversy and the Responsibility of American Intellectuals* (New Brunswick: Rutgers Univ. Press, 1999); Jan Best, 'Racism in Classical Archaeology', supra.

The negative reaction reminds me of Francis Bacon's dictum that 'the forbidden writing is always thought to be certain sparks of a truth that fly up into the faces of those that seek to choke it and tread it out.' Bacon, *An Advertisement Touching the Controversies of the Church of England*, in, *An Introductory Sketch to the Martin Marprelate Controversy, 1588-1590*, ed. Edward Arber (London: Southgate 1879), The English Scholars Library of Old and Modern Works, No. 8) at 151.

[225] By 'racism' I mean the construction of visible or quantitative difference in the human biological species as *necessarily* qualitative difference. If, as intellectual history suggests, reason first appeared in Greece, 'reason has compromised itself with racism from its appearance in Greece until the present day. It continues': Christian Delacampagne, 'Racism and the West: From Praxis to Logos,' in, *Anatomy of Racism*, ed. David Theo Goldberg (1992) 83 at 87.

The great Greek philosopher, Aristotle, is *the fons et origo* of racism. Subsequent theorists, theologians, and physician-philosophers like Galen – the principal authority in medical science until the modern times – merely conjoined a series of powerful footnotes to Aristotle's opinion. See, e.g., Aristotle, *Physiognomonica* 6.812a-12, in, *The Works of Aristotle*, ed. W.D. Ross (1928) Vol. VI, where Aristotle states that 'cowardice' is attributable to 'too black a hue', and proffered *Egyptians* and *Ethiopians* as proof. Coming as it did from the pen of Alexander's teacher, the militaristic context of Aristotle's characterization is unmistakable. The unexceptionable (from a medical point of view) 'environmental determinism' espoused by the patron of the medical profession, Hippocrates, probably started this mode of thought. See, Hippocrates, 'Airs, Waters, Places', XII-XXIV, in, 1 *Hippocrates*, trans. W.H.S. Jones (Loeb Classical Library) (London: Heinemann, 1923) 105-137. In the eighteenth century, 'almost every serious discussion of the character of the Negro relies upon acceptance of, or opposition to, the theory that climate influences man' – Wylie Sypher, *Guinea's Captive Kings: British Anti-Slavery Literature of the Eighteenth Century* (Chapel Hill: Univ. of North Carolina Press, 1942) at 52. On Galen, and the popularity of physiognomy generally, see, Elizabeth C. Evans, 'Galen, the Physician as Physiognomist', *Transactions of American Philological Association* 76 (1945) 287, 'The Study of Physiognomy in the Second Century A.D.', *Transactions of American Philological Association* 72 (1941) 96.

In the modern world, 'the dreams of racism ... have their origin in ideologies of class, rather than in those of nation: ... in claims to divinity among rulers and to 'blue' or 'white' blood and 'breeding' among aristocracies ... they justify ...domestic repression and domination. Where racism developed outside Europe in the nineteenth century it was always associated with European domination': Benedict Anderson, *Imagined Communities: Reflections on the Origin and Spread of Nationalism*, rev. ed. (London and New York: Verso, 1991) at 149-50. See, also, William B. Cohen, *The French Encounter with Africans: White Response to Blacks, 1530-1880* (Bloomington & London: Indiana Univ. Press, 1980) at 96.

[226] See, generally, David Theo Goldberg, *Racist Culture: Philosophy and the Politics of Meaning* (London: Blackwell, 1993); Seymour Drescher, 'The Ending of the Slave Trade and the Evolution of European Scientific Racism', in *The Atlantic Slave Trade: Effects on Economies, Societies, and Peoples in Africa, the Americas, and Europe* ed. Joseph E. Inikori & Stanley L. Engerman (Duke Univ. Press, 1992) at 361-396; Richard H. Popkin, 'The Philosophical Basis of 18th Century Racism,' *Studies in Eighteenth Century Culture* 3 (1974) 245; Claudine Hunting, 'The Philosophers and Black Slavery, 1748-1765,' *Journal of the History of Ideas* 39 (1978) 405; Thomas E. Kebel, 'Scientific Racism in the Philosophy of Science: Some Historical Examples', *Philosophical Forum* 22 (1990) 1; P. Brantlinger, 'Victorians and Africans: The Genealogy of the Myth of the Dark Continent,' *Critical Inquiry* 12 (1985) 166; Hugh A. MacDougall, *Racial Myth in English History* (Montreal: Harvest House, 1982); O.A. Ladimeji, 'Nationalism, Alienation and The Crisis of Ideology', 46 *Transition* 38; V.Y. Mudimbe, *The Invention of Africa* (Indianapolis: Indiana Univ. Press 1988); Frederick Grimke, *The Nature and Tendency of Free Institutions* (1848) ed. J.W. Ward (Cambridge, Mass.:, 1968) (who declared that Anglo-Saxon civilization would ensure the complete disappearance of the Negro); William W[ilson] Cook, *American Institutions and Their Preservation* (New York: Norwood Press, 1927); A. McLaren, *Our Own Master Race: Eugenics in Canada, 1885-1945* (Toronto: McClelland & Stewart, 1990); Allison Blakely, 'Blacks in the Dutch Color Spectrum: Lexicography and Racial Imagery,' *The Historian* 54 (1991) 656; Eduardo Bonilla-Silva, 'This is a White Country: The Racial Ideology of the Western Nations of World System,' *Research in Politics and Society* 6 (1999) 85.

227. See, *inter alia*, Frank Dikotter, *The Discourse of Race in Modern China* (Hong Kong Univ. Press, 1992); Bernard Lewis, *Race and Slavery in the Middle East: An Historical Enquiry* (New York: Oxford Univ. Press, 1990); Michael Weiner, *Race and Migration in Imperial Japan* (New York: Routledge 1994); Cedric Dover, 'The Racial Philosophy of Ibn Khaldun', *Phylon* XIII (No. 2) (1952) 107; Cedric Dover, 'The Racial Philosophy of Jehuda Halevi', *Phylon* XIII (No. 4) (1952) 312; A.J. Arberry, *Classical Persian Literature* (London: George Allen & Unwin, 1958) at 255; Hellmut Riter, 'Irrational Solidarity Groups: A Socio-psychological Study in Connection with Ibn Khaldun', *Oriens* 1 (1948) 1; Aziz Al-Azmeh, 'Barbarians in Arab Eyes,' *Past and Present* 134 (1992) 3; Norman F. Cantor, *The Sacred Chain: The History of the Jews* (New York: HarperCollins, 1994) at 336.

228. Habib Tawa, 'Historical Aspects of the Question of Science and Racism', in, *Racism, Science and Pseudo-Science (Proceedings of the Symposium to Examine Pseudo-scientific theories invoked to justify racism and racial discrimination,* Athens 1981 (UNESCO).
229. Joseph Raz, 'Facing Diversity: The Case of Epistemic Abstinence', in, *Ethics in the Public Domain: Essays in the Morality of Law and Politics* (Oxford: Clarendon Press, 1994) 45; R. Ely, 'Democracy and the Right to be Different', *New York Univ. L.R.* 56 (1981) 397; D.L. Bazelon, 'The Morality of the Criminal Law', *South Cal. L.Rev.* 49 (1976) 385; Arthur Mitzman, 'On the Historicity of High Culture' [Book Review*], Journal of the History of Ideas* 55 (1994) 159.
230. 'The fundamental problem is ... how to reconcile one's identity and the actualities of one's own culture, society, and history to the reality of other identities, cultures, peoples. This can never be done simply by asserting one's preference for what is already one's own: tubthumping about the glories of "our" culture or the triumphs of "our" history is not worthy of the intellectual's energy, ... the public realm in which intellectuals make their representations is extremely complex and contains uncomfortable features, but the meaning of an effective intervention in that realm has to rest on the intellectual's unbudgeable conviction in a concept of justice and fairness that allows for differences between nations and individuals, without at the same time assigning them to hidden hierarchies, preferences, evaluations. Everyone today professes a liberal language of equality and harmony for all. The problem for the intellectual is to bring these notions to bear on actual situations where the gap between the profession of equality and justice, on the one hand, and the rather less edifying reality, on the other, is very great.': Edward W. Said, *Representations of the Intellectual* (New York: Pantheon Books, 1994) at 94. Cf. the interesting exchange between the anthropologist-ethnographer, Clifford Geertz and the pragmatist-post-modernist liberal philosopher, Richard Rorty on 'The Uses of Diversity' and 'On Ethnocentrism: A Reply to Geertz,' in *Michigan Quarterly Review* 26 (1986), 105-123 and 525-534.
231. Michael Howard, *The Lessons of History* (Oxford: Clarendon Press 1991) at 63: 'among the fiends in the liberal demonology today, imperialism, racism, militarism reign supreme; an evil trinity at whose collective door most of the wrongdoing in the world can conveniently be laid. Yet, little more than three decades ago, ... these words and the ideas associated with them evoked, even among professed liberal thinkers, a very different response.' See, inter alia, R. Cover, *Justice Accused: Antislavery and the Judicial Process* (New Haven: Yale Univ. Press 1975); Bruce Wright, *Black Robes, White Justice* (New Jersey: Lyle Stuart, 1987) at 54; P. Radin, *The Racial Myth* (New York: Whittlesey House, 1934); Charles C. Miller, 'Constitutional Law and The Rhetorics of Race', in, *Law in American History*, ed. D. Fleming & B. Bailyn (Boston & Toronto: Little, Brown, 1971) at 147-200; W.D. Jordan, *White Over Black*, supra; P. Curtin, *The Image of Africa: British Ideas and Actions 1780-1850*, supra; R.A. Huttenback, 'The British Empire as a "White Man's

Country" – Racial Attitudes and Immigration Legislation in the Colonies of White Settlement', *Journal of British Studies* 13 (1973) 108; James W. St. G. Walker, *'"Race", Rights, and the Law in the Supreme Court of Canada: Historical Case Studies* (Osgoode Society & Wilfrid Laurier Univ. Press, 1997); Constance Backhouse, *Colour-Coded: A Legal History of Racism in Canada, 1900-1950* (Toronto: Univ. of Toronto Press, 1999); Thomas B. Berger, *A Long and Terrible Shadow: White Values, Native Rights and the Americas, 1492-1992* (Vancouver: Douglas & McIntyre, 1991); Donald Avery, *"Dangerous Foreigners": European Immigrant Workers and Labour Radicalism in Canada, 1896-1932* (Toronto: Mclelland & Stewart, 1979); Abraham L. Davis and Barbara L. Graham, *The Supreme Court, Race and Civil Rights* (Thousand Oaks, California: Sage Publications, 1995). After the American civil war, 'antebellum law and racist ideology' rapidly metamorphosed into 'postbellum law and racist ideology': Barbara Ladd, *Nationalism and The Color Line in George W. Cable, Mark Twain and W. Faulkon* (Lousiana State Univ. Press, 1996) at 117.

232. Alexis de Tocqueville, *Democracy in America*, Vol. I at 322. Rousseau underscored the provincial character of the concept of man in European discourse when he wrote: 'though the inhabitants of Europe for three or four hundred years past have overrun the other parts of the world, and are constantly publishing new collections of voyages, I am persuaded that those of Europe are the only men we are as yet acquainted with; nay, to judge by the ridiculous prejudices which to this day prevail even among men of letters, very few, by the pompous title of the study of mankind, mean any thing more than the study of their own countrymen…': *Discourse on Inequality*, supra note 78 at 231.

As 'a believing Catholic' or rather 'a deviant Protestant', and being prone 'like many of his German contemporaries to make rash and sweeping generalization,' Lord Acton 'describes … as a 'great absurdity' …[the] view that 'the original distinctions of race are altogether hypothetical': E.L. Woodward, 'The Place of Lord Acton in the Liberal Movement of the Nineteenth Century', *Politica* (1939) 248 at 254, 261. The phrase 'deviant Protestant' is Richard Tuck's, 'Grotius & Selden,' in *The Cambridge History of Political Thought 1450-1700* ed. J.H. Burns (Cambridge Univ. Press, 1991) at 521.

233. Not even the Enlightenment, which happened exclusively in a 'world of white men, … founded on Christianity and on the culture of the classical age', is exempt from these strictures. The quotation is from Ulrich Hof, *The Enlightenment*, trans. from the German (Oxford: Blackwell, 1994) at 7.

234. Richard Rorty, *Philosophy and the Mirror of Nature*, supra note 33 at 359.

235. Michael Novak, *The Spirit of Democratic Capitalism* (1982) (New York: Madison Books, 1991) at 27.

236. Tacitus, *Agricola and Germania*, trans. M. Hutton at 245; William D. Gairdner, *The Trouble With Canada: A Citizen Speaks Out* rev. ed. (Toronto: Stoddart Publishing Co., 1994) at 277: 'men the world over despise victims – especially their own – whereas women tend to take pity on them.'

237. Luciano Canfora, *The Vanished Library*, trans. Martin Ryle (Berkeley: Univ. of California Press, 1990) at 71; Debora Shuger, 'Irishmen, Aristocrats and Other White Barbarians', *Renaissance Quarterly* 50 (1997) 494 at 515.
238. Michael Oakeshott, 'The Voice of Poetry in the Conversation of Mankind', in, *Rationalism in Politics*, supra note 54 at 207.
239. Chinua Achebe, *Anthills of the Savannah* (1987) at 100: 'orthodoxy whether of the right or of the left is the graveyard of creativity .. a genuine artist, no matter what he says he believes, must feel in his blood the ultimate enmity between art and orthodoxy.'
240. For a subtle acknowledgment (and celebration) of the rhetorical character of contemporary modern liberal political philosophy, see, Richard Rorty, *Philosophy and the Mirror of Nature*, supra note 33 at 157 et seq; Richard Rorty, 'Solidarity or Objectivity,' in *Post Analytic Philosophy* ed. J. Rajchman & Cornel West (New York: Columbia Univ. Press 1985).
241. F.A. Hayek, *The Road to Serfdom*, supra note 54 at 138.
242. D. Thomson, 'Rousseau and the General Will', in, *Political Ideas*, ed. D. Thomson (London: Penguine Books 1966) at 105; John E. Smith, *The Spirit of American Philosophy* (1962) rev. ed. (Albany: State Univ. of New York Press, 1983) at 4.
243. Morris R. Cohen, 'The Place of Logic in Law', *Harvard L.Rev.* (1916) 622 at 638.
244. J.M. Keynes, 'Economic Possibilities for Our Grandchildren', in, *Essays in Persuasion* (London: MacMillan, 1932) at 369. Keynes went on to suggest that we should continue the pretension for another 100 years. A noted American conservative scholar, Russell Kirk, after distinguishing between 'two great elements in any society, its Permanence and its Progression,' identified the former with 'the conservative interest' and the latter with 'the liberal interest.' He then added, 'there are ages in which intelligent people would do well to ally themselves with the Progression of their nation, to contend against stagnation, for society without the means of renewal is not for this world ... But our time is not such an age... our modern peril ... is that of vertiginous speed ... in the twentieth century, it is our Permanence, not our Progression, which needs the adherence of thinking men and women': Russell Kirk, *Enemies of the Permanent Things: Observations of Abnormity in Literature and Politics* (New York: Arlington House, 1969) at 26.
245. Shakespeare, *Merchant of Venice*, Act III Sc. I, Lines 80-94: 'The world is still deceived with ornament. In law, what plea so tainted and corrupt. But, being season'd with a gracious voice, Obscures the show of evil? In religion, What damned error, but some sober brow Will bless it and approve it with a text, Hiding the grossness with fair comment?'
246. Joseph M. Levine, *Humanism and History: Origins of Modern English Historiography* (Ithaca: Cornell Univ. Press, 1987) at 151: 'it is clear from the second book of the *Advancement of Learning* that Bacon was pretty well satisfied with the achievements of the humanities, including moral and political philosophy, though he had many specific recommendations for their

improvement'. See also Neal Wood, 'Tabula Rasa, Social Environmentalism and the English Paradigm,' *Journal of the History of Ideas* 53 (1992) 647 at 665. Julian Martin, *Francis Bacon, the State, and the Reform of Natural Philosophy* (Cambridge: Cambridge Univ. Press, 1992) notes that Bacon was 'deeply conservative and elitist in his political views'.

247. 'Whenever there come a philosopher who tells you that he has found the ultimate truth, do no trust him. If he tells you that he knows the ultimate good or has a proof that the good must become reality, do not trust him, either. The man merely repeats the errors which his predecessors have committed for two thousand years. It is time to put an end to this brand of philosophy': H. Reinchenback, *The Rise of Scientific Philosophy* (Berkeley: Univ. of California Press 1951) at 302. See also, Ved Mehta, *Fly and the Fly Bottle* (Boston: Little Brown, 1962) at 269.

248. See, generally, Thomas S. Kuhn, *The Structure of Scientific Revolutions*, 3rd ed. (Chicago: Univ. of Chicago Press, 1996)

249. Plato, *Phaedrus* 227.

250 See, particularly, Allan Bloom, *The Closing of the American Mind*, supra note 8; Francis Fukuyama, *The End of History and the Last Man* (New York: Free Press, 1992). For the supposed indictment of 'liberal democracy' which implicitly or explicitly shape the intellectual agenda of (some) contemporary old and libertarian (modern) liberalism, see the succinct confession and avoidance by Werner J. Dannhauser, 'The Problem of the Bourgeois,' in *The Legacy of Rousseau* ed. Clifford Orwin & Nathan Tarcov (Chicago: Univ. of Chicago Press, 1997) 3 at 15: '... The charges against the bourgeois have not only continued but in some cases become more strident. Much of that stridency directs itself at the moderation liberal democracies recognize as the political virtue par excellence. In doing so, bourgeois democracy becomes part of the great tradition of Western civilization. It becomes the heir, perhaps the sole surviving heir, of both Jerusalem and Athens. It is one thing to say that liberal or bourgeois democracy is the corrupted heir of that tradition... it is another thing to say that it is the corrupt heir to a tradition that is itself corrupt because it is dominated by dead white European males, and because it was always defaced and disgraced by sexism, racism, homophobia, elitism, ethnocentrism, and other evils. That is the charge against the bourgeois today, a charge that must be refuted ...' See also, Arthur Asher Shenfield, 'The Ideological War Against Western Society,' in, *Limited Government, Individual Liberty, and the Rule of Law: Selected Works of Arthur Asher Shenfield* ed. Norman Barry (London: Edward Elgar Publishing Ltd, 1998) at 321-340.

251. F.A. Hayek, *The Road to Serfdom*, supra note 54 at 70.

252. On the distinction between 'convergent' and 'divergent' problem, see, E.F. Schumacker, *A Guide for the Perplexed* (New York: Harper and Row, 1977)

253. The belief that 'the ancients' were against 'democracy' may well be a result of a myth fostered by associating political philosophy with *forms* of government. See, Arlene W. Saxonhouse, *Athenian Democracy : Modern*

Mythmakers and Ancient Theorists (Notre Dame: Univ. of Notre Dame Press, 1997); Lisa Kallet-Marx, 'Institutions, Ideology, and Political Consciousness in Ancient Greece: Some Recent Books in Athenian Democracy' [Book Review] *Journal of the History of Ideas* 55 (1994) 307.

[254] Robert Unger, *What Should Legal Analysis Become?,* supra note 53 at 72. But see, Jeremy Waldron, *Law and Disagreement* (Oxford: Clarendon Press, 1999)

255. Plato, *Phaedrus* 270.

256. See, particularly, Allan Bloom ed. *Confronting the Constitution* (Washington, D.C.: AEI Press 1990); Harry V. Jaffa, *Original Intention and the Framers of the Constitution: A Disputed Question* (Washington, D.C.: Regnery Gateway, 1994)

257. I. Kant, *Logic*, trans. Robert S. Hartman & Wolfgang Schwartz (New York: Dover Publications, 1988) at 76.

258. B. Farrington, *Science and Politics in the Ancient World* (London: George Allen & Unwin 1939) at 218.

259. Ian Harris, *The Mind of John Locke: A Study of Political Theory in its Intellectual Setting* (Cambridge: Cambridge Univ. Press 1994) at 192; Ian Harris, 'Locke's Political Theory,' in *British Philosophy and the Age of Enlightenment* ed. Stuart Brown (London & New York: Routledge, 1996) 96 at 99.

260. F.H. Eterovich, *Approaches to Natural Law* (New York: Exposition Press 1972) at 160; A. Cobban, *In Search of Humanity*, supra note 45 at 212-213. For the political context of Kant's 'absolutism,' see, Frederick C. Beiser, *Enlightenment, Revolution, and Romanticism: The Genesis of Modern German Political Thought 1790-1800* (Cambridge, Mass.: Harvard Univ. Press, 1992).

261. Kant later castigated the commercial, Christian countries of his time for 'drinking up iniquity like water', in their interaction with the peoples of Asia, Africa and the Americas: Kant, 'To Perpetual Peace: A Philosophical Sketch', (1795) in, *Perpetual Peace and Other Essays*, trans. T. Humphrey (Indianapolis: Hackett Publishing Co. 1983) at 119.

262. William James, 'The Moral Philosopher and the Moral Life', in, *Essays in Pragmatism* ed. A. Castell (New York: Hafner, 1948) at 81.

263. R. Rorty, *Philosophy and the Mirror of Nature*, supra note 33 at 5.

264. *Montaigne in Movement*, tr. A. Goldhammer (Chicago, 1958) at 293, cited, D.R. Kelley, '"Second Nature": The Idea of Custom in European Law, Society, and Culture', supra note 32 at 160. Cf: 'It was not the intention of most of the great scientists of the sixteenth and seventeenth centuries to diminish the power of traditional institution ... They accommodated themselves to traditional political institutions; when the traditions of liberalism and democracy prospered in the 19th century they also accommodated themselves to these newly ascendant traditions. Most scientists were not themselves explicitly antitraditional. 'Scientism' which was antitraditional and hence critical of all beliefs and institutions which were not demonstrably true or valuable according to scientific criteria, was largely the work of nonscientists, publicists,

philosophers, social scientists, and social reformers': Edward Shils, *supra* note 63 at 103-4.

265. William James, supra note 262 at 80-1: 'If the philosopher is to keep his judicial position, he must never become one of the parties to the fray ...The philosopher must be a conservative, and in the construction of his casuistic scale must put the things most in accordance with the customs of the community on top.

And yet if he be a true philosopher, he must see that there is nothing final in any actually given equilibrium of human ideals...'

266. 'Locke's state of nature evokes a condition in which neither social convention, temporal authority nor inherited belief confounds the human capacity to discover the moral law': Kirstie M. McClure, *Judging Rights: Lockean Politics and the Limits of Consent*, supra note 66 at 62; David Resnick, 'Locke and The Rejection of the Ancient Constitution,' *Political Theory* 12 (1984) 97 at 102: 'according to Locke, it is reason that identifies what is truly obligatory, and custom does not necessarily embody reason. The way to discern whether an action or rule is truly obligatory is to discern its rationality, not to dwell upon its antiquity, its universal acceptance in the community, or the number of people, past and present, who say it is right or good or praiseworthy.'

267. Clifford Geertz, *Local Knowledge: Further Essays in Interpretive Anthropology* (New York: Basic Book, 1985)

268. Pierre Vidal-Naquet, *The Black Hunter: Forms of Thought and Forms of Society in the Greek World,* trans. Andrew Szegedy-Maszak (Baltimore: Johns Hopkins, 1986) at 252. See also, Jean Pierre Vernant, *The Origins of Greek Thought* (1962) trans. from the French, (Ithaca, New York: Cornell Univ. Press 1982).

269. Ulrich Hof, *The Enlightenment,* supra note 233 at 161.

[270] Francis Fukuyama, *The End of History and the Last Man,* supra note 250 at 305.

271. See, Michael S. Moore, supra note 20.

272. Thomas S. Kuhn, *The Structure of Scientific Revolutions,* supra note 248 at 122.

273. Michael Oakeshott, 'The Voice of Poetry in the Conversation of Mankind', in, supra note 54 . (Emphasis added)

274. I have run together here Peter Novick, *"That Noble Dream": The Objectivity Question and the American Historical Profession* (Cambridge: Cambridge Univ. Press 1988); R. Rorty, 'Solidarity or Objectivity', *in Post-Analytic Philosophy*, supra; R. Rorty, *Contingency, Irony, and Solidarity* (Cambridge: Cambridge Univ. Press 1989); George P. Fletcher, *Loyalty: An Essay on the Morality of Relationships* (New York: Oxford Univ. Press 1993).

[275] See, e.g. R. Dworkin, *Taking Rights Seriously*, supra note 3 at 182.

276. I refer to hermeneuticists generally, and Richard Rorty, in particular. Cf: David A. Hollinger, 'How Wide the Circle of the "We"? American Intellectuals

and the Problem of the Ethnos since W.W. II,' *American Hist. Rev.* 98 (1993) 317.
277. Reuven Brenner, 'Economics – An Imperialist Science?' *Journal of Legal Studies* 9 (1980) 170; R. Cooter & J. Gordley, 'Economic Analysis in Civil Law Countries: Past, Present, and Future' *International Rev. of Law and Economics* 11 (1991) 261; Neil Duxbury, supra note 178 at 310: 'Economics is considered by its jurisprudential advocates to be not just an old social science, but the queen of the social sciences, the only social science capable of providing analytical models which facilitate the discovery of precise, verifiable answers to many difficult questions about legal policy and decision-making'.
278. Michael Novak, supra note 235 at 18.
279. Ernest Barker, in supra note 36 at XXVI.
280. J.S. Swain, 'What is History', *Journal of Philosophy* 20 (1920) at 349.
281. Ernst Troeltsch, 'The Ideas of Natural Law and Humanity', Appendix to Otto Gierke, supra note 35; D.G. Ritchie, 'Philosophy and the Study of Philosophers', *Mind* 8 (1899) (N.S.) 1 at 24: '.... We can only face the problems rightly if we face them for ourselves. And, for that reason one of the dangers we've to guard against is the scholastic habit of becoming the mere expositors of any one master, however great'.
282. J.B. Skemp, 'The Permanent Importance of Greek Studies,' *Durham University Journal* LXXIII (N.S.) (1980) 1 at 7. 'The Greek mind was free to think about the world as it pleased, to reject all traditional explanations, to discard all the priests taught, to search unhampered by any outside authority for the truth': Edith Hamilton, *The Greek Way* (New York: W.W. Norton, 1930) at 35.
283. B. Schwatz, *In Search of Wealth and Power: Yen Fu and the West* (Cambridge, Mass. Belknap Press, 1964) at 240.
[284] John A. Hall, *Powers and Liberties: The Causes and Consequences of the Rise of the West* (Oxford: Basil Blackwell, 1985) at 258.
[285] Patricia J. Williams, *The Rooster's Egg* (Cambridge, Mass.: Harvard Univ. Press, 1995) at 25.
286. D. Spitz, *The Real World of Liberalism* (Chicago & London: Univ. of Chicago Press, 1982) at 196.
287. Aristotle, *Politics* 1302a25-30.
288. St. Augustine, *The City of God* Bk. 4 Chap. 4.
289. Allan Bloom, *The Closing of the American Mind*, supra note 8.
290. Marke DeWolfe Howe, 'The Positivism of Mr. Justice Holmes', *Harvard L.R.* 64 (1951) at 534.
291. B. Kaplan, 'Encounters with O.W. Holmes, Jr.', in, *Holmes and The Common Law: A Century Later* (Holmes Lectures, 1981) at 24.
292. H.E. Yntema, 'The Rational Basis of Legal Science', *Columbia L.R.* 31 (1931) 925 at 943.
293. W.T. Murphy, 'Memorizing Politics of Ancient History,' [Book Review] *Modern Law Rev.* 50 (1987) 384.

[294] Roger Poole, *Towards Deep Subjectivity* (London: Penguin Press, 1972) at 70; William J. Bouwsma, 'From History of Ideas to History of Meaning,' *J. of Interdisciplinary Hist.* 12 (1981) 279.

295. Nathaniel Weyl, *Karl Marx: Racist* (New Rochelle, New York: Arlington House, 1980); C. Zirkle, *Evolution, Marxian Biology and The Social Scene* (Philadelphia: Univ. of Penn. Press, 1959); George Watson, *The English Ideology: Studies in the Language of Victorian Politics* (London: Allen Lane, 1973) at 210-212.

296. Sir Ernest Barker, 'Reflections on English Political Theory', *Political Studies* 1-2 (1953-4) 6. This phrase has been credited to an anonymous correspondent in *The Times*, 16th August, 1790: D. Winch, 'Adam Smith: Scottish Moral Philosopher and Political Economist,' in *Adam Smith: International Perspectives* ed. H. Mizuta and C. Sugiyama (New York: St. Martins Press, 1993) at 85.

297. B. Schwarzchild, *The Red Prussian: The Life and Legend of Karl Marx*, trans. M. Wing (New York: Charles Scribner's Sons, 1947) at 84.

298. J. Dunn, 'The Identity of the History of Ideas,' *Philosophy* 43 (1968) 85 at 98.

Chapter 2

The Eye of the Intellect

> A man's vision concerning such things is dullest when he is young and at its sharpest when he is old[1]

> Through want of years when men are not indifferent but partial, then their judgment is weak and unripe; and when it growth to strength and ripeness, by that time it is forestalled with such a number of prejudicate opinions as it is made unprofitable[2]

Introduction

After several years of wandering on his way back from the Trojan War, Odysseus, the hero of Homer's *Odyssey,* returned home. Disguised as a wretched old beggar, Odysseus watched the actions of Penelope's suitors in his own household. He discovered, for instance, that the soothsayer, Leodes, had not discouraged or refused to identify with the schemes of the suitors. When the time came for Odysseus to mete out punishments to the *dramatis personae* he had good reason to deal harshly with the soothsayer. But the soothsayer had a different perception of the role he had played. The soothsayer wrapped his arms around Odysseus legs and beseeched Odysseus to refrain from striking him. The latter retorted:[3]

> If verily thou dost declare thyself the soothsayer among these men, often, I ween, must thou have prayed in the halls that far from me the issue of a joyous return might be removed, and that it might be with thee that my dear wife should go and bear thee children; wherefore thou shalt not escape grievous death.

But not everyone suffered as the soothsayer. Among those who escaped the fate of the suitors was the bard, Phemius. A credible witness corroborated Phemius' plea that he did not willingly blow the flute and played the lyre for the enjoyment of the suitors. That convinced the warrior of the bard's innocence; the bard was spared.

The first two sections of this chapter is concerned with the intellectual universe constructed by a different species of bard, 'the ancients', when they originated the form of liberalism that we called 'old' liberalism in the first chapter. The third section critiques the use made of 'the ancients' by some contemporary republican political philosophers. As in the previous chapter, the purpose of this chapter is neither to bury nor to sing the praises of old liberalism. Rather, it puts the ancients' intellectual universe in perspective, and underscores its ramifications for 'visible' minorities and 'the south' when deployed by some contemporary republican political theorists.

The ancients fashioned and established an intellectual universe that seemingly banished the liberal idea[4] from the world of man. Yet, when viewed against the realities of the ancient world, 'the ancients' intellectual universe appears to be more a strategic reflection of the political necessity of the age than a desire to overthrow the liberal idea. In a nutshell, 'the ancients' were concerned not so much with the liberal idea as with the noble intellectual task of how to unify, conserve, and preserve the political existence and independence of the *free* peoples of antiquity, that is, the Greeks.

Except, perhaps, the turbulent and short-lived Athenian democracy, everywhere the ancients looked they saw stable, durable, and peaceful republics only in ethnically and culturally homogenous, class-based socioeconomic polities.[5] And, they apparently concluded that that was the form that republics *necessarily* assume. With that rationalistic premise, the ancients proceeded to construct a corresponding hierarchical socioeconomic and political model. With the probable exception of the flicker of light in modern times, philosophy, as well as literature, affords no counter-example to this model.[6] In pre-modern times, the inevitability of class-based sociopolitical and economic world was expressed in the language of natural law. In modern times, the repertoire of natural society was used. Sometimes, however, it was presented as the 'teachings of history'[7] or wrapped up in romantic consciousness. With the ascension of science in the nineteenth century, thinkers hit on the strategy of 'seeking the clue to the social pyramid in cranial bumps.'[8] The thesis of this chapter is that the deployment, at the domestic or internal level, of the intellectual universe invented by the ancients always compels the choice of sociopolitical and economic institutions that freeze individuals into 'higher and lower orders.'[9] The adoption of the same conceptual framework at the international or external level results in assigning some peoples and/or states to the apex of the pyramid and others to the base of 'the great chain of being.'[10] Unless the intellect is re-knead it would be impossible to confront the belief in hierarchical sociopolitical and economic world. But the aim of this chapter is not to undertake the task of re-kneading the intellect. Rather, it emphasizes that we cannot embark on that task unless and until we heed some Baconian admonitions.

First, we shall have to abandon intellectual piety, by which certain philosophers become 'dictators instead of consuls.'[11] Intellectual piety makes scholars line up behind one master or another. The zeal and brilliance with which scholars prosecute the resultant controversy shroud their 'self-imposed immaturity,'[12] and, consequently, their dogmatism. The resultant refusal to open their own eyes[13] has soporific effect on speakers and hearers alike.[14] Consequently, the conclusions made by the passive or rather actively constrained intellect are passed on, like an incurable disease, from one generation of scholars to another.

Secondly, we cannot embark on the task of re-kneading the intellect merely by picking or choosing between 'the ancients' and 'the moderns'[15] or old and modern liberalism respectively. Contemporary political theorists give the impression that any sociopolitical and economic problem can be resolved within the conceptual framework of either old or modern liberalism. But this is as erroneous as it is misleading. For, both thc variegated contemporary advocates of old liberalism and the disunited proponents of modern liberalism believe that their respective predecessors somehow managed to design a miraculously 'gapless system of rights or entitlements of what people are entitled to have as a matter of distributive justice.'[16] Their common foe is 'positivism,' which is sometimes depicted as not merely relativistic, but a 'dangerous form of relativism.'[17] In this scenario, advocates of old liberalism designate the ancients as nature's amanuensis. They charge that the moderns had torn several leafs off from the book of nature that the ancients had deciphered. Contemporary proponents of modern liberalism reverse these claims. To them, the ancients had made an artificial and untrue veil for nature; the moderns had pierced the veil and revealed nature's true face. Both portray positivists as sophists who, like Protagoras, would have us believe that 'man is the measure of all things'.

This is not a brief for positivism, but the self-assurance and pugilism of the other schools of thought are frightening. Contemporary old and modern liberal political theorists believe that their respective theses are true. The result is an array of 'imperial intellects,'[18] sealed up, hermetically, and its scholars moving with ease, in their own separate 'universe and library,' with the books in their library constituting 'cognitive authority.'[19] They, therefore, choose 'the doctrinal' as opposed to 'the initiative' method of teaching.[20] Scholars in the different schools are, jointly and severally, anxious to convince readers of the ideality of their paradigms. Each of the schools insists that its 'judgment is fittest to be the intellectual standard'.[21]

The voluminous literature generated by the scholars' debate papers over the sociopolitical and economic malaise that called the controversy into being in the first place. In particular, there has been little, if any, appreciable improvement in sociopolitical and economic institutional practices, especially as they relate to very 'visible' minorities in liberal polities on the one hand, and, on the other, between advanced, industrialized nations and the 'the south.' In fact, for the first time since the end of the Second World War, very 'visible' minorities within liberal democracies, and 'Third World' polities have witnessed rapid reversals and degeneration of their sociopolitical and economic fortune. The role of the revived political ideals in this matter cannot be underestimated. Political theorists seek to channel the practice of freedom into paths constructed when the concepts of 'visible minorities' and 'third-world' were nonexistent.

Although an established conceptual framework facilitates increased intellectual activity, this occurs within the limits imposed by the paradigm. This makes the growth, in contradistinction from the paradigmatic advancement, of knowledge difficult, if not impossible. Yet, dominant contemporary political theorists see the question of the possibility of the growth of political knowledge as one of paradigm choice, a contest between old and modern liberalism. But we know that 'when paradigms enter into a debate about paradigm choice, their role is necessarily circular' for 'each group uses its own paradigm to argue in that paradigm's defense.'[22] Notwithstanding that the established conceptual frameworks possess liberal valence, and although they are far from being grounded in an 'atmosphere of accredited mendacity,'[23] a skeptical attitude to established conceptual frameworks is necessary for the growth of knowledge.

Thirdly, it will be necessary to dispel a misconception, fostered by racial and gender critiques of political philosophers, that because of the gender bias of the ancients and the racism of the moderns, we can profit neither from the one nor the other. But we need not throw the baby out with the bath water. Perhaps, political philosophers embraced androcentric and racial prejudices not because political philosophy is inherently gender and racial biased but because philosophers pandered to the vanities of their immediate societies and times. Gender and racial prejudices heighten some of the weaknesses of old and modern liberalism, but they say nothing about their strength.[24] Their strength lies in the firm conviction that the world is intelligible, and human beings have the capacity to understand it; that philosophy is possible, even though *certainty* is unattainable. Specifically, although we can know *how* we know what we *believe* that we know, we cannot know tha*t* we *know*. To know that we know is to know as God, but we are mortals. The real problem lies in the unarticulated premise that the founders of liberalism, old or modern, had discovered or mapped out ultimate intellectual universe. One of the central points of this chapter is that the intellectual universe articulated by the ancients rests as much on truncated history as the conceptual framework of modern liberalism rests on 'congealed history.'[25] In that truncated history, the so-called 'colored' peoples are subjects acted upon rather than objects acting in their own right.

Standard histories seldom contain the totality of experience that significantly influenced political theories. Part I of this chapter suggests that a long view of history will throw into bold relief the optics of the ancients. In the ancient world, the practice was widespread for commonwealths to invade commonwealths, for the invaders to slaughter resisters along with the eminent citizens, and enslave the remainder. I shall call this phenomenon 'perianderism.'[26] Part II suggests that the ancients aimed at and designed an ideal Greek republic immune to perianderism, but in so doing they fashioned an intellectual universe that elevated the few and depressed the many: they designated some as natural rulers and others as born to be ruled. Part III examines the subtle attempt made by some contemporary republican political theorists, as exemplified by Francis Fukuyama's *The End of History and the Last Man,*[27] to once more naturalize hierarchy.

I

THE RELEVANCE OF A LONG VIEW OF HISTORY

Until recently, the intellectual history of the ancient world was little more than encomium for the Greeks. Reverence for and admiration of the Greeks have always involved a particular brand of historical consciousness that, in turn, entailed certain unarticulated beliefs. Prominent among such unspoken assumptions is that Greece was the home of the arts and sciences, of philosophy, of all learning. Sir Henry Maine captured this sentiment when he remarked that 'nothing moves in this world which is not Greek in its origin.'[28] Another unspoken assumption was that history attests to the fact that fair-skinned peoples alone, specifically, Indo-Europeans, have been the sole, creative, and thinking portion of mankind. The fact that Christianity had long been the established religion in European societies necessitated a third unspoken assumption. It is that biblical historiography and cosmogony furnish sacred history and facts.[29] 'Jerusalem is the fountain-head of religious knowledge – a more sacred oracle of truth, and the source of another sort of knowledge, high and supernatural as Athens is of secular' were the high words of John Henry Newman in the nineteenth century.[30] However, from the time when archeological and geological researches began to contradict sacred history,[31] the last mentioned assumption was increasingly confined to and continued to be made only by those who refused to regard Greece as the spiritual, in contradistinction to the intellectual, home of Europe.[32]

These and several other complacent beliefs have been shaken. We have learned, for instance, that history began at Sumer;[33] that the arts and sciences were cultivated long before the historic Greeks and the noble Romans ruled the earth;[34] that the account of Egypt in Genesis and Exodus is almost certainly mistaken;[35] that, notwithstanding the pious credulity of the Christian Fathers[36] - who were largely 'men of one book only'[37]- Egypt bears witness to 'the antiquity of knowledge or the knowledge of antiquity.'[38] In short, 'archeological researches have disclosed infinitely long and important perspectives stretching back to a much more remote point in time than the Greece that seemed to be revealed by classical literature,'[39] or the historiography of Near Eastern books of religion that uniformly attributed whatever passed in the world to Divine Providence.[40]

The civil history of the world crafted by European scholarship surpassed Near Eastern books in traducing the history of other commonwealths. For instance, the consistency with which Hebrew myths and legends[41] and the ethnocentric history of Near Eastern books of religion underline the marked contrast between Semites and Egyptians is marched by the obdurate audacity of European scholars that the people who ancient annalists classified and described as 'Hamites' were necessarily fair-skinned peoples. They turned the biblical classification on its head, and hypothesized that Hamites were fair-skinned peoples who initiated and diffused civilization in the ancient world.[42] When, in the face of contradictory evidence, the thesis could not be sustained, they simply denied that Egypt had had a genuine civilization.[43] Since the place of Greece in the history of civilization is assured, scholars shifted their attention to Mesopotamia. In no time, however, disturbing snippets of long forgotten history came to the surface. Specifically, archeological research revealed that the great civilization that flourished between the rivers Tigris and Euphrates, a civilization which, until the late decades of the nineteenth century, was credited to a Semitic people, was initiated by a non-Semitic, non-Indo-European people, the Sumerians. The semitic Amorites, 'the people known to history as the Babylonians because they had their capital at Babylon,'[44] were usurpers in the area.[45]

The activities of usurpers are well documented in antiquity. Leaving aside earlier and, particularly the so-called 'battleless' conquest of Egypt by the somewhat mysterious Hyksos[46] in the eighteenth century before the Christian era,[47] and the endemic attacks by the 'sea peoples'[48] in the latter part of the second millenium before the Christian era, Egypt played unwilling host to 'a dreary file of foreign conquerors:'[49] Assyrians,[50] 672 B.C., Persians, 525 B.C., Greeks, 333 B.C., Romans, 50 B.C. This culminated with the moslem Arabs, who, in the seventh century A.D. finally put out the light of Egyptian civilization.[51] In short, until the descendants of the peoples of the so-called 'heroic age'[52] (whose supposed aristocratic ideals would later influence political philosophy)[53] had 'outgrown the barbarous habits'[54] of the past, they were the principal destroyers of settled commonwealths.[55]

At various times, through assimilation and the pursuit of knowledge, the conquered in turn conquered the conquerors. But, as long as there were would be conquerors, the conservation of acquired knowledge or the pursuit of new ones was precarious. The peoples of the heroic age did not abandon their vocation until after they had destroyed the commonwealths they incessantly pillaged. Like the later Germanic tribesmen,[56] it was probably in the prosecution of wars that they first came into contact with letters and all that that entailed. The passion for war and booty,[57] and the designation of its results as just,[58] was a widespread belief in warrior societies.[59] In fact, ancient and some modern political philosophers saw war as a constant redeemer of the polis.[60] We shall return to this point in the third part of this chapter.

History is not reticent on the implications of the ethic of war for civilization. It meant the successive invasion and destruction of settled, highly developed civilizations. Where the conquerors belonged to a relatively homogenous political or ethnic group, as was the case with the Amorites, the pen rapidly completes the destruction started with the sword. Consequently, history preserves no trace of the conquered peoples. This was what happened in Mesopotamia:

> the very existence of a Sumerian people was forgotten until [in the twentieth century] a succession of European and American scholars filtered, from the mixture of Persian, Assyrian and Babylonian elements the sedimental culture of Sumer.[61]

Where those who spelled the death knell for other commonwealths belonged to more than one distinct or homogenous ethnic or political group, the multiplicity of sources makes it impossible for one group to succeed in fooling history. This was the case with Egypt. In spite of the erasures and obliterations in Egyptian inscriptions, the *tabula* could not be made *rasa*; vestigial traces of the commonwealths that played hosts to so many hordes of conquerors were preserved. For instance, the testimony of an ethnically semitic people – a people that probably migrated into the valley of the Nile and rapidly ascended during the Hyksos period - emphasized that Egyptians were different from their (Hebrews') hosts. In the sacred history books (the earliest of which, in their present form, dates to the first millenium B.C.[62]) the Hebrews classified Egyptians as a 'hamitic' people. Another ethnically semitic people, the Assyrians, who conquered Egypt long before they carried the Hebrews into captivity, could not have mistaken the identity of the people they displaced from Egypt. And, Greek historians and philosophers specifically alluded to the hue of the people of the Nile.[63] Further, traders and mercenaries, Greeks or non-Greeks, who later settled in Egypt[64] must have been familiar with the men with whom they traded or fought with or against. The successive invasions and the attendant assumption of the reins of power over Egypt by various conquerors had domino effect on Ethiopia, a fact that made Pliny[65] conclude that Ethiopia was reduced to tatters by continuous warfare with Egypt.[66] But modern scholars, bent on constructing and edifying racialized history of the world, dismiss Pliny's conclusion as mere allusions to 'mythical splendours of the hoary past.'[67] Indeed, Egypt and Ethiopia were known to Sumerians. In Sumerian mythology Egypt and Ethiopia, called Magan and Meluhla(?), were objects of blessing by the Sumerian god, Enlil.[68] Perhaps, Magan and Meluhla were to the Sumerians (or vice versa) what, until the 'modern fabrication of ancient Greece,' Egypt had been to Greece.[69]

The foregoing is not a contribution to the misplaced and futile quest for a 'racial' origin of civilization. Rather, the relevance of this sort of excursus is that if, as intellectual history suggests, philosophy generally, and political philosophy in particular, began with the Greeks, it evolved only long after many cities in the ancient world had succumbed before the might of the so-called heroic peoples. The intellectual universe and the conceptual framework fashioned by philosophers and theologians of the triumphant societies elevated the winners and depressed the losers of those ancient wars. Their optics, reflected in what we earlier characterized as 'the metaphysics of political conservatism,'[70] has exerted influence down to the present times. Indeed, there is renewed interest and faith in ancient political ideal.

Ancient political ideal seem to have been premised on 'cultural primitivism.'[71] More pertinently, it presupposed the existence of various ethnically or culturally divergent political societies warring against one another. The ancients recognized that survival in such a world required nurturing a particular type of personality, namely, the citizen who is secure in and is virtually devoted to the republic. To put it starkly, old liberalism saw individuals only as members of a unit, and that unit was the republic. Thus, the subject of ancient political thought, even in its democratic dimension, was not the individual qua individual but the individual as a member of a *free* political community; in ancient times, the free political community, not the free individual, was the locus of liberty. Hence, the fundamental difference between the liberty of the ancients and that of the moderns popularized by Benjamin Constant.[72]

Since the nineteenth century when the reaction against unrestrained individualism set in, the communitarian orientation of classical republicanism has made old liberalism seductively attractive to critiques of modern liberalism. The 'possessive individualism' and the capture of law and politics by the economic doctrine of *laissez faire* fostered by the ideological twist to modern liberalism, have made it easy for critiques of modernity to pose as crusaders seeking to recover holy lands from infidels. They see as irredeemably soulless the sociopolitical world created and dominated by the 'economic man' otherwise known as the bourgeois. Perhaps the critics are right, perhaps they are wrong. But this humanistic judgment and the sociopolitical and economic plight of many individuals within liberal democracies and 'the increasing entrenchment of poverty and misery'[73] in the Third World tend to draw 'the south' like a magnet into the fold of old liberalism.

Yet, old liberalism is an extremely slippery slope. The republican ideal of the ancients is like Lewis Carroll's mushroom: nibbling on one of its sides makes a political society grow tall, the other shortens it because it freezes the citizens like flies in amber. In short, old liberalism purchases political stability, greatness, and prosperity at the expense of individual freedom and equality.[74] It is this doubleedgedness that has always made 'the palmy days 'of humanism' coincide with the 'age of despots.'[75] Nonetheless, when considered against the background of the ancient world in which it was fashioned, there were good reasons why old liberalism could not but reject individualism. To do otherwise would leave the door open for fractious alliances between and among individuals along 'selfish' social, political, and economic lines or, worse, such political and economic alliances between the same class of citizens of different republics. That would be detrimental to the cohesiveness of the republic, and undermine its ability to further its own public interest, and defend its people against aggression and oppression by others.

II

PERIANDERISM, OLD LIBERALISM, AND THE LIBERAL IDEA

We have alluded to the prevalence in antiquity of the sacrilegious practice of pillaging, sacking, and scattering political entities. The invading horde slaughter the eminent citizens of the invaded polity, confiscate the land, and their leader assumes the title hitherto reserved for the Creator, 'King of kings'. Nobody knows when this started, but archeology, literature, and ethnography hint that 'barbarians' and 'civilized' alike practiced such usurpation, conquest, and savagery. However, probably because the literary accounts that survived were those 'written by the intellectuals of settled societies' only barbarians 'are pictured as cruel, destructive and murderous.'[76] In the annals of ancient commonwealths, the term 'slavery' was often used restrictively to denote the pervasive misfortune - the sociopolitical and economic calamities - that inevitably followed the invasion and conquest of one commonwealth by another. From early times, the love of freedom and the desire to throw off the yoke of national slavery inspired poets, philosophers, and statesmen, and roused cities to rebellion.

Conquering, pillaging, and enslaving of commonwealths by commonwealths began at the dawn of history; the chronicles of ancient communities testify eloquently to the prevalence of such a practice.[77] Indeed, what is called ancient history is little more than a record of the series of the bloody wars fought by various political societies; in ancient times, political societies were little more than 'symchaies or permanent alliances for cooperation in wars.'[78] When that was the case, the cause of the 'liberal idea,' of individual freedom and equality, was precarious.

With the birth of political philosophy, the liberal idea was overshadowed. Although before the Greeks man was not intellectually quiescent, the conventional wisdom is that philosophy generally, and political philosophy particularly, is coeval with the Greeks.[79] Now, Greek political philosophy, in contradistinction from Greek political thought, is almost synonymous with the political ideas of the Socratics.[80] In fact, some scholars still regard the socratics as 'the absolute origin of thinking on various topics,'[81] and some contemporary advocates of old liberalism take classical political philosophy as the quintessential product of the intellect.[82] But what does this intellect see? The answer is both short and simple: it espies hierarchy boldly etched out in nature, and it boldly constructs a sociopolitical and economic intellectual universe that closely mirrors the perceived image. This ancient counterpart of the 'bell curve' was sketched by the socratics with consummate intellectual skill.

However, the socratics did not use their own bell curve to *explain* an existing sociopolitical structure. Rather, they used it as a remedy for the instability of Greek city-states. The Greeks were fragmented into, lived in, and owed political allegiance to different city-states. As a result, they were doubly exposed to perianderism: one, at the hands of fellow Greeks, two, at the hands of barbarians, that is, non-Greeks. In order to curb this double helliom, the socratics conceived an ideal Greek republic. Put differently, classical political philosophy was a blueprint for *unifying* Hellenes into a single republic.

It is common knowledge that the intellectual history of the Greek political ideal begins with 'the humane Plato.'[83] In the *Republic* Plato explicitly formulated the 'noble-lie'[84], according to which the citizens would be made to believe that although they were all brothers, some (the rulers) were made of gold, some (the helpers) of silver, and some (farmers and craftsmen) of iron and brass. Further, each class would, for the most part, breed after its own kind. The resultant natural division of labor would banish political aspiration, suppress economic ambition, and obviate social mobility. This 'phoenician tale,' as the great philosopher himself called it, was taken over by Aristotle. The latter first *naturalized*[85] the *republic*, and then cast the concept of division of labor into a logical mould. This enabled Aristotle to arrive at the seemingly irrefutable notions of natural masters and natural slaves. Significantly, only non-Greeks could be slaves; Greeks were born to rule.[86] It is not surprising that the most renowned conqueror of the ancient world - Alexander the great - was Aristotle's pupil.

By a curious development in intellectual history, Aristotle was early elevated, by theologians and philosophers alike, into the enviable position of the philosopher par excellence.[87] It was taken for granted that Aristotle had designed an intellectual universe that accurately captured reality, and that he had defined once and for all times all the operative concepts in all fields of learning, including political philosophy. In short, Aristotle was designated 'the oracle of nature and of truth.'[88] In the later Middle Ages, which marked the 'psychological and intellectual adolescence of the new races in Europe',[89] European scholars imbibed and internalized Aristotlean intellectual world. Thus, until the twilight of modernity in the fifteenth century, the task of the intellect was limited to disputing and expounding issues within the confines established by an Aristotlean intellectual world – a phenomenon more widely known as scholasticism.[90]

We have noted that the received political ideal was refractory to individualism and equality. As a result, distrust of individualism and equality passed insensibly into the corpus of knowledge and became one of those 'implicit or incompletely explicit assumptions operating in the thought'[91] of those who followed, consciously or unconsciously, the political ideals ultimately traceable to the socratics. As we saw in the first chapter, it was in the seventeenth century that the moderns broke with the ancient conceptual framework. Again, as we suggested in that same chapter, from the eighteenth century onwards, one of the striking patterns exhibited by political theorists was reverence for ancient political thought. This had mixed blessings, for the totality of ancient political thought included both the notions of hierarchy and the inflammatory ideas of individual freedom and equality.[92] But following the reaction to the French Revolution, and relying on history and anthropology, the principle of hierarchy gained an upper hand. This was especially the case in Germany where the study of and reliance on history reached its apogee.[93] The turn to history was so pervasive that scholars thought, taught, and wrote 'as if philosophy had been superseded by history.'[94]

The outbreak of the Second World War and the role of ancient political ideal in facilitating the dissemination and wide acceptance of the ethic of war prompted some modern epistemics to take a hard look at the intellectual universe constructed by the ancients. The result was astonishing. Classical political philosophy was found wanting. It was castigated as profoundly anti-democratic,[95] authoritarian, and uncompromisingly against 'the open society'.[96] As well, Periclean Athens did not emerge unscathed: it was exposed as 'a slave-owning aristocracy' and an imperialistic democracy.[97] In short, as Laocoon had cautioned his fellow Trojans,[98] scholars suddenly realized that the Greeks were to be feared, whatever gifts they might have brought to the modern world.[99] Although it is inconceivable that scholars would cease serenading the Greeks, half century of relative peace seems to have washed away that lesson from intellectual consciousness.

III

THE SPIDER'S WEB

History is the neuronal databank of peoples. When remote descendants look back to remote ancestors, the real or imagined accomplishments of the latter might inspire the former to embark on political speculations that would manifestly improve existing sociopolitical and economic practices. That is one possibility. Another possibility is that such looking-back could turn out to be a source of exalted savagery and stilted barbarity. It all depends on what the past discloses, or rather, which aspect of the past the present finds interesting, and how it uses what it appropriates. From the perspective of 'visible' minorities in liberal constitutional polities and 'the south', Fukuyama's Straussian[100] orientation raises the spectacle of the second possibility.

Fukuyama first articulated his thesis in a journal article in 1989. Three years later, he published an elaborate version of the same thesis as *The End of History and the Last Man.*[101] The argument of the book rests on the belief in the existence of 'a Universal History of mankind' - a cleverly crafted euphemism for intellectual parochialism. Specifically, Fukuyama critiques modern liberalism from an intellectual disposition that portends and glorifies the return of perianderism. Although some famous philosophers will be mentioned, we shall be concerned solely with Fukuyama's ideas as he presents them or as they stand on their own.[102] We shall not be concerned with whether or how Fukuyama's thesis fits or does not fit into the political thought of the famous philosophers who he uses as a peg on which he hangs his arguments.

The ensuing discussion shows three things. First, that Fukuyama's theory rests ultimately on truncated historical consciousness. Second, that this genre of scholarship invariably exalts some commonwealths and inevitably depresses others. And third, that the resultant political ideal is inherently antithetical to modernity. In what follows, I will first identify and outline the thesis of the book. Second, I will briefly show that Fukuyama's 'universal history of mankind' is an abridged history, and that, contrary to Fukuyama's claim, it does not necessarily contain a transhistorical moral or political standard. Third, I will show that, far from being superior to Anglo-Saxon liberalism, Fukuyama's Greco-

German liberalism is covertly anti-modern and a thickly veiled attempt to resuscitate the so-called heroic world of antiquity.

The theme of *The End of History and the Last Man* can be put shortly. It is that despite 'the current worldwide liberal revolution,' modern liberalism does not appear to have the ability to satisfy a primordial desire for recognition.

Fukuyama calls the desire for recognition a thymotic desire. According to him, there are two types of such desire. These are isothymia or 'the desire to be recognized as the equal of other people', and megalothymia or 'the desire to be recognized as superior to other people.'[103] Fukuyama calls contemporary democracies 'the universal homogenous state.'[104] He essays that the former type of thymotic desire – isothymia – permeates the universal homogenous state. He writes that the apparent triumph of the liberal idea in the universal homogenous state has lulled men into thinking that the latter type of thymotic desire – megalothymia – is dead. Fukuyama's thesis is that if megalothymia is truly dead then 'liberal democracy' itself is doomed. Fortunately, megalothymia is alive. However, it is denied full reign by the universal homogenous state. Fukuyama looks into the attic of history and he uncovers the irrepressible megalothymia; he brilliantly articulates preference for sociopolitical structures that accord due recognition to megalothymia. He outlines the Homeric character of the world that would be bred by a resurgence of megalothymia. Far from shrinking from the brutal implications of such a world, he depicts it as the tonic of progress. A resurgence of megalothymia would assuredly give rise to what he cryptically calls 'immense wars of the spirit.'[105] In the aftermath of such wars, some warriors would make it back home, like Odysseus, after many tribulations; some would be destroyed while many others would be simply lost. Nevertheless, some of those who eventually make it safely home would not find their new surroundings adequate. Instead, they would 'set their eyes once more on a new and more distant journey'. In this way, the human spirit would continually soar; the wheel of history would continue to turn. The dominance of megalothymia ensures permanent progress.

The End of History is an extensive dilation on the meaning of *thymos*, and its manifestation and application in many areas of human endeavors. Fukuyama finds thymos at work and at the base of liberal revolutions worldwide, and he minces no words that megalothymia is superior to isothymia. He puts the former at the base of excellence in many areas of human endeavors.[106] Indeed, he sees a residue of 'irrational thymos', that is, megalothymia, as the mainspring of the most successful capitalistic societies.[107] But megalothymia seems to be absent from sociopolitical life. He blames this on the universal homogeneous state. Fukuyama's project is to recover megalothymia from limbo, and set it up as the principle of sociopolitical philosophy.

Fukuyama lays claims to intellectual legitimacy by reminding his readers that 'the first extended *analysis* of the phenomenon of desire for recognition in Western philosophical tradition appears ... in the book that stands at the very head of that tradition – Plato's *Republic*.'[108] 'Thymos', he says, 'is a Greek word that may somewhat awkwardly be translated as 'spiritedness.'[109] He likens 'thymos' to an 'innate human sense of justice: people believe that they have a certain worth, and when other people act as though they are worth less – when they do not recognize their worth at its correct value – then they become angry.'[110] More importantly, thymos is 'characteristic of the guardians in Plato's *Republic*.'[111] It is pertinent to remark here that the 'guardians' constitute the warrior class in *The Republic*. Fukuyama builds a bridge linking *The Republic* with the early nineteenth century German philosopher, G.W.F. Hegel. He does this by identifying the Greek *thymos* as 'the psychological seat' of Hegel's 'aristocratic master.'

The concept of the aristocratic master is one of the key strands in Hegel's philosophy of history. Hegel saw in history the gradual unfolding and concretizing of the Idea of freedom. He delineated world-historical realms into four: the Oriental, the Greek, the Roman, and the Germanic. He (Hegel) construed the ascendance and decline of each of the first three world-historical realms, as the successive movement of the Idea of freedom to a 'higher principle and hence the transition of world history to another nation.'[112] But how did world history begin? Fukuyama appropriately reminds us that, in the *Phenomenology of Mind*, Hegel postulated that history was set into motion by an initial violent encounter between 'first men'.

Unlike the social contract constructs of the moderns, the outcome of the first encounter between the 'first men' was the establishment of the political relationship of masters and slaves: 'a highly unequal relationship of lordship and bondage.'[113] Fukuyama assures the reader that Hegel did not 'approve' such a political structure. On the contrary, Hegel knew that such a political structure was both primitive and oppressive. Nevertheless, Fukuyama points out that he (Hegel) understood that 'it was a necessary stage of human history in which both terms of the class equation, masters and slaves, preserve something importantly human.'[114] In short, in Fukuyama's intellectual universe, 'the master' preserved one type of thymotic desire while 'the slave' preserved the other. Further, 'the consciousness of the master is ... higher and more human than that of the slave ... [hence there is] something morally praiseworthy in the pride of the aristocrat-warrior…'[115] According to Fukuyama, the aristocrat-warrior disdains the things of this world. Indeed, this creature scorns life itself; unlike the 'slave', the aristocrat-warrior is always willing, ready and able to risk his life in a prestige battle for recognition of his superior worth. In sum, the aristocratic master is the real stuff from which the universal historian or philosopher plucks materials for a 'trans-historical concept of man.'[116] From this premise, Fukuyama poises comfortably, like Achilles on the back of the Tortoise,[117] on the *intellectual* foundation of modern liberalism, and attempts to kill it with ease.

Fukuyama essays that any political institutional arrangement that does not pander to the vainglorious ambitions of 'the aristocratic master' cannot be completely satisfying. To be sure, the founders of modern liberalism were not so unreflective as to fail to see that Hegel's honored creature, 'the aristocratic master,' was indeed an anthropological type – 'an authentic human type.'[118] But, according to Fukuyama, they saw the problem of political philosophy as that of how to persuade this 'would-be master to accept the life of the slave in a kind of classless society of slaves.'[119] Fukuyama says they are wrong. In Fukuyama's intellectual universe, political society necessarily consists of masters and slaves! To use Kant's phrase,[120] this sort of speculation makes political philosophy a recipe for 'drinking up iniquity like water.'[121]

Fukuyama professes the universality of megalothymia. Nonetheless, he leaves no doubt that he writes as one of the self-styled 'faithful defenders of the Western Alliance.'[122] That this secular theology is a counterpane for intellectual parochialism is evident from the following passages. 'For our purposes,' he writes, 'it matters very little what strange thoughts occur to people in Albania [Eastern Europe] or Burkina Faso [Africa], for we are interested in what one could in some sense call *the common ideological heritage of mankind.*'[123] And, again, 'the universal historian must be ready to discard entire peoples and times as essentially pre- or non-historical, because they do not bear on the central 'plot' of his or her story.'[124] Since, according to conventional wisdom, intellectual history begins with the Greeks, Fukuyama consigns to pre-history the intellectual adventures of men before the Greeks. Moreover, he conceives political philosophy as consisting essentially of the *analysis* of, and abstracting from, this abbreviated history of mankind.

For him, the plot for a universal history begins with the Greeks, stretches through Western Europe (excluding, however, the Judeo-Christian interlude),[125] and ends in the first half of the twentieth century. He abstracts from this 'plot' the trans-historical standard with which he evaluates the goodness or badness of any regime or social system, namely, whether and to what extent it allows or gives full reign to the instincts of the so-called 'aristocratic master'. To put it starkly, it is only by insisting that authentic political education means taking notes from the various Homeric characters discernible from history that Fukuyama arrives at the so-called 'common ideological heritage of mankind'. What is this but stilted psychologism and banal intellectual provincialism?

When erstwhile barbarous people become intellectualized, they barbarize the intellect. And, when the musing of the barbarized intellect is adorned with the name of philosophy and religion, the savage character of its postulates become veiled with a veneer of sublimity. The barbarian's concept of right that 'might is right' constituted the *historical* basis of right.[126] The historical basis of right could be sophistically identified with the *philosophical*, but only scholars who identify poetry with history and history with philosophy would take the historical for the philosophical. Fukuyama elides the distinction between the historical and the philosophical basis of right. This enables him to discreetly underscore the 'might is right' rule by captioning Chapter 23 of his book with the notorious speech of the imperial Athenians to the Melians, and by pointing out that we are blinded to this reality by the unreality of contemporary realism.[127]

Now, Fukuyama uses the word 'barbarian' in an uncommon sense. To him, 'barbarian' denotes peoples unaware of the immense and superior advantage that the deployment of the scientific method in the service of military and economic pursuits confers on the State. As there are no such ignorant peoples in Europe, America, or Asia, and as even the bourgeois particularly appreciates the immense powers of science, Fukuyama declares that there are 'no true barbarians at the gates'[128] of modern civilization.

But that usage is not the only possible meaning of the word 'barbarian'. It is well known that Greeks used the word 'barbarian' as an ethnolinguistic term to refer to non-Greeks. Although 'barbarian' did not necessarily mean culturally nude or morally depraved, the word could also mean simply rude men, that is, men without learning. It is certain that, in Fukuyama's pre-historical period, the Greeks were once barbarians in this latter sense. A nodding acquaintance with history also shows that the Germanic peoples, who constitute the nucleus of modern civilization, were once barbarians, indeed 'super-barbarians,'[129] in that same sense. In fact, 'wherever we first meet Indo-Europeans in history, they were barbarians, and their invasions often produced a serious decline in the civilizations they encountered.'[130]

The sporadic foray of invading barbarian hordes was the continual scourge of commonwealths in the ancient world. However enormous their subsequent advancement of the arts and sciences, it requires little reflection to see that such invaders were predators, not producers, destroyers not builders. But in Fukuyama's intellectual universe, they were early exemplars of ethnically homogenous, group-oriented political societies, and 'tightly knit economic organizations.'[131] Nonetheless, Fukuyama conceded, in truly Machiavellian vein, that these so-called prototypes of integrated political and economic organizations subdued their victims only 'through superior ruthlessness, cruelty, and bravery'.[132] Barbarism may have preceded civilization, but is might ever necessarily right?

It is a 'lying invention'[133] for a universal historian or philosopher of history to characterize predators as bunches of 'aristocratic masters', and their victims as 'slaves'. History suggests that erstwhile barbarians rose to prominence partly through the power of the broad sword and partly through the acquisition and cultivation of the arts and sciences. As Tocqueville[134] succinctly puts it,

> An attentive survey of history demonstrates that, in general, barbarous nations have raised themselves to civilization by degrees and by their own efforts. Whenever they derived knowledge from a foreign people, they stood towards them in the relation of conquerors, and not of a conquered nation … the power that victory bestows upon the barbarian is sufficient to keep up his importance among civilized men and permit him to rank as their equal … The one has might on his side, the other had intelligence; the former admires the knowledge and the arts of the conquered, the latter envies the power of the conquerors. The barbarians at length admit civilized man into their palaces, and he in turn opens his schools to the barbarians…

When the emergent intellectuals came to reflect on the past, they correctly divined that their ancestors owed their greatness to 'megalothymia'. But it would have been tactless to put matters so bluntly. So they resorted to subterfuges. In the 'east', religion played the hideous role of reconciling ethics with barbarity; hence the notion of slavery as an integral part of a divinely ordained sociopolitical and economic world. In the 'west', philosophy surrogated for religion; hence such 'phoenician tales' as the myth of the metals and the notion of 'slaves by nature' or the conviction that 'no society can properly function without classification, without an arrangement of things and men in classes and prescribed types.'[135] It was largely the result of the barbarous practices[136] of the past that were taken over and cast into intellectual figures. In displacing traditional poets, the ancients converted what was initially a 'pragmatic acceptance' into a 'normative acceptance.'[137]

Conventional wisdom maintains that these notions were elaborated 'in societies dedicated to the proposition that all men are not created equal.'[138] Whatever may be said for or against that view, that proposition is a direct opposite of 'the zodiac sign' under which, intellectually speaking, modern liberal constitutional polities were born. They reflect the conviction, based on victory in the past, that some individuals and/or peoples are natural masters, others are natural slaves. And, because 'nothing is so seldom found among the writings of men as true and perfect civil history',[139] these conclusions of triumphal history were perpetuated and transmitted to posterity. Specifically, they passed imperceptibly into Europe during the later Middle Ages, and became part of the unarticulated major premises of political philosophy. After a period of eclipse in the seventeenth and eighteenth centuries, they were revamped and entrenched anew by 'scientific naturalism'[140] and imperialism in the nineteenth and early twentieth centuries. It required the trauma of such a monstrous proportion as the Nazi holocaust before scholars explicitly began to exercise any serious doubt that 'war is the father of all and king of all.'[141]

Fukuyama maintains that without the thymotic strivings of the first men, that is, without the continual prosecution of wars of recognition, humanity would lapse into lethargious stupor. Generalizing, I suspect, from the history of nationalism[142] and, particularly, the reaction to 'the German desire for military world dominion' in the first part of the twentieth century, Fukuyama writes that 'the possibility of war is a great force for the rationalization of societies, and for the creation of uniform social structures across cultures.' War is the fuel of progress, for its threat 'forces states to restructure their social systems along lines most conducive to producing and deploying technology'.[143] Since war is driven by thymos, whether it is iso- or megalo-thymia, it follows that if thymos ceases, historical progress will come to an end. Since liberal constitutional polities recognize one another at the correct value, they seldom go to war against one another.[144] As well, isothymia pervades the universal homogenous state, and so political stirrings within such polities are strictly limited to the demand for the recognition of the equal worth of those hitherto denied such recognition. In short, if we discount the economic realm there is no room for megalothymia in contemporary sociopolitical world. In Fukuyama's intellectual universe, the lack of an outlet for megalothymia does not augur well for civilization; it makes impossible the cultural wars necessary for the continual surge in civilization, and the attendant separation of masters from slaves, of slave states from master states.

In plain terms, the so-called 'aristocratic master' who desires nothing but the recognition of his supposedly superior worth terrorizes his fellow creatures into submitting to an unequal relationship. No amount of phenomenological depiction or universal historical construct can conceal the fact that in doing that the 'aristocratic master' alienates and extinguishes the sense of human fellowship. It follows that if the consciousness of this creature is set up as the principle of sociopolitical action we take away the 'hue' in 'man' and bid farewell to humane virtues. Any political philosophy that relies on the megalothymotic consciousness of the so-called aristocratic master would glorify war and, like the bellicose religious beliefs of the Teutonic peoples of old, among others, connect 'the passions of humanity with its continual prosecution.'[145] Fukuyama hankers after, and reminds so-called aristocratic masters in world historical societies of the necessity of continual quest for unlimited conquest. But whatever positive implications it may have for scientific advancement and economic prosperity, any resurgence of megalothymia would portend doom for those who would be the moral outsiders - visible minorities generally, and very visible minorities in particular - in such sociopolitical and economic world. By fastening on the consciousness of the so-called aristocratic-master – the archetypal 'ever-victorious hero that goes to war in order to exercise and to show his might'[146] - Fukuyama portrays the practice of evil as the rejuvenation of humanity. He seeks to enchant the world by the supposed 'common ideological heritage of mankind.'

In this 'old age of mankind'[147] it requires more than the *ipsissima verba* of an avowed philosopher of history to convince humankind of the superiority of the 'very Teutonic and perverse'[148] megalothymotic consciousness of the so-called aristocratic master. Notwithstanding the fact that Fukuyama brilliantly touts it as a better, viable, and nobler liberalism, Greco-German liberalism is wedded to the metaphysics of political conservatism, and the heady brew of the superiority of one's ethnic and ethnos. The involvement of old liberalism in derailing the course of the liberal idea is one of the grave aberrations of the human intellect; the advent of modern liberalism and the institutionalization of procedural democracy are its albatross. Assuredly, Anglo-Saxon liberalism has its shortcomings. But to maintain, as Fukuyama does, that the love of hierarchy or 'the dissatisfaction with liberty and equality'[149] by those with the megalothymotic disposition of the so-called aristocratic master signifies the possibility of a higher, purer and profounder culture is symptomatic of intellectual amnesia. It is the high road to civic barbarism.

Mortals concoct 'universal histories,' and as Eben-Ezra pointed out to Hypathia,[150] philosophers are first and foremost men, and men of a particular time and place. Under the cloak of the concept of universal history, Fukuyama exalts some peoples/individuals and marginalizes others. Nay, Fukuyama's head is in Sparta while his feet are on Athenian soil; he relishes aristocratic liberalism while writing under the canopy of, and ostensibly for, a modern democratic republic. Of course, like Socrates, modern democracies recognize that 'even the wolf has the right to be heard.'[151] But citizens of what John Rawls called 'well ordered' polities should beware lest they swallow wolverine potions from the vessels of republican intellectualism. In any event, history suggests that nations that prosecute bloody wars and scholars who formulate and disseminate bloody instructions, somehow get hoisted by their own petards. For, even-based justice ensures that a bloody instruction assumes a life of its own and, later or sooner, returns to plague its inventors.[152] Whatever its shortcomings, modern liberalism preaches the same message that the first philosopher relayed to the Erewhons: 'that we ought by this time to have outgrown the barbarous habits of our ancestors; and if, as we believe, we know better than they, we should do better.'[153] What is more the spirit of the common law has long made scholars aware that, however much it may be seen as an organizational necessity, the principle of hierarchy is simply one of the invidious intellectual legacies of the ancients particularly[154] and pre-modern thought generally.

Conclusion

It is common knowledge that the only recorded instance of 'liberal democracy' in the ancient world originated and flourished, albeit briefly, in a southern Greek city-state, Athens, not from northern Greece, and certainly not on Mount Olympus. Familiar as they were with the 'megalothymotic' disposition of the Olympians,[155] 'the ancients' banished Homerics from the ideal Greek world. Or, more accurately, wherever the Olympian type might be found, they would be co-opted into republics under law and presided over by 'philosopher-kings' or 'natural rulers' rather than the irrational godhead on Mount Olympus. Homer would be reversed. The result would be that the reckless marring and jarring of persons, properties, promises, and polities that characterized the Olympians' suzerainty would permanently become things of the past. Law, right, and justice would reign on earth whatever might be the state of affairs in heaven. Put differently, the Olympians were to 'the ancients' what the state of nature was to 'the moderns'. It may well be that 'the ancients' trusted any form of government except democracy, but there is little doubt that Plato and Aristotle were the founders of political philosophy as we know it. In the seventeenth century, Hobbes revived the basic equality of human beings, and Locke renewed the reconciliation of liberty with the state. With the exception of Enlightenment thought, all the turns made since then have been variations on the construal of political theory as the idealizing of one's cultural, political morality. Be that as it may, nobody, except the headstrong creatures on Mount Olympus or their counterparts in political societies and their intellectual myrmidons, has anything to fear from 'philosopher-kings', 'sovereign princes,' or the right of the individual to 'life, liberty, and estate' under the rule of law.

The philosophic figure behind Straussian intellectualism was one of the first political theorists to broach and explicitly propose a return to 'the ancients,' and to reopen the question of 'tyranny.'[156] Now, from the point of view of the 'liberal idea', tyranny may be described as the suspension, curtailment, negation, abrogation, disregard, frustration of or trampling on or indifference and hostility to the right of the individual as individual or as a member of a group to optimal development. In this sense, tyranny is tyranny whether under monarchy, aristocracy, or democracy. In brief, any political theory that, for whatever reasons, covertly or overtly substitutes a hierarchical sociopolitical *intellectual* universe for the *perpetually potential flat world of man* discards the very tool against tyranny forged by political philosophy. Perhaps, it was the latter – the idea of a perpetually potential flat world – that 'the ancients' interpreted negatively and formalized as natural inequality, which they embedded in their political ideals. Be that as it may, it is only if the ancients were infallible interpreters of the nature of things that their theoretical webs could be surrogated for the study of phenomena and their conceptual structures substituted for fresh philosophical investigations. The fact is that the ancients' political ideals have traditionally been and are still commonly used as props for humanistic 'schools of thought that despise democracy and equality.'[157]

It is as much idolatrous to idealize the Greeks, Romans, a 'Caucasian-Semitic clan'[158] or any portion of mankind or human anthropological type as it was for the Hebrews to fall down before 'the golden calf'.

Although Fukuyama artfully draped Greco-German liberalism in the mystic *persona* of the so-called 'aristocratic master,' the so-called 'common ideological heritage of mankind' is a magus' ploy for substituting the remains of the north, 'the politics of Olympus,'[159] and its 'datum' supposedly 'supplied by divine authority,'[160] for the world of (ir)rational men and women, the kingdom of political philosophers. Only an anthropocentric intellectualism would make scholars take poetry for history and history for philosophy. The best way to imitate 'the ancients' is *not* to be mythmakers, mystics, or romantics. By exalting megalothymia, Fukuyama replaces philosophy with psychology and relegates philosophers to the hapless role of super-slaves.

Centuries of political consciousness and decades of post-Enlightenment research and experience have inured scholars to diversity, if not plurality. As a result, it is unlikely that those who see things differently than the dominant regimes of truth will be invariably branded as Amalekites fit to be 'smitten hip and thigh.'[161] This may therefore be an auspicious time for new learners to 'plunge again and again in the water of doubt.'[162] Bereft of intellectual ideologies they might be able to see that, like the men castigated by Micah,[163] many political philosophers have made crooked what is straight in itself while all the time proclaiming that theirs is the voice of reason. In any event, and although it may be that 'a view is not refuted by the fact that it happens to have been shared by Hitler,'[164] it seems certain that 'whom Helena has paralyzed, His reason hardly shall regain.'[165] Or, perhaps more accurately, wherever people listen to and *believe* Phoenician tale carriers (whether such tales are bruited in villages, palaces, salons, educational institutions, or the market place) they are doomed to continually constructing and perpetually refurbishing hierarchical sociopolitical and economic world. Just as children learn by believing adults, scholars learn by believing their predecessors. The crucial point is for scholars to recognize 'the groundlessness'[166] of their belief.

Notes

---

[1] Plato, *Laws* 715D-E

[2] F. Bacon, *An Advertisement Touching the Controversies of the Church of England*, in, *The English Scholars Library of Old and Modern Works,* No. 8, ed. Edward Arber, (Southgate, London 1879) at 161.

[3] Homer, *The Odyssey*, trans. A.T. Murray (Loeb Classical Library) (London: Heinemann, 1919) Bk. XXII at 361.

[4] See Chapter 1 at 2.

[5] Aristotle explicitly stated that 'it is not a new or recent discovery of political philosophers that the State ought to be divided into classes, and that the warriors ought to be separated from the husbandman. The system has continued in Egypt and in Crete to this day, and was established, as tradition says, by a law of Sesostris in Egypt and of Minos in Crete.... The very best thing of all would be that the husbandmen should be slaves taken from among men who are not all of the same race and not spirited ...' Aristotle, *Politics* Bk. VIII Ch. 10, 1329 b1-5; 1330a25. As history makes clear, the sad fact is that that model derived from conquest.

[6] See, inter alia, Arthur O. Lovejoy, *The Great Chain of Being* (Cambridge, Mass.: Harvard Univ. Press, 1936); Page duBois, *Centaurs and Amazons: Women and the pre-History of the Great Chain of Being* (Ann Arbor: Michigan Univ. Press, 1982); E.M.W. Tillyard, *The Elizabethan World Picture: A Study of the Idea of Order in the Age of Shakespeare, Donne and Milton* (New York: Vantage Books, 1967); Alice Chandler, *A Dream of Order: The Medieval Ideal in Nineteenth Century English Literature* (Lincoln: Univ. of Nebraska Press, 1970); H. Craig, *The Enchanted Glass* (Oxford: Basil Blackwell, 1960); R.J. Smith, *The Gothic Bequest: Medieval Institutions in British Thought 1688-1863* (Cambridge: Cambridge Univ. Press, 1987)

[7] William E. Hearn, *The Government of England: Its Structure and Its Development*, 2nd Ed. (Melbourne: George Robertson & Co.1886) at 442: 'the history of the countries of Western Europe ... knows nothing of a time in which there were no nobles as well as freemen and serfs ... The more minutely the institutions of these countries are examined, the more strongly do they confirm the teachings of history.'

[8] S.G. Checkland, 'Growth and Progress: The Nineteenth Century View in Britain,' *Economic Hist. Rev.* 12 (1959) 49 at 56. The outstanding contemporary example is Richard J. Herrnstein and Charles Murray, *The Bell Curve: Intelligence and Class Structure in American Life* (New York: Free Press, 1994)

[9] D. Spitz, *The Real World of Liberalism* (Chicago: Univ. of Chicago Press, 1982) at 196.

[10] Arthur O. Lovejoy, *The Great Chain of Being*, supra note 6.

[11] Francis Bacon, *The Advancement of Learning*: '...credulity in respect of certain authors, and making them dictators instead of consuls, is a principal cause that the sciences are no further advanced ... For as water ascends no higher than the level of the first spring, so knowledge derived from Aristotle will at most rise no higher again than the knowledge of Aristotle. And therefore, though a scholar must have faith in his master, yet a man well instructed must judge for himself: for learners owe to their masters only a temporary belief, and a suspension of their own judgment till they are fully instructed, and not an absolute resignation or perpetual captivity. Let great authors, therefore, have their due, but so as not to defraud time, which is the author of authors, and the parent of truth...' 'We can say Cicero says thus;

these were the manners of Plato; these are the very words of Aristotle. But what do we says ourselves? What do we judge? ... though we could become learned by other men's learning, a man can never be wise but by his own wisdom': Montaigne, 'Of Pedantry', in, *Essays* 25 *Great Books of the Western World* at 57.

[12] '... immaturity is the inability to use one's understanding without guidance from another. This immaturity is self-imposed when its cause lies not in lack of understanding, but in lack of resolve and courage to use it without guidance from another...' Immanuel Kant, *Perpetual Peace and Other Essays*, trans. T. Humphrey (Indianapolis: Hackett Publishing Co., 1983) at 41.

[13] 'He who is unwilling to open his eyes is as prone to error as he who is born blind, even if by chance his road were free of obstacles and his power of vision sufficiently acute': John Locke, *Questions Concerning the Law of Nature* trans R. Horwitz, *et al*, (Ithaca: Cornell Univ. Press, 1990) at 233.

[14] David Hume, *Philosophical Works*, ed. T.H. Green and T.H. Grose, Vol. III at 79: 'Eloquence when at its highest pitch, leaves little room for reason or reflections; but addressing itself to the fancy or the affections captivates the willing hearers, and subdues their understanding'.

[15] For an excellent introduction to the fundamental differences between 'the ancients' and 'the moderns', see, *Liberalism and Its Critics*, ed. M.J. Sandel (New York: New York Univ. Press, 1984). For the protracted controversy as to the choice between the ancients and the moderns in seventeenth century world of science, see, R.F. Jones, *Ancients and Moderns* 2nd ed. (Berkeley: Univ. of California Press, 1965)

[16] H.L.A. Hart, 'American Jurisprudence Through English Eyes: The Nightmare and the Noble Dream,' *Georgia L.Rev.* 11 (1977) 969 at 986.

[17] Frederick Vaughan, 'On Being a Positivist: Does it Really Matter?', *Osgoode Hall L.J.* 29 (1991) at 404.

[18] I do not use the phrase, 'imperial intellect' in a pejorative sense. Rather, I use it in the sense identified by John H. Newman, *The Idea of a University* (1852) (London: Longmans, Green, 1929) at 461: '...the philosophy of an imperial intellect ... is based, not so much on simplification as on discrimination. Its true representative *defines*, rather than analyzes.' (Emphasis added).

[19] Susan Mann, 'The Universe and The Library: A Critique of James Boyd White as Writer and Reader,' *Stanford L.Rev.* 41 (1989) 959 at 961. The phrase, 'cognitive authority' is from P. Wilson, *Second-Hand Knowledge: An Inquiry into Cognitive Authority* (Westport, Conn.: Greenwood Press, 1983) at 15.

[20] 'The doctrinal method teaches, the initiative method ... intimates, the doctrinal method requiring a belief of what is delivered, but the initiative rather that it should be examined': F. Bacon, supra note 11.

[21] Joseph Glanvill, *The Vanity of Dogmatizing: The Three 'Versions'* (with an introduction by Stephen Medcalf) The Harvester Renaissance Library I, Harvester Press, 1970) III at 31.

[22] Thomas S. Kuhn, *The Structure of Scientific Revolutions*, 3rd ed. (Chicago: Univ. of Chicago Press, 1996) at 94

[23] The phrase is Acton's. Lord Acton, 'Inaugural Lecture on the Study of History', (1895) in, *Essays in the Liberal Interpretation of History* ed. William H. McNeill (Chicago: Univ. of Chicago Press, 1967) at 306.

[24] Cf: 'When we find a thinker reflecting or echoing an apparently erroneous, narrow, or even illogical thought that was popular or authoritative in his time, we must never rule out the possibility that what we have discovered is not the limit of his vision but only an example of his deliberate rhetorical accommodation to reigning prejudice which he does not share but thinks it best not to expose. If the entertaining of such a hypothesis draws a cloud over all claims to definitive intellectual history, the loss will be compensated … by the fact that our intellectual histories … will be more honest and closer to the truth.': Thomas L. Pangle, *The Spirit of Modern Republicanism: The Moral Vision of the American Founders and the Philosophy of Locke* (Chicago & London: Univ. of Chicago Press, 1988) at 38. But see, Hans Georg Gadamer, *Truth and Method* (New York: Seabury Press, 1975) at 488.

[25] George A. Kelly, 'Veils: The Poetics of John Rawls,' *J. of the History of Ideas* 57 (1996) 343 at 360.

[26] From Periander, king of the Corinthians (625 B.C.). When this prince assumed the reins of government, he was desirous to learn 'the safest political establishment for administering the city best'. He, therefore, sent a herald to another king, Thrasybulus, prince of Miletus. Instead of making a direct answer to the herald, 'Thrasybulus led out Periander's messenger outside the city, and with him entered a sown field; then he walked through the corn, questioning, and again questioning the herald about his coming from Corinth. And ever and again as he saw one of the ears of corn growing above the rest he would strike it down, and what he struck down he threw away, until by this means he had destroyed all the fairest and strongest of the corn. So he passed through the whole place and having added no suggestion, sent the herald away.

When the herald came back to Corinth, Periander was anxious to know what suggestion Thrasybulus had made. But the man said that Thrasybulus had made no suggestion at all, and indeed he wondered what sort of a man this was … a madman and a destroyer of his own property; for he recounted all that he had seen Thrasybulus do. But Periander understood the act of Thrasybulus and grasped in his mind that what he was telling him was that he should the most eminent of the citizens …': Herodotus, *Histories*, trans. David Grene, (Chicago: Univ. of Chicago Press, 1987) Bk. V. 92.

[27] Francis Fukuyama, *The End of History and the Last Man* (New York: Free Press, 1992)

[28] Henry S. Maine, *Village Communities in the East and West* 7th Ed. (London: John Murray 1913) at 238.

[29] See, Mark Pattison, 'Tendencies of Religious Thought in England, 1688-1750', in, *Essays and Reviews* ed. Jowett 4th ed. (London: Longman & Green,

1861); Harry P. Kroitor, 'Cowper, Deism, And the Divinization of Nature', *Journal of the History of Ideas* (1960) 511.

[30] John Henry Newman, *The Idea of a University*, supra, note 18 at 264.

[31] Amy Cruse, *The Victorians and Their Books* (London: George Allen & Unwin, 1935) at 84-107.

[32] See, generally, *Essays and Reviews*, supra note 29; David J. DeLaura, *Hebrew and Hellene in Victorian England* (Texas: Austin Univ. Press, 1969). The Victorian religious establishment strongly disapproved of the *Essays and Reviews*. See, J. Ellis, *Seven Against Christ: A Study of 'Essays and Reviews'* (Leiden: E.J. Brill, 1980); Josef L. Athohz, 'The Mind of Victorian Orthodoxy: Anglican Responses to 'Essays and Reviews', 1860-1864,' in *Religion in Victorian Britain, Vol. IV Interpretation* ed. Gerald Parson (Manchester Univ. Press, 1988) 128.

[33] Sir I. Kramer, *History Begins at Sumer* 2nd ed. (London: Thames and Hudson, 1961)

[34] See, e.g. George Sarton, *A History of Science: Ancient Science Through the Golden Age of Greece* (Harvard Univ. Press, 1960).

[35] Ben Gurion, *Israel, A Personal History*

[36] See, e.g. Tertullian, *Apology*, in, *Apologetical Works and Minucius Felis Octarius*, trans. R. Arbemann et al (New York: Fathers of the Church Inc., 1950); St. Augustine, *The City of God*, Bk XVIII. 38, 39, 40: '...their [Egyptian] learning ... did not antedate that of our Patriarchs ... how utterly unconvincing is the presumptuous prattling of those who maintain that Egyptian astronomical science has a history of more than 100,000 years! From what books, pray did they cull this number... Besides since 6,000 years have not yet elapsed from the days of Adam, the first man, should we not ridicule ... those who strive to convince us of a temporal duration so different and so utterly contrary to this established truth?' Cf. (1) Aristotle, *De Caelo*, 270b 'For in the whole range of time past, so far as our inherited records reach, no change appears to have taken place either in the whole scheme of the outmost heaven or in any of its proper parts. [note 1] Simplicius says he "has been told" that there are written astronomical records in Egypt for the past 630,000 years and in Babylon for the past 1,440,000 years[!!].' (2) Herodotus, *The Persian Wars* Bk II, 143: 'when Hecataeus ... was at Thebes, and discoursing his genealogy, traced his descend to a god in the person of his 16th ancestor, the priests of Zeus did to him exactly as they did to me, though I made no boast of my family. They led me into the inner sanctuary ... and showed me a multitude of colossal statues in wood, which they counted up. When Hecataeus ... mentioned a god as his 16th ancestor, the priests opposed their genealogy to his, going through the list, and refusing to allow that any man was ever born of a god. Their colossal figures were each, they said, a Piromis, born of a Piromis, and the number of them was 345: through the whole series Piromis followed Piromis ...'

[37] E.J. Bickerman, 'The Jewish Historian Demetrios,' in, *Christianity, Judaism and Other Greco-Roman Cults*, 3 Vols. 3 at 72.

[38] Francis Bacon, *Novum Organum* Bk. I. 71.
[39] K. Clark, *The Critical Historian* at 132.
[40] W.G. Lambert, 'History and the Gods: A Review Article,' *Orientalia* 39 (1970) 170 [Review of, Albrektson Bertil, *History and the Gods: An Essay on the Idea of Historical Events as Divine Manifestations in the Ancient Near East and in Israel*, 1967]; Mark W. Hamilton, 'The Past as Destiny: Historical Visions in Samal and Judah Under Assyrian Hegemony,' *Harvard Theological Rev.* 91 (1998) 215. See, further, Peter L. Berger, *The Sacred Canopy: Elements of a Sociological Theory of Religion* (Anchor Books, 1966); E.A. Speiser, 'The Biblical Idea of History in Its Common Near Eastern Setting,' in *The Jewish Expression*, ed. Judah Goldin (New York: Bantam Books, 1970); Grant Frame, *Rulers of Babylonia From the Second Dynasty of Isin to the End of Assyrian Domination, 1157-612 B.C.* (Toronto: Univ. of Toronto Press, 1997).
[41] See, e.g. Josephus, *Antiquities of the Jews*, Bk I, Ch. VI, 2; Bk. II, Ch. X, 1-2; Louis Ginzberg, *The Legends of the Jews*, trans. by Henrietta Szold, (Philadelphia: The Jewish Publication Society of America, 1909) 6 vols. *Bible Times and Character, From the Creation to Jacob* Vol. 1 at 169 et seq; H. Polano, *The Talmud (Selections)* (London: Fredrick Warne & Co. 1892) at 27-28.
[42] On the 'Hamitic Hypothesis,' see, Edith R. Sanders, 'The Hamitic Hypothesis: Its Origin and Functions in Time Perspective,' *J. of African History* 10 (1969) 521; I.R. Amadi, 'The Northern Factor in the History of Sub-Saharan Africa: The Hamitic Hypothesis Revisited,' *Transafrican J. of Hist.* 18 (1989) 80; Phillip S. Zachernuk, 'Of Origins and Colonial Order: Southern Nigerian Historians and the 'Hamitic Hypothesis' c. 1870-1970', *J. of African History* 35 (1994) 427. On diffusionism, see particularly, George Elliot Smith, *The Diffusion of Culture* (London: Watts, 1933).
[43] See, generally, Martin Bernal, *Black Athena: The Afroasiatic Roots of Classical Civilization* Vol. I (The Fabrication of Ancient Greece 1785-1985) (London: Free Association Books, 1987); Cheik A. Diop, *The African Origin of Civilization: Myth or Reality* trans. Mercer Cook (Chicago: Lawrence Hill Books, 1974). (The point here is not to endorse Afrocentric diffusionism which, in a bid to turn the tables on Hellenocentric diffusionism, replaced the supposed singular culture bearers or white colonists' of antiquity with 'blacks and turn[ed] their ships to sail northwards.' The quoted phrases are from Pekka Masonen, 'The Negroland Revisited: Discovery and Invention of the Sudanese Middle Ages,' *Annales Academiae Scientiarum Fennica* (2000) at 59).
[44] Samuel N. Kramer, *The Sumerians: Their History, Culture and Character* (Chicago: Univ. of Chicago Press, 1963) at 288.
[45] George Smith, *The Chaldean Account of Genesis*, rev. ed. A.H. Sayce (London, 1880); Sir Isaac Kramer, *History Begins at Sumer*, supra; L. Cottrell, *The Quest for Sumer* (New York: G.P. Putnam's, 1965); George Sarton, *A History of Science: Ancient Science Through the Golden Age of Greece* (Harvard Univ. Press, 1960) 59-72.

[46] On the ethnic identity of the Hyksos, see, Robert M. Engberg, *The Hyksos Reconsidered* (Chicago: Univ. of Chicago Press, 1939) University of Chicago Studies in Ancient Oriental Civilization No. 18; John Van Seters, *The Hyksos: A New Investigation* (New Haven: Yale Univ. Press, 1966) at 181-190; S. W. Baron, *A Social and Religious History of the Jews* 2nd ed. (New York: Columbia Univ. Press, 1952) Vol. I at 36; Battiscombe Gunn & Alan H. Gardiner, 'New Renderings of Egyptian Texts,' *Journal of Egyptian Archaeology* V (1918) 36 at 37.

[47] Manetho, the Egyptian historian's grim description of the Hyksos' conquest (as quoted by Josephus, *Against Apion*, I.73) deserved reproduction: 'Tutimaeus. In his reign, I know not why, a blast of God's displeasure broke upon us. A people of ignoble origin from the east, whose coming was unforeseen, had the audacity to invade the country, which they mastered by main force without difficulty or even a battle. Having overpowered the chiefs, they then savagely burnt the cities, razed the temples of the gods to the ground, and treated the whole native population with the utmost cruelty, massacring some, and carrying off the wives and children of others into slavery ... The continual growing ambition of ... their first rulers, was to extirpate the Egyptian people. Their race bore the generic name of Hyscos ... Some say that they were Arabians.' The Hyksos were anathematized in later Egyptian tradition. See, D.B. Redford, 'The Hyksos Invasion in History and Tradition', *Orientalia* (n.s.) 39 (1970) 1.

Parallel accounts to the Hyksos conquest abound from the so-called Jihad wars waged in nineteenth century West Africa. See, *inter alia*, Jamil M. Abun-Nasr, *The Tijaniyya: A Sufi Order in the Modern World* (Oxford: Oxford Univ. Press, 1965), Chapter 5; Richard L. Roberts, *Warriors, Merchants, and Slaves: The State and the Economy in Middle Niger Valley, 1700-1914* (Stanford: Stanford Univ. Press, 1987), Chapter 3; Merryn Hiskett, *The Sword of Truth: The Life and Times of Shehu Usuman Dan Fodio*, 2nd ed. (Northwestern Univ. Press, 1994), Chapter 6.

[48] See, Alessandra Nibbi, *The Sea Peoples and Egypt* (Park Ridge: N.J: Noyes Press 1975); N.K. Sandars, *The Sea Peoples: Warriors of the Ancient Meditarenean, 1250-1150 B.C.* (London: Thames & Hudson, 1985); R d'A Desborough, *The Last Mycenaeans and Their Successors* (Oxford: Clarendon Press, 1964) Chapter 10; H.R. Hall, 'Keftiu and the Peoples of the Sea,' *Annual of the British School at Athens* 8 (1901-2) 157-189 at 173-188; Gerhard Herm, *The Phoenicians: The Purple Empire of the Ancient World*, trans. Caroline Hillier (London: Victor Gollowicz, 1975) at 41 et seq.

[49] R. Sullivan, *The Story of Ramses* (Edwin Mellin Press, 1986) at 195.

[50] The Assyrians have been aptly described as 'a ruthless fighting machine that struck terror through the civilized world' in the first half of the first millenium before Christ: *The Epic of Man*, at p. 136.

[51] Alfred J. Butler, *The Arab Conquest of Egypt and the Last Thirty Years of the Roman Dominion* (Oxford: Clarendon Press, 1902); J.B. Condliffe, *The Commerce of Nations* (New York: W.W. Norton, 1950) at 21: 'The moslems

did the greatest damage of all to the more highly developed Mediterranean countries. In their first cruzading zeal ... the moslems from their central strongholds in the Arabian peninsula extended their sway as far east as India, Indonesia, and even parts of China. African civilization never recovered from their onslaught.'

[52] The 'heroic age' of Hebrews and Greeks, is placed between the sixteenth and the tenth century B.C.: Cyrus H. Gordon, *Before the Bible: The Common Background of Greek and Hebrew* (London: Collins Clear-Type Press, 1962). We should note, in passing, that unlike Greeks, the ancient Egyptians 'did not pay divine honors to heroes.': Herodotus, *Histories*, Book II, 50.

[53] See, e.g. W. Jaeger, *Paiedia: The Greek Ideal of Culture*, trans. G. Highet, 2nd ed. (New York: Oxford Univ. Press, 1945) Vol. I at 11: 'in many details, the ethical doctrines of Plato and Aristotle were founded on the aristocratic morality of early Greece ... The class limitations of the old ideals were removed when they were sublimated and universalized by philosophy: while their permanent truth and their indestructible ideality were confirmed and strengthened by that process ... in many respects Aristotle, like the Greeks of all ages, has his gaze fixed on Homer's characters, and he develops his ideals after the heroic patterns ...' Elizabeth Rawson, *The Spartan Tradition in European Thought* (Oxford: Clarendon Press, 1969), *passim.*

[54] The phrase is from Samuel Butler, *Erewhon* ed. P. Mudford at 229.

[55] As if he had forgotten the so-called curse on Canaan's descendants, Josephus, for instance, wrote that 'the Hebrews took all the cities of the land of Canaan by right of war': Josephus, *Wars of the Jews*, Bk. IV Ch. IX.3. See further, Ivar Lissner, *The Living Past* trans. from the German by J. Maxwell Brownjohn (New York: G.P. Putnam & Sons, 1957); G. Goldin, 'Jericho: The Archeological Problem,' 50 *Hibbert Journal* 130; William McKae Evans, 'From the Land of Canaan to the Land of Guinea: The Strange Odyssey of the "Sons of Ham"' *American Hist. Rev.* (1980) 15.

It is said that Jericho was an urban site as early as 8,000 B.C. and 'had massive walls and a temple shrine as early as c.6500 B.C.': Herbert Schutz, *The Prehistory of Germanic Europe* (Yale Univ. Press, 1983) at 57; S.E. Finer, *The History of Government from the Earliest Times, Vol. I: Ancient Monarchies & Empires* (Oxford: Oxford Univ. Press, 1999) at 99.

A renowned protestant biblical scholar, orientalist, and philosopher of history, W.F. Albright, had no qualms about the rightness of the conquest and expulsion of Canaanites. See, W.F. Albright, *From the Stone Age to Christianity* (New York, 1957) at 280-1, cited, Robin Blackburn, *The Making of New World Slavery, 1492-1800* (London: Verso, 1997) at 88 note 83.

[56] M. Todd, *The Northern Barbarians, 100 B.C. – A.D. 300* (London: Hutchinson Univ. Library, 1975); Johannes Brousted, *The Vikings*, trans. (Penguine Books, 1995); P.J. Heather, *Goths and Romans 352-489* (Oxford: Clarendon Press, 1991).

The ancient Teutonic religious beliefs had no ties with the 'pure and benevolent virtues of life'. Instead, they 'sanctified all the horrors of war, and connected all the hopes, energies, and passions of humanity with its continual prosecution': S. Turner, *The History of the Anglo-Saxons: From the Earliest Period to the Norman Conquest* 7th ed., 3 vols. (London: Longmans, 1852) I at 200.

[57] 'We have learned from authors worthy of confidence that entire nations have been, on their own admissions, pirates and brigands; "for the ancients, piracy was not something strange and unexpected, but something reputable', Didymus says in his comment on Homer... And in truth, the Romans themselves, who are held up as having displayed examples of virtue for the entire world, how did they acquire for themselves honors, triumphs, glory, and an immortal memory for their own name, if not from robbery and rapine by which they laid the entire world to waste? What else is that great "virtue" so celebrated among them with so many panegyrics, what else is it, I ask, but violence and wrong?': J. Locke, *Questions Concerning the Law of Nature*, trans. R. Horwitz et al., (Ithaca, N.Y., and London: Cornell Univ. Press, 1990) at 185-7. For the modern period, see, inter alia, C.H. Karraker, *Piracy Was a Business* (1953); J.H. Parry, *Europe and a Wider World 1415-1715* (London: Hutchinson Univ. Library, 1949); J.H. Parry, *The Age of Reconnaissance*, 2nd ed. (London: Weindenfeld and Nicholson, 1966).

[58] The clearest statement of this morality is by the imperial Athenians to the Mileans. See, Thucydides *History of the Polynnesian Wars*, and Callicles (as portrayed by Plato) in *Gorgias*, 489c, 490a. Warner Jaeger, supra note 53 at 323 insinuates that although 'Plato is fundamentally opposed' to Callicles' blunt assertion of the 'might is right' morality, 'he [Plato] states them with the ease and sympathy of a man who has suppressed them in himself, or has yet to suppress them.' This is probably tantamount to identifying representational clarity of a position with moral commitment to it.

[59] H. Frisch, *Might and Right in Antiquity*, trans C.C. Martindale (Denmark, Gyldendalsk Boghandil, 1950). Warriors believed that their vocation is superior to scribes and their works: '...that warriors were superior to writers and to all their works seems to have been part of the traditional ideology of the barbarians who had conquered the Roman empire... Matthew Paris ... recorded one formulation of this idea in a declaration allegedly made by some of the French baronage against the Clergy in 1247. They declared that 'all of us, the King's chief men, perceive by applying our minds that the kingdom was not won by written law, nor by the arrogance of clerks, but by the sweat of war'. To the Normans ...who were usurpers wherever they triumphed – whether in France, England, Italy or Syria – the righteousness of conquest was part of a mythology...': M.T. Clanchy, *From Memory to Written Record: England 1066-1307* (London: Edward Arnold, 1979) at 23.

[60] See, *Republic*, V.470c-d, where, speaking for and to Greeks, the philosopher declares that Greeks and non-Greeks are enemies by nature. Aristotle, 'the ablest moralist of antiquity' (Lord Acton's words) conceived war as a natural art of acquisition that Greeks should practice against non-Greeks. See, Aristotle, *Politics* I, 1256b 23-26. Heraclitus summed up the history of the

ancient world when he declared that 'war is father of all and king of all; and some he has shown as gods, others men; some he has made slaves, others free': Charles H. Kahn, *The Art and Thought of Heraclitus*, p. 67. Among the moderns, Immanuel Kant, for instance, postulated that '... at the stage of culture at which the human race still stands, war is an indispensable means for bringing it to a still higher stage, ... and, since culture had scarcely begun, Holy Scripture is completely correct in portraying the welding together of peoples into a society and the complete freedom from external danger (that results from it) as a hindrance to all further culture and as a fall to unredeemable corruption', 'An Answer to the Question: 'What is Enlightenment?'', (1784) supra note 12 at 58; G.W.F. Hegel, *The Phenomenology of Spirit*, trans. A.V. Miller (Oxford: Oxford Univ. Press, 1977) at 272; *Philosophy of Right*, supra, S.324.

[61] L. Cottrell, *The Quest for Sumer*, supra note 45 at 201.

[62] See, e.g. George A Barton, *The Religion of Israel* (Philadelphia: Univ. of Penn. Press, 1928) at 20; Bishop John William Colenso, *The Pentateuch & Book of Joshua Critically Examined* (New York: D. Appleton, 1863) Vol. 1; J.B. Bury, *A History of Freedom of Thought*, 2nd ed. (London: Oxford Univ. Press, 1952) at 154; Richard E. Friedman, *Who Wrote the Bible?* (New York: Summit Books, 1987); W.O.E. Oesterley, *The Jews and Judaism During the Greek Period: The Background of Christianity* (London: S.P.C.K., 1941) at 43; Eugene Ulrich, *The Dead Sea Scrolls and the Origins of the Bible* (William B. Eerdmans Publishing Co, 1999). Historians allude to the plurality of Egypt in patriarchal times. See, e.g. A.H. Sayce, *The Races of the Old Testament* (1925) rev. ed. (The Religious Tract Society) at 149: '... the Egypt referred to in the old testament was already full of foreign elements. In the age of the patriachs Northern Egypt was governed by Hyksos Kings, and the princes who received Abraham and Joseph, though they may have adopted Egyptian titles and customs and even called themselves by Egyptian names were Asiatics in race ... It was the subjects of the Pharaohs, the scribes and the peasantry, and not the Pharaohs themselves, to whom the Israelite had to look for the essential characteristics of the Egyptian race.'

[63] See, e.g. Herodotus, *The Histories*, Bk. II, 57, 104; Aristotle, *The Works of Aristotle*, ed. W.D.Ross (1928), Vol. VI, *Physiognomica* 6.812a-12; *Problemata* Bk. XIV 909a-4; *Historia Animalium* Bk. III, 9.517a12-20.

[64] Greek contact with the surrounding world intensified in the first half of the last millenium B.C.. See, particularly, Jan Paul Crielaard, 'Homer, History, and Archaeology,' in *Homeric Questions: Essays in Philology, Ancient History, and Archaeology* ed. Jan Paul Crielaard (Amsterdam: J.C. Gebe, 1995) 201 at 224-235. On the settlement of Greeks and others in Egypt, see, particularly, Richard D. Sullivan, 'Psammetichus I and the Foundation of Naukratis' in, *Ancient Naukratis*, ed. William D.E. Coulson Vol. II (Oxford: Oxbow Books, 1996) at 179-195; John Boardman, *The Greeks Overseas: Their Early Colonies and Trade* New enlarged ed (London: Thames & Hudson, 1980) Chapter 4; Astrid Moller, *Naukratis: Trade in Archaic Greece* (Oxford: Oxford Univ.

Press, 2000) at 32-38. On inscriptions by and fortunes of mercenaries, see, e.g., Russell Meiggs & David Lewis ed. *A Selection of Greek Historical Inscriptions To the End of the Fifth Century B.C.* (Oxford: Clarendon Press, 1969) at 12-13; Emil G. Kraeling, *The Brooklyn Museum Aramaic Papyri: New Documents of the Fifth Century B.C. from the Jewish Colony at Elephantine* (New Haven: Yale Univ. Press, 1953); Peter Schafer, *Judeophobia: Attitudes toward the Jews in the Ancient World* (Cambridge, Mass.: Harvard Univ. Press, 1997) at 121-125.

[65] Pliny, *Histories*

[66] While Ethiopians conquered Egypt in the eighth century B.C., 'Egypt's' harassment of 'Ethiopia' stretches through two millennia. See, E.A. Wallis Budge, *Annals of Nubian Kings (With a Sketch of the History of the Nubian Kingdom of Napata)* (London: Kegan Paul, 1912) at pp. xxi et seq; George A. Reisner, *Harvard African Studies Vol. VI (Excavations at Karma)* (Cambridge, Mass., 1923) at 541-554; *The Myths of Hyginus, Poetica Astronomica*, trans, & ed. Mary Grant, (Univ. of Kansas Publications, Humanistic Studies, No. 34. 1960) II.20; Walter B. Emery, *Egypt in Nubia* (London: Hutchinson, 1965) at 125; Jean Vercoutter, 'Upper Egyptian Settlers in Middle Kingdom Nubia', *Kush* V (1957) 61; K.A. Kitchen, *The Third Intermediate Period in Egypt, 1100-650 B.C.*; William McKee Evans, 'From the Land of Canaan to the Land of Guinea: The Strange Odyssey of the "Sons of Ham"', *American Hist. Rev.* 15 (1980); Laszlo Torok, 'Kush: An African State in the First Millennium B.C.' *Proceedings of the British Academy* 87 (1994) 1.

[67] J.W. Crowfoot, *The Island of Meroe* (London, 1911) at 34. 'Much of Ethiopia's history is still shrouded in myth and legend, but we know that in the second millenium B.C., it was dominated by the Egyptian Empire and was known as Kush, its people as Kushites. ...Between 750 and 500 B.C., tribes of Sabaeans – Semites from Southern Arabia – migrated to the area...By the second century B.C., Ethiopia was ruled by a dynasty of Arabian origin, who called themselves the Negus-Nagast, or 'king of kings'. The seat of this dynasty was at Axum, an Ethiopian city founded almost a millenium earlier by the first of the native Ethiopian emperors...': Israel Drapkin, *Crime and Punishment in the Ancient World* (Toronto: Lexington Books, 1989) at 291.

[68] Samuel N. Kramer, *Sumerian Mythology* rev. ed. (New York: Harper & Bros, 1961)

[69] J.G.A. Pocock recently suggested that historiographical and/or cultural assumptions rather than 'racial' prejudice account for the exclusion of Egyptians and Phoenicians from accounts of the origins of Greek civilization, *Barbarism and Religion, Vol. II: Narratives of Civil Government* (Cambridge: Cambridge Univ. Press, 1999) at 356.

[70] See chapter 1.

[71] 'Cultural primitivism is the discontent of the civilized with civilization, or with some conspicuous and characteristic feature of it. It is the belief of men living in a relatively highly evolved and complex cultural condition that a life far simpler and less sophisticated in some or in all respects is a more desirable

life ...' Arthur O. Lovejoy and George Boas, *Primitivism and Related Ideas in Antiquity* (1935) (New York: Octagon Books, Inc. 1965) at 7. The modern equivalent of 'cultural primitivism' is 'reactionary modernism,' on which, see Jeffrey Herf, *Reactionary Modernism: Technology, Culture, and Politics in Weimar and The Third Reich* (1984); Herman Lebovics, *Social Conservatism and the Middle Classes in Germany, 1914-1933* (Princeton, N.J.: Princeton Univ. Press, 1969).

[72] B. Constant, 'The Liberty of the Ancients compared with that of the Moderns,' in B. Constant, *Political Writings* ed. Biancamaria Fontana (Cambridge: Cambridge Univ. Press, 1988) 308-328.

[73] The phrase is from Patrick C. Osode, 'State Contracts, State Interests and International Commercial Arbitration: A Third World Perspective' *African J. of International and Comp. Law* 9 (1997) 107 at 128.

[74] For a concise articulation of the 'political risks of the return to the ancients,' see, Luc Ferry, *Political Philosophy, Vol. 1: Rights – The New Quarrel Between the Ancients and the Moderns*, trans. Franklin Phillip (Chicago: Univ. of Chicago Press, 1990) at 20-21.

[75] James H. Robinson, *Petrarch, The First Modern Scholar and Man of Letters* 2nd ed. (New York: G.P. Putnam's Sons, 1914) at 107.

[76] Isaac Asimov, *In the Beginning* (New York: Crown Publishers, 1981) at 124. Cf. A 'barbarian's view' of the Romans: '... these more deadly Romans, whose arrogance you shun in vain by obedience and self-restraint. Harriers of the world, now that earth fails their all-devastating hands, they probe even the sea: if their enemy have wealth, they have greed; if he be poor, they are ambitious; East nor West has glutted them; alone of mankind they behold with the same passion of concupiscence waste alike and want. To plunder, butcher, steal, these things they misname empire: they make a desolation and they call it peace': Tacitus, *Agricola*, trans Maurice Hutton (Cambridge, Mass.: 1946) at 219.

[77] See, inter alia, Paulus Orosius, *The Seven Books of History Against the Pagans*, trans. J. Deferrari (Washington: The Catholic Univ. of America Press, 1964) Books II and III; Charles Rollin, *Ancient History* 11th ed. trans from the French (London, 1808) 8 vols., passim; Herodotus, *The Histories*, passim; Thucydides, *History of the Peloponnesian Wars*; Xenophon, *Hellenica*; G. Smith, *Assyrian Discoveries* (London, 1875)

[78] J.A.O. Larsen, 'The Origin and Significance of the Counting of Votes', *Classical Philology* 44 (1949) 164 at 172.

[79] Wilhelm Windelband, *A History of Philosophy Vol. 1 (Greek, Roman, and Medieval* (New York: Harper & Row, 1958) at 23; H.A. Frankfort, *Before Philosophy: The Intellectual Adventures of Ancient Man* (1946); Edmund Husserl, 'Philosophy and the Crisis of European Man,' in *Phenomenology and the Crisis of Philosophy* trans. Quentin Lauer (New York: Harper & Row, 1965); Charles H. Kahn, 'Some Remarks on the Origins of Greek Science and Philosophy,' in *Science and Philosophy in Classical Greece* ed. Alan C. Bowen (New York & London: Garland Publishing, 1991) 1.

[80] F. Boas, 'Who Were the Greeks?' *Classical Philology*; I.T. Irwin, 'Socrates and the Athenian Democracy' [Book Review] *Philosophy and Public Affairs* 18 (1989) 184.

[81] P. duBois, *Centaurs and Amazons: Women and The Pre-History of the Great Chain of Being*, supra note 6 at 11.

[82] Outstanding contemporary examples include, Allan Bloom, *The Closing of the American Mind* (New York: Simon & Schuster, 1987); A. MacIntyre, *After Virtue* (Notre Dame: Univ. of Notre Dame Press, 1981).

[83] Adam Smith, *Theory of Moral Sentiments* ed. D.D. Raphael & A.L. MacFie (Oxford: Clarendon Press, 1976) at 210

[84] Plato, *Republic*, III, 414

[85] 'Aristotle consciously used the concept of 'nature' in laying down the fundamental themes of his moral philosophy, his politics and his ethics ...': M.B. Crowe, *The Changing Profile of the Natural Law* (Martinus Nijhoff, The Hague, 1977) at 19; 'No Greek writer whose works have come down to us was more prone than Aristotle to use the word "nature," in a eulogistic or normative sense': Arthur O. Lovejoy and George Boas, *Primitivism and Related Ideas in Antiquity*, supra note 71 at 185.

[86] Aristotle, *Politics* Bk. 1, Chapter 5, 1254a-1255b. For the social and cultural underpinning of Greek slavery, see, A.J. Raymer, 'Slavery – The Graeco-Roman Defence,' *Greece & Rome* 10 (1940-41) 17; Vincent Rosivach, 'Enslaving Barbaroi and the Athenian Ideology of Slavery,' *Historia* 48 (1999) 129; Paul Cartledge, 'Like a Worm I' the Bud? A Heterology of Classical Greek Slavery,' *Greece & Rome* 40 (1993) 163.

[87] '[Until the end of] the thirteenth century ... the translators of Aristotle, the Arabs and the Jews added stone upon stone to the legacy of ancient thought, and all, in greater or less degree, were of opinion that philosophy was a subject that could be taught and learned, and that the master of the wise was Aristotle. Upon and above this basis of philosophy stood theology...': David Knowles, *The Evolution of Medieval Thought* (London: Longmans, 1962) at 338. 'No doctrine vindicated itself in so wide a variety of contexts as did Aristotelianism: Greek, Islamic, Jewish and Christian ... Aristotelianism is philosophically the most powerful of pre-modern modes of moral thought': A. MacIntyre, *After Virtue*, supra note 82 at 118.

[88] John Henry Newman, *The Idea of a University*, supra note 18 at 109.

[89] D. Knowles, *The Evolution of Medieval Thought*, supra note 87 at 83. For a 'third world' version of Aristotlean political universe, see the account given by Wole Soyinka, *The Open Sore of a Continent* at 104-107.

[90] Scholasticism was characterized by 'a close connection between philosophy and religion, and a close dependence upon ancient philosophy, especially as presented by Aristotle, and this philosophy is regarded as a corpus rational of natural truths which are ascertainable and valid in their degree as the body of revelation': David Knowles, *ibid.* at 89. 'There were two scholasticisms in Europe, one Christian, the other Judaic ... when Greek came to be known and acquaintance with Aristotle to be intimate, the Church had to decide whether to

turn her back on Greek science and thought or accept them as auxiliaries and allies. She adopted the latter course ... The Jewish synagogue did likewise ... All the same, the alliance between Church doctrine and philosophical speculation had not been struck on a footing of equality. The Church claimed the upper hand – she was mistress; and philosophical research, free within certain limits, was not expected to overstep them ...': Adrien Naville, *Revue de theologie et de Philosophie*, Sept-Oct. 1915 at 7-8, cited, Vilfredo Pareto, *The Mind and Society: A Treatise on General Sociology*, trans. A. Bongioruo and Arthurs Livingston (New York: Dover Publications, 1963) Vol. I at 34n; Norman F. Cantor, *Imagining the Law: Common Law and the Foundations of the American Legal System* (New York: HarperCollins, 1997) at 45: '... The scholastic temperament inclined to deep learning, synthesis, system building, and looking backward. It brought together the text of Greek philosophy with the Christian Bible and the theology and ethics propounded by the church fathers of the fourth and fifth centuries, primarily Saint Augustine. It used logic to solidify this intellectual pastiche into a vast intellectual system that uttered definitions and theories on everything – metaphysics, natural science, psychology, ethics, politics...'

[91] A.O. Lovejoy, *The Great Chain of Being*, supra note 7 at 7.

[92] K.R. Popper, *The Open Society and Its Enemies* 5th ed. (London: Routledge & Kegan Paul, 1966) 2 vols. passim; A.H.M. Jones, 'The Athenian Democracy and Its Critics', *Cambridge Historical Journal* 11 (1953) 1; I.T. Irwin, 'Socrates and the Athenian Democracy' [Book Review], supra note 80.

[93] D.F.S. Scott, 'Growth of Classical Tradition in Germany', *Durham University Journal* 49 (1957) 51; Ulrich J. Schneider, 'The Teaching of Philosophy at German Universities in the 19th Century,' *Hist. of Universities* 12 (1993) 197 at 246-260; Konrad H. Jarausch, 'The Institutionalization of History in 18th Century Germany,' in, *Aufklarung Und Geschichte Studien zur deutschen Geschichtswissenschaft in 18.Jahrhundert* ed. H.E. Bodeker, et al, (Vandenhoeck & Ruprecht) 625.

[94] Mark Hewitson, *National Identity and Political Thought in Germany: Wilhelmine Depiction of the French Third Republic, 1890-1914* (Oxford: Clarendon Press, 2000) at 31.

[95] See, e.g., D. Spitz, *Patterns of Anti-Democratic Thought* (New York: MacMillan, 1949); Alban D. Windspear, *The Genesis of Plato's Thought* 3rd ed. (Montreal: Harvest House, 1974); H. Kelsen, 'The Philosophy of Aristotle and the Hellenic-Macedonian Policy', *International Journal of Ethics* XLVIII (1937) 1; G. Vlastos, 'Equality and Justice in Early Greek Cosmology', *Classical Philology* 42 (1947) 156 (cf: G. Vlastos, *Plato's Universe* (Seattle: Univ. of Washington Press, 1975); George F. Hourani, 'The Education of the Third Class in Plato's Republic', *Classical Quarterly* XLIII (1949) 58; H.B. Parkes, *Gods and Men: The Origins of Western Culture* (New York: Knopf, 1959); John H. Hallowell, 'Plato and His Critics', *Journal of Politics* 27 (1965) 273; M.I. Finley, 'Athenian Demagogues,' *Past and Present* 21 (1962) 3.

[96] K.R. Popper, *The Open Society and Its Enemies*, supra note 92.

[97] W. Warde Fowler, *The City-States of the Greeks and Romans* (London: MacMillan, 1913) at 177; M.I. Finley ed. *Slavery in Classical Antiquity* (Cambridge: W. Heffer & Sons, 1960); James Vogt, *Ancient Slavery and The Ideal of Man*, trans. Thomas Wiedemann (Oxford: Blackwell, 1974).

[98] Virgil, *Aeneid*, ed. C.H. Sisson (Carcanet Press, 1986), BK III, 28: 'Do you think any present from the Greeks/Could come without a trick in it? You know Ulysses … I fear the Greeks/ Whatever presents they may bring to us?'

[99] Of course, the Greeks were vigorously defended. See, for example, *Plato, Popper and Politics: Some Contributions to a Modern Controversy*, ed. Renford Bambrough (Cambridge, W. Heffer & Sons Ltd, 1967)

[100] In terms of contemporary polarities, Straussians are 'republicans', not 'democrats'; 'neo-conservatives, not 'neo-liberals'; 'the new right', not 'the new left.' 'Straussians … believe that a community of men can rise above the egalitarianism of western democracies and achieve a higher level of understanding of the world through careful study of a small number of political philosophers, particularly Plato, Machiavelli, Hobbes, Rousseau, Marx, and Nietzsche. Straussians believe that material prosperity in itself, means little. They would have us believe that Western-style democracies can successfully generate the wealth necessary to satisfy man's material cravings but can do nothing to satisfy man's craving for things deeper and more profound': Jonathan R. Macey and Geoffrey P. Miller, 'The End of History and the New World Order: The Triumph of Capitalism and the Competition Between Liberalism and Democracy', *Cornell International L. J.* 25 (1992) 277 at 278-9. See, further, Gordon S. Wood, 'The Fundamentalists and the Constitution,' *New York Review of Books* 35 (No.2) (1988) 33; Shadia B.Drury, *The Political Ideas of Leo Strauss* (London: Macmillan, 1988), Shadia B. Drury, *Leo Strauss and The American Right* (New York: St. Martins Press, 1997); Ted V. McAllister, *Revolt Against Modernity: Leo Strauss, Eric Voegelin, and the Search for a Post-liberal Order* (Lawrence, Kansas: Kansas Univ. Press, 1996). But see, Harry A. Jaffa, 'The Truth About Leo Strauss,' *Chronicle of Higher Education*, December 5, 1997, B.11; Jurgen Gebhardt, 'Leo Strauss: The Quest for Truth in Times of Perplexity' in, *Hannah Arendt & Leo Strauss: German Emigres and American Political Thought After World War II* ed. Peter Graf Kielmansegg, *et al.* (Washington, D.C.: German Historical Institute, 1995) 81; Peter Berkowitz, 'Liberal Zealotry,' [Book Review] *Yale L.J.* 103 (1994) 1363 at 1375-79; Susan Orr, *Jerusalem and Athens: Reason and Revelation in the Works of Leo Strauss* (Rowman & Littlefield Publishers, 1995); Nasser Behnegar, 'The Intellectual Legacy of Leo Strauss, 1899-1973,' *Annual Rev. of Political Science* 1 (1998) 95.

[101] Francis Fukuyama, *The End of History and the Last Man*, supra note 27.

[102] For reviews, see, *inter alia*, Stephen Lukes, 'Hegel's Recurrence,' *The New Republic*, March 6, 1992; Jonathan R. Macey & Geoffrey P. Miller, 'The End of History and the New World Order: The Triumph of Capitalism and the Competition Between Liberalism and Democracy,' supra note 100; Samuel P. Huntington, 'No Exit: The Errors of Endism,' *National Interest* 17 (1989) 3;

Leon Wieseltier, 'Spoilers at the Party', *National Interest* 17 (1989) 12; Kenneth Minogue, 'Classy But Shaky', *National Interest* 26 (1991/2) 71; Harold Perkin, *European History Quarterly* 24 (1994) 327; Michael S. Roth, *The Ironist's Cage: Memory, Trauma, and the Construction of History* (New York: Columbia Univ. Press, 1995) Chapter 9.
[103] Supra note 101 at 182.
[104] Ibid.
[105] Ibid. at 328-339.
[106] Ibid. 315ff
[107] Ibid. 229. This essentially Nietzschean explanation *used* to be proffered by scholars who condemn 'liberal democracy' as an incorrigible bourgeois order. See, e.g., Georg Sorel, *Reflections on Violence*, trans T.E. Hulme & J. Roth (New York: Collier Books, 1965) Chapter 7.

In *Trust: The Social Virtues and the Creation of Prosperity* (London: Hamish Hamilton, 1995), Fukuyama reiterates that 'economics is the arena in which modern recognition struggles plays themselves out', and that 'liberal democracy works because the struggle for recognition that formerly had been carried out on a military, religious, or nationalist plane is now pursued on an economic one,' at xiii, 359. See also, Francis Fukuyama, *The Great Disruption: Human Nature and the Reconstitution of Social Order* (New York: Free Press, 1999).
[108] Ibid. at 163. (Emphasis added).
[109] Ibid.
[110] Ibid. at 165.
[111] Ibid.
[112] G.W.F. Hegel, *The Philosophy of Right*, SS.354, 347; *The Philosophy of History* [Introduction].
[113] Fukuyama, supra note 27 at 147.
[114] Ibid. at 155. Other Straussians express the same notion more cryptically. They write about 'the necessary harshness of beginnings,' and, for good measure, of 'the necessity of the more productive rescuing the earth from the less so': Clifford Orwin and James R. Stoner, Jr., 'Neoconstitutionalism? Rawls, Dworkin and Nozick,' in, *Confronting The Constitution* ed. Allan Bloom (Washington, D.C.: AEI Press, 1990) 437 at 466.
[115] Ibid. at 156.
[116] Ibid. at 138
[117] See, Lewis Carroll, 'What the Tortoise Said to Achilles', *Mind* (N.S.) 4 (1895) 278.
[118] Fukuyama, supra note 27 at 159.
[119] Ibid.
[120] Immanuel Kant, 'To Perpetual Peace: A Philosophical Sketch', (1795) in, *Perpetual Peace and Other Essays* trans T. Humphrey (Indianapolis: Hackett Pub. 1983) at 119.
[121] MacIntyre is right when he pointed out that 'whenever those immersed in the bureaucratic culture of the age try to think their way through to the moral

foundations of what they are and what they do, they will discover suppressed Nietzschean premises,' Alasdair MacIntyre, *After Virtue,* supra note 82 at 114.
[122] Allan Bloom, *National Interest*, No. 16, Summer 1989 at 19.
[123] Ibid. at 9. (Emphasis added).
[124] Fukuyama, supra note 27 at 139.
[125] Francis Fukuyama, *Trust: The Social Virtues and the Creation of Prosperity*, supra note 107 at 286.
[126] H. Frisch, *Might and Right in Antiquity*, supra note 59.
[127] Fukuyama, supra note 27 at 245-265.
[128] Ibid. at 88.
[129] The phrase is Patricia Vertinsky, 'Body Matters: Race, Gender, and Perceptions of Physical Ability from Goethe to Weininger,' in *Identity and Intolerance: Nationalism, Reason, and Xenophobia in Germany and the U.S.* ed. Norbert Finsch & D. Schirmar (Cambridge: Cambridge Univ. Press, 1998) 331 at 356.

For an exposition of 'the richness and impoverishment of the term barbarian', see, Maurizio Lupoi, *The Origins of the European Legal Order* trans. Adrian Belton (Cambridge: Cambridge Univ. Press, 2000), Chapter 3.
[130] Chester G. Starr, *A History of the Ancient World* 4th ed. (New York: Oxford Univ. Press, 1991) at 81. But see, Donald A. MacKenzie, *Crete and Pre-Hellenic Europe* (1917) (Random House, 1995).
[131] Fukuyama, supra note 27 at 295.
[132] Ibid. at 148.
[133] Petrarch, 'Religion does not Require us to Give up Literature', in, *Petrarch, The First Modern Scholar and Man of Letters*, ed. James H. Robinson (New York: G.P. Putnam's Sons, 1914) at 388.
[134] Alexis de Tocqueville, *Democracy in America*, Vol. I at 46. Cf. Jean Bodin, *Method for the Easy Comprehension of History* trans. Beatrice Reynolds (New York: Octagon Books, 1966) at 145: 'Was there ever a race so huge and savage which, when it had found leaders, was not carried forward along the path of civilization? What race, once instructed in the most refined arts, but ceasing to cultivate the humanities, did not sink sometime into barbarity, and savagery? Although innumerable of this exists, yet none is more illustrious than that of the Germans, who as they themselves confess were once not very far from the level of wild beasts. Then they wandered in marshes and forests like animals and by some rooted dislike they avoided letters. Nevertheless, they have now so far advanced that in the humanities they seem superior to the Asiatics; in philosophy, ... to the Greeks; in geometry to the Chaldeans; and in various crafts they seem to be superior to all peoples.'
[135] Hannah Arendt, [Introduction] in, Walter Benjamin, *Illuminations* ed. Hannah Arendt, trans. Harry Zohn (New York: Harcourt, Brace and World, 1968) at 3.
[136] For a speculative description of the brutal nature of Greek megalothymia, see, Watsuji Tetsuro, *Climate and Culture*, trans. Geoffrey Bownas (New York: Greenwood Press, 1988) at 80-85.

[137] Michael Mann, 'The Social Cohesion of Liberal Democracy', *Am. Sociological Rev.* 35 (1970) 423 at 425: 'pragmatic acceptance, where the individual complies because he perceives no realistic alternative, and normative acceptance, where the individual internalizes the moral expectations of the ruling class and views his own inferior positions as legitimate.'

[138] Fukuyama, supra note 27 at 305. In, *Trust: The Social Virtues and the Creation of Prosperity,* supra note 107 at p. 252, Fukuyama points out, and explains, a supposed paradox of such societies, namely, that they 'treat their members more equally in practice.' According to him, 'the answer is related to the fact that the egalitarianism in communally oriented societies is often restricted to the homogeneous cultural groups that tend to comprise them and does not extend to other human beings, even if they share their society's dominant cultural beliefs. Moral communities have distinct insiders and outsiders; insiders are treated with respect and equality that is not extended to outsiders. Indeed, there is an inverse proportion between the solidarity of those inside the community and the hostility, indifference, or intolerance shown to those on the outside...' In 'Social Capital, Civil Society, and Development,' *Third World Quarterly* 22 (2001) 7 at 8, Fukuyama writes that the insider-outsider division is underpinned by 'a natural human proclivity for dividing the world into friends and enemies, that is the basis of all politics.'

The 'insider-outsider' syndrome is a staple *historical* fact, and the subject of constant rhetorical endorsement. See, *inter alia*, Numa Denis Fustel de Coulanges, *The Ancient City: A Study on the Religion, Laws, and Institutions of Greece and Rome* (1885) (Baltimore: Johns Hopkins, 1980) at 86-92; B. Snell, *The Discovery of the Mind: The Greek Origins of European Thought*, trans. by T.G. Rosenmeyer (Oxford: Basil Blackwell, 1953) at 165-7; W. Sombart, *The Quintessence of Capitalism: A Study of the History and Psychology of the Modern Business Man,* trans. M. Epstein (London: T. Fisher Unwin, 1915) at 265: 'all early peoples had double-barrelled morality, with one code of conduct towards the tribesman and another towards the stranger'; F. Boas, *The Mind of Primitive Man* (1938) (Westport, Conn.: Greenwood Press, 1983) at 202; H. Spencer, *The Principles of Ethics*, 2 vols. (New York: D. Appleton, 1903), Vol. I at 322: 'From the earliest times ... rude tribes and civilized societies ... had had continually to carry on external self-defence and internal cooperation – external antagonism and internal friendship. Hence, their members have acquired two different sets of sentiments and ideas, adjusted to these two kinds of activity'; Max Weber, *The Protestant Ethic and the Spirit of Capitalism* trans. Talcott Parson (New York: Charles Scribner's, 1955) at 57: '... like war and piracy, trade has often been unrestrained in its relations with foreigners and those outside the group. The double ethic ... permitted ...what was forbidden in dealings among brothers'; Anthony M. Ludovici, *A Defence of Aristocracy: A Text Book for Tories* (London: Constable & Co. 1933) 2nd ed. at 282 et seq.

[139] F. Bacon, *The Advancement of Learning.*

[140] Frank M. Turner, *Contesting Cultural Authority: Essays in Victorian Intellectual Life* (Cambridge Univ. Press, 1993).

[141] See, note 60.

[142] 'From the very beginning the principle of nationalism was almost indissolubly linked, both in theory and practise, with the idea of war. For Hegel, for Fichte and Arndt, those Prussian thinkers whose ideas were to be archtypical for so much of the nineteenth century nationalism, war was the necessary dialectic in the evolution of nations. As one deputy at the Frankfort Assembly of 1848 put it, 'mere existence does not entitle a people to political independence; only the force to assert itself as a state among others'. In nation-building as in revolution, force was the midwife of the historical process': Michael Howard, *The Lessons of History* (Oxford: Clarendon Press, 1991) at 39.

[143] Fukuyama, supra note 27 at 73. On the Anglo-American reaction to 'the German desire for military world dominion,' see the succinct essay by Elihu Root, 'The Need for Organization in Scientific Research', *Bulletin of the National Research Council* 1 (1919) 7 at 9, 10: '... the impulse which has called in the power of organization to multiply the effectiveness of scientific and industrial research to the highest degree is the German desire for military world dominion. All the world realizes now the immense value in preparing for the present war of the German system of research ... That realization is plainly giving a tremendous impetus to movements for effective organization of scientific power both in England and in the United States ... Germany had the advantage at the start, because she had long been consciously making this kind of preparation with a settled purpose to bring on the war when she was ready. It would be the height of folly for the peaceable, law-abiding nations of the earth ever to permit themselves to be left again at a disadvantage in that kind of preparation ...Without it, the most civilized nation will be as helpless as the Aztecs were against Cortez. We are not limited, however, to a military objective, for when the war is over the international competitions of peace will be resumed. No treaties or leagues can prevent that, and it is not desirable that they should, for no nation can afford to be without the stimulus of competition. In that race the same power of science which has so amazingly increased the productive capacity of mankind ... will be applied again and the prizes of industrial and commercial leadership will fall to the nation which organizes its scientific forces most effectively.'

[144] Fukuyama, supra note 27 at 263

[145] S. Turner, *The History of the Anglo-Saxons (From the Earliest Period to the Norman Conquest* 7th ed. (London: Longmans, 1852) Vol. I at 200.

[146] Bustenay Oded, *War, Peace and Empire: Justifications for War in Assyrian Royal Inscriptions* (Wiesbaden: Reichert, 1992) at 155.

[147] Fukuyama, supra note 27 at 334.

[148] Ibid. at 159.

[149] Ibid. at 334. In *The Great Disruption: Human Nature and the Reconstitution of Social Order*, supra note 107 at 227, Fukuyama claims that "... human beings *by nature* like to organize themselves hierarchically – or to put it more precisely, those on the top of hierarchies find the satisfaction that recognition of

the social status brings so enjoyable that it frequently outweighs money and material wealth as a source of happiness. *Those on the bottom of hierarchies like it less, but they usually have no choice.'* (Emphasis added).

[150] Charles Kingsley, *Hypathia*

[151] Plato, *Phaedrus* 272

[152] This sentence paraphrases Shakespeare, *Macbeth*, I, vii, 8-12.

[153] Samuel Butler, *Erewhon*, supra note 54.

[154] R. Pound, *The Spirit of the Common Law* (Francestown, N.H. Marshall Jones, 1931) at 87.

[155] The Greeks soundly believed that the Homerics were historical personalities. See, M.I. Finley, *The World of Odysseus* 2nd ed. (London: Penguine Books, 1991) 22-5; A.W. Gomme, *The Greek Attitude to Poetry and History* (Berkeley: Univ. of California Press, 1954), Chapter 1; Hermann Strasburger, 'The Sociology of the Homeric Epics', in *Homer: German Scholarship in Translation* ed. P.V. Jones and G.M. Wright (Oxford: Clarendon Press, 1997) 47.

[156] Leo Strauss, *Natural Right and History* (Chicago: Univ. of Chicago Press, 1953); *On Tyranny*

[157] Allan Bloom, *The Closing of the American Mind* (New York: Simon & Schuster, 1987) at 90.

[158] The phrase is from Blaudine Kriegel, *The State and the Rule of Law* trans. March A. LePain & Jeffrey C. Cohen (Princeton, N.J.: Princeton Univ. Press, 1995) at 54.

[159] Jenny Strauss Clay, *The Politics of Olympus: Form and Meaning in the Major Homeric Hymns* (Princeton, N.J.: Princeton Univ. Press, 1989)

[160] The phrase is from B. Willey, *The Seventeenth Century Background* (London: Chatto & Windus, 1957) at 17.

[161]The phrase is from R.H. Tawney, 'The Rise of the Gentry, 1558-1640', in, *Essays in Economic History*, ed. E.M. Carus-Wilson (London: Edward Arnold Publishers, 1954) at 214.

[162] L. Wittgeinstein, *Remarks on Frazer's Golden Bough* ed. Rush Rhees, (trans. A.C. Miles) (The Brynmill Press, 1979) at 1e.

[163] Micah 3: 9-11.

[164] Leo Strauss, *Natural Right and History*, supra note 156 at 42-3.

[165] E.M. Butler, *The Tyranny of Greece Over Germany* (Cambridge Univ. Press, 1935) at 154.

[166] L. Wittgenstein, *On Certainty* ed. G.E.M. Anscombe & G.H. von Wright trans. Denis Paul & G.E.M. Anscombe (Oxford: Basil Blackwell, 1963) at 160, 166.

Chapter 3

Analytical Jurisprudence and Legal Theory

> I imagine the world of men as a race of children marooned on an island of hard facts, most of them with their backs to the sea busily digging or building in the sand. They squabble a good deal; they achieve considerably less, and the little they accomplish is often wholly or partly obliterated by the waves, so that they have to move their pitch and begin all over again ....[1]

Introduction

This chapter makes explicit what is implicit in the preceding chapters, namely, that moral philosophy is not so much about theorizing or interpreting local practices as with uncovering *right* practice. Its argument rests on three postulates. First, that the philosophy of law is quintessentially the philosophy of right. Second, that the philosophy of law is 'expository', not 'censorial.' And third, that analytical jurisprudence is not coterminous with the philosophy of law. The argument itself is two-pronged: analytical jurisprudence is inherently provincial and ethnocentric, and its theory of jurisprudence precludes the possibility of ascertaining and articulating putatively universal legal norms. The chapter is divided into four parts. Part I posits the philosophy of law as the paradigmatic ethical philosophy. Part II outlines the advent and nature of modern legal theory and analytical jurisprudence, and distinguishes between the former and the latter on the one hand, and, on the other, between analytical jurisprudence and theories of law. Part III uses the concept of crime as forceps in adducing some of the reasons why analytical jurisprudence is not co-extensive with the philosophy of law. Part IV complements this by underscoring the inherent localism of analytical jurisprudence in its hermeneutic dimensions.

I

PHILOSOPHY OF LAW AS PHILOSOPHY OF RIGHT

Philosophy may be described as a never-ending attempt to grasp the nature of things, natural or human. The corpus of understanding of the nature of things at any given time is positive knowledge. Understanding, of course, pertains to things as they are *mediately* not as they are *immediately*. This distinction goes back to ancient times. The world of immediate perception is the 'physical' world; the world of mediated perception is the 'metaphysical' world. Philosophy dwells in the metaphysical realm.

The first recorded philosopher who underscored the distinction between the physical and the metaphysical worlds was the great Plato. Plato set up (or he is understood as having set up) the metaphysical world as separate and distinct from the physical world. Further, he regarded (or he is interpreted as having regarded) the metaphysical world as the real world, and the physical world as at best only a pale copy of the metaphysical.

It is to the everlasting glory of Aristotle (or so intellectual history suggests) that he realized that the contrast between the metaphysical and the physical worlds was not between the real and the unreal, the transient and the permanent, but between the material and the immaterial. In other words, Aristotle saw that the physical world is as much real as the metaphysical. To speak accurately, the physical and the metaphysical are two sides of the same coin, existence.

Moreover, the metaphysical is logically prior to the physical while the physical is experientially prior to the metaphysical. Indeed, but for immediate perception mortals would never have surmised the existence of the metaphysical world. It follows that to depreciate or abandon the physical world (as Plato allegedly did or counseled) is to barricade the route to the metaphysical. In short, Aristotle receives the honor of recognizing that the distinction between the physical and the metaphysical worlds is itself a philosophical invention. In the medieval period, the difference between Plato and Aristotle on this point was understood as the divergence between the heavenbound and the earthbound philosopher.

It was those who grasped Aristotle's point who resuscitated philosophy at the beginning of the modern era. However, their unexceptionable anti-authoritarian epistemology issued in nominalism.[2] Among the outstanding philosophers in the modern world, it is perhaps only Immanuel Kant who explicitly underscored the significance of the distinction between the physical and the metaphysical worlds. In his inaugural lecture, Kant aptly characterized the distinction as the 'noblest enterprise of Antiquity.'[3]

Unless one belongs to a tribe that collapses existence into perception, one would have no difficulty with recognizing that neither the physical nor the metaphysical world is constituted as such by man. To put it starkly, philosophy supposes Being or Existence independent of human perception. The Greeks, who intellectual history has made the originators of philosophy, embraced that fundamental supposition. It can only be called 'theological'. In fact, before the Greeks, the activity called philosophy was a priestly vocation; philosophers were theologians.[4]

The subject of philosophy may be divided into two classes: natural and ethical. Accordingly, there are two broad divisions of philosophy, namely, natural and ethical philosophy. Duty is the subject matter of ethical philosophy. When it is not superseded by or subsumed under political philosophy or deflected by history, tradition, or theories of law, the philosophy of law is the form that ethical philosophy assumes in the civil world. Its subject matter is the juridical dimension of Duty. Specifically, the philosophy of law deals with *necessary* Duties and their correlation, namely, *perfect* Rights. From the juridical point of view, therefore, the philosophy of law is 'the principal and most perfect branch of ethics.'[5] 'Jurisprudence' is a sobriquet for the philosophy of law.

The analysis of the totality of experience for the purpose of discerning and formulating the stable, invariable, or structural elements is 'philosophical analysis.'

There are two types of philosophical analysis: universal and general. General philosophical analysis is therapeutic. It is either negative or positive. Positive therapeutic philosophical analysis entails the identification and articulation of the structural elements of specific (cultural) ethical experience. Negative therapeutic philosophical analysis is sociology of error. It entails 'the detection of the sources in linguistic idioms of recurrent misconstructions and absurd theories'[6] of or about specific (cultural) ethical experience. In the English-speaking world, negative therapeutic philosophical analysis dominated ethical philosophy between the fifties and the seventies of the last century, but few legal philosophers were bewitched by it in its unstinted form. At any rate, it no longer commands the heights.[7] General philosophical analysis is the compliment of reason to tradition.

At least two things distinguish universal from general philosophical analysis. First, their respective frames of reference are different.

Whereas general philosophical analysis works within the framework of specific (cultural) ethical experience, universal philosophical analysis takes within its ken the totality of all experience. Secondly, their respective aims are different. Whereas general philosophical analysis aims at ascertaining and elaborating the structural elements of specific (cultural) ethical experience, universal philosophical analysis aims at discovering and articulating putatively universal ethical kinds. Universal philosophical analysis – inventive discovery via the analysis of the totality of experience - is the quest of reason for the reason of things.

An understanding of the nature of things is formalized in concepts, and the 'resolutive-compositive'[8] method is utilized to deepen knowledge of concepts. Concepts in turn become the tools of exposition. Now, the subject of exposition is not necessarily identical with the subject of philosophy. Whereas the subject of exposition is an understanding of things, things themselves are the subjects of philosophy. In other words, while the subject of philosophy exists independently of an understanding of it, the subject of exposition does not necessarily coincide with the subject of philosophy. I am not suggesting that the subject of exposition can never be identical with the subject of philosophy (though it may be that we have no way of knowing if and when that happens). No. I only want to underscore, for pedagogic purposes, that it is only if an intellect grasps and accurately represents the object of study that the subject of exposition might be identical with the subject of philosophy. It is easy to elide the distinction between the two. Often times, deference to great teachers compels learners to identify the understanding of things by the former with the things themselves. The most common way of doing this is the scholastic habit of setting up certain philosophers as 'cognitive authority.'[9] We lose the subject of philosophy momentarily if we substitute an understanding of things for the things themselves. We lose it irretrievably if we concentrate on explicating the understanding of things by some great teacher(s) instead of investigating the things themselves or if we take the 'coherence' of a particular formulation as evidence of its truth or correctness.[10]

The explication of concepts is 'conceptual analysis.' Conceptual analysis 'takes its material (i.e., the concepts to be analyzed) as antecedently ready made.' Put simply, conceptual analysis involves the 'equating of one concept with a certain configuration of a number of others'; it may, therefore, 'be described somewhat figuratively as a breaking down of the *original* concept into its component parts.'[11]

An original concept is the result rather than the cause of philosophical investigation. Although language apparently lends phenomenality to concepts, concepts are products of understanding. Put differently, concepts are forms with determinate content. Or, put differently still, concepts are units of understanding, and content is the substance of these self-same units. Far from being optical entities, concepts are reflective configurations. In short, concepts are mind-dependent.[12] It is the mind that formulates things; things themselves are formless. In short, concepts are intellectual products. But, in societies where philosophy is entirely or almost entirely learned or transmitted in writing[13] or where philosophy acquires 'a strong flavour of secularised theology' such that the products of human understanding are 'withdrawn from the questioning mind,'[14] concepts are depicted as Platonic forms.[15]

The content of concepts may be divided into two: material and immaterial. The material is that component of a concept that is directly or inferentially observable. The immaterial is the component of a concept that is observable neither directly nor inferentially. We shall call the material component of concepts the 'formal' element, and the immaterial component, the 'rational' element. In other words, conceptual analysis simultaneously generates two structural properties.

The theoretical function of the philosophy of law is to formulate legal concepts, and coordinate the structural elements of concepts into juridical *facts* or *norms*. Its practical function is to deploy such facts or norms in regulating individual behavior and superintending and systematizing institutional practice. For reasons that will be made clear shortly, it is my thesis that analytical jurisprudence abridges these tasks, that it is an incomplete philosophy of law.

II

MODERN LEGAL THEORY AND ANALYTICAL JURISPRUDENCE

It is common knowledge that until the nineteenth-century, jurisprudence was permeated by natural law theory, and was pursued by political philosophers.[16] Another characteristic of pre-nineteenth century legal philosophy was that law, morals, and politics were not analytically distinguished. All that changed in that most scientific of all centuries when philosophy spun off so many separate sciences. Specifically, in the nineteenth century, modern legal theory emerged from the crucible of political philosophy; legal philosophy was severed from political philosophy, and was quickly established as a separate discipline.

Modern legal theory sharply distinguished law, morals, and politics. That move necessitated another distinction, namely, the division of philosophy of law into two distinct branches: the 'expository' and the 'censorial' or the *exposition* of what the law *is* and the *exposition* of what the law *ought* to be.[17] The former was hiked off from the latter, and allocated to different intellectual workers; one is the function of the jurist, the other is the function of the legislator or its under-laborer, the law reformer. This division of labor is the backbone of modern jurisprudence. It sets for jurists the singular task 'of sharpening and deepening our understanding of legality, law, and their relationship to each other and to human society.'[18]

However, the founders of modern jurisprudence were fervent legal positivists. As such, it is not always easy to differentiate modern legal theory from legal positivism. In fact, if seen through the prism of positivistic intellectuality, modern jurisprudence looks like the *alter ego* of legal positivism. Yet the character of modern jurisprudence is different from that of legal positivism. One is a theory or school of law whose views of the nature of law shape the meaning of the concept of law, legal concepts, and the task of legal theory. Specifically, legal positivism maintains that law is made, not discovered, that law is separate and distinct from morals and politics, and that the task of legal theory is to ascertain, describe, and systematize the law as it is in positive systems of law. The other is an approach to legal philosophy. As an approach rather than a theory or school of law, modern jurisprudence specifies 'a scientific methodology for the study of law.'[19] This is the possibly age-old[20] analytic or resolutive-compositive[21] method.

Now, analysis supposes the existence or at least the possibility of the existence of the subject of analysis. As such, modern jurisprudence assumes the existence of law and focuses on its understanding. Further, as a discipline born in the scientific age, modern legal theory insists on the study of law as a phenomenon separate and distinct from such related phenomena as morals and politics. In other words, both modern legal theory and legal positivism harp on the distinction between law and morals or law as it *is* and law as it *ought* to be. But its significance for modern legal theory is different from that of legal positivism.

The positivistic distinction between law as it is and law as it ought to be or between law and morals is not the same thing as the *analytic* distinction between law and morals or the exposition of law as it *is* and the exposition of law as it *ought* to be. The former is theory-laden. It makes 'the study of laws into an autonomous science by making it morally neutral.'[22] The latter is agnostic; it neither asserts nor denies that law or its study is morally neutral or that law lives in moral and political vacuum. But after this initial different starting points, both the theory-laden and theory-neutral position converge in that they conceive the function of the jurist as the identification and study of law as a phenomenon on its own rather than as an appendage of morals or politics. In short, modern jurisprudence enjoins jurists to study positive laws 'scientifically' rather than 'to participate in the system' by arguing that a particular interpretation or theory of law affords 'the correct view.'[23]

Modern jurisprudence is a phoenix from the ashes of pre-modern moral philosophy, for it acknowledges that 'the principles and distinctions which the mere *being* of Law supposes'[24] are the focus of legal theory. But the fact that modern jurisprudence emerged together with legal positivism conceals the significance of the phrase 'principles and distinctions which the mere being of law supposes'. Yet, no matter how difficult it may be to sever modern jurisprudence from the theory of law with which its birth is closely associated modern legal theory cannot be identified with a particular theory or school of law. The point here is that the key to understanding the nature of legal theory or the science of law does not lie in its link with this or that theory or school of law, but in the historical fact that it used to be part of political philosophy. The separation of law and morals is as much integral to modern jurisprudence as it is to legal positivism, but we shall underscore the fact that it has different valence for legal theory. This requires a brief history of modern jurisprudence.

Although John Austin wrote the first English text on modern jurisprudence in 1832,[25] the story of the emergence of modern jurisprudence in the English-speaking world began with Jeremy Bentham. We have already noted that Bentham divided jurisprudence into two branches: expository and censorial. After stating that an expositor ascertains what the law is while the censor inquires after what the law ought to be, Bentham added that the law ascertained by the former might be those of a particular nation or a number of nations, or the laws of all nations. He called the former expository (local) jurisprudence, and the latter expository (universal) jurisprudence.[26] Next, Bentham noted that the diversity of nations and languages ensured that there were hardly any two nations that agreed or used the same words in formulating their laws. But the diversity of nations and its seemingly attendant tower-of-babel atmosphere did not preclude discerning convergence or correspondence of otherwise divergent legal language and laws. In Bentham's own words,

> '... among the words that are appropriated to the subject of law, there are some that in all languages are pretty exactly correspondent to one another: which comes to the same thing nearly as if they were the same. Of this stamp ... are those which correspond to the words *power*, *right*, *obligation*, *liberty*, and many others.'

Since correspondent legal terms indicate identity of otherwise divergent legal forms or string of words, the exposition of law as it is must focus on the analysis of the indicia of such identity. That is, in order to know what the law is the universal expositor has to determine the meaning of convergent legal terms. Expository (universal) jurisprudence is thus concerned with the seemingly narrow task of analyzing the concept of law and legal concepts common to all systems of law; Bentham, at least, gave that impression. As he puts it,

> if there are any books which can ...be styled books of universal jurisprudence, they must be looked for within very narrow limits... To be susceptible of an universal application, all that a book of the expository kind can have to treat of, is the *import*[27] of words: to be, strictly speaking, universal, it must confine itself to terminology.[28]

On the surface of it, this does not even hint that law is amoral or that the import of legal words invariably rules out morals from the sphere of law. As well, it does not suggest that the expositor makes or invents the meaning of law and legal concepts. On the contrary, it suggests that the task of the expositor is to discover existent, convergent meaning of legal words. And, unlike the traditional philosopher or 'the man of system'[29] the modern jurist does not hanker after what ought to be. Rather, the modern jurist studies the laws and legal language of nations for the singular purpose of discerning what the law *is* by focusing on and exploring the implications of common distinctions or convergent meaning of otherwise divergent legal terms.

However, universal expository jurisprudence does not require the investigation of the laws of all nations. In practice, it suffices if one investigates the laws of one's immediate society and that of a few other nations with which it is closely connected.[30] However, Bentham himself had minimal interest in expository jurisprudence, both local and universal. Instead, he took the 'principle of utility' as a foundation and he engaged almost exclusively on universal censorial jurisprudence; his was a science of law as it ought to be, not the juristic science of what the law is. Nonetheless, Bentham attempted to fix, once and for all times, the nature of juristic science of law, that is, expository jurisprudence.

It is trite to say that Bentham was an avowed enemy of natural law theory in all its manifestations. In Bentham's schema, one of the functions of the distinction between the exposition of law as it is and the exposition of law as it ought to be was to undermine the supposedly inherently anarchical and reactionary implications of natural law theory and, conversely, to strengthen 'juridical positivism.'[31] Unlike natural law theorists who postulated that law had 'a divine parent,'[32] positivists regarded law as human command, specifically, the expression of the will of the legislature.[33] To legal positivists it is cant to suggest that the law, whether wholly or partly, is grounded on morals and, *pro tanto* normative. On the contrary, the *ipsissima verba* of the political sovereign are law, whatever words the sovereign chooses to utter.

It would have been uncharacteristic for Bentham, the philosopher who arguably 'supplied a formula under which indiscriminate opposition could be generalised,'[34] to have failed to prize criticism.[35] Accordingly, although Bentham maintained that the sovereign's command is law, he also insisted that the sovereign's words were not *ipso facto* above criticism. As Bentham realized, what the political sovereign wills does not necessarily coincide with what ought to be. To preserve the censor and to effectively criticize the law, we need to know what the law is, as the sovereign willed it. This requires the exposition of law as it is which should be kept separate and distinct from the exposition of law as it ought to be. In short, to Bentham knowledge of the 'ought' presupposes knowledge of the 'is.'[36] Thus, the 'is' would not be confounded with the 'ought'; the business of criticizing and censoring the law would be preserved. In particular, the expositor would be prevented from meddling with the job of the censor, that is, the exposition of the law that ought to be. As William Twining succinctly puts it, 'Bentham distinguished the is and the ought for the sake of the ought.'[37] Hence, Bentham laid it down, 'on normative grounds,' that the expositor elucidates law and legal concepts 'in "flatly descriptive and morally neutral" terms.'[38] The positivistic theory of law and its concomitant insistence on separating the expositor from the censor culminated in the characterization of law and its exposition as purely descriptive and morally neutral.

Although we shall see shortly that Austin's description of the nature of legal theory is by no means unambiguous, he picked up the gauntlet and developed jurisprudence along descriptive and morally neutral lines. Austin's starting point was Bentham's distinction between universal and local *expository* jurisprudence. However, from the onset

Austin defines jurisprudence as a science. 'Jurisprudence,' Austin writes, 'is the *science* of what is essential to law, combined with the science of what it ought to be.'[39] But Austin immediately proceeded to confine himself to the former. He then divided jurisprudence into two: general and particular. He describes the latter as 'the science of any system of positive law as now actually obtains, or once actually obtained, in a specifically determined nation, or specifically determined nations.'[40] In other words, particular jurisprudence deals exclusively with national laws. Further, it is practice-based, for it expounds the law from the point of view of ordinary legal practice. The Roman lawyers' art[41] and, perhaps, 'the textbook tradition'[42] that emerged in the latter part of the nineteenth century exemplify particular jurisprudence. Like Bentham, Austin mentioned particular jurisprudence only to dismiss it. In fact, Austin did not dignify particular jurisprudence with the name of philosophy of law.

Austin introduced general jurisprudence by emphasizing that it is the science of law, and here law means positive law, not natural or divine law. Specifically, general jurisprudence is the philosophy of law as it is in systems of positive law.[43] Unlike particular jurisprudence, general jurisprudence derives its materials from a comparative source – systems of particular and positive law. Further, general jurisprudence is theoretical: it deals with the peculiarly legal - what is essential to law. And, it deals with law *qua* law in contradistinction to morals and politics or with law as it is rather than with law as it ought to be. At first sight, this resonates with Bentham's distinction between the exposition of law as it is and the exposition of law as it ought to be. But Austin may not have made the distinction in the same context or for the same purpose as Bentham.

Austin delineated the province of jurisprudence more definitively than Bentham did. According to Austin, general jurisprudence is directly concerned with the exposition of the elements common to various systems of particular and positive law. In Austin's own words,[44]

> general jurisprudence ... is concerned directly with principles and distinctions which are *common* to various systems of particular and positive law; and which each of those various systems inevitably involves, let it be worthy of praise or blame, or let it accord or not with an assumed measure or test. Or (changing the phrase) general jurisprudence ... is concerned with law as it necessarily *is*, rather than with law as it *ought* to be: with law as it be, *be it good or bad*, rather than with law as it must be, *if it be good*.

Of course, Austin was a legal positivist, and it is tempting to interpret these words as those of a legal positivist *simpliciter*. But, I submit that, in this passage, Austin couched *analytic* distinctions in seemingly positivistic vocabulary. Put differently, while the context suggests that Austin penned these words as a modern jurist, the italicized phrases give the impression that he was thinking as a positivist.[45] Once that ambiguity is located and resolved, and the positivist baggage is discarded, it becomes clear that the phrase 'law as it necessarily *is*, rather than law as it *ought* to be' does not, in terms, mean that law is normatively neutral. In other words, if we purge Austin's formulation of expository jurisprudence of its positivistic phraseology, it becomes manifest that modern jurisprudence does not necessarily rule out the possibility that the exposition of law might be a description of what is perhaps essentially normative. The task of expository general jurisprudence is to show what the law *is* whatever 'indignant moralists,'[46] howling politicians, and underdog earthlings might say. It is the theory-laden depiction of law and its study, in contradistinction from the theory-neutral depiction, that makes 'analytical jurisprudence,' to use the sobriquet for English jurisprudence, a purely descriptive and normatively neutral science of law.

We saw above that Bentham pointed out that universal (that is, general) expository jurisprudence need not address the laws of all nations. As he practiced it, Austin restricted general jurisprudence to the determination and coherent exposition of 'the principles, notions and distinctions' common to 'ampler and maturer systems of positive law'. By 'ampler and maturer systems of positive law,' Austin, like many a nineteenth century scholar, meant the systems of positive law 'of all civilized European Nations.'[47] This, in effect, referred to the common law and the continental civil law systems. In short, although Austin realized that 'the subject of [general] jurisprudence is law, not some laws or the law of this or that country,'[48] he decidedly restricted the philosophy of law to the analysis of the positive systems of law of European nations he deemed worthy of study. Thus, whether or not Austin believed that 'primitive' and 'developed' societies are entirely different,[49] he excluded systems of positive laws of pre-modern and non-European nations.

The coherent exposition of the principles, notions, and distinctions common to ample and mature systems of positive law requires prior determination and elucidation of leading legal terms. That is, analytic jurisprudence requires the prior identification and careful analysis or determination of the meaning of the concept of law and other legal concepts employed in legal discourse in contradistinction to morals and politics.[50] Put differently, general jurisprudence entails two expository exercises:

> General jurisprudence ... involves the exposition of two different kinds of principles or notions. Concepts that are essential for the study of any legal system are one type. To this extent, the business of general jurisprudence is to formulate what today would be called a 'conceptual framework.' Empirical generalizations are the other type. Their presence means that general jurisprudence entails more than the elucidation of basic legal terms or concepts. Beyond this, it also involves the exposition of substantive similarities between different legal systems.[51]

Austin remarked that he was following in the steps of earlier philosophers,[52] but that did not mean that it was the function of the legal philosopher to censor the law, as earlier philosophers reputedly did. Nor did it mean that legal philosophy seeks to mirror some platonic legal forms or Kantian legal categories. On the contrary, the function of the legal philosopher is to ascertain the meaning of law and fundamental legal concepts embedded in, and to articulate coherently the principles, distinctions, and notions common to various systems of 'developed' systems of positive law. In short, general jurisprudence is expository, not censorial.

It cannot be overemphasized that Bentham distinguished expository from censorial jurisprudence primarily to differentiate the vocation of the expositor of law as it is from the vocation of the expositor of law as it ought to be. As noted earlier, such division of labor did not imply that the subject of exposition itself is morally neutral any more than it meant that the study of law could not reach such values. But both Bentham and Austin muddied expository jurisprudence by dipping the concept of law into the 'cynical acid' of legal positivism - law is simply what the political superior sets for the political inferior. The point here is that the positivistic intellectuality of the founders of modern jurisprudence made them rule out the possibility that the exposition of law might be the formulation of *normative* rules - a fact that accounted in no small measure for the skeptical reception of analytical jurisprudence in Victorian England.[53] But the roots of the conception of law and its study as normatively neutral run deeper than juridical positivism.

One of the working beliefs of nineteenth century scholarship was that words, standing by themselves, are meaningless.[54] Just as one's character might be determined by knowing the company one keeps, the meaning of a word could be fixed by knowing the group of words in which it occurs. To know the meaning of a word, one has to know how it is used in a meaningful unit. And, a meaningful unit, 'the smallest unit of understanding is ... the sentence or proposition.'[55] As Frege succinctly puts it, 'only in a proposition have the words really a meaning.'[56] It follows that the proposition or sentence, not the individual word or the term in isolation, is the archetype of thought or locus of understanding.

Bentham and Austin subscribed to that fundamental belief. They both knew that words and phrases 'taken by themselves are the work of abstraction, the produce of refined analysis.'[57] Specifically, Bentham pointed out that 'every man who speaks, speaks in propositions, the rudest savage, no less than the most polished orator,'[58] and Austin remarked that legal terms are 'short marks for long series of propositions.'[59] A corollary of this is that legal terms and concepts are propositional idioms or shorthand representations of otherwise lengthy lexical discourse. It follows, therefore, that to determine the meaning of the concept of law and leading legal terms, one has to ascertain the propositions they embody.

We might take Alfred Whitehead's characterization of a proposition as an accurate description of its meaning. According to Whitehead, 'a proposition is the abstract possibility of some specified nexus of actualities realizing some eternal object, which may either be simple or may be a complex pattern of simpler objects. It is a *notion* about actualities, a suggestion, a *theory*, a supposition about *things*.'[60] (We will leave aside the platonic notion that actualities realize eternal object). If we conjoin this with the delineation of the expositor from the censor, it becomes clear that, in examining and exploring the philosophical implications of legal propositional idioms or concepts, jurists are not ventriloquists mimicking the views of this or that subject of law. Specifically, jurists are not, in principle, agents of the state, whether democratic or not, but savants of the *law*. Like judges who apply the law as it is in positive law, jurists study the law and legal terms as they are in positive systems of law. It follows that impartiality is as much a requisite for jurists as it is for judges. In short, jurists are independent subjects of the law or rather impartial, though not necessarily Martian, observers who investigate legal phenomena for the singular purpose of ascertaining what the law *is*.

Leo Strauss has rightly pointed out that philosophical inquiry begins by considering not what one sees of the subject of inquiry, 'but in what is said about them or in opinions about them.'[61] Opinions about law and its rules are commonly formed and expressed in ordinary language by participants in positive systems of law. But when it comes to philosophical inquiry, ordinary language is merely a language of investigation, for, 'things,' not words, are the objects of philosophical scrutiny. This means that we have to separate the '*things*' under investigation from the words used to describe them.[62] We might make the same point differently by saying that verbal sounds or written signs, the language of investigation, is purely descriptive while the subject of investigation, non-verbal sound or unwritten signs, is 'both descriptive and normative in character,'[63] and so must be the result of philosophical investigation itself.

That words are not really the objects of study, coupled with the fact that the study of law had to rest on experience, forces jurists to become 'natural historians who explore' the logic of 'the concealed or forgotten *uses* of everyday [legal] words'.[64] In other words, jurists endeavor to determine the philosophical meaning of legal terms and concepts by excavating the propositions concealed by ordinary legal language. And, they expound such propositions unvarnished and unadorned by the desire to determine what ought to be. Thus, jurists are concerned not so much with the ordinary or speculative meaning of legal terms and words, as with the idea of law encapsulated in linguistic labels. It is little wonder that the reputed founders of juristic science, the Romans, neither conceived law as a speculative science nor engaged in 'a linguistic analysis of their framework juristic concepts.'[65]

In exploring the logic of the concealed or forgotten uses of everyday legal language, a philosophical analyst searches for their *legal* meaning as distinct from, and undistorted by, political usage and moral embellishment. The goal of philosophical investigation into systems of positive law is to discover what is *law*, not what is agreeable to some political form and moral interests or what is conformable with established opinion, authoritative practice or speculative thought. Consequently, in explicating the results of philosophical inquiry into systems of positive law, the expositor does not expand or abridge the law. Rather, the expositor re-presents what s/he apprehends the law to be. Hence, while the expositor begins with common opinions about law, s/he ends by making clear and definite the *idea* of law buried in strings of ordinary legal language or practice. In Bentham's succinct but anthropocentric formulation, exposition is the art of finding 'clear ideas to annex to the expressions of a man whose ideas were not clear.'[66] But how far can the expositor go in bypassing the gossamer of speculative reasoning, institutional morality, politics, and ordinary language to find the clear ideas misted by legal terms and words?

Bentham gave a clear answer to that epistemological question. According to Bentham, analysis terminates at the sensible objects to which a thing relates. 'To find the limits of any subject,' Bentham wrote, 'nothing more can be done than to ascertain the real or semi-real entities, the substances or motions or situations it relates to.'[67] By 'real or semi-real entities' Bentham meant things that are directly or indirectly perceptible. To use his own words, 'real or semi-real entities' are 'either perceptible or inferential: perceptible either *impressions* or *ideas*; inferential, either *material*, i.e., *corporeal*, or *immaterial*, i.e., *spiritual*.'[68] Significantly, Bentham eliminated the immaterial or spiritual altogether[69] and he tied up expository work with a type of empiricist epistemology that insists that all ideas derive from the senses,[70] thus putting strict limits on the pursuit of knowledge. To Bentham, philosophical inquiry is complete as soon as one reaches the directly or inferentially perceptible substances to which a thing relates. Accordingly, the jurist can only trace the ideas of law embedded in legal terms and language up to the sensible objects to which they relate. This is another way of saying that juristic inquiry perforce terminates at the formal elements of law and legal concepts, for formal elements are properties that are 'either directly perceptible or knowable by inference based on perception.'[71]

Bentham described concepts as 'fictitious entities,' and he remarked that the ideas annexed to concepts arise ultimately from sensible impressions by 'real entities.'

> The ideas annexed to … words … are ideas copied immediately from the impressions made by real entities, the ideas annexed to words and phrases, act of will, sign of an act of will, physical act or act of the body, event, circumstance etc, are either like the former, ideas copied immediately from impressions made by real entities or copies of the sensible affections of determinate real entities.'[72]

As Bentham conceived it, the art of exposition could not go beyond explicating the impressions made by real entities. As a piece of epistemology, this is unexceptionable, but as a definition of the limits of knowledge it is insufferable, and perhaps wrong. Put simply, Bentham shortened the intellectual vision when he set the limits of philosophical inquiry into law at those entities that are perceptible either directly or inferentially. This might be controversial, but it is doubtful that the content of the structural elements of law and fundamental legal concepts is exhausted by directly or indirectly perceptible entities.

There is no gainsaying that modern jurisprudence is expository, not censorial or 'evaluative.'[73] Perhaps, Bentham and Austin did for the philosophy of law in the modern world what Socrates did for moral philosophy in the ancient world – they brought jurisprudence from heaven down to earth. It may even be that the philosophy of law has always been expository, that only the failure to demarcate the censor from the expositor fostered the illusion that jurisprudence was censorial. Be that as it may, unless we allow theories or schools of law or moral and political theories to determine the perspective of legal theory, the fact that jurisprudence is expository does not, in itself, mean that law is normatively neutral. Nor does it mean that the expositor of law is committed in advance to this or that institutional morality or sociopolitical and economic configuration. It appears, as well, that it does not mean that expository jurisprudence is inherently incapable of determining and capturing any normative attributes the law might possess.

As we have seen, Austin's *Lectures on Jurisprudence* was the first in the series of modern essays that transformed the philosophy of law from a normative to a descriptive science. Austin mapped out the nature of modern legal theory but, as he practiced it, he turned the philosophy of law from the principal and most perfect branch of ethics into 'descriptive sociology.'[74] Be that as it may, the departure has one enormous intellectual advantage: it makes continually possible 'a fresh start'[75] at the analytical characterization or interpretive construction of the legal experience of civilized nations or developed system(s) of positive law.

It is well known that Austin's imperative theory of law has been considerably modified, weakened, or displaced. However, the English-speaking world is wedded to analytical jurisprudence. Now, the label, 'analytical jurisprudence', is equivocal; it is liable to confuse method with theory. As we have seen, analytical jurisprudence is neither a theory of or about law nor is the 'resolutive-compositive' method peculiar to legal theory. Rather, analytical jurisprudence is a theory of jurisprudence. As such it identifies a subject of study (law), embraces 'scientific' methodology, and specifies the task of legal theory (the exposition of law). Analytical jurisprudence is therefore a discipline[76] that should not be identified with a particular school or theory of law.

Particular theories or schools of law no less than analytical jurisprudence often formulate definitive meanings of law and legal concepts. Of course, neither the definition of law and legal concepts fostered by a school or theory of law nor that formulated by analytical jurisprudence can 'settle any fundamental question.'[77] Nevertheless, since the analytical method is esteemed the scientific method *par excellence*, the definition of law and legal concepts fostered by analytical jurisprudence are more likely to command assent than those fostered by theories or schools of law. Therefore, it is necessary to keep separate and distinct the definition of law and other legal concepts fostered by a theory or school of law from the definition of the same concepts generated by analytical jurisprudence. Further, the definition of law and other legal concepts proffered by a particular analytical jurist should not be identified with law and legal concepts themselves, for, as pointed out earlier, the subject of exposition is not necessarily identical with the subject of philosophy. H.L.A. Hart makes the point succinctly: it is a mistake to fail 'to distinguish between, on the one hand, law and legal concepts and, on the other, theories of or about law, and definitions of legal concepts.'[78] Put differently, analysis of legal phenomena can be carried out independently of a theory of or about law. Nor do we have to underwrite the definition of law and other legal terms by the theory of law we somehow happen to hold. In short, like analytic philosophy generally, analytical jurisprudence is 'ethically and politically neutral *formally*.'[79]

As we have seen, Austin worked in the alembic of 'the positive systems of law of all civilized European nations.' Subsequent analytical jurists demurred on this point. Instead of seeking the highest common factor of the positive systems of law of all civilized European nations, Austin's successors confined themselves to the materials of the positive laws of English-speaking nations. Although they moved within a smaller orbit, the 'new' analytical jurists were faithful to Austin's conception of the task of legal theory.[80] Of course, analytical jurists in the common law world proffer theories and definitions of law and legal concepts. But, following the 'linguistic turn,' they arrive at such theories and definitions on the basis of acute analysis of the language of law in English-speaking nations. Although both the 'interpretive turn' and 'rhetorical turn' that succeeded the 'linguistic turn' emphasize that the materials of the positive system of law with which they deal contain substantive values, they are also hermetically sealed up in the Anglo-American legal culture. In short, Austin's comparative conceptual framework is simply superseded by the conceptual framework revealed by interpretive or rhetorical analysis of law within the common law system. Thus, unlike Austin, the new analytical 'jurisprudes'[81] do not pursue a [common] definition, but rather an account of a concept that is already implicitly defined in [the common law] language.'[82]

Analytic philosophy does not postulate the creation of knowledge *ex nihilo*. Rather, it assumes that 'knowledge in any sphere must be based on knowledge.'[83] Unlike the supposed classical epistemology (and post-classical epistemology tinctured, as it were, by theology) which assumed that any foundational knowledge must be 'natural' and 'divine' respectively, modern epistemological belief assumes that any foundational knowledge must be 'empirical'. That is, the product of observation and reflection, not an emanation of natural or divine intelligence. Accordingly, analytical jurisprudence rests on empirical foundation.

Austin gave analytical jurisprudence a solid empirical[84] foundation by deriving the data for the philosophy of law from what he called 'the ampler and maturer' systems of positive law. After identifying and isolating the leading terms from such empirical sources, he subjected them to rigorous analysis and then proceeded to make the generalizing claim that the meaning of such necessary terms (concepts) are the ultimate basis on which must rest the subsequent systematization work.[85] When the succeeding generations of analytical jurists limited the field of observation, so to speak, to the common law system, they thereby effectively particularized general jurisprudence.

Earlier we differentiated two types of philosophical analysis, universal and general. As well, we noted that the latter is therapeutic, and that it is either negative or positive. We further pointed out that positive philosophical analysis entailed determining and formulating the structural elements of specific ethical experience. Positive philosophical analysis is especially suited for understanding law as it is in a positive system of law. Since the antecedently ready-made concepts of a positive system of law are embedded in the language of the relevant legal jurisdiction, the first concern of positive philosophical analysis is the clarification of the language in which the concepts are hidden in linguistic idioms. This is usually an ordinary language. Ordinary languages normally consist of words, which, of course, symbolize thought. In short, while positive philosophical analysis is immediately concerned with language, its ultimate aim is to retrieve the thought embodied in local language. Put differently, positive philosophical analysis aspires to recover local, traditional wisdom. Positive philosophical analysis - the retrieval of traditional wisdom via the analysis of the language in which it is embedded - is the concept of philosophy that the scholastics derived from 'the ancients'.

The scholastic concept of philosophy waned in the seventeenth century at the outset of the modern period, and was overshadowed by Enlightenment thinkers in the eighteenth century. It is one of the paradoxes of intellectual history that the scholastic concept of philosophy was revamped in the wake of the romantic reaction to the revolutionary impulse in late eighteenth and early nineteenth centuries. Instead of pre-modern scholasticism, which was 'dominated by theology,'[86] the new scholasticism was dominated by history. The point here is that, as Austin defined it, general jurisprudence is the manifestation in the legal domain of the renewed scholastic concept of philosophy. Analytical jurisprudence is positive philosophical analysis is descriptive sociology.

Recall that analytical jurisprudence explicitly anchors itself on experience. In practice, an invisible 'our' has been almost always invariably inserted before 'experience'. This has almost always given analytic philosophy generally, and analytical jurisprudence particularly, not only an ethnocentric tinge but also a present-mindedness and provincial slant.[87] A corollary of this is that the concepts deployed in the exposition of law, morals and politics, are almost always generalized account of law, morals and politics based on the experience of certain societies. The distinction between 'civilized' and 'uncivilized' communities or 'developed' and 'primitive' societies (which, in more recent times, has metamorphosed into the distinction between 'literate' and 'oral' cultures[88]) conspired to confine ethical philosophy to the analysis of the legal, moral, and political experience of 'civilized' or 'developed' societies. Indeed, in the nineteenth century it was explicitly maintained that 'it is out of the *beliefs* and *judgments* only of the civilized that rational consensus is to be constructed.'[89]

If 'all science is cosmology,'[90] all philosophy tends to be cosmography. Since analytical jurisprudence demarcates the legal cosmos in a way that excludes the legal experience of pre-modern societies generally and the so-called 'primitive' societies in particular, it is impossible for analytical jurisprudence to encircle the totality of *all* experience. Or, rather, analytical jurisprudence takes the legal experience of 'civilized' societies as constitutive of the totality of legal experience. This suggests that its concept of law and other fundamental legal concepts are those *conceivable* in 'developed' legal orders. It is primarily concerned with recovering and clarifying the conceptual meaning of law and other legal concepts, and with elaborating coherent conceptual conclusions, principles and rules generated by such legal orders.

Of course, it is rash to deny that developed systems of positive law contain sediments from the legal worlds which analytical jurisprudence formally excludes from its purview. Nevertheless, the definitive meanings of law and other fundamental legal concepts fashioned by analytical jurisprudence are *relative* to the world that supplied the furniture for its intellectual universe. Consequently, except when analytical jurists are expounding their own theories of or about law and the definitions of law and legal concepts in 'developed' systems of positive law, any claim to *universality* would be an ill-conceived supererogation. Besides, there is always the possibility that the meaning of law and other fundamental legal concepts embedded in mature systems of positive law that one analyst comes up with may be disputed by another analytical jurist. Hart's critique of, and divergence from, Austin's definition of law is a well-known instance of this;[91] Ronald Dworkin's critique of, and departure from, Hart is another.[92]

III

LIMITATIONS OF ANALYTICAL JURISPRUDENCE

The foregoing might suggest that the argument that analytical jurisprudence is not coextensive with the philosophy of law rested on the claim that it is implicitly provincial. This is not so. Analytical jurisprudence is a deficient philosophy of law partly because of its provinciality and partly because of a prejudice from within analytic philosophy itself as manifested in analytical jurisprudence.

We noted in the first part above that the notion of 'the concept' implied two structural properties, and in the second part that analytical jurisprudence is a theory of jurisprudence. As a theory of jurisprudence, analytical jurisprudence rests on an epistemological belief that limits the concept of 'the concept' to formal properties only. Put differently analytical jurisprudence denies the dual character of concepts. This shrinking of 'the concept' is a diminution that neither could have been intended nor would it have been endorsed by the methodological nominalism of the adversaries of Aristotleanism. This is the core of the thesis that analytical jurisprudence is not coterminous with the philosophy of law. I want to demonstrate this with a relatively uncontroversial legal concept, the concept of crime.

Richard Tur has suggested that 'the criminal law throws up so much grist for the jurisprudential mill.'[93] He might have added that that is because the concept of crime best demonstrates that law is ultimately ethical in nature. To show this, we have to trace briefly the history of the law of crimes.

One of the leading criminal law scholars in the twentieth century, the late Professor Glanville Williams, pointed out long ago that the student of the criminal law need not go beyond Sir Edward Coke.[94] This is because, historically, a clear, general and distinct principle of liability did not emerge in the criminal law until after the sixteenth century.[95] Assuming, for present purposes, that legal theory does not stand to lose if one ignores the history of the criminal law up until the seventeenth century, let us ask (and answer) the usual analytic question: 'what is crime?'

As everyone acquainted with law knows, the pivotal element of crime is 'intent', and the quintessence of 'intent' is *malice prepense* or malice aforethought. Pollock and Maitland essay that when the term *malitia* first came into use in English law, it hardly signified a state of mind; rather, it meant wrongdoing.[96] Or, as F. B. Sayre puts it, 'malice was construed in its popular sense as meaning general malevolence or cold-blooded desire to injure, and referred to the underlying motive rather than to the immediate intent of the actor.'[97] To make *malitia* refer to a state of mind, some qualifying adjective, like *praemedita* or *ex cogitata*, was needed.[98] When this was done, the phrase 'designated a purely psychical element,' that is, 'the immediate intent of the actor.'

By the time Sir Edward Coke was 'reporting the unwritten law'[99] of England, *malice prepense* had acquired a technical connotation. It was used as a term of art to discriminate the capital crime of murder from other forms of punishable but lesser homicide. Accordingly, Coke refused to restrict the meaning of the phrase to its earlier and 'popular, purely psychical sense.' As a 'common law's Aristotle,'[100] Coke faithfully described *malice prepense* as 'when one compasseth to kill, wound, or beat another and doth it *sedato animo*,' adding that 'this is said in law to be malice aforethought, prepensed, malitia praecogitata.'[101] And, he described murder as 'when a man of sound memory and of the age of discretion, unlawfully killeth an reasonable creature ... with malice forethought either expressed by the party, or implied by law.'[102] Leaving aside the notion of 'implied malice,' what distinguished the malice for murder from the malice for manslaughter was the environment in which the criminal intent or *mens rea* was formed. If the intention to kill arose on a sudden falling out or provocation it would still be malice but not prepensed.[103] In short, to constitute a crime under the common law 'there must be, first, a vicious will [i.e., intent]; and secondly, an unlawful act consequent upon such vicious will.'[104]

Following the advent and ascendance of analytical jurisprudence, the analytical scalpel was brought to bear on the concept of crime embedded in the common law. Analytical jurists label the twin requirements of 'vicious will' and 'unlawful act' *mens rea* and *actus reus* respectively. *Actus reus* is often defined residually as all the elements of the offence except the mental element, and *mens rea* is described as the mental element or simply 'intention' or 'recklessness'.[105] In other words, the content of the concept of crime is not really certain enumerated acts but the notion of intentional unlawful act. And, 'intentional unlawful act' ultimately resolves into two real or semi-real entities, 'intent' and 'act'.

But the analytic exercise is not complete as soon as one resolves a concept into its parts. Resolution is merely the way down. The way up is to compose the whole from its parts. Accordingly, analytical jurists have taken the further step of composing 'crime' from bottom upwards. In doing so, they have had to determine the meaning of the concept of crime. And, they invariably frame the meaning of crime in 'conceptualist' terms, that is, they hold that the meaning of the concept generated by the process of resolution and composition can be generalized.[106]

They followed the intellectual tradition that construes the question, 'what is x?' as a demand for definition, and which requires that the definition be predicated on the 'essence' of the thing being defined. An essential property is that formal attribute that is regarded as the central or indispensable component of that thing. The definition is then framed in such a way that its denotation invariably includes the essential property. In short, the essentialist method of definition hinges the meaning of a concept on its essence and decrees that the stipulated meaning should be the ultimate basis from which argument commences and ends. The essentialist method of definition is as old as Aristotle;[107] the difference between 'the ancients' and 'the moderns' is that while the latter regarded 'essences' as nominal,[108] the former regarded them as real.

The father of analytical jurisprudence, John Austin, employed the essentialist method of definition; indeed, as already noted, he conceived the science of law as the determination of what is essential to law. Although he emphasized that an 'essential part is not the complex whole of which it is an essential part,' Austin concluded the analysis of the concept of 'wrong' (under which he subsumed 'crime') by stating that,

> intention, negligence, heedlessness or rashness, is *an essentially component part* of injury or wrong ... intention, negligence, heedlessness or rashness, is *of the essence* of injury or wrong; is *of the essence* of breach of duty; is *a necessary condition precedent* to the existence of that plight or predicament which is styled guilt or imputability.[109]

Analytical criminal jurists take the same essentialist position. However, unlike Austin, analytical common law scholars have had to exclude 'negligence' from the notion of criminal guilt, for the simple and obvious reason that the common law concept of crime does not include 'negligence.' Analytical jurisprudence claims to have fathomed the meaning of crime: crime means an intentional or reckless violation of legal duty imposed by that species of public law known as the criminal law in mature systems of positive law.

But 'crime' is an ordinary word, and its utilization to describe intentional or reckless breach of duty imposed by a species of law is an act of linguistic appropriation which does not suffice to confer the right to decree that usage. That usage gives the misleading impression that crime is a department rather than a concept of law. Unlike concepts, which are intellectual products that serve as fixed reference points, ordinary words have neither 'absolute permanent meanings'[110] nor are they integral parts of the thought they express. Rather, words are instruments of expression, and the particular letters that make up a word have no logical relation to the thought the word expresses. This is a by-product of the conventional nature of ordinary languages in general, and ordinary legal language is not an exception. In short, while words are necessarily employed in philosophical inquiry, the thing, 'the idea'[111] encoded in words can be descried, described and preserved without having recourse to the services of such linguistic labels.[112] Unfortunately, the radar of analytical jurisprudence was not designed to catch such entities.

As we have seen, John Austin took his bearings from Bentham, and he described general jurisprudence as the theoretical study of law as it is in positive systems of law.[113] We have already noted that Bentham regarded concepts as 'fictitious entities', and that he fixed the limits of philosophical inquiry at the 'the real or semi-real entities, the substances or motions or situations' to which a thing relates. In other words, Bentham confined the notion of the concept to material substances or formal properties only. This somewhat 'bizarre twist in the hermeneutic spiral'[114] veiled the implicit shortening of the intellectual vision. There is nothing in Austin's *Lectures* that suggests that he disagreed with Bentham on this point. To put it starkly, analytical jurisprudence denies the dual character of concepts; its theory of the nature of knowledge forecloses the possibility of ascertaining the dual content of law and legal concepts, and casting them into *juridical* facts or norms.

In truth, the immaterial components of concepts are not analytically recoverable things. Rather, they are rationally discernible entities. On this view, which is at least as old as Plato and Aristotle,[115] the difference between the subject of natural and ethical philosophy is not one between fact and value, but between natural and ethical kinds which are both 'facts' capable of being unraveled by the intellect.

This means that there is another sense in which legal concepts have essences, namely, the ethical sense. Unlike the analytic sense, the function of the ethical essence is not the formal one of marking off one concept from another, but the normative one of distinguishing 'right' from 'wrong'. Save for an apparent exception discussed elsewhere,[116] the normative function of 'intent' is that it is *wrong* to impose extraordinary sanctions on a legal actor for breach of a legal duty or obligation unless the act or omission was intentional or at least reckless. And, the normative function of 'act' is that it is *wrong* to regard a legal person as a responsible actor unless one had, and did exercise, the capacity (or failed to exercise the capacity when one could and should have done so) in breach of one's legal duties or obligations. These are the probable juridical *facts* to which the 'real or semi-real entities' of 'intent' and 'act' relate. To deny the dual content of concepts and to limit, as analytical jurisprudence does, the philosophy of law to the retrieval and description of the formal properties of the concepts embedded in, and the coherent exposition of the principles, distinctions and notions common to 'developed' systems of positive law is to define rational inquiry out of existence.

We noted earlier that analytical jurisprudence is morally and politically neutral formally. We have just seen that a formal, amoral philosophy of law is not only incomplete but is also a contradiction in terms. This is confusing. It ceases to be so if we add that the formal neutrality of the analytical approach does not imply that the materials on which it is brought to bear are themselves morally and politically neutral. Rather, 'formal neutrality' underscores the methodological requirement that the formulation of the concept of law and other fundamental legal concepts should be influenced neither by the theory of law held by an analyst nor by any particular moral or political theory. That way, the moral or political ramifications of law and other fundamental law concepts can constitute the subject matter of particular moral and political theories or theories of law. In other words, the function of particular moral and political theories or theories of law is not the abstract one of defining law and other fundamental legal concepts, but the practical one of designing, maintaining, and superintending the institutional rules and practices necessary for the optimal effectuation of the law. This is why political theorists have traditionally focused not so much on forms of government as on the best administration, and why legal philosophy continually converges on law's dominion: the rule of law.[117] It also explains why law is often (misleadingly) characterized as moral or political much to the discomfiture of (some) positivists[118] and (some) idealists[119] alike.

IV

HERMENEUTICS AND LEGAL THEORY

While the immediately preceding pages considered the limitations of analytical jurisprudence the previous part showed that the founders of modern jurisprudence in the English-speaking world effected a 'paradigm shift'[120] in legal theory. They did so, first, by emphasizing the necessity of distinguishing law from morals and politics, and second, by reviving the age-old analytic method of inquiry. As well, Bentham and Austin displaced the theory of law prevalent until their own time, and they not only substituted another theory, legal positivism, but they also superimposed that theory of law on modern jurisprudence, as they practiced it. Despite sustained assault on legal positivism since the nineteenth century, its hold on the legal imagination, both on the Continent and in English-speaking countries, has been astonishingly tenacious.[121]

Insofar as the present study is concerned, the development in legal theory following the triumph of legal positivism may be usefully divided into three periods. These are the period between the birth of modern jurisprudence in the nineteenth century and the two cataclysmic European wars otherwise known as the first and second world wars, the period immediately after the second world war up to the nineteen-sixties, and the period since the nineteen-seventies. Of course, these periods witnessed shifting currents in theories and schools of law, but we shall not be concerned with theories and schools of law as such. The analytic method was energetically utilized by (mostly) self-conscious positivists in the study of law during the first period. The second period was little different from the first, except that it witnessed the adaptation and application in legal theory of the supposedly distinctive methodology of the human sciences developed on the continent in the nineteenth century. I have in mind here the incursion of hermeneutics into modern legal theory. The third period is characterized by the 'return of grand theory'[122] that boldly seeks to overcome the alienation of the normative in the human sciences by positivistic intellectuality.

Undoubtedly, there is much to celebrate, as Quentin Skinner does, in grand theory, but its immediate effect on the study of law was to plunge legal theory into 'ideological chaos.' From the point of view of our present concerns, the return of grand theory in law threatened to return jurisprudence to a pre-scientific or 'neolithic'[123] age.

This part focuses on the influence of 'hermeneutics'[124] on modern legal theory. While analytical positivism reigned in the Anglo-

American legal world, the continental world developed and promoted hermeneutics as the appropriate approach to the human sciences, including law. Hermeneutics is thus the second leg on which rests modern jurisprudence. The aim here is to pinpoint the intellectual insight which hermeneutics brought into the study of law, and to underscore its limitations. The discussion does this by showing three things, among others. First, it shows that hermeneutics is not incompatible with different schools or theories of law. Second, it shows that hermeneutics construes legal theory as 'expository.' Third, and perhaps most importantly, it shows that hermeneutics emphasizes 'the indispensability of tradition'[125] for the human sciences generally, and law particularly.[126]

Because it emphasizes the indispensability of tradition for the study of law, hermeneutics modified or appeared to have modified the amoral-ness of analytical positivism or the classical positivist-inspired belief that the study of positive laws can generate only descriptive theory of law and normatively neutral rules of law. However, legal hermeneutics seems to have achieved that feat at the enormous cost of reducing the law and its rules to outright creatures of convention or mere products of local knowledge.

H.L.A. Hart[127] introduced hermeneutics into the study of law in the second of the three periods outlined above, that is, the period following the Second World War.[128] Since then Anglo-American 'legal theory has been attempting to make the hermeneutic paradigm prevail in its approach to its object.'[129] There is no doubt that H.L.A. Hart's 'peerless contributions'[130] to modern jurisprudence inadvertently exposed 'the groundlessness'[131] of institutional legality, and led to new anxiety about the nature and foundation of law. The attempt to dispel the resultant intellectual uneasiness culminated in the emergence of interpretive theories of law in the third period identified above.

Hart was, of course, an ardent legal positivist, but both his hermeneutic[132] or methodological[133] positivism and the anti- or post-positivist hermeneutics of some of his critics and successors generally,[134] and Ronald Dworkin[135] particularly, derive from the same Anglo-American variant of this aspect of continental philosophy, namely, 'analytic hermeneutics.'[136] Analytic hermeneutics itself derives from one of the foremost philosophers of the twentieth century, Ludwig Wittgenstein, who had the exceptional chance of showing the English-speaking world 'how to think philosophically and historically.'[137]

According to some commentators, the later Wittgenstein[138] (for there is an 'early' Wittgenstein, with whom we are not here concerned) subtly and simultaneously dissimulated both *subject*ive and *object*ive foundations of knowledge, and filled the vacuum with *tradition* or *convention*. According to others, Wittgenstein repudiated all foundations whatsoever, including tradition and convention. According to still others, Wittgenstein was neither a traditionalist nor a conventionalist nor an anti-foundationalist. Rather, he was the philosophers' therapist who realized the errors of earlier philosophers generally, and particularly the futility of platonic yearnings, and so he confined philosophy to the elucidation of *language-games* or the clarification of 'conceptual structures.'[139] I am neither competent nor willing to arbitrate among these protean interpretations. At this juncture, three observations will suffice. First, Wittgenstein was an eminent member of the outstanding Viennese intelligentsia, and although his training was not primarily humanistic, he received his initial education from outside the cultural orbit of the original home of modern hermeneutics.[140] Second, Wittgenstein did not attempt to redefine philosophy, but only claimed to have found a new way or method of practicing the ancient art.[141] Third, it is not unknown that, as in other areas of human endeavor, intellectual disciples seldom possess the catholicity of their master.

Hermeneutics claims uniqueness for the human sciences. Specifically, it insists that its object of study, 'the human species in all its manifold activities, presents features, such as consciousness and culture, that are not captured in the nets of natural science.'[142] In other words, according to hermeneutics, the human species, as conscious cultural being, is not amenable to the causal-explanatory mode of analysis that typifies the natural sciences.[143] When it is *not* coupled with positivism or a social scientific orientation, hermeneutics rejects the view that the concepts used in the human sciences, including law, are purely descriptive or that theoretical study of positive law can yield only normatively neutral rules.

Because it emphasizes the normativity of law, hermeneutics putatively strengthens the rule of law. It follows that hermeneutics is capable of providing a firm basis for rights. Yet, whether in the hands of contemporary positivists, anti- or post-positivists, analytical legal hermeneutics does not appear to have the power to inoculate the rule of law against the vagaries of conventional morality any more than the classical positivists shielded law from the whimsical caprice of sovereign princes. To put it starkly, it is not implausible to deny that analytic legal hermeneutics fosters 'enthusiast[s] of the rule of law.'[144] Any belief to the contrary may well be an 'undeserved reputation,' to use Leslie Green's words again. But we should not attempt to cross the bridge before we get to it.

Before lapsing into leisurely exposition, it is necessary to make some remarks on the nature of modern hermeneutics. However much mystified by talks of '*volksgeist*' [145] '*weltansicht,*' '*weltanschauung,*' '*forms of life,*' '*language-games*', etc., modern hermeneutics is neither the nadir nor the summit of Teutonic mysticism any more than metaphysics is a Gothic fantasy. Rather, modern hermeneutics was a weapon forged and effectively wielded by a heterogeneous but powerful 'backward-looking reformist movements'[146] on the continent in the early nineteenth century. Just as modern natural rights theories were originally developed by politically 'conservative thinkers as a defence of property, competition and other related values,'[147] modern hermeneutics was initially developed by 'the eminent conservatives who founded the historical school'[148] of thought in Germany in the early nineteenth century. Hermeneutics was the methodological means by which the eminent conservatives interceded for tradition against the alleged annihilation or attempted annihilation of 'the spirit' by 'scientism.'[149]

The wrongs committed by an intellectual movement could be corrected, if at all, only by resorting anew to life and its processes. In the late eighteenth and early nineteenth centuries, an incipient *a priori* rationalism had threatened to impose itself on and color all intellectual activities, including legal philosophy. This was not a peccadillo, but a cardinal epistemological sin. Specifically, the 'truth' about law and its rules as *a priori* rationalists portrayed it threatened to overwhelm *life*. Before the development of modern hermeneutics, *a priori* rationalism looked triumphant; it stood at the portals of philosophy, including legal theory. In reality, legal theory was moribund, or rather, modern legal theory was about to be born.

When the inevitable reaction set in, in the form of romanticism,[150] the conflation of theory and method ensured that the attack could be immediately or retrospectively portrayed as an assault on theory or method or both or a concerted effort to substitute one theory or method for another. This is not so much a mistake as an obfuscating characterization. Unfortunately, that perception was reinforced and, indeed, perpetuated by the fact that the emergence of romanticism, 'between 1789 and 1848'[151] with 'its built in conservative tendency,'[152] was the result of recoiling from the revolutionary impulse on the continent.[153] As a politically conservative movement, romanticism aimed primarily at retrieving, describing and systematizing 'the robust vitalising spirit which fortified and preserved the legitimate organs, institutions, and traditions of the past'[154] in order to shape the present and influence the future.

Out of romanticism came the historical school of thought[155] which, in scholarly imagination, is the archenemy of Enlightenment rationalism. Hermeneutics itself descended directly from the historical school. And, of course, '*geist*'[156] was the controlling[157] concept of the historical school of thought generally, and particularly of the influential historical school of law founded by F.C. von. Savigny.[158] Put differently, the historical school was the intellectual arm of romanticism, and hermeneutics was its methodological expression. Thus, romanticism, historicism, and hermeneutics are inseparable.[159]

Ludwig Wittgenstein, the reputed fountainhead of analytic hermeneutics, was probably a romantic,[160] though certainly not of a nostalgic stripe.[161] However, Wittgenstein himself was, strictly speaking, not an analytic hermeneutics philosopher.[162] What is more, although postmodernists are wont to depict him otherwise, and contrary to the cultural relativism implicit in analytic hermeneutics, Wittgenstein was not 'a cultural relativist.'[163] Indeed, Wittgenstein's philosophy was not a philosophy of culture or language or history, but a resolute attempt to purify philosophical analysis by dispelling the cause of philosophical bewilderment. Wittgenstein had located the roots of philosophical puzzlement in language-, history-, and culture-based *thought*. To dissolve the puzzles created by language, history, and culture-based thought, Wittgenstein fashioned, and put to at least three uses, the notions of 'language-games' and 'forms of life'.

One, to underline the relativity of linguistic, historical, and cultural thought without, however, asserting that thought itself is necessarily relative to language, history, and culture. Two, to underline the importance of history, language, and culture for any theoretical study without, however, asserting that the former binds the latter. And three, to illuminate the process of discerning the stable in the flux of linguistic, historical, and cultural experiences without, however, claiming that the stable replicates reality. Each of these assumes that it is possible for scholars to be 'objective,' in the sense that they are able to look and see with unprejudiced eyes the stable in the totality of linguistic, historical, and cultural experiences. Specifically, they imply that it is not impossible for scholars to overcome the ethnocentrism and relativism inherent in their own linguistic, cultural, and historical worldviews. As Plato[164] pointed out long ago, it is only in polities without rigorous philosophical tradition that scholars remain cocoon in their own linguistic nests, and flutter about like ensnared birds in their own dialectic cages. Wittgenstein philosophized precisely because he was convinced that scholars could escape from, and soar above, their immediate linguistic, historical, and cultural iron cages. In

Wittgenstein's own poignant phrase, he philosophized because he wanted to show 'the fly the way out of the fly bottle.'[165]

The historical school of law focused on the question of the nature of law as an object of scientific study. As such, it sought the answer not to 'a historical or methodological question but to a *philosophical* one: what is law, and what constitutes its foundation.'[166] This means that the interest of the methodological expression of the historical school, hermeneutics, was 'more ontological than technical.'[167] Both on the Continent, where it originated, and the Anglo-Saxon world, where it was warmly received, at least until after the first World War,[168] the historical school of law was neither an assault on legal theory *qua* theory nor was it a root-and-branch rejection of 'reason.' Rather, the historical school of law raised the cry of distress, so to speak, that summoned jurists to rehabilitate positive law as an object of scientific study rather than abandon it to its fate in the hands of a seemingly triumphant *a priori* rationalism on the continent, and an incipient social scientific approach on the British island.

As parts II and III above imply, modern legal theory, with its 'scientific' methodology, does not entail the theoretical conclusion that law is normatively neutral or that legal theory can fashion only normatively neutral rules of law. We have noted that legal hermeneutics, when it is not underwritten by positivistic intellectuality, explicitly affirmed the normativity of law. But that is not what or all that hermeneutics contributed to law and its study. In fact, the distinctive contribution of hermeneutics to legal theory does not lie in the particular, affirmative answer it gives to the question, 'is law normative?' Nor does it lie in where it says we should look for the telltale signs of the normativity of law. Rather, it consists of the exaltation of mind, of the timely reminder that 'reality is primarily spiritual, not material,'[169] if not in all disciplines, at least in the human sciences, including law.

However, we should not overlook the rider. To the historical school of thought, the 'spiritual' that constitutes 'reality' is the national spirit, the *volksgeist* of this or that political entity, 'the concrete generally shared cultural characteristics of a people.'[170] Even when due allowance is made for the fact that, contextually, 'the *volksgeist*' denotes the 'intellectual life'[171] of a people, not its animal existence, it is still as much anthropocentric as Bentham's[172] notion that, ultimately, what the expositor does is to find clear ideas for the nebulous expressions of another. In other words, insofar as the study of law is concerned, the difference between the positivist and the historical schools of law is not that one is ahistorical while the other is not, but in their different derivation and characterization of positive law as an object of scientific study.

The historical school of law was not a reaction to rationalism *per se,*[173] but to *a priori* rationalism, and advocates of legal change through legislation and codification. In opposition to *a priori* rationalists and hasty codifiers,[174] the historical school insisted on leaving legal development to the silent force of evolutionary processes. Specifically, the legal theorist was not to look for the principles of law in *a priori* fashion as hitherto, but in tradition, the sedimentary deposit of the intellectual life of a people. Like English analytical jurists, the German school of historical jurisprudence conceives the task of legal theory as *expository*, the study of law as it *is* (or rather, as it had come to be) not the study of law that *ought* to be. Unlike legal positivism, however, it is the totality of the legal experience of a people - the text and the spirit of the laws and much else - not the congealed decrees of arbitrary sovereign political powers, which determine the character of positive law as an object of scientific study.

Nonetheless, stripped of its somewhat mystical and mythical clusters, the historical school is a first cousin of positivism; indeed, it is at bottom a humanistic reinstatement of positivistic intellectuality. The intellectual goal of the historical school of law was neither to substitute a theory of law for the positivist's or another method for scientific methodology. Rather, the historical school craved for and established to its own philosophical satisfaction a new basis for a more accurate description of moral phenomena as objects of scientific study. It was clear to the historical school that *a priori* rationalists had forsaken the authentic springs of wisdom when they by-passed experience and purported to ground law on 'reason' alone. As well, Bentham[175] and the secular utilitarians had made a 'bizarre twist in the hermeneutic spiral'[176] when they methodically defined 'the spiritual' out of existence. The historical school put 'the spiritual' back on the intellectual canvas by fashioning or rather reviving a humanistic concept of knowledge.

Analytical hermeneutic jurists in general, and H.L.A. Hart in particular, endorse the humanistic concept of knowledge. Seen in this light, Hart's *The Concept of Law* which, until the return of grand theory in the human sciences in the seventies of the last century, was the newest fountainhead of modern jurisprudence in the English-speaking world, is an extended essay on the humanistic character of the subject of legal theory. Hart reinforced Austin's classical thesis that the matter of jurisprudence is positive law, not natural or divine law, but unlike Austin, hermeneutics enabled Hart to identify and underline a humanistic notion of the normative character of law. 'The most prominent general feature of law at all times and places,' Hart wrote, 'is that its existence means that certain kinds of human conduct are no longer optional, but in *some* sense obligatory.'[177] Austin had overlooked or misrepresented that general feature of law; Hart set out to correct the anomaly.

We are not here concerned with Hart's solution, but it follows that legal theory must be of such a character that it could capture the fact that and the sense in which law is normative.[178] In short, although it is often times portrayed as a *methodological*, *philosophical*, or *critical* challenge to positivism, hermeneutics generally, and analytic legal hermeneutics particularly, is best seen as an *epistemological* corrective of positivism; it is a redefinition of the *positive*, not a renunciation of it. In brief, while romanticism historicized 'reason' and historicism humanized (not moralized) 'scientific' methodology, hermeneutics delineated and successfully established ''separate but equal' epistemological realms'[179] for the human sciences.

Specifically, instead of the one-dimensional perspective of an incipient social scientific orientation in the English-speaking world, and the censorial orientation of erstwhile continental *a priori* rationalists, hermeneutics invited meditation on the objects of study in the human sciences as cultural wholes, not simply as parts, however salient.[180] Thus, hermeneutics is neither an alternative to 'scientific' *methodology* nor is it an attempt to determine what *ought* to be. [181] Rather, it is a re-description of moral phenomena to capture what the romantics saw as a better characterization of the object of study in the human sciences generally, and law in particular.

The historical school defined *what is* in accordance with its own humanistic phenomenological postulates. But it cannot be overemphasized that both analytical and historical jurists were averse to *censorial* jurisprudence. That is, neither the English nor the Germans conceived legal theory as the study of the law that *ought* to be; that is the province of censorial jurisprudence, and the preserve of rationalists. As David Granfield[182] succinctly puts it, both schools of law 'effectively bypassed rationalism.'

A starker, though profane, way of putting it is to say that the historical school resuscitated humanism, and hermeneutics made that humanism 'scientific' by divesting it of its specifically postclassical and all subsequent theological encrustation. To the German romantics, who saw themselves as the obvious 'residual legatees of classical civilization,'[183] humanism/ historicism was more a fulfillment of, than a reaction against 'the Enlightenment.'

Historians have disaggregated 'the Enlightenment.' As a result, the Enlightenment is best described as a coat of many colors with distinct national embroideries and long cosmopolitan draperies.[184] Although some Enlightenment thinkers, notably French *philosophes* and radical English Whigs,[185] were thoroughly against the established religion and the received moral establishment, neither the Enlightenment nor the historical school was amoral. In fact, humanism/historicism was a kind of morality or religion, with its own ontological commitments.

However, hermeneutics was subsequently transformed into philosophy, and became amoral. The amoral-ness of hermeneutics does not stem from early nineteenth century German romantics, who saw hermeneutics primarily as an approach necessitated by the character of the objects of study in the human sciences. Rather it is due to the work of their successors, the existential philosophers or new humanists, who, by going farther back in history than the eighteenth century continental humanists had done, surreptitiously relieved humanism of its specifically classical metaphysical underpinnings. In this respect, existential philosophy is to historicism what deontological ethics is to social contract theory: it sets man adrift from all erstwhile ontological suppositions. However, unlike deontological ethics, which not only left man with both 'will' and 'reason' but also, like the ancients, subjected the former to the superintendence of the latter, existential philosophy left men without any standard or guide except their own brute spirit.[186] And, unlike their immediate predecessors, existential philosophers, with their apparent ahistorical historicity, apparently discounted tradition. This is just another way of saying that existential philosophers introduced or reintroduced the absolutely free man – man unconscious of any internal or external constraints - into the moral, political, and legal world. The resultant irrationalism, which verges on nihilism, was the consequence, whether intended or unintended, of the work, among others, of the outstanding German existential philosopher, Martin Heidegger. Significantly, a prominent neo-Wittgensteinian legal scholar, Dennis Patterson, has referred to Martin Heidegger rather than Wittgenstein as 'the master of hermeneutics.'[187] Heidegger, the principal existential philosopher who features prominently in Gadamer's philosophical hermeneutics, veered into nihilistic consciousness by simply leaving the 'sphere of 'morality'' out of 'the truth of Being'[188] as their predecessors had portrayed it. Like the logical positivists who denied the reality of moral distinctions, and who instead held that morality was 'a matter of the will, not of the understanding,'[189] Heidegger and his followers saw morality as 'merely another way of expressing reified values.'[190] Without tradition as foundation, philosophical hermeneutics is seemingly the acme of nihilistic intellectuality; with tradition as foundation, philosophical hermeneutics is apparently 'a form of tempered dogmatism'[191] or rather 'an apologia for humanistic learning.'[192]

The point of this somewhat condensed and seemingly digressive excursus is neither to slight[193] philosophical hermeneutics nor to exalt early continental romantics or the historical school, but to underline one of the marked differences between early nineteenth century and subsequently dominant continental hermeneutics. In the eighteenth and early nineteenth centuries, historical consciousness impelled political thinkers to 'dissolve all history into the poetics of self-creation.'[194] Deep historical awareness had convinced the thinking class that man, not nature or God, was the center of the moral universe. Historically, men speak different languages, belong to different ethnic groups, worship different gods, were organized into different polities, and ruled by different laws. In short, except when herded into a sprawling empire, men evolved divergent cultures, that is, they were differently *natured* or *humanized*. Since, according to the historical school, the historical is all there is and could be it followed that there was no human nature or history as such, but only a number of discrete natures or self-created histories. Hermeneutics, the methodological expression of the historical school, fortified historicism by emphasizing that the study of self-created histories must be free from universalistic prejudices. Their successors, who formulated philosophical hermeneutics, carried to its logical conclusions the theoretical premises of historicism in at least two notable ways. First, they completed the destruction of the specific concept of natural right propagated by social contract theorists and, second, they converted hermeneutics into a regal philosophy. Grounding itself on the 'substance'[195] of the unique continental tradition generated by 'real history,'[196] philosophical hermeneutics describes 'what is the case,'[197] with the imperialistic consequence that only those who accept that 'what is the case' is as philosophical hermeneutics describes it are or 'ought to be taken seriously.'[198] The spirit of analytic hermeneutics is closer to early nineteenth century understanding of the role of hermeneutics than it is to hermeneutics as philosophy.

The trajectory of modern legal theory runs from 'the historical view of law' that emerged in the early nineteenth century to the 'formal conceptual jurisprudence'[199] characteristic of leading jurists on the continent and on both sides of the Atlantic later in the nineteenth and early twentieth centuries. This points to the strong intellectual bond between the historical and the analytic schools of law. Although it may be that the founder of the historical school of law would not have approved the transition,[200] it was the historical view of law that cascaded into theoretic moulds later in the nineteenth and early twentieth centuries. The resultant formal legal science, which 'rigorously and absolutely excluded from the purview of jurisprudence the moral, social, and political conditions''[201] in which law manifests itself - thus making law into an autonomous discipline[202] - is known on the continent as 'general theory of law'. It is what is called 'analytical jurisprudence' in the English-speaking world.[203]

Now, the analytical 'nineteenth century English school of jurisprudence,'[204] especially as manifested in 'the textbook tradition,'[205] was intertwined with the law of the land as it crystallized in the nineteenth century.[206] In the same way, continental general theorists of law were aligned with the accredited 'natural laws'[207] of their own immediate societies. In other words, as between historical and analytical jurisprudence, the question is not 'whether positivism?' Rather, it is quite simply 'which positivism?', to use the apt words of a recent commentator.[208] I conclude that, as *philosophy*, legal hermeneutics is 'a normative version of legal positivism.'[209] As *critique*, legal hermeneutics is an epistemological corrective of 'scientism' in the study of law. In the former case, legal hermeneutics assumes a positivistic *theory* of law. However, as *method*, hermeneutics does not presuppose a particular theory of law any more than analytical jurisprudence presupposes the imperative theory of law. Hence, just as there are analytical or general theorists who reject the imperative theory of law, there are analytical hermeneutic jurists who are not legal positivists.

Even as a methodology hermeneutics is not congruent with a scientific approach, for at least two reasons. In the first place, hermeneutics is inherently holistic,[210] and holism undoubtedly 'encourages points of view, which in a general sense can be called *relativistic*.'[211] Specifically, legal hermeneutics confines theorists to the analysis of legal phenomena as they are conveyed in a particular language or related languages or as they are in particular legal traditions or cultures. In the second place, hermeneutics circumscribes philosophical investigations by ruling out in advance certain possibilities. Specifically, just as Bentham and the secular utilitarians methodically disregarded the 'spiritual', the German school of historical thought and its progenies systematically eschewed the quest for 'the abstract and universal.'[212] Indeed, the historical school explicitly denied 'the significance, if not the existence, of universal norms.'[213] In fact, the practitioners of hermeneutics, whether as method, critique, or philosophy, have 'seldom pretended to "scientific" status.'[214] Instead, they have always been concerned with the interpretation of language and texts - the words and thought of traditional wise men and local or adopted deities. In short, hermeneutics is inherently local and present-minded. This last – localism and present-mindedness - if nothing else, makes hermeneutics infirm as an approach in the scientific study of law.

This is not to deny that the historical school made permanent contributions to the theoretical study of law. Aside from the fact that it impressed on the legal mind that the object of legal scholarship is essentially normative, hermeneutics firmly implanted the belief that 'it is 'legal experience' that gives rise to what one *recognises* to be law; not the contrary.'[215]

Wittgenstein had strengthened that fundamental intellectual insight not by showing that it is impossible to see beyond the smoke of one's own cultural chimney or the limits of our own local language, but by showing that 'we can see *only* because we do so from a particular perspective.'216 This is the perspective of distinct human groups or 'forms of life'. Put differently, Wittgenstein showed that understanding works within a frame through whose window one sees. Once scholars see the necessity of a frame of reference that perforce includes traditional knowledge,[217] they could listen silently to the clear, though oftentimes mythical, explanation of the nature of things and things of nature by old wise men without in any way implying that the old men are fools.[218] But, unperturbed by the old-men's lucid exposition, scholars would not hesitate to subject even traditional knowledge to fresh philosophical analysis not with a view to confuting the old men but for the singular purpose of seeing whether their 'crystalline clarity will survive immersion in sceptism.'219 That, however, does not mean that philosophical analysts worship the scientists' idol which portrays the result of human understanding as 'objective' truth. The reason is simple. Aside from the hubris involved in such claims, the study of moral phenomena is not amenable to practical experiments, to falsification or verification. Hence any belief that a particular understanding of moral phenomena is 'the truth, the whole truth, and nothing but the truth' stultifies genuine philosophical dialogues.220 Assuredly, defensive interrogation of local, cultural patrimony, especially by highly competent, scientifically or philosophically-trained individuals, indirectly 'stabilize [traditional] knowledge against scepticism.'[221] But, if they are *philosophers*, scholars are always skeptical, to put it mildly, of any claim to knowledge of reality, of 'the objective truth', whether it is made in the name of 'revelation,' 'nature,' 'reason,' 'tradition,' 'science,' or what not. And, if they are true to their vocation, philosophical analysts make no assertions about 'the truth.' Rather, they merely report their findings. Professionally, philosophers are skeptics; intellectually, they are conservatives, though conservatives of a judicial kind, for they scrupulously abstain from descending into the arena or becoming one of the parties to the fray.[222]

To say then that we can see only because we do so from a particular perspective is not necessarily tantamount to enjoining scholars to pursue the type of 'intellectual career of stately conservative sobriety'[223] that culminates in Panglossian grand interpretive theories; the aim of philosophical inquiry is not to make the institutional fruits of a scholar's political tradition the best it can be or to prove that the scholar's immediate world 'is really the best of all possible worlds'.[224] Moreover, it does not necessarily require or endorse any 'ism'. Specifically, it recommends neither traditional*ism* nor conventional*ism* nor relativ*ism*. More precisely, because 'all 'isms' is a monism,'[225] and all 'monisms' is an 'absolute,' which in turn implies certainty, (knowledge of which philosophical analysts disclaim) Wittgenstein eschewed all 'ism.' Instead, Wittgenstein latched on to a precondition of understanding, namely, that discourse takes place against the background of the totality of experience as a unified whole.[226] In his schema, tradition was not so much a foundation as a ladder that one could graciously discard after using it to ascend. Tradition is indeed indispensable, but it is not the terminal point. Put differently, Wittgenstein directed attention to the type of philosophical investigation that utilizes existing, interpretive or traditional materials but which frees itself from 'the institutional weight of a hermeneutic enterprise.'[227]

In the study of law, the overall result of that methodological innovation was the reaffirmation of the sound epistemological notion that what is *law* can not be known a priori. This harks back to the core of the historical school of law and legal hermeneutics, namely, that 'legal discourse has essential characteristics only when it is part of an ordered system in which it receives and manifests meaning.'[228] It is the virtue of the historical school of law and its methodological expression that they affirmed the indispensability of tradition for legal theory. It is a vice that they made traditional legal knowledge into a loadstone that dragged down and, in the guise of analytic and grand interpretive theoretical models, continues to impede legal theory.

The aim of legal theory is neither to fathom supposedly absolute or natural laws nor to formulate general or interpretive theories of law. (Too often, the former culminates in some ideal or ideological formulations that masquerade as 'objective' laws, as Hans Kelsen[229] pointedly remarked while the latter tends to terminate in 'an ultimately very Herderian'[230] or social scientific attitude that makes jurists belief that juristic inquiry is, by and large, descriptive sociology, or, Immanuel Kant[231] notwithstanding, interpretive anthropology under a different sobriquet). Rather, the purpose of legal theory is to analyze the totality of experience with a view to discovering and expounding principles of legal *right.* Contrary to the hermeneutic impulse, the totality of legal experience is not limited to or by a particular historical epoch or culture(s). The function of juristic inquiry is to traverse the totality of legal experience with a view to understanding law independently of the tradition and language that embroidered it in the course of time in particular culture(s).

Conclusion

It is common knowledge that the founders of analytical jurisprudence were first and foremost utilitarian-positivists. The fact that they treated moral, political, and legal philosophy in the same works even though they insisted that morals, politics, and law are analytically distinct makes it difficult to dissociate analytical jurisprudence from the moral theory and the theory of law propounded by these analytical jurists. Yet, no matter how difficult it may be to distinguish analytical jurisprudence from the school of law to which an analyst belongs, intellectual sanity requires that they be kept separate and distinct. As moral theorists, Bentham and Austin insisted that utility constituted the moral standard; as political theorists they were moderns, and as theorists of law they were positivists.

As positivists Bentham and Austin insisted on the separation of law and morals, on law as it is and law as it ought to be. As analytical jurists, however, they insisted not so much on the separation of law and morals as on distinguishing the *exposition* of law as it is in positive systems of law from the exposition of the same phenomena as it would be if it conforms with a particular moral or political standard. In other words, as analytical jurists they insisted on freeing the exposition of law from the trammels of theories of or about law. But their main target was natural law theory. It is an astonishing paradox that they failed to see the inconsistency involved in their own insistence on separating law and morals prior to analyzing law, thus foisting their positivist definition of law on legal theory.

Until the advent of interpretive theories of law in the seventies of the last century, the coupling of these incommensurable approaches to the study of law gave analytical jurisprudence an apparently distinctive characteristic: moral and political neutrality. But, the analytic separation of law, morals, and politics, in contradistinction to the positivist separation does not entail the conclusion that law is amoral or apolitical. If we refrain from addling modern legal theory and theories of law generally, and legal positivism particularly, it would not follow from the fact that law is distinguishable from morals and politics that it is morally and politically neutral. Law is regulative, morals is hortative, and politics is formative. Put differently, law relates to necessary duties, morals to discretionary duties, and politics to organizational duties. In short, the separation of law, morals, and politics is an analytic necessity. But in their battles against natural law theorists, positivists made it into a conceptual one, thus determining the terms of the endless debate between positivists and anti- or non-positivists. In sum the conceptual separation of law and morals is a positivist plank that was somehow thrust into the analytic block mainly because the early myrmidons of analytical legal philosophy were fervent legal positivists.

The identification and removal from the analytical approach of this and other interpolations derived from theories of or about law will not, however, suffice to make analytical jurisprudence a complete philosophical approach in the study of law. This is because analytical jurisprudence is infested with an epistemological bathos that dichotomizes formal and rational inquiries, and which confines legal philosophy to the former.

Legal hermeneutics is incapable of remedying the mischief. When historicism triumphed, and hermeneutics was grafted on the analytical approach, expository jurisprudence was transmuted into interpretive sociology, which involved the construction of the 'ideal-types' or the ascertainment of the meaning of the concepts embedded in a particular legal culture or a number of related systems of positive law. In other words, analytic legal hermeneutics or interpretive theories of law are to modern legal theory what scholasticism was to pre-modern thought. Because it sees the objects of study in the human sciences as 'reality-posits',[232] of which there are different cultural forms, hermeneutics compounds the provincial bias of analytical jurisprudence. It reinforces and conceals the underlying subjectivism or conventionalism that has always been the Achilles heel of even the best form of empiricism. A theory of jurisprudence that confines the philosophy of law to the exposition or interpretive construction of the systems of law of civilized nation(s) or one's own cultural legal experience, and which programmatically denies or excludes the possibility of winning the '*form* of rationality'[233] immanent in legal phenomena is radically deficient. Law, the reason of things, binds all private and public institutional actors. There is no assurance that any claim to knowledge of the reason of things is true, but it is unlikely that a soul that seeks the reason of things will 'find that wrong is right.'[234]

Notes

[1] E.M. Butler, *The Tyranny of Greece Over Germany* (Cambridge: Cambridge Univ. Press, 1935) at 3.

[2] Whatever the development in the succeeding centuries, including twentieth-century post-analytic philosophy, at the beginning of the modern period, nominalism did not entail the rejection of metaphysics. Rather, nominalism was a strategy necessitated in part and devised by men intent on repudiating Aristotleanism (in contradistinction from Aristotle) in order to revive the activity which goes by the name of 'philosophy'. In the context of the socioeconomic, religious, and political order of the time, the only way to revive philosophy was to shrink Aristotle, that is, reduce him to a mortal. (This is not a tautology!) Methodologically, this required proceeding on an inquiry *de novo* (in the hypothetical sense) that is, *as if* one had no intellectual predecessors, as Rene Descartes particularly recommended in his *Discourse on Method*, and Francis Bacon preached so vehemently in his works, especially, *The Advancement of Learning*. Epistemologically, it involved showing, as Locke particularly set out to do in the *Essay Concerning Human Understanding*, the probable 'Original, Certainty, and Extent of humane Knowledge.' The nominalism of the pioneers of philosophy in the modern world was, therefore, dictated neither by any doubt about the existence of a world independent of perception nor by any skepticism as to the capacity of the human mind to understand phenomena, but simply by the desire to make room for the liberty of examination – a liberty which was last exercised in classical Greece but was subsequently swamped by the dogmatic systems/theories spawned by the prodigious intellectual product of the Socratics. Raymond Aron has identified liberty of examination or intellectual freedom as the 'essence' of Western culture: *The Opium of the Intellectuals* trans. Terrence Kilmerton (London: Secker & Warburg, 1957) at 258.

[3] Immanuel Kant, 'On the Forms and Principles of the Sensuous and Intellectual Worlds,' (1770) in, Gabriele Rabel, *Kant* (Oxford: Clarendon Press, 1963) at 89.

[4] Before the close of the ancient world, however, the political societies of philosopher-theologians succumbed before the might of Greek and Roman arms. See particularly, Donald B. Redford, *Egypt, Canaan, and Israel in Ancient Times* (Princeton, N.J.: Princeton Univ. Press, 1991). Amongst these

victorious societies, philosophy was not a priestly vocation. Nevertheless, Greek philosophy was redolent with theological ramifications.

At the close of the ancient world, which marked the beginning of the Holy Roman Empire, philosophy lost its preeminence to theology. Although the theological implications of Greek philosophy subsequently recommended first Plato, and later, Aristotle, to the intelligentsia of the Holy Roman Empire, philosophy became the handmaiden of theology, i.e., 'it supplied the latter with the conceptual, logical, physical and metaphysical materials it needed': P. Hadot, *Philosophy as a Way of Life* (trans. from the French) (Oxford: Blackwell, 1995) at 270. Theology reinforced law, which in turn reinforced politics and economics. Intellectually speaking, that position was unaffected by the Renaissance. It was not until the onset of the secularization process in post-renaissance Europe, and its acceleration in the eighteenth and nineteenth centuries, that philosophy gradually ceased to be the handmaiden of theology. As soon as the process of divesting philosophy of its specifically post-classical theological encrustations began, and law, politics and economics were no longer subject to the superintendence of theology, even extremely perceptive thinkers were no longer able to appreciate why the schools as well as adherents of the 'religions of the book' had been partial to ancient philosophy as embodied in the works of Aristotle. As the bond which united law, politics and economics loosened each of these disciplines evolved its own separate and independent worlds. In contemporary parlance, each organized itself around Kuhnian paradigms.

[5] William Blackstone, *Commentaries* I, 27. '...Aristotle himself has said, speaking of the laws of his own country, that Jurisprudence, or the knowledge of those laws, is the principal and most perfect branch of ethics.' Note that Blackstone adroitly invokes Aristotle's authority in limiting Jurisprudence to the knowledge of the laws of one's own country.

[6] G. Ryle, 'Systematically Misleading Expressions,' in *Logic and Language* (First and Second Series) ed. A. Flew (New York: Anchor Books, 1954) 13-40 at 39.

[7] In its heyday, negative therapeutic philosophical analysts appeared to be playing Aristotle against Plato, but in fact they were themselves cultural Platonists.

[8] John H. Randall, Jr., 'The Development of the Scientific Method in the School of Padua,' *Journal of the Hist of Ideas* 1 (1940).

[9] P.Wilson, *Second-Hand Knowledge: An Inquiry into Cognitive Authority* (Westport, Conn.: Greenwood Press, 1983) at 15: 'Cognitive authority is influence on one's thoughts that one would consciously recognize as proper... The authority's influence on us is thought proper because he is thought credible, worthy of belief.' See further, Hans Georg Gadamer, *Truth and Method* (New York: Seabury Press, 1975) at 248-51.

[10] Since it relates mainly to the interconnectedness of propositions within a system of thought, 'coherence' or any of its synonyms such as 'consistency', 'fitness', 'integrity,' 'harmony', 'unity,' etc. are a criterion of stability or

validity rather than truth or rationality. See, Michael Polanyi, *Personal Knowledge: Towards a Post-Critical Philosophy* (New York: Harper & Row Publishers, 1964) at 294: '... what earlier philosophers have alluded to by speaking of coherence as the criterion of truth is only a criterion of *stability*. It may equally stabilize an erroneous or a true view of the universe...'

'Coherence' metamorphoses into a criterion of truth or rationality only if we are 'Idealists'. See, *inter alia*, William Ewald, 'Comparative Jurisprudence (I): What Was it Like to Try a Rat?' *Univ. of Pa L.R.* 143 (1995) 1889 at 1933-4; Alexander Rosenberg, *Economics – Mathematical Politics or Science of Diminishing Returns?* (Chicago & London: Univ. of Chicago Press, 1992) at 15; Steven B. Smith, *Hegel's Critique of Liberalism: Rights in Context* (Chicago and London: Univ. of Chicago Press, 1989) at 220-1.

On how 'coherence' first assumed the status of 'rationality' or 'truth,' see, Stephen Toulmin, *Human Understanding* 2 vols. (Oxford: Clarendon Press, 1972) I at 44; Mott T. Greene, *Natural Knowledge in Pre-Classical Antiquity* (Baltimore & London: Johns Hopkins Univ. Press, 1992) at 141.

[11] K. Wiredu, *Philosophy and an African Culture* (Cambridge: Cambridge Univ. Press, 1980) at 162. (Emphasis added). The 'antecedently ready-madeness' of concepts gives conceptual analysis an *ostensible* Platonic ring.

[12] Jerry A. Fodor, *Concepts: Where Cognitive Science Went Wrong* (Oxford: Clarendon Press, 1998)

[13] For penetrating analysis of the cognitive advantages of writing, see, Jack Goody, *The Domestication of the Savage Mind* (Cambridge: Cambridge Univ. Press, 1977); Jack Goody, *The Logic of Writing and the Organization of Society* (Cambridge: Cambridge Univ. Press, 1986); Walter J. Ong, *Orality and Literacy: The Technologizing of the Word* (London: Methuen, 1982). Of course, the intellectual harvest of writing comes into being only if the sociopolitical, religious and other factors are conducive to its realization: See, Jonathan Parry, 'The Brahmanical Tradition and the Technology of the Intellect,' in, *Reason and Morality* ed. Joanna Overing (London: Tavistock Publication, 1985) 200-225; Edward Shils, *The Intellectual Between Tradition and Modernity: The Indian Situation* (The Hague: Moutm & Co, 1961).

[14] The phrases are from O. Kahn Freund, 'Reflections on Legal Education,' *Modern L.R.* 29 (1966) 121 at 126.

[15] The doctrine of Platonic forms has both positive and negative tendencies. Its positive tendency is that it underscores the oneness of knowledge. Its negative tendency is that it fosters 'imperial intellects.'

[16] For general surveys, see, *inter alia*, Huntington Cairns, *Legal Philosophy from Plato to Hegel* (Baltimore: The Johns Hopkins Press, 1949); Carl J. Friedrich, *The Philosophy of Law in Historical Perspective* 2nd ed. (Chicago & London: Univ. of Chicago press, 1963). (This and the next part draw on Adekemi Odujirin, *The Normative Basis of Fault in Criminal Law: History and Theory* (Toronto: Univ. of Toronto Press, 1998)).

[17] Jeremy Bentham, *The Principles of Morals and Legislation* (New York: Prometheus Books, 1988) at 323-24: 'To know what is meant by jurisprudence

we must know ... what is meant by a book of jurisprudence. A book of jurisprudence can have but one or the other of two objects: 1. To ascertain what the law is. 2. To ascertain what it ought to be. In the former case it may be styled a book of expository jurisprudence; in the latter, a book of censorial jurisprudence ...' (Emphases original); Jeremy Bentham, *A Comment on the Commentaries and a Fragment on Government*, ed. J.H. Burns and H.L.A. Hart (London, 1977) at 397-8.

[18] Roger A. Shiner, *Norm and Nature: The Movements of Legal Thought* (Oxford: Clarendon Press, 1992) at 1.

[19] Richard C. Cosgrove, 'The Reception of Analytical Jurisprudence: The Victorian Debate on the Separation of Law and Morality, 1860-1900,' *Durham Univ. Journal* 74 (1981) 47; Wilfrid E. Rumble, *The Thought of John Austin* (London: Athlone Press, 1985) at 3.

[20] See, James Bryce, *Studies in History and Jurisprudence*, 2 Vols. (Oxford: Clarendon Press, 1901) Vol. 2 at 179.

[21] John H. Randall, Jr., supra note 8.

[22] Steven Beller, *Vienna and the Jews 1867-1938: A Cultural History* (Cambridge: Cambridge Univ. Press, 1989) at 21.

[23] A.W. B. Simpson, 'Common Law and Legal Theory,' in *Legal Theory and Legal History* at 379.

[24] Austin's description of his Course of *Lectures on Jurisprudence* cited, infra note 47. (Emphasis added).

[25] In actual fact, the full text of his *Lectures* did not appear until 1863.

[26] Bentham, *Principles of Morals and Legislation*, supra note 17 at 325.

[27] Emphasis added.

[28] Ibid. (Emphasis in the original).

[29] Adam Smith, *The Theory of Moral Sentiments* ed. D.D. Raphael and A.L. Macfie (Oxford: Clarendon Press, 1976) at 233.

[30] Bentham, *Principles of Morals and Legislation*, supra note 17 at 326.

[31] Paul Lucas, 'Ex Parte Sir William Blackstone, 'Plagiarist': A Note on Blackstone and the Natural Law,' *Am. J. of Legal Hist.* 7 (1963) 142.

[32] Hans Kelsen, *General Theory of Law and State* trans. Anders Wiedberg (Cambridge, Mass.: Harvard Univ. Press, 1946) at xv.

[33] 'The primitive sense of the word *law*,' Bentham wrote, 'and the ordinary meaning of the word is – the will or command of a legislator.' J. Bentham, *The Theory of Legislation*, ed. C.K. Ogden (London: Kegan Paul, 1931) at 83. (Interestingly, Bentham was silent on the primitive sense of the latter word, 'legislator'). Or, as O.W. Holmes Jr. put it in an unsigned note, law is the 'will of the de facto supreme power of the community.' Cited in David A. Hollinger, 'The "Tough-Minded" Justice Holmes, Jewish Intellectuals, and the Making of an American Icon,' in *Science, Jews and Secular Culture: Studies in Mid-Twentieth Century America Intellectual History* (Princeton, N.J.: Princeton Univ. Press 1996) at 46.

[34] C.H.S. Fifoot, *English Law and Its Background* (London: G. Bell & Sons, 1932) at 155

[35] Bentham's injunction to the citizen under a government of Laws was 'to obey punctually, and censure freely': *A Comment on the Commentaries and a Fragment on Government,* supra note 17 at 399.
[36] 'Inasmuch as the knowledge of what ought to be, supposes a knowledge of what is, legislation supposes jurisprudence, but jurisprudence does not suppose legislation. *What laws have been and are, may be known without a knowledge of what they ought to be.* Inasmuch as a knowledge of what ought to be, is bottomed on a knowledge of antecedents *cognato genere*, legislation supposes jurisprudence.' Austin, *Lectures* II at 1112. (Emphasis supplied). The italicized sentence which suggests that Austin had historical laws only in mind betrays the equivocation that permeates Austin's formulation of the task of legal theory.
[37] William Twining, 'General and Particular Jurisprudence – Three Chapters in a Story,' in *Positivism Today*, ed. Stephen Guest, (Aldershot: Dartmouth Publishing Co., 1996) at 121.
[38] Gerald J. Postema, *Bentham and the Common Law Tradition* (Oxford: Clarendon Press, 1986) at 331.
[39] Austin, *Lectures* 2 at 1112. Emphasis added.
[40] Austin, *Lectures* I at 33; 2 at 112.
[41] 'the great Roman lawyers', he wrote, ' were, in truth, expositors of a positive or technical system' of law: Ibid. 2 at 1115.
[42] David Sugarman, 'Legal Theory, the Common Law Mind and the Making of the Text-book Tradition,' in, *Legal Theory and Common Law*, ed. William Twining (Oxford: Basil Blackwell, 1986); A.W.B. Simpson, 'The Rise and Fall of the Legal Treatise', in *Legal Theory and Legal History*, supra.
[43] Austin, *Lectures* I at 33
[44] Ibid.
[45] Cf. the seemingly unequivocal positivist passage: 'The existence of law is one thing, its merit or demerit is another. Whether it be or be not is one enquiry; whether it be or be not conformable to an assumed standard, is a different enquiry. A law, which actually exists, is a law, though we happen to dislike it, or though it vary from the text, by which we regulate our approbation and disapprobation. This truth, when formally announced as an abstract proposition, is so simple and glaring that it seems idle to insist upon it....' *Lectures,* I at 220.
[46] The phrase is F.A. Hayek, *Law, Legislation and Liberty*, 3 Vols. (Chicago: Univ. of Chicago Press, 1981) Vol. 3: at 166.
[47] 'Taken in its literal import, it [universal jurisprudence] lies within a narrow compass. So different is Law amongst barbarians from Law amongst civilised men, Law amongst Asiatics from Law amongst Europeans, Law in Mahometan from Law in Christian countries, that Jurisprudence would be confined to the definitions of a few leading terms, supposing it confined to the matter which is common to *all* systems. But in the positive systems of Law which are worthy of accurate examination (in the positive systems, that is, of all civilized European Nations) *common* distinctions and principles, though they take very various

forms, are sufficiently numerous to constitute the subject of a science. Accordingly, these are the subjects of the universal Jurisprudence which it is the purpose of the Lectures to expound' – Catalogue description by Austin of his course of lectures (Second Statement by the Council of the University of London Explanatory of the Plan of Instruction. 1828) cited, Wilfrid E. Rumble, *The Thought of John Austin* (London: Athlone Press, 1985) at 75.

[48] Jerome Hall, *Foundations of Jurisprudence* (Indianapolis: The Bobbs-Merrill Co., 1973) at 14.

[49] See Wilfrid Rumble, 'John Austin and His Nineteenth Century Critics: The Case of Sir Henry Sumner Maine' *Northern Ireland Law Quarterly* 39 (1988) 119 at 139.

[50] '...it will be impossible, or useless, to attempt an exposition of these principles notions and distinctions, until by careful analysis, we have accurately determined the meaning of certain leading terms which we must necessarily employ; terms which recur incessantly in every department of the science: which, whithersoever we turn ourselves, we are sure to encounter. Such, for instance, are the following: Law, Right, Obligation, Injury, Sanction: Person, Thing, Act, Forbearance. Unless the import of these are determined at the outset, the subsequent speculations will be a tissue of uncertain talk.' 'By a careful analysis of leading terms, law is detached from morals, and the attention of jurisprudence is confined to the distinctions and divisions which relate to law exclusively.' *Lectures* 2 at 1110, 1111.

[51] Rumble, supra note 47 at 74.

[52] 'the subject and scope of general jurisprudence, as contradistinguished to particular jurisprudence, are well expressed by Hobbes ... My design is to show, not what is law here or there, but what is law: as Plato, Aristotle, Cicero, and divers others have done, without taking upon them the profession of the study of law': Austin, *Lectures*, I at 33.

[53] See, Richard C. Cosgrove, 'The Reception of Analytic Jurisprudence: The Victorian Debate on the Separation of Law and Morality, 1860-1900,' supra note 19; Wilfrid E. Rumble, 'John Austin and His 19th Century Critics: The Case of Sir Henry Sumner Maine,' supra note 49.

[54] W. David Shaw, *The Lucid Veil: Poetic Truth in the Victorian Age* 2nd rev. ed. (London: Athlone Press, 1987).

[55] Ibid. at 75.

[56] G. Frege, *The Foundations of Arithmetic* (1884) trans. J.L. Austin (Illinois: Northwestern Univ. Press, 1968) at x, 71.

[57] Bentham, *Essay on Language*, 321, cited, Ross Harrison, *Bentham* (London: Routledge and Kegan Paul 1983) at 65.

[58] Ibid.

[59] Austin, *Lectures*, 2 at 1111.

[60] A. N. Whitehead, *Adventures of Ideas* (Cambridge: Cambridge Univ. Press, 1933) at 312. (Emphasis added).

[61] Leo Strauss, *Natural Right and History* (Chicago & London: Univ. of Chicago Press, 1953) at 124.

[62] As Locke puts it, 'if we but separate the Idea under consideration from the sign that stands for it, our Knowledge goes equally on in the discovery of real Truth and Certainty, whatever Sounds we make use of.' *Essay Concerning Human Understanding*, IV, Chap. IV, 9.27-30.
[63] Mario Jori, 'Revolutions in Legal Science: Back to the Concept of Law,' in, *Enlightenment, Rights, and Revolution: Essays in Legal and Social Philosophy* ed. Neil MacCormick and Zenon Bankowski (Aberdeen Univ. Press, 1989) 337 at 339: 'as it is well known, legal science ... has to be a rather monstrous double character: it has to be both descriptive and normative in character.'
[64] W. David Shaw, *The Lucid Veil*, supra note 54. (Emphasis added).
[65] John Finnis, *Natural Law and Natural Rights* (Oxford: Clarendon Press, 1980) at 206; W. Ullmann, *The Medieval Idea of Law as Represented by Lucas de Penna* (London: Methuen, 1946).
[66] J. Bentham, *Of Laws in General* ed. H.L.A. Hart (London: Athlone Press 1970) at 232.
[67] J. Bentham, *The Limits of Jurisprudence Defined* ed. Charles W. Everett (New York: Columbia Press, 1945) at 85. [This book is a version of *Of Laws in General*]
[68] Bentham, *Chrestomathia* III, 126n. cited in R. Harrison, *Bentham*, supra note 56 at 56. (Emphasis in the original).
[69] See, generally, James E. Crimmins, *Secular Utilitarianism: Social Science and the Critique of Religion in the Thought of Jeremy Bentham* (Oxford: Clarendon Press, 1990); James E. Crimmins, 'Bentham and the Critique of Religion,' *Journal of the Hist. of Ideas*. J. Bentham, *Essay on Language* 321, cited, Ross Harrison, *Bentham*, supra note 57 at 58.
[70] 'If it be true that our ideas are derived all of them from our senses and that the only way of rendering any of our ideas clear and determinate is to trace it up to the sensible objects in which it originates the only method that can be taken for explaining them to the purpose is the method .. of paraphrasis.' Bentham, *Of Laws in General*, supra at 294. And, 'A word may be said to be expounded by paraphrasis when not that word alone is translated into other words, but some whole sentence of which it forms a part is translated into another sentence; the words of which latter are expressive of such ideas as are simple, or are more immediately resolvable into simple ones than those of the former.' Bentham, *Comment on the Commentaries and a Fragment on Government*, supra note 17 at 495n.
[71] Harrison, supra note 57 at 58.
[72] Bentham, *Of Laws in General*, at 251-2.
[73] H.L.A. Hart, 'Austin, John,' in, *International Encyclopedia of the Social Sciences*, Vol. I (Macmillan, 1968) at 472.
[74] H.L.A. Hart, *The Concept of Law*, (Oxford: Clarendon Press, 1961), Preface.
[75] Ibid. at 78
[76] Robert S. Summers, 'The "New" Analytical Jurists,' *N.Y.U.L.Rev.* 41 (1966) 861 at 888; Wilfrid E. Rumble, *The Thought of John Austin*, supra note 47 at 3.

---

77 John Rawls, *A Theory of Justice* (Cambridge, Mass.: Harvard Univ. Press, 1971) at 130; Joseph Raz, *The Morality of Freedom* (Oxford: Univ. Press, 1986) at 14.

78 H.L.A. Hart, 'Analytical Jurisprudence in Mid-20th Century: A Reply to Professor Bodenheimer,' *Univ. of Penn. L.R.* 104 (1957) at 954. Both Rawls and Dworkin describe the distinction as the difference between 'concept' and 'conception'. John Rawls, *A Theory of Justice*, supra note 77 at 5-6; R. Dworkin, *Taking Rights Seriously* (Cambridge, Mass.: Harvard Univ. Press, 1977) at 134-6.

79 Ernest Nagel, 'Impressions and Appraisals of Analytic Philosophy in Europe,' *Journal of Philosophy* 33 (1936) 5 at 9. (Emphasis original).

80 Pre-World War II analytical jurists 'believe[d] in a descriptive theory of the fundamental structures of positive law as a possible and philosophically interesting task, which is neutral between controversial political and ideological options and alternative moral systems': J.S. Brito, 'Hart's Criticism of Bentham in Contemporary Concepts of Law,' *Archives for Phil of Law and Social Philosophy* (Supplement no. 1, Pt 4) (1983) 531 at 532. As we noted in Chapter 1, non-descriptive theorists of law and politics, which sought to reunite law with modern political philosophy emerged in the 1970s, beginning with Rawls, *A Theory of Justice*, supra note 77. And, as noted in the same chapter, advocates of republican political philosophy promptly challenged them. By the 1980s, the jurisprudential landscape had become a bedlam of explicitly political philosophies, such as 'liberal', 'conservative', 'critical legal studies,' 'economic analysis of law', 'law and literature', 'feminist analysis of law' etc. See, Gary Minda, *Postmodern Legal Movements: Law and Jurisprudence at Century's End* (New York: New York Univ. Press, 1995); William W. Fisher III, 'The Development of Modern American Legal Theory and the Judicial Interpretation of the Bill of Rights,' in *A Culture of Rights: The Bill of Rights in Philosophy, Politics and Law, 1791-1991* ed. Michael J. Lacey & Knud Haskonssen (Cambridge: Cambridge Univ. Press, 1991) 266 at 295-318.

81 For the history and meaning of the word 'jurisprude,' see, N.E.H. Hull, 'The Romantic Realist: Art, Literature, and the Enduring Legacy of Karl Llewellyn's "Jurisprudence"', *Am. J. of Legal Hist.* 40 (1996) 115.

82 George P. Fletcher, *Rethinking Criminal Law* (Toronto: Little, Brown, 1978) at 449. Fletcher recently clarified what is involved in this type of philosophical analysis of law. See George P. Fletcher, *Basic Concepts of Legal Thought* (New York: Oxford Univ. Press, 1996) at 36.

83 Timothy M.S. Baxter, *The Cratylus: Plato's Critique of Naming* (New York: E.J. Brill, 1992) at 76.

84 On Austin's empiricism, see, *inter alia*, Wilfrid Rumble, 'John Austin and His 19th Century Critics: The Case of Sir Henry Sumner Maine', supra note 53, rep. Wilfrid Rumble, *The Thought of John Austin*, supra note 47 at 96 et seq; W.L. Morison, John Austin (Stanford Univ. Press, 1982) at 179-207. On the nature of Austin's empiricism, see, *inter alia*, Jerome E. Bichenbach, 'Empiricism and Law,' [Book Review] *U.T.L.J.* 35 (1985) 94; Robert N.

Moles, *Definition and Rule in Legal Theory* (London: Basil Blackwell, 1987) at 30-34; Michael Lobban, *The Common Law and English Jurisprudence, 1760-1850*, Chapter 8. It should be emphasized, however, that there is 'no necessary connection between empiricism and analytic philosophy,': J.O. Urmson, 'The History of Philosophical Analysis,' in, *The Linguistic Turn* ed. Richard Rorty (Chicago: Univ. of Chicago Press, 1967) at 295.

[85] That claim probably derived from Aristotle, *Analytica Posteriora*. See, A.W.B. Simpson, 'The Rise and Fall of the Legal Treatise,' *Univ. of Chic. L.R.* 48 (1981) 632 at 642; 'Legal Iconoclasts and Legal Ideals,' *Univ. of Cincinnati L.R.* 58 (1990) 819 at 834.

[86] P. Hadot, *Philosophy as a Way of Life*, supra note 4.

[87] For a celebration of the ethnocentricity of analytic philosophy, see, Richard Rorty, 'Solidarity or Objectivity,' in, *Post-Analytic Philosophy* ed. J. Rajchman & Cornel West (New York: Columbia Univ. Press, 1985); Richard Rorty, *Contingency, Irony and Solidarity* (Cambridge: Cambridge Univ. Press, 1980), 189-198.

[88] Leroy Vail and Landig White, *Power and The Praise Poem* (Charlottesville: Univ. Press of Virginia, 1991). See, for instance, Walter J. Ong, *Orality and Literacy: The Technologizing of the Word*, supra note 13 at 175.

[89] Alasdair MacIntyre, *Three Rival Versions of Moral Enquiry: Encyclopaedia, Genealogy, and Tradition* (Notre Dame: Univ. of Notre Dame Press, 1990) at 177. (Emphasis added). Edward Shils pointedly reiterates this belief when he wrote that 'the Third World [is] backward rather than ... the locus of major moral and political values...' 'The Antinomies of Liberalism' in *The Relevance of Liberalism* (Boulder, Colorado: Westview Press, 1978) 134 at 194.

[90] Karl R. Popper, *A World of Propensities* (Bristol: Thoemmes, 1990) at 7.

[91] See, H.L.A. Hart, *The Concept of Law*, supra note 74.

[92] See, particularly, R. Dworkin, *Taking Rights Seriously*, supra note 78, especially Chapters 2 & 3.

[93] Richard Tur, 'Criminal Law and Legal Theory,' in, *Legal Theory and Common Law*, ed. William Twining (London: Basil Blackwell, 1986) at 198.

[94] Glanville Williams, *Criminal Law: The General Part*, 2nd ed. (London: Stevens & Sons, 1961) at 30. See also, J. F. Stephen, *History of the Criminal Law of England*, 3 vols. (London: Steven & Sons, 1883) 2: at 295.

[95] David J. Seipp, 'The Structure of English Common Law in the Seventeenth Century,' in, *Legal History in the Making: Proceedings of the Ninth British Legal History Conference, 1989* ed. W.M. Gordon & T.D. Fergus, (London: Hambledon, 1991) at 83.

[96] Pollock & Maitland, *History of English Law*, Vol. II, 2nd ed. (Cambridge: Cambridge Univ. Press, 1923).

[97] F.B. Sayre, 'Mens Rea', *Harvard L.R.* 45 (1945) 974 at 997.

[98] Pollock & Maitland, supra note 96, Vol. I; T.A. Green, *Verdict According to Conscience* (Chicago: Univ. of Chic Press, 1992) at 56.

[99] Richard Helgerson, *Forms of Nationhood: The Elizabethan Writing of England* (Chicago & London: Univ. of Chic. Press, 1991) at 78.

[100] Richard A. Posner, '"Conventionalism": The Key to Law as an Autonomous Discipline?' *U.T.L.J.* 30 (1988) 333 at 347.
[101] Coke, *Third Institute* 51.
[102] Ibid. at 47.
[103] As Coke puts it, 'some manslaughters be voluntary, and not of malice forethought, upon some sudden falling out. And this for distinction sake is called manslaughter. There is no difference between murder and manslaughter; but that the one is upon malice forethought, and the other upon a sudden occasion, and therefore is called chance-medley. As if two meet together, and striving for the wall the one kill the other, this is manslaughter and felony …' Ibid. at 55. See also. Hale, *History of the Pleas of the Crown* Vol. I at 449.
[104] 4 Blackstone *Commentaries* 20.
[105] In explicating the mental element in crime, analytical jurists do not necessarily employ identical terms and phrases. But it seems that there is general agreement that 'the bottom of the psychological kit [has been] reached,' such that we 'may substitute various synonyms' for 'intention' and 'recklessness'. Jerome Hall, *General Principles of Criminal Law*, 2nd ed. (New York: Bobbs-Merill, 1960) at 113.
[106] C.K. Odgen & I.A. Richards, *The Meaning of Meaning,* 8th ed. (New York: Harcourt, Brace & World Inc., 1923) at 100.
[107] Karl L. Popper, *The Open Society and Its Enemies*, 5th ed. 2 Vols. (London: Routledge & Kegal Paul, 1966) 2 at 9.
[108] Locke pithily expresses the nominalist position: '…essential, and not essential, relate only to our abstract Ideas, and the names annexed to them; which amounts to no more but this, That whatever particular Thing, has not in it those Qualities which are contained in the abstract Idea, which any general Terms stands for, cannot be ranked under that species, nor be called by that name since that abstract Idea is the very Essence of that Species,' *Essay Concerning Human Understanding*, III, vi, s.4. Wittgenstein puts it tersely, 'the mathematician creates essences': Wittgenstein, *Remarks on The Foundations of Mathematics* ed. G.H. von Wright et al, trans. G.E.M. Anscombe (Oxford: Basil Blackwell, 1956) at 50.
[109] Austin, *Lectures*, 1 at 474. (Emphases original).
[110] Rodolfo Sacco, 'Legal Formants: A Dynamic Approach to Comparative Law,' *Am. J. of Comp. Law* 39 (1991) 1 at 12.
[111] '"The idea" signifies the concept of the absolute totality of all conceivable experiences,': R. Stammler, 'Fundamental Tendencies in Modern Jurisprudence,' *Mich. L.R.* 21 (1922-23) 623 at 639.
[112] John Locke, *Essay Concerning Human Understanding*, supra note 62.
[113] See above.
[114] Richard Helgerson, supra note 99 at 190.
[115] See, Ralph Cudworth, *A Treatise Concerning Eternal and Immutable Morality* (1731) (New York: Garland Publishing, 1976 rep), passim.

[116] Adekemi Odujirin, 'The Resilience of the Common Law: Negligence, Criminal Responsibility, and the Canadian Charter of Rights and Freedoms,' *Common Law World Review* 30 (2001) 169.

[117] Legal positivism defines the concept of law in terms of its own theory of law, and then identifies the 'rule of law' with fidelity to positive law. Legal idealism also defines the concept of law in terms of its own theory of law, and then identifies the 'rule of law' with fidelity to the posited ideal law. This sleight of hand fosters, on the one hand, the positivist's insistence that 'an ideal of fidelity to law [is] possible only within the framework of legal positivism' and, on the other hand, the idealist's conviction that 'the only meaningful sense of fidelity [to law] is fidelity to the common opinions and not some independently existing object.' This impales the understanding on the horns of immanence and narcissism. But, 'if legal understanding, in an effort to achieve authentic contact with its object, defers to the internal standpoint of the practice, it achieves immanence at the price of an uncritical accommodation to the given norms of the tradition ... If, however, understanding attempts to construct the practice in accordance with an ideal having independent normative force, then it sacrifices immanence and becomes an external imposition...' The quoted words are Alan Brudner's *The Unity of the Common Law: Studies in Hegelian Jurisprudence* (Berkeley: Univ. of California Press, 1994) at 267, 266, 14.

[118] See, for instance, H.L.A. Hart, 'Positivism and the Separation of Law and Morals,' *Harvard L. Rev.* 71 (1958); Hans Kelsen, *General Theory of Law and State* (Cambridge, Mass.: Harvard Univ. Press, 1945).

[119] See, for instance, Ernest J. Weinrib, 'Legal Formalism: On the Immanent Rationality of Law,' *Yale L.J. 97* (1988) 949; Lon L. Fuller, 'Positivism and Fidelity to Law: A Reply to Professor Hart,' *Harvard L. Rev.* 71 (1958) 630.

[120] On 'paradigm shift,' see, Thomas S. Kuhn, *The Structure of Scientific Revolutions* 3rd ed. (Chicago & London: Univ. of Chicago Press, 1996)

[121] Not even the 'pirate kingdoms of the twentieth century' which momentarily made legal positivism 'morally untenable' succeeded in dislodging it from the center of the legal universe. The phrases are Stig Stromholm, *A Short History of Legal Thinking in the West* (Stockholm: Norstedts Forlage, 1985) at 276.

[122] Quentin Skinner ed. *The Return of Grand Theory in the Human Sciences* (Cambridge: Cambridge Univ. Press, 1985)

[123] Geoffrey Samuel, 'Science, Law and History: Historical Jurisprudence and Modern Legal Theory,' *N.I.L.Q. 41* (1990) 1 at 18: '...The twentieth century is witnessing 'ideological chaos' because philosophers, in trying to abandon history, are in truth 'neolithic' in their attachment to historical premises...'

[124] 'Two fundamental connotations ... are attached to the word *hermeneutics*: a mythical-religious origin and the notion of a translator or carrier of messages. The word itself comes from the Greek for 'interpretation.' *Interpretation*, in turn, comes from the Latin for 'agent, negotiator, or the act of giving meaning.' The word *meaning*, to take the last step, derives from Old English and signifies the thing that one intends to convey, especially by language; it carries with it

also the sense of something intervening or intermediate... The end result is a form of understanding that is distinct from and independent of ordinary scientific explanation.' Bruce Mazlish, *The Uncertain Sciences* (New Haven & London: Yale Univ. Press, 1998) at 89; 'The word "hermeneutics" points back ... to the task of ...interpreting and communicating something that is unintelligible because it is spoken in a foreign language...': Hans-Georg Gadamer, 'Hermeneutics and Historicism', in *Truth and Method* (1960) 2nd Ed. (New York: Crossroad, 1986) at 486; 'Hermes transmitted the messages of the gods to the mortals, that is to say, he not only announced them verbatim but acted as an 'interpreter' who renders their words intelligible ... Hermeneutics is consequently engaged in two tasks: one, the ascertaining of the exact meaning-content of a word, sentence, text, etc.; two, the discovery of the instructions contained in symbolic forms.': Josef Bleicher, *Contemporary Hermeneutics: Hermeneutics as Method, Philosophy and Critique* (London & New York: Routledge & Kegan Paul, 1980) at 11.

[125] Hans Georg Gadamer, *Truth and Method,* supra note 124 at 249.

[126] On hermeneutics, see generally, Hans-Georg Gadamer, *Truth and Method,* supra note 124; Hans-Georg Gadamer, *The Beginning of Philosophy,* trans. Rod Coltman (New York: Continuum, 1998) Chapter 2; Josef Bleicher, *Contemporary Hermeneutics: Hermeneutics as Method, Philosophy and Critique,* supra note 124; Gayle L. Ormiston and Alan D. Schrift ed. *The Hermeneutic Tradition: From Ast to Ricoeur* (New York: State Univ. of New York Press, 1990); Richard J. Bernstein, *Beyond Objectivism and Relativism: Science, Hermeneutics, and Praxis* (Philadelphia: Univ. of Pennsylvania Press, 1983), pp. 109-169; Roy J. Howard, *Three Faces of Hermeneutics: An Introduction to Current Theories of Understanding* (Berkeley: Univ. of California Press, 1982); Stig Stromholm, 'Legal Hermeneutics – Notes on the Early Modern Development,' *Scandinavian Studies in Law* 22 (1978) 213-241; Aulis Aarnio, 'Outline of a Hermeneutic Approach in Legal Theory,' *Acta Philosophica Fennica* 36 (1983) 47; S. Levinson and Steven Maillox ed. *Interpreting Law and Literature: A Hermeneutic Reader* (Evaston, Il: Northwestern Univ. Press, 1988); George Wright, 'On a General Theory of Interpretation: The Betti-Gadamer Dispute in Legal Hermeneutics,' *Am. J. of Jurisprudence* 32 (1987) 243; Brad Sherman, 'Hermeneutics in Law,' [Review Article] *Modern L.Rev.* 51 (1988) 386-402; Stephen M. Feldman, 'The New Metaphysics: The Interpretive Turn in Jurisprudence,' *Iowa L.R.* 76 (1991); Stephen M. Feldman, 'Republican Revival/Interpretive Turn,' *Wis. L.R.* 679 (1992); Timothy O'Hagan, 'Gadamer, Hermeneutics and the Law,' *Archiv fur Rechts und Sozialphilosophie* 76 (1996) 197.

[127] H.L.A. Hart, *The Concept of Law,* supra note 74; H.L.A. Hart, *Essays in Jurisprudence and Philosophy* (Oxford: Clarendon Press, 1983).

[128] P.M.S. Hacker, 'Hart's Philosophy of Law,' in, *Law, Morality, and Society: Essays in Honour of H.L.A. Hart,* ed. P.M.S. Hacker & J. Raz (Oxford: Clarendon Press, 1977) 1; Brian Bix, 'H.L.A. Hart and the Hermeneutic Turn in Legal Theory,' *SMU L.R.* 52 (1999) 167.

[129] Jacques Lenoble, 'Narrative Coherence and the Limits of the Hermeneutic Paradigm,' in, *Law, Interpretation, and Reality: Essays in Epistemology, Hermeneutics, and Jurisprudence* ed. P. Nerhot (Dordrecht: Kluwer Academic Publishers, 1990) 127-168 at 128.

[130] Quentin Skinner, *The Return of Grand Theory in the Human Sciences*, supra note 122 at 15 [Introduction].

[131] L. Wittgenstein, *On Certainty* ed. G.E.M. Anscombe & G. H. von Wright, trans. Denis Paul & G.E.M. Anscombe (Oxford: Basil Blackwell, 1974) at 166.

[132] H. Hamner Hill, 'H.L.A. Hart's Hermeneutic Positivism: On Some Methodological Difficulties in The Concept of Law,' *Canadian Journal of Law and Jurisprudence* 3 (1990) 113.

[133] Stephen R. Perry, 'Hart's Methodological Positivism,' *Legal Theory* 4 (1998) 427.

[134] See, *inter alia*, Andrei Marmor ed. *Law and Interpretation: Essays in Legal Philosophy* (Oxford: Clarendon Press, 1995); W.J.T. Mitchell ed. *The Politics of Interpretation* (Chicago & London: Univ. of Chicago Press, 1983); Roger Shiner, *Norm and Nature: The Movements of Legal Thought* (Oxford: Clarendon Press, 1992) Chapter 5; Vittorio Villa, 'Legal Science and Hermeneutic Point of View,' in *Theory of Legal Science* (Proceedings of the Conference on Legal Theory and Philosophy of Science, Lund, Sweden, Dec. 11-14, 1983) ed. Aleksander Peczenic *et al.* (Dordrecht: D. Reidel Co. 1984) 509; Massimo La Torre, 'Meaning, Norm and Legal Science: An Institutionist Approach,' in, *Normative Systems in Legal and Moral Theory* (Festchrift for Carlos E. Alchournon and Eugenio Bulygin ed. Ernesto Garzon Valden *et al* (Berlin: Duncker & Humblot, 1997) 394; Brian Slattery, 'Law's Meaning,' *Osgoode Hall Law Journal* 34 (1996) 553; Brian Slattery, 'Three Concepts of Law: The Ambiguous Legacy of H.L.A. Hart,' *Saskatchewan L. Rev.* 61 (1998) 323.

[135] See, particularly, Ronald Dworkin, 'How Law is Like Literature,' in, *A Matter of Principle* (Cambridge, Mass.: Harvard Univ. Press, 1985) 146; *Law's Empire* (Cambridge, Mass.: Harvard Univ. Press, 1986) esp. pp. 45-87, 228-238.

[136] Aulis Aarnio, 'Outline of a Hermeneutic Approach in Legal Theory,' supra note 126 at 59; Aulis Aarnio, *Reason and Authority: A Treatise on the Dynamic Paradigm of Legal Dogmatics* (Aldershot: Dartmouth, 1997) at 106: 'Analytic hermeneutics offers (one) philosophical method to understand the essential features of legal interpretation. A very important means in the use of this method is the concept of the *language-game* introduced by Wittgenstein.' '...the addition of 'analytic' to 'hermeneutics' ... indicate[s] a preference for formal or logicist ways of elucidating the problems of intersubjective understanding. There is an enormous variation in ways of doing this... Behind most of [them] ... lies the seminal work of Wittgenstein.': Roy J. Howard, *Three Faces of Hermeneutics*, supra note 126 at 38.

[137] Norman F. Cantor, *The Sacred Chain* (New York: HarperCollins, 1994) at 364. For an early, formal acknowledgement of the centrality of Wittgenstein's

thought, see, particularly, A.G.N. Flew, 'Introduction', in *Essays on Logic and Language*, First Series (Oxford: Basil Blackwell, 1963) at 10.

[138] See, *inter alia*, Allan Janik and Stephen Toulmin, *Wittgeinstein's Vienna* (New York: Simon & Schuster, 1973) at 167-201, 202-238 (early and later Wittgeinstein respectively); Ray Monk, *Ludwig Wittgenstein: The Duty of Genius* (New York: Free Press, 1990) at 62-166, 298-327 (early and later Wittgenstein respectively); P.M.S. Hacker, *Wittgenstein's Place in Twentieth-Century Analytic Philosophy* (Oxford: Blackwell, 1996) at 22-38, 76-136 (early and later Wittgeinstein respectively); Dale Jacquette, *Wittgenstein's Thought in Transition* (West Lafayette, Indiana: Purdue University Press, 1998) Parts I and III (early and later Wittgeinstein respectively).

[139] See, *inter alia*, Roger A. Shiner, 'Wittgenstein and the Foundations of Knowledge,' *Proceedings of Aristotlean Society* (N.S.) 78 (1978) 78-103; Dennis M. Patterson ed, *Wittgenstein and Legal Theory* (Boulder: Westview Press, 1992); G.H. von Wright, 'Analytical Philosophy: A Historico-Critical Survey,' in Georg Henrik von Wright, *The Tree of Knowledge and Other Essays* (Leiden: E.J. Brill, 1993) 25-52 at 45-6; P.M.S. Hacker, *Insight and Illusion: Themes in the Philosophy of Wittgenstein*, rev. ed. (Oxford: Clarendon Press, 1989) Chapter VI.

[140] For biographical information on Wittgenstein, see, particularly, Georg Henrik von Wright, *Wittgenstein* (Oxford: Blackwell, 1982) pp. 15-34; Allan Janik and Stephen Toulmin, *Wittgenstein's Vienna,* supra note 138 at 169-176.

[141] P.M.S. Hacker, *Insight and Illusion*, supra note 139 at 147.

[142] Bruce Mazlish, *The Uncertain Sciences*, supra note 124 at 67; Hans-Georg Gadamer, *Truth and Method*, supra note 124 at xii.

[143] See, generally, Charles Taylor, 'Interpretation and the Sciences of Man,' *Review of Metaphysics* 25 (1971) 3; Charles Taylor, 'Understanding in Human Science,' *Review of Metaphysics* 34 (1980) 25; Hans-Georg Gadamer, *Truth and Method,* supra note 124 at xii; Georg Henrik von Wright, 'Humanism and the Humanities,' in Georg Henrik von Wright, *The Tree of Knowledge and Other Essays*, supra note 139 at 164-7.

[144] Leslie Green, '*The Concept of Law* Revisited' [Book Review] *Mich. L. R.* 94 (1994) 1682 at 1698.

[145] 'Embodying a unique genius, or *Geist*, each *Volk*' supposedly 'formed an organic whole, the values, beliefs, traditions, and language of which could only be understood from within by entering into the viewpoint of the members.' Thus, 'history as an observable process, occurred not on a universal level, but only among particular social entities': Matti Bunzl, 'Franz Boas and the Humboldtian Tradition: From Volksgeist and Nationalcharakter to an Anthropological Concept of Culture,' in *Volksgeist as Method and Ethic: Essays on Boasian Ethnography and the German Anthropological Tradition*, ed. George W. Stocking, Jr., (History of Anthropology) Vol. 8 (Madison: Univ. of Wisconsin Press, 1996) 17-78 at 20.

[146] James Q. Whitman, *The Legacy of Roman Law in the German Romantic Era: Historical Vision and Legal Change* (Princeton, N.J.: Princeton Univ. Press, 1990) at 98.
[147] R. Tuck, *Natural Rights Theories: Their Origin and Development* (Cambridge: Cambridge Univ. Press, 1979) at 22.
[148] Leo Strauss, *Natural Right and History*, supra note 61 at 14.
[149] Richard J. Bernstein, *Beyond Objectivism and Relativism*, supra note 126 at 112: 'Nineteenth century hermeneutics developed as a reaction against the intellectual imperialism of the growth of positivism, inductivism, and *the type of scientism that claimed that it is the natural sciences alone that provide the model and the standards for what is to count as genuine knowledge*. The character of hermeneutics was shaped by the assault on the integrity and autonomy of the human sciences…' (Emphasis added).
[150] See, generally, Lilian R. Furst, *Romanticism in Perspective: A Comparative Study of Aspects of the Romantic Movements in England, France and Germany* 2nd ed. (London: MacMillan, 1979); Maurice Cranston, *The Romantic Movement* (Oxford: Basil Blackwell, 1994); Roy Porter and Mikulas Teich, ed. *Romanticism in National Context* (Cambridge: Cambridge Univ. Press, 1988).
[151] Roy Porter and Mikulas Teich, *Romanticism in National Context*, supra note 150 [Introduction] at 2.
[152] Klaus Epstein, *The Genesis of German Conservatism* (Princeton, N.J.: Princeton Univ. Press, 1966) at 674; David Eastwood, 'Robert Southey and The Intellectual Origins of Romantic Conservatism,' *English Hist. Journal* 105 (1989) 308 at 315.
[153] 'Throughout a Europe recoiling from a French domination which could pretend to advance *universal* progress and rationality, Romantics aimed to uncover a national character and even 'racial' continuities through which the past, embodied in living memory, could speak to, guide, and nurture the present … one common thread to Romanticism across Europe was the forging of historical myths to bolster indigenous national cultures…' Roy Porter and Mikulas Teich, *Romanticism in National Context*, supra note 150 at 5. See, further, Hedva Ben-Israel, 'The French Revolution and the Romantic Movement in Historiography', in, *English Historians and the French Revolution* (Cambridge: Cambridge Univ. Press, 1968) at 110-126.
[154] H.R. Trevor-Roper, *The Romantic Movement and the Study of History* (London: Athlone Press, 1969) at 9.
[155] Hans-Georg Gadamer, *Truth and Method*, supra note 124 at 244.
[156] See, supra note 145.
[157] James Whitman, 'From Philology to Anthropology in Mid-Nineteenth Century Germany,' in, *Functionalism Historicized: Essays on British Social Anthropology* ed. George W. Stocking, Jr. (History of Anthropology) Vol. 2 (Madison: Univ. of Wisconsin Press, 1984) 214-229 at 218; Matti Bunzl, 'Franz Boas and the Humboldtian Tradition: From Volksgeist and Nationalcharakter to an Anthropological Concept of Culture,' in *Volksgeist as*

Method and Ethic: Essays on Boasian Ethnography and the German Anthropological Tradition, supra note 145 at 17.

[158] On Savigny and the historical school of law, see, generally, James Q. Whitman, *The Legacy of the Roman Law in the German Romantic Era*, supra note 146, Chapter IV; Herman Kantorowicz, 'Savigny and the Historical School of Law,' *Law Quarterly Rev.* 37 (1937) 326; Susan Gaylord Gale, 'A Very German Legal Science: Savigny and the Historical School,' *Stanford J. of International Law* 18 (1982) 123. That Savigny and the school of law he founded were inherently *conservative* seems to be beyond doubt. See, e.g., Mathias Reimann, 'Nineteenth Century German Legal Science,' *Boston College L. Rev.* 31 (1990) 837 at 866: 'Savigny's jurisprudence fit particularly well with the strongly conservative mood of the German aristocracy after the Napoleonic wars. And Savigny himself, a nobleman who loathed and feared radical innovation, became a symbol for the preservation of traditional structure.'

[159] See, generally, James Q. Whitman, *The Legacy of the Roman Law in the German Romantic Era*, supra note 146; Theodore Ziolkowski, *German Romanticism and Its Institutions* (Princeton: Princeton Univ. Press, 1990); Mathias Reimann, 'Nineteenth Century German Legal Science,' supra note 158; Georg G. Iggers, *The German Conception of History: The National Tradition of Historical Thought from Herder to the Present* Rev. Ed. (Middletown, Conn.: Wesleyan Univ. Press, 1983).

[160] Michael Peters and James Marshall, *Wittgenstein: Philosophy, Postmodernism, Pedagogy* (Westport, Conn.: Bergin & Garvey, 1999) at 44; Yuval Lurie, 'Culture as a Human Form of Life: A Romantic Reading of Wittgenstein' *International Philosophical Quarterly* 32 (1992) 193.

[161] von Wright, supra note 139 at 89.

[162] von Wright, 'Wittgenstein and The Twentieth Century', in supra note 139 at 86; Allan Janik and Stephen Toulmin, *Wittgenstein's Vienna*, supra note 138 at 258.

[163] Peter Levine, *Nietzsche and the Modern Crisis of the Humanities* (Albany, N.Y.: State Univ. of New York Press, 1995) at 65.

[164] Plato, *Republic*

[165] Ludwig Wittgenstein, *Philosophical Investigations*, trans. G.E.M. Anscombe (Oxford: Basil Blackwell, 1967) at 103e.

[166] Ernst-Wolfgang Bockenforde, 'The School of Historical Jurisprudence and the Problem of the Historicity of Law,' in, *State, Society and Liberty: Studies in Political Theory and Constitutional Law* trans. J.A. Underwood (New York & Oxford: Berg Publishers, 1991) at 3. (Emphasis original). It would be noticed that this is the question that philosophers of law generally pose for themselves. It was precisely the question that John Austin set for himself when he outlined the contours of general jurisprudence. It is appropriate to point out here that, before Austin, who was himself not a product of university education, composed his *Lectures on Jurisprudence*, he took a trip to Germany, which was then the reputed home of civil law studies; he was much influenced by the

budding German historical school. For a brief description of the legal intellectual climate in Germany at the time of Austin's visit, see, Andreas B. Schwartz, 'John Austin and the German Jurisprudence of His Time,' *Politica* (1934) 178; Michael Lobban, *The Common Law and English Jurisprudence, 1760-1850*, (Cambridge: Cambridge Univ. Press, 1991) Chapter 8; Michael Lobban, 'Was There a Nineteenth Century 'English School of Jurisprudence?'' *J. of Legal Hist.* 16 (1995) 34.

[167] Gerald L. Bruns, 'Law and Language: A Hermeneutics of the Legal Text,' in *Legal Hermeneutics: History, Theory, and Practice*, ed. Gregory Leyh (Berkeley: Univ. of California Press, 1992) 23-40 at 27: 'As for law, one can begin with the proviso that hermeneutics does not think of it in terms of the conceptual or methodological interests of the legal theorist, still less in terms of the strategic interests of legal or judicial practice; rather, the concern is with the conditions in which these interests are pursued. Put it [differently] that the interests of hermeneutics are more ontological than technical.' See further, Gadamer, *Truth and Method*, supra 124 at 345 et seq.

[168] See, particularly, Mathias Reimann, 'A Career in Itself: The German Professoriate as a Model for American Legal Academia,' in *The Reception of Continental Ideas in the Common Law World, 1820-1920* ed. M. Reimann (Berlin: Duncker & Humblot, 1993) 165-202 at 194; Mathias Reimann, 'Nineteenth Century German Legal Science,' supra note 158 at 897 n.208; Jurgen Herbst, *The German Historical School in American Scholarship: A Study in the Transfer of Culture* (Ithaca, N.Y.: Cornell Univ. Press, 1965) Chapter 8. For short accounts of the larger context for the change, see, e.g., Henry J. Schmidt, 'The Rhetoric of Survival: The Germanists in America from 1900 to 1925,' in *America and the Germans: An Assessment of a Three Hundred Year History* ed. Frank Tromurler & Joseph McVeigh, Vol. II (The Relationship in the Twentieth Century) (Philadelphia: Univ. of Pennsylvania Press, 1985) 204-216; N.E.H. Hull, *Roscoe Pound & Karl Llewellyn: Searching for an American Jurisprudence* (Chicago & London: Univ. of Chic. Press, 1997) at 108-112, 116-117.

[169] Bruce Mazlish, *The Uncertain Sciences*, supra note 124 at 88: 'In the particular German tradition of [the nineteenth century] ... reality is primarily spiritual, not material, and the method necessary to reach it, hermeneutical. By *spiritual*, ... the German hermeneutic thinkers generally meant the domain of religion and myth ...'

[170] Mathias Reimann, 'Nineteenth Century German Legal Science,' supra note 158 at 853.

[171] Ibid. at 854; Ernst-Wolfgang Bockenforde, *State, Society and Liberty*, supra note 166 at 6-10; M. Bellomo, *The Common Legal Past of Europe, 1000-1800*, trans. L. Cochrane (Washington, D.C.: Catholic Univ. of America Press, 1995).

[172] See Part II above.

[173] 'the rejection of abstract reason by German historicists does not ... mean a rejection of all rationality in scientific inquiry. On the contrary ... historicism is predominantly a scholarly movement which seeks rational understanding of

human reality. Recognizing the emotional qualities of all human behavior, it seeks to develop a logic that takes into account the irrational aspects of human life.': Georg W. Iggers, *The German Conception of History*, supra note 159 at 10.

[174] Although the historical school of law was initially averse to legislation and codification as tools of legal development, from mid-nineteenth century onwards it became reconciled with the movement for legislation and codification. See, generally, Michael John, *Politics and the Law in Late Nineteenth-Century Germany: The Origins of the Civil Code* (Oxford: Clarendon Press, 1989).

[175] See Part II above.

[176] Richard Helgerson's, *Forms of Nationhood: The Elizabethan Writing of England*, supra note 99 at 190.

[177] H.L.A. Hart, *The Concept of Law*, supra note 74 at 6. (Emphasis original).

[178] Hart clarified 'the nature of legal theory' in a 'Comment' in R. Gavison ed. *Issues in Contemporary Legal Philosophy* (Oxford: Clarendon Press, 1987) 36, and in the posthumously published postscript to *The Concept of Law*. In the former, Hart wrote that there is 'a standing need for a form of legal theory or jurisprudence that is descriptive and general in scope, the perspective of which is not that of a judge ... but is that of an external observer of a form of social institution with a normative aspect, which in its recurrence in different societies and periods exhibits many common features of form, structure and content...' In the latter, (at p. 239-40) Hart added that such a theory of law is general in that 'it is not tied to any particular legal system or legal culture.' It is descriptive in that 'it is morally neutral and has no justificatory aims...'

[179] The phrase is Anne Harrington's, *Reenchanted Science: Holism in German Culture From Wilhelm II to Hitler* (Princeton, N.J.: Princeton Univ. Press, 1996) at 27.

[180] Josef Bleicher, *Contemporary Hermeneutics*, supra note 124 at 120: 'Hermeneutic philosophy focuses not on the methodology of the [human sciences], but on their relationship to the whole of our experience of the world; by evidencing understanding as a fundamental characteristic of existence it does not intend to restrict the disciplined and skilled understanding of texts, but only hopes to free it from a false self-understanding.'

[181] The 'leading authority on hermeneutic from the philosophical point of view,' Hans-Georg Gadamer, categorically asserts that the hermeneutics he develops 'is not ... a methodology of the human sciences ...' And, in a reply to one of his most perceptive critics, he writes that 'fundamentally I am *not proposing a method* ...' *Truth and Method*, supra note 124 at xiii, 465. (Emphasis original). See also, James R. Robinson, 'Hermeneutic Since Barth,' in, *New Frontiers in Theology: Discussions among Continental and American Theologians*, Vol. II (*The New Hermeneutic*) ed. James M. Robinson & John B. Cobb, Jr. (New York: Harper & Row, 1964) 1-77 at 76; Jerry H. Stone, 'Christian Praxis as Reflective Action,' in, *Legal Hermeneutics: History, Theory, and Practice*, supra note 167, 103-126 at 105-6.

Richard Rorty also forcefully argued against hermeneutics as method. See, particularly, Richard Rorty, 'Method and Morality,' in, *Social Science as Moral Inquiry* ed. Norman Haan *et al* (New York: Columbia Univ. Press, 1983) 155-176. Elsewhere, Rorty playfully described hermeneutics as an 'attitude': Richard Rorty, 'A Reply to Dreyfus and Taylor,' *Review of Metaphysics* 34 (1980) 39-46.

[182] David Granfield, *The Inner Experience of Law: A Jurisprudence of Subjectivity* (Washington, D.C.: Catholic Univ. of America Press, 1988) at 24, 26: '...rationalism, relying on reason focused on *what the law ought to be*, the Historical School in Germany, studying customs, focused on *what the law was*, and the Analytic School in England, using logic, focused on *what the law is...* These two schools effectively bypassed rationalism...'

[183] George Wright, 'On a General Theory of Interpretation: The Betti-Gadamer Dispute in Legal Hermeneutics,' supra note 126 at 202. Cf. 'a *studium humanitas*, which in a certain way reaches back to the ancients and thus also becomes a revival of Greek civilization always adheres to *historically understood humanism.* For Germans this is apparent in the humanism of the eighteenth century...': Martin Heidegger, *Letter on Humanism*, in *Basic Writings*, 193-242 at 201. (Emphasis added).

[184] Roy Porter and Mikulas Teich (ed.) *The Enlightenment in National Context* (Cambridge: Cambridge Univ. Press, 1981); J.G.A. Pocock, *Barbarism and Religion, Vol. I: The Enlightenments of Edward Gibbon, 1737-1764* (Cambridge: Cambridge Univ. Press, 1999) at 6-9, 138, 300-302; Richard B. Sher, *Church and University in the Scottish Enlightenment: The Moderate Literati of Edinburgh* (Princeton, N.J.: Princeton Univ. Press, 1985) at 9-11, 151, 211; James R. Jacob & Margaret C. Jacob, 'The Anglican Origins of Modern Science: The Metaphysical Foundations of the Whig Constitution,' *Isis* 71 (1980) 251 at 265-6; Donald Greene, 'Augustianism and Empiricism: A Note on Eighteenth Century English Intellectual History,' 1 *Eighteenth Century Studies* 33; Hugh Trevor-Roper, 'The Scottish Enlightenment,' *Blackwood's Magazine* 322 (1977) 371.

[185] See, generally, Margaret C. Jacob, *The Radical Enlightenment: Pantheists, Freemasons and Republicans* (London: George Allen & Unwin, 1981); Frank E. Manuel, *The Eighteenth Century Confronts the Gods* (Cambridge, Mass.: Harvard Univ. Press, 1959).

[186] Karl Lowith, *Martin Heidegger and European Nihilism* ed. Richard Wolin, trans. Gary Steiner (New York: Columbia Univ. Press, 1995).

[187] Dennis Patterson, *Law and Truth* (New York and Oxford: Oxford Univ. Press, 1996) at 73 n.16.

[188] Werner Marx, *Is There a Measure on Earth? Foundations for a Nonmetaphysical Ethics*, trans. Thomas J. Nenon and Reginald Lilly (Chicago & London: Univ. of Chicago Press, 1987) at 25.

[189] F. Waismann, 'Ethics and Science,' (1939) in, F. Waismann et al. *Ethics and the Will: Essays* ed. B. McGuinness and J. Schulte, trans. Hans Kaal (Dordrecht: Kluwer Academic Publishers, 1994) 35 at 45.

[190] J. Habermas, 'Work and Weltanschauung: The Heidegger Controversy from a German Perspective,' in, J. Habermas, *The New Conservatism: Cultural Criticism and the Historians' Debate*, ed. & trans. S. W. Nicholsen (Cambridge, Mass.: MIT Press, 1989) 140 at 148.
[191] Brad Sherman, 'Hermeneutics in Law,' supra note 126 at 396.
[192] Richard J. Bernstein, *Beyond Objectivism and Subjectivism*, supra note 126 at 180.
[193] Gianluigi Palombella, 'The Cognitive Attitude: About a Structural Character in Law Interpretation,' *Archiv fur Rechts und Sozialphilosophie* 85 (1999) 151 at 169: '... the achievements of dialectic and philosophical hermeneutics ... should not be slighted.'
[194] The phrase is from J.G.A. Pocock, *Barbarism and Religion, Vol. Two: Narratives of Civil Government* (Cambridge: Cambridge Univ. Press, 1999) at 159.
[195] Gadamer, *Truth and Method*, supra note 124 at 269.
[196] David Hume, Essay XI, 'On the Populousness of Ancient Nations,' in *Philosophical Works*, Vol. III, ed. T.H. Green and T.H. Gros (1886) at 414: 'The first page of Thucydides is ... the commencement of real history.'
[197] Hans-Georg Gadamer, *Truth and Method*, supra note 124 at 465.
[198] Leslie Armour and Elizabeth Trott, *The Faces of Reason: An Essay on Philosophy and Culture in English Canada, 1850-1950* (Waterloo, Ontario: Wilfrid Laurier Univ. Press, 1981) at 26: 'Philosophically, reason has been thought of in many different ways (1) as a formal foundation out of which knowledge may be spun; (2) as *a kind of force for determining and showing what ought to be taken seriously and what derided;* (3) as a device... by which one may generate rules of one's own making for one's own pleasure; or (4) as something revealed in the natural order of things.' (Emphasis added).
[199] Ernst-Wolfgang Bockenforde, supra note 166 at 12.
[200] See, *inter alia*, Manlio Bellomo, *The Common Legal Past of Europe, 1000-1800*, trans. Lydia G. Cochrane (Washington, D.C.: The Catholic Univ. of America Press, 1995) at 19; Harold J. Berman, 'Origins of Historical Jurisprudence,' *Yale L.J.* 103 (1994) 1653 at 1737; Reinhard Zimmermann, 'Savigny's Legacy: Legal History, Comparative Law, and the Emergence of a European Legal Science,' *L.Q.R.* 112 (1996) 576 at 598-600; Peter Stein, *Roman Law in European History* (Cambridge: Cambridge Univ. Press, 1999) at 120.
[201] Manlio Bellomo, *Ibid.*
[202] The practice of making law an autonomous discipline is very old. See, Bruce W. Frier, 'Autonomy of Law and the Origins of the Legal Profession,' *Cardozo L. R.* 11 (1990) 259.
[203] Gustav Radbruch, 'Anglo-American Jurisprudence Through Continental Eyes,' *Law Quarterly Rev.* 52 (1936) 530.
[204] Michael Lobban, 'Was There a 19th Century 'English School of Jurisprudence,'' supra note 166.

[205] David Sugarman, 'Legal Theory, the Common Law Mind and the Making of the Text-book Tradition,' in, *Legal Theory and Common Law*, supra note 42.
[206] For the political attitude of John Austin and scholars in the 'text-book tradition', see, *inter alia*, Eira Ruben, 'John Austin's Political Pamphlets, 1824-1859,' in *Perspectives in Jurisprudence*, ed. E. Attwooll (Glasgow: Univ. of Glasgow Press, 1977) 20; Lotte & Joseph Hamburger, *Troubled Lives: John & Sarah Austin* (Toronto: Univ. of Toronto Press, 1985), Chapters 8 & 9; Phillip Schofield, 'Utilitarian Politics and Legal Positivism: The Rejection of Contractarianism in Early Utilitarian Thought,' in *Legal Positivism Today*, supra note 37.
[207] 'Maitland extolled Savigny as 'the herald of evolution, the man who substitutes development for manufacture, organism for mechanism, *natural laws* for *Natural law*" C.H.F. Fifoot, *Judge and Jurist in the Reign of Victoria* (1959) at 9, cited. Mathias Reimann, 'A Career in Itself: The German Professoriate as a Model for American Legal Academia', supra note 168. (Emphasis added). For an exploration of the affinities between hermeneutics, *a fortiori* the historical school, and 'natural law', see, Francis J. Mootz, III, 'Law in Flux: Philosophical Hermeneutics, Legal Argumentation, and the Natural Law Tradition,' *Yale J. of Law & the Humanities* 11 (1999) 311. For the identity of the 'natural law tradition' in question, see, Max Weber, *Economy and Society: An Outline of Interpretive Sociology* (New York: Bedminster Press, 1968) Vol. 2 at 867.
[208] Sebastian Urbina, *Reason, Democracy, Society: A Study on the Basis of Legal Thinking* (Dordrecht: Kluwer Academic Publishers, 1996) Chapter 1.
[209] Martin Loughlin, *Public Law and Political Theory* (Oxford: Clarendon Press, 1992) at 22.
[210] Hubert L. Dreyfus, 'Holism and Hermeneutics,' *Review of Metaphysics* 34 (1980) 3; von Wright, supra note 139 at 48; Margret Jane Radin, 'Reconsidering the Rule of Law,' *Boston Univ. L.R.* 69 (1989) 781 at 813.
[211] von Wright, supra note 139 at 46. (Emphasis in the original).
[212] Hans-Georg Gadamer, *Truth and Method*, supra note 124 at 490.
[213] Leo Strauss, *Natural Right and History*, supra note 61 at 14.
[214] Donald.R. Kelley, *The Human Measure: Social Thought in the Western Legal Tradition* (Harvard Univ. Press, 1990) at 13: 'Hermeneutics has seldom pretended to scientific status: bound to language and to literary texts, hence to human convention and empirical scholarship (if not myth), it has been content to be regarded as an art (techne), at most a form of practical wisdom (phronesis, prudentia), and in this sense 'local knowledge''.
[215] P. Nerhot, *Law, Writing, Meaning: An Essay in Legal Hermeneutics*, trans. Ian Fraser (Edinburgh: Edinburgh Univ. Press, 1992) at 28. (Emphasis added).
[216] Sybil Schlesinger, 'Working Definitions: A Critique of H.L.A. Hart's Use of Wittgenstein in The Concept of Law,' *Archiv fur Rechts und Sozialphilosophie* 83 (1997) 103 at 124. (Emphasis added).
[217] Because of certain background political doctrines, some prominent social scientists and legal scholars acknowledge the indispensability of traditional

knowledge only to see tradition as a place of intellectual refuge rather than a starting-point. As a result they more or less idealize tradition, and condemn any attempt to go behind or beyond tradition as an intellectual sin called 'rationalism.' See, *inter alia*, Michael Oakeshott, *Rationalism in Politics* (London: Methuen, 1962); F.A. Hayek, *The Constitution of Liberty* (London: Routledge & Kegal Paul, 1960); Michael Polanyi, *Personal Knowledge: Towards a Post-Critical Philosophy*, supra note 10; Daniel Bell, *The End of Ideology: On the Exhaustion of Political Ideas in the Fifties* (1960) (Cambridge, Mass.: Harvard Univ. Press, 1988); Edward Shils, *Tradition* (London & Boston: Faber & Faber, 1981); Anthony T. Kronman, 'Precedent and Tradition,' *Yale L.J.* 99 (1990) 1029.

[218] See, Plato, *Parmenides*.

[219] E.P. Thompson, *Whigs and Hunters: The Origin of the Black Act* (N. Y.: Pantheon Books, 1975) at 262.

[220] Cf: 'When some standard, principle, norm, duty, or quality is set up as "objective", it is then claimed that criticism has come to an end, for if the standard, principle, norm, duty, or quality is taken to be "objective", then the need for conversation is over. We would know "the answer." Yet any such endpoint is inimical to the practice of criticism itself, for there remains the question whether that end has been realized in practice.' David M. Frankford, 'The Critical Potential of the Common Law Tradition,' [Book Review] *Col. L.R.* (1994) 1076 at 1123.

[221] Michael Polanyi, *Personal Knowledge*, supra note 10 at 245.

[222] William James, 'The Moral Philosopher and the Moral Life', in *Essays in Pragmatism* ed. A. Castel (New York: Hafner, 1948) at 81: 'If the philosopher is to keep his judicial position, he must never become one of the parties to the fray ... The philosopher must be a conservative, and in the construction of his casuistic scale must put the things most in accordance with the customs of the community on top. And yet if he be a true philosopher, he must see that there is nothing final in any actually given equilibrium of human ideals ...'

[223] Benedict Anderson, *The Spectre of Comparisons: Nationalism, Southeast Asia, and the World* (London: Verso, 1998) at 362. Anderson was referring to the famous German sociologist, Max Weber.

[224] M.H. Watkins, 'Economics and Mystification,' *Journal of Canadian Studies* 4 (1969) 55.

[225] Leo Strauss, 'Jerusalem and Athens: Some Preliminary Reflections,' in *Studies in Platonic Political Philosophy* (Chicago: Univ. of Chic. Press, 1983) at 149.

[226] 'All testing, all confirmation and disconfirmation of a hypothesis takes place already within a system. And this system is not a more or less arbitrary and doubtful point of departure for all our agreements: no, it belongs to the essence of what we call an argument. The system is not so much the point of departure, as the element in which arguments have their life.' Ludwig Wittgenstein, *On Certainty*, supra note 130, S.105.

[227] The phrase is James A. Boon, *Other tribes, other scribes: Symbolic anthropology in the comparative study of cultures, histories, religions, and texts* (Cambridge: Cambridge Univ. Press, 1982) at 221.
[228] Donald H.J. Hermann, 'Phenomenology, Structuralism, Hermeneutics, and Legal Study: Applications of Contemporary Continental Thought to Legal Phenomena,' *Univ. of Miami L.R.* 36 (1982) 379 at 408.
[229] Hans Kelsen, *General Theory of Law and State*, supra note 118.
[230] William Ewald, 'Comparative Jurisprudence (I): What Was it Like to Try a Rat?', supra note 10 at 2039
[231] I. Kant, *The Metaphysics of Morals*, trans. Mary Gregor (Cambridge: Cambridge Univ. Press, 1991) at 44.
[232] 'A reality posit is a *representation* of a particular state of the world ... that functions as the content, the topic, the object or the aim for any of the various states of the mind that we designate with such labels as fantasizing, or wishing or believing or perceiving or remembering that or what have you... Through their content reality-posits ... refer or point beyond themselves to another realm, the exteriorized framework, that we call 'reality' or the 'world', connecting us to it by positing *of* it (as in fantasy or in memory or in belief) or positing *for* it (as in desire) a particular state of the realm' Richard A Shweder, 'Post-Nietzschian Anthropology: The Idea of Multiple Objective Worlds,' in *Relativism: Interpretation and Confrontation* ed. Michael Krauz (Notre Dame Univ. Press, 1989) 99 at 107 (Emphasis original).
[233] G.W.F. Hegel, *The Philosophy of Right* 46 Great Books of the Western World (Chicago: Encyclopaedia Britannica, Inc., 1952) at 2 (Preface). (Emphasis in the original).
[234] The phrase is from James G. Hershberg, *James B. Conant: Harvard to Hiroshima and the Making of the Nuclear Age* (New York: Alfred A. Knopf, 1993) at 27.

Conclusion: The City Dwellers

> … we are three brothers born by Rheia to Kronos, Zeus, and I [Poseidon], and the third is Hades, … All was divided among us three ways, each given his domain. I when the lots were shaken drew the grey sea to live in forever; Hades drew the lot of the mists and the darkness, and Zeus was allotted the wide sky, in the cloud and the bright air. But earth and high Olympos are common to all three. Therefore I am no part of the mind of Zeus. Let him in tranquility and powerful as he is stay satisfied with his third share.[1]

The preceding chapters rest on the premise that a modicum of epistemological distance from institutional morality is indispensable for ethical philosophy. Up until the eighteenth century, nature and/or reason played that indispensable role. In the eighteenth and early nineteenth centuries, history displaced nature/reason, and the twentieth century substituted tradition. Assuredly, history and tradition are not incapable of offering firm ground upon which to develop sophisticated legal and political theories. However, fidelity to history and tradition tends to culminate in intellectual narcissism.

Scholars are the silent legislators in society. Now 'every society allocates powers and profits, to which the adherents of the intellectual *status quo* lend a measure of support.'[2] But allegiance to the sociopolitical and economic institutions that make possible the practice of professional scholarship should not be so total as to overwhelm the philosophic spirit itself. While tradition is not necessarily rationalized irrationality and history is not perforce congealed reason, it diminishes learning when some scholars reconcile themselves with history and tradition, only to assert with perfect equanimity that 'respect for tradition *inevitably* shields also some iniquitous social relations'.[3] Nor should a scholar's devotion to the immediate polity and its socioeconomic and legal institutions be merely prudential, a pretentious cover for subverting them, for propagating and disseminating or simulating atheistic teachings. Rather, the scholar's role is to labor ceaselessly inside and outside the walls of the city. Such shuttling is not for the purpose of justifying or vilifying the city's ways or effecting 'rational reconstruction'[4] of institutional practice or coherently expounding a society's convictions of justice or idealizing its morality. On the contrary, it is for the singular purpose of seeing whether, and if so, to what extent, institutional practice can 'survive immersion in skepticism.'[5] In performing that task scholars will often work on what poets praise and tradition cherishes and historians catalogue. But if scholars are content and feed the public with the phenomenological poetics of historical tradition then the old and young alike will believe that 'what is is right'. Scholars would be unmitigated traditionalists, even if they disagree among themselves on the correct interpretation of or the theory that best explains the tradition. This is the bypass to the quintessential unexamined life which Socrates declared unworthy of man. That was why Plato would banish Homer from the *republic*, for poetry does not leave room for the class of scholars called philosophers. It is also why the prosecution, conviction, or execution of Socrates is a permanent blot on Athenian democracy. J.S. Mill made the point differently when he argued that if we lacked nonconformists we should nonetheless constantly invent arguments that agitate institutional beliefs and practices. In short, an examined life becomes unexamined if it ceases to be the subject of fresh examination, but is instead shielded by cultural intellectualism.

We noted in the third chapter that philosophy is a perennial intellectual activity that supposes *being*. We can do no more here than to add that 'being' is a-historical, a-cultural, and nonlinguistic. But that does not mean that learning generally, and particularly the science of being, theology, is mute or that it takes place outside cultures, histories, or language games. Theology teaches that phenomena are manifestations of the rule of gods that are themselves the handiwork of God. Theology lends its voice to philosophy or rather philosophy borrows the language of theology. In short, when philosophy speaks, it speaks the language of theology. In some localities philosophical speech was transfigured into historical muse. Specifically, Homer picked up the conventional names of gods and God, and he used the language of theology to describe the deeds of largely willfully irrational beings. Ditto for the professional scribes who standardized the books of religion and historical theologians or philosophers of history, 'that class in which Germany has been so rich,'[6] who cunningly represent worldly events as the trail of Divine perambulations. But, in the seventh century before Christ or thereabout men with Grecian lineaments were exposed or re-exposed to scholarship free from such mystifying encumbrances, and they boldly sidestepped not theology or religion but history and poetry, the social sciences of antiquity. And, instead of immersing themselves in the life of the traditional mind they steeped themselves in philosophical investigation, inquiry free from scribal authority, myths, and miens. The result was what we know as Greek civilization.

Greek civilization was already moribund at the time the immortal Socrates appeared in historic Athens. It is commonplace that Socrates wrote nothing, but between them Plato and Aristotle codified the philosophical approach, even though they themselves were rooted in the Greek hearth. Until the modern period when the philosophical approach was revived and bifurcated into *foundational* rationalism and empiricism, scholasticism reigned supreme. Enlightenment thinkers reinvigorated philosophical investigation, but like its Grecian counterpart European enlightenment culminated in and provoked a reaction so forceful that scholars scuttled back into their historical and traditional intellectual nests. In the nineteenth century, Nietzsche announced the demise of the ahistorical; God has since pronounced Nietzsche dead, much to the consternation of academic philosophers. The conventional wisdom now is that ethical philosophy is invariably historical, that there is no transcultural standard, and the domain of Hermes, the god messenger of the gods, is simply the interpretation of local knowledge.

It is obvious that this book demurs on that point. While history, tradition, and language are indispensable for learning, they need not cripple philosophical investigations. We should forget neither the 'theo' in theory or the 'holy' in scholarship nor substitute the local for the global or the particular for the universal. Ethical philosophy is a science of universal norms, though usually applied locally. As such, it must always be critical exercise of practical reason, the local quest for the universal; it must be neither complacent nor hypocritical nor utopian. In short, liberal analytic intellectuality must be liberal and analytic enough to suspect its own paradigms. The ascendance of historicism and traditionalism and, perhaps, the absence of 'barbarians' within the gates of modern civilization are the principal reasons why ethical philosophy wallows in abject naturalism, much to the detriment of liberal learning and the prejudice of 'the south.'

Notes

[1] Homer, *The Iliad* trans. Richmond Lattimore (Chicago Univ. Press, 1951) XV, 187-194.

[2] Michael Polanyi, *Personal Knowledge: Towards a Post-Critical Philosophy* (New York: Harper & Row, 1964) at 322.

[3] Ibid. (Emphasis added).
[4] On the meaning of this phrase, see, M.P. Golding, 'Kelsen and the Concept of "Legal System"' *Archiv fur Rechts Und Social Philosophie* 47 (1961) 355; D. Neil MacCormick & Robert S. Summers, 'On Method and Methodology,' in, *Interpreting Statutes: A Comparative Study*, ed. D. Neil MacCormick & Robert S. Summers (Dartmouth, 1991) 18-23 at 19: 'By "rational reconstruction" we mean the activity of explaining fragmentary and potentially conflicting data by reference to theoretical objects in the light of which the data are seen as relatively coherent, because presented as parts of a complex, well-ordered whole'; Neil MacCormick, 'The Ideal and the Actual of Law and Society,' in *Law, Values, and Social Practices* ed. John Tasioulas (Aldershot: Dartmouth, 1997) 15 at 23-6; H.L.A. Hart, 'Kelsen Revisited,' in, *Essays in Jurisprudence and Philosophy* (Oxford: Clarendon Press, 1983) at 287-295.
[5] E.P. Thompson, *Whigs and Hunters: The Origin of the Black Act* (New York: Pantheon Books, 1975) at 262.
[6] Elizabeth Rawson, *The Spartan Tradition in European Thought* (Oxford: Clarendon Press, 1969) at 307.

Bibliography

Aarnio, Aulis. 'Outline of a Hermeneutic Approach in Legal Theory'. *Acta Philosophica Fennica* 36 (1983) 47.

---------------- *Reason and Authority: A Treatise on the Dynamic Paradigm of Legal Dogmatics*. (Aldershot: Dartmouth, 1997)

Aarsleff, Hans. 'The State of Nature and the Nature of Man in Locke.' In *John Locke: Problems and Perspectives* ed. John W. Yolton (Cambridge: Cambridge Univ. Press, 1969)

Abun-Nasr, Jamil M. *The Tijaniyya: A Sufi Order in the Modern World* (Oxford: Oxford Univ. Press, 1965)

Achebe, Chinua. *Anthills of the Savannah* (1987)

Acton. *Essays in the Liberal Interpretation of History* ed. W.H. McNeill (Chicago & London: Univ. of Chicago Press, 1967)

Al-Azmeh, Aziz. 'Barbarians in Arab Eyes.' *Past and Present* 134 (1992) 3.

Amadi, I.R. 'The Northern Factor in the History of Sub-Saharan Africa: The Hamitic Hypothesis Revisited.' *Transafrican J. of History*. 18 (1989) 80.

Anderson, Benedict. *Imagined Communities: Reflections on the Origin and Spread of Nationalism* rev. ed. (London & New York: Verso, 1991)

---------------- *The Spectre of Comparisons: Nationalism, Southeast Asia and the World* (London: Verso, 1998)

Appleby, Joyce. 'Republicanism in Old and New Contexts.' *William & Mary Quarterly* 43 (3rd Series) (1986) 20.

Arberry, A.J. *Classical Persian Literature* (London: George Allen & Unwin, 1958)

Arendt, Hannah, 'Introduction', in Walter Benjamin, *Illuminations*, trans. Harry Zohn (New York: Harcourt, Brace and World, 1968)

Aristotle, *The Collected Works of Aristotle* ed. W.D. Ross (1928)

Armour, Leslie and Tott, Elizabeth. *The Faces of Reason: An Essay on Philosophy and Culture in English Canada, 1850-1950* (Waterloo: Ontario: Wilfrid Laurier Univ. Press, 1981)

Arnold, T.W. *The Symbols of Government* (New Haven: Yale Univ. Press, 1935).

Aron, Raymond, *The Opium of the Intellectuals*, trans. Terrence Kilmerton (London: Secker & Warburg, 1957)

Ashcraft, Richard. 'Locke's State of Nature: Historical Fact or Moral Fiction?' *American Pol. Sc. Rev.* 62 (1968) 898

Asimov, Isaac. *In the Beginning* (New York: Crown Publishers, 1981)

Athohz, Josef L. 'The Mind of Victorian Orthodoxy',

Atiyah, P.S. *The Rise and Fall of the Freedom of Contract* (Oxford: Clarendon Press, 1979)

Augustine, St. *The City of God.*

Austen, Ralph A. 'The Trans-Saharan Slave Trade: A Tentative Census.' In, *The Uncommon Market: Essays in the Economic History of the Atlantic Slave Trade* ed. Henry A. Geney & Jan S. Hogerborn (New York: Academic Press, 1979) 36.

Austin, J. *The Province of Jurisprudence Determined and the Use of the Study of Jurisprudence* (1832) (London: Weidenfeld & Nicolson, 1954).

---------------- *Lectures on Jurisprudence* 2 Vols. 3rd and 4th eds. Ed. R. Campbell (London: John Murray 1869, 1873)

Avery, Donald. *"Dangerous Foreigners" European Immigrant Workers and Labour Radicalism in Canada, 1896-1932* (Toronto: McClelland & Stewart, 1979)

Avramides, Anita. ed. *Women of Ideas* (London: Duckworth, 1995)

Awolowo, O. *The Problems of Africa* (Ibadan: Macmillan Education, 1977)

Ayandele, E.A. *African Historical Studies* (London: Frank Cass, 1979)

Ayres, Philip. *Classical Culture and the Idea of Rome in 18th Century England* (Cambridge: Cambridge Univ. Press, 1997)

Azurara. *Chronicle of the Discovery and Conquest of Guinea*, trans. C. Beazley and E. Prestage (London: Hakluyt Society, 1896)

Babbitt, Irvin. *Rousseau and Romanticism* (1919) (New York: World Publishing, 1955)

Backhouse, Constance. *Colour-Coded: A Legal History of Racism in Canada, 1900-1950* (Toronto: Univ. of Toronto Press, 1999)

Bacon, F. 'An Advertisement Touching the Controversies of the Church of England.' In, *An Introductory Sketch to the Martin Marprelate Controversy, 1588-1590* ed. Edward Arber (London: Southgate 1879).

Bacon, F. *The Advancement of Learning* Great Books of the Western World 30.

Baker, Ernest. 'Some Foreign Influences in Greek Thought.' *Greece and Rome* 5 (1935-6) 2.

Bakir, A.M. 'Slavery in Pharaonic Egypt.' *Annales Service des Antiquites de L'Egypte* 45 (1947) 135.

Baron, S.W. *A Social and Religious History of the Jews*, 2nd ed. (New York: Columbia Univ. Press, 1952)

Barrett, Harold. *The Sophists: Rhetoric, Democracy and Plato's Idea of Sophistry* (Novato, California: Chandler & Sharp Publishers, 1987)

Baxter, Timothy M.S. *The Cratylus: Plato's Critique of Naming* (New York: E.J. Brill, 1992)

Bazelon, D.L. 'Civil Liberties – Protecting Old Values in the New Century.' *New York Univ. Law Rev.* 51 (1976) 505.

----------------- 'The Morality of the Criminal Law.' *South Cal. L.Rev.* 49 (1976) 385.

Bedarida, Francois. *A Social History of England 1851-1975* trans. A.S. Forster (London & New York: Methuen, 1979)

Behnegar, Nassser. 'The Intellectual Legacy of Leo Strauss, 1899-1973.' *Annual Rev. of Pol. Science* 1 (1998) 95.

Beiser, Frederick. C. *Enlightenment, Revolution, and Romanticism: The Genesis of Modern German Political Thought, 1790-1800* (Cambridge, Mass.: Harvard Univ. Press, 1992)

Bell, Daniel. *The End of Ideology: On the Exhaustion of Political Ideas in the Fifties* (1960) (Cambridge, Mass.: Harvard Univ. Press 1988).

Beller, Steven. *Vienna and The Jews, 1867-1938: A Cultural History* (Cambridge: Cambridge Univ. Press, 1989)

Bellomo, M. *The Common Legal Past of Europe, 1000-1800.* Trans. L. Cochrane (Washington, D.C.: Catholic Univ. of America Press, 1995)

Ben-Gurion, David. *Israel: A Personal History* (1972)

Ben-Israel, Hedva. *English Historians and the French Revolution* (Cambridge: Cambridge Univ. Press, 1968)

Benson, Robert L. and Constable, Giles ed. *Renaissance and Renewal in the 12th Century* (Harvard Univ. Press, 1982)

Bentham, Jeremy. *A Fragment on Government* ed. F.A. Montague (Westport, Conn.: Greenwood Press, 1980 rep.)

--------------------- *An Introduction to the Principles of Morals and Legislation* ed. J.H. Burns and H.L.A. Hart (London: Athlone Press 1970)

--------------------- *Of Laws in General* ed. H.L.A. Hart (London: Athlone Press, 1970)

---------------------- *The Limits of Jurisprudence Defined* ed. Charles W. Everett (New York: Columbia Press, 1945)

Berger, Peter L. *The Sacred Canopy: Elements of a Sociological Theory of Religion* (Anchor Books, 1966).

Berger, Thomas B. *A Long and Terrible Shadow: White Values, Native Rights and the Americas, 1492-1992* (Vancouver: Douglas & McIntyre, 1991)

Berkowitz, Peter. 'Liberal Zealotry.' [Book Review] *Yale L.J.* 103 (1994) 1363.

Berlin, I. *Slaves Without Masters: The Free Negro in the Antebellum South* (1974) (Oxford: Oxford Univ. Press, 1981)

Berlin, Isaiah. 'Two Concepts of Liberty'

Berlinerblau, Jacquies. *Heresy in the University: The Black Athena Controversy and the Responsibility of American Intellectuals* (New Brunswick: Rutgers Univ. Press, 1999)

Berman, Harold J. 'The Origins of Historical Jurisprudence'. *Yale L.J.* 103 (1994) 1653.

Bernal, Martin. *Black Athena: The Afroasiatic Roots of Classical Civilization: The Fabrication of Ancient Greece 1785-1985* Vol. I (London: Free Association Books, 1987)

Berns, Walter. *Taking the Constitution Seriously* (New York: Simon and Schuster, 1987)

Bernstein, Richard J. *Beyond Objectivism and Relativism: Science, Hermeneutics, and Praxis*. (Berkeley: Univ. of California Press, 1982)

Best, Jan. 'Racism in Classical Archaeology.' *Talanta* 24 (1992) 7.

Bhabha, Homi K. *The Location of Culture* (London & New York: Routledge, 1994)

Bichenbach, Jerome E. 'Empiricism and Law.' *University of Toronto Law Journal* 35 (1985) 94.

Bickerman, E.J. 'The Jewish Historian Demetrios.' In, *Christianity, Judaism and Other Greco-Roman Cults.* ed. Jacob Neusner (Leiden: Brill, 1975)

Bix, Brian. 'H.L.A. Hart and the Hermeneutic Turn in Legal Theory'. *SMU L.R.* 52 (1999) 167.

Blackburn, Robin. *The Making of New World Slavery, 1492-1800* (London: Verso, 1997)

Blackstone, William. *Commentaries on the Laws of England*

Blakely, Allison. 'Blacks in the Dutch Color Spectrum: Lexicography and Racial Imagery.' *The Historian* 54 (1991) 656.

Bleicher, Josef. *Contemporary Hermeneutics: Hermeneutics as Method, Philosophy and Critique*. (London & New York: Routledge & Kegan Paul, 1980)

Bloom, Allan, ed. *Confronting the Constitution* (Washington, D.C.: AEI Press 1990)

------------------ *The Closing of the American Mind* (New York: Simon & Schuster, 1987)

Boas, F. *The Mind of Primitive Man* (1938) (Westport, Conn.: Greenwood Press, 1983 rep.)

Bockenforde, Ernst-Wolfgang. *State, Society and Liberty: Studies in Political Theory and Constitutional Law.* Trans. J.A. Underwood (New York & Oxford: Berg Publishers, 1991)

Bodin, Jean. *Method for the Easy Comprehension of History*. Trans. Beatrice Reynolds (New York: Octagon Books, 1966).

Bolgar, R.R. ed. *Classical Influences on Western Thought A.D. 1650-1870* (Cambridge: Univ. Press, 1978)

Boon, James A. *Other tribes, other scribes: Symbolic anthropology in the comparative study of cultures, histories, religions, and texts* (Cambridge: Cambridge Univ. Press, 1982)

Bonilla-Silva, Eduardo. '"This is a White Country": The Racial Ideology of the Western Nations of World System.' *Research in Politics and Society* 6 (1999) 85.

Brantlinger, P. 'Victorians and Africans: The Genealogy of the Myth of the Dark Continent.' *Critical Inquiry* 12 (1985) 166.

Brito, J.S. 'Hart's Criticism of Bentham in Contemporary Concepts of Law.' *Archives for Phil. of Law and Social Philosophy* (Supplement No. 1, Pt. 4) (1983) 531.

Brudner, Alan. *The Unity of the Common Law: Studies in Hegelian Jurisprudence* (Berkeley: Univ. of California Press, 1994)

Bruns, Gerald L. 'Law and Language: A Hermeneutics of the Legal Text'. In *Legal Hermeneutics: History, Theory and Practice* ed. Gregory Leyh (Berkeley: Univ. of California Press, 1992) 23.

Bryce, James. *Studies in History and Jurisprudence* 2 Vols. (Oxford: Clarendon Press, 1902)

Budge, E.A. Wallis. *Annnals of Nubian Kings* (London: Kegan Paul, 1912)

Bunzl, Matti. 'Franz Boas and the Humboldtian Tradition: From Volksgeist and Nationalcharakter to an Anthropological Concept of Culture.' In *Volksgeist as Method and Ethic: Essays on oasian Ethnography and the German Anthropological Tradition.* Goerge W. Stocking, Jr. ed. (History of Anthropology) Vol. 8 (Madison: Univ. of Wisconsin Press, 1996) 17.

Bury, J.B. *A History of the Freedom of Thought*, 2nd ed. (London: Oxford Univ. Press, 1952)

Busia, K. *Africa in Search of Democracy* (Oxford: Univ. Press, 1967)

Butler, Alfred J. *The Arab Conquest of Egypt and the Last Thirty Years of the Roman Dominion* (Oxford: Clarendon Press, 1902)

Butler, E.M. *The Tyranny of Greece Over Germany* (Cambridge: Univ. Press, 1935)

Buxton, William. *Talcott Parsons and the Capitalist Nation-State: Political Sociology as a Strategic Vocation* (Toronto: Univ. of Toronto Press, 1985)

Cairns, Huntington. *Legal Philosophy from Plato to Hegel* (Baltimore: Johns Hopkins Press, 1949)

Campbell, 'German Influences in English Legal Education Jurisprudence in the 19th Century.' *Univ. of Western Australia Annual L.R.* 4 (1957-9) 357.

Canfora, Luciana. *The Vanished Library*. Trans. Martin Ryle (Berkeley: Univ. of California Press, 1990)

Canovan, Margaret. 'Paternalistic Liberalism: Joseph Priestley on Rank and Equality.' *Enlightenment and Dissent* 1 (1983) 23.

Cantor, Norman F. *The Sacred Chain: The History of the Jews* (New York: HarperCollins, 1994)

--------------------- *Imagining the Law: Common Law and the Foundations of the American Legal System* (New York: HarperCollins, 1997)

Caroll, Lewis. 'What the Tortoise Said to Achilles.' *Mind* (n.s.) 4 (1895) 278.

Cartledge, Paul. '"Like a Worm I" the Bud? A Heterology of Classical Greek Slavery.' *Greece and Rome* 40 (1993) 163.

Chandler, Alice. *A Dream of Order* (Lincoln: Univ. of Nebraska Press, 1970)

Checkland, S.G. 'Growth and Progress: The Nineteenth Century View in Britain.' *Economic Hist. Rev.* 12 (1959) 49.

Chinweizu. *The West and the Rest of Us* (New York: Random House 1975)

Chloros, A.G. 'Some Aspects of the Social and Ethical Elements in Analytical Jurisprudence.' *Juridical Review* 67 (1955) 79.

Churchill, Sir Winston. *My Early Life* (New York: Manor Books, Inc. 1972).

Clanchy, M.T. *From Memory to Written Record: England 1066-1307* (London: Edward Arnold, 1979)

Clay, Jenny Strauss. *The Politics of Olympus: Form and Meaning in the Major Homeric Hymns* (Princeton, N.J.: Princeton Univ. Press, 1989)

Clive, John & Bernard Bailyn. 'England's Cultural Provinces: Scotland and America.' *William and Mary Quarterly* (3rd Series) 11 (1954) 200.

Cobban, Alfred. *In Search of Humanity* (New York: G. Braziller, 1962)

Cohen, I. Bernard. *Science and the Founding Fathers: Science in the Political Thought of Jefferson, Franklin, Adams, and Madison* (New York: W.W. Norton, 1991)

Cohen, William B. *The French Encounter with Africans* (Bloomington & London: Indiana Univ. Press, 1980)

Coke, Edward Sir. *Third Institute*

Colbourn, H. Trevor. *The Lamp of Experience: Whig History and the Intellectual Origin of the American Revolution* (Chapel Hill: Univ. of North Carolina Press, 1965)

Colenso, John William (Bishop). *The Pentateuch & Book of Joshua Critically Examined* (New York: D. Appleton, 1863)

Condliffe, J.B. *The Commerce of Nations* (New York: W.W. Norton, 1950)

Constant, B. 'The Liberty of the Ancients Compared with that of the Moderns'. In B. Constant, *Political Writings* ed. Biancamaria Fontana (Cambridge: Cambridge Univ. Press, 1988) 308.

Cook, William W. *American Institutions and Their Preservation* (New York: Norwood Press, 1927)

Cooper, Frederick. *Plantation Slavery on the East Coast of Africa* (New Haven & London: Yale Univ. Press, 1977)

Cosgrove, Richard A. 'The Reception of Analytic Jurisprudence: The Victorian Debate on the Separation of Law and Morality, 1860-1900.' *Durham University Journal* 74 (1981) 47.

Cottrell, L. *The Quest for Sumer* (New York: G.P. Putnam's, 1965)

Coupland, Reginald. *East Africa and Its Invaders: From the Earliest Times to the Death of Seyyid Said in 1856* (Oxford: Clarendon Press, 1938)

Cover, R. *Justice Accused: Antislavery and the Judicial Process* (New Haven: Yale Univ. Press 1975)

Craig, H. *The Enchanted Glass* (Oxford: Basil Blackwell, 1960)

Craig, Leo H. *The War Lover: A Study of Plato's Republic* (Toronto: Univ. of Toronto Press, 1994)

Crielaard, Jan Paul. 'Homer, History and Archaeology.' In *Homeric Questions: Essays in Philology, Ancient History and Archaeology*. Ed. Jan Paul Crielaard (Amsterdam: J.C. Gebe, 1995) 201.

Crimmins, James E. 'Bentham's Political Radicalism Re-examined' *Journal of the Hist. of Ideas* 55 (1994) 259.

------------------------ *Secular Utilitarianism* (Oxford: Clarendon Press 1990)

Crowe, M.B. *The Changing Profile of the Natural Law* (The Hague: Martinus Nijhoff, 1977)

Crowfoot, J.W. *The Island of Meroe* (London: Egypt Exploration Fund, 1911)

Cruse, Amy. *The Victorians and Their Books* (London: George Allen & Unwin, 1935)

Cudworth, Ralph. *A Treatise Concerning Eternal and Immutable Morality* (1731) (New York: Garland Publishing, 1976 rep.).

Curtin, P. *The Image of Africa: British Ideas and Action 1780-1850* (Madison: Univ. of Wisconsin Press 1964)
D'Entreves, A.P. *Natural Law* (New York: Harper & Row 1965)
D'Souza, Dinosh. *The End of Racism* (New York: Free Press, 1995)
Dannhauser, Weyner J. 'The Problem of the Bourgeois.' In *The Legacy of Rousseau* ed. Cliford Orwin & Nathan Tarcov (Chicago: Univ. of Chicago Press, 1997) 3.
Davidson, B. *Black Mother: Africa, the Years of the Slave Trade* (Boston: Little Brown, 1961)
Davis, Abraham L. & Graham, Barbara L. *The Supreme Court, Race and Civil Rights* (Thousand Oaks, California: Sage Publications, 1995)
Dawson, Christopher. 'The Historic Origins of Liberalism.' In, *The Image of Man* ed. M.A. Fitzimons et al (New York: Books for Libraries Press, 1971)
De Coulanges, Fustel. *The Ancient City: A Study on the Religion, Laws, and Institutions of Greece and Rome* (1885) (Baltimore: Johns Hopkins, 1980)
De Man. Paul. *Romanticism and Contemporary Criticism*. Ed. E.S. Butt, et al (Baltimore: Johns Hopkins Press, 1993)
Delacampagn, Christian. 'Racism and the West: From Praxis to Logos.' In, *Anatomy of Racism* ed. David Theo Goldberg (Minneapolis: Univ. of Minnesota Press, 1990) 83.
DeLaura, David J. *Hebrew and Hellene in Victorian England* (Texas: Austin Univ. Press, 1969)
Demetriou, K. 'In Defence of the British Constitution: Theoretical Implications of the Debate on Athenian Democracy in Britain, 1770-1850.' *History of Political Thought* 17 (1996) 200.
Desborough, V.R. d'A. *The Last Mycaneans and Their Successors* (Oxford: Clarendon Press, 1964)
Dicey, A.V. *Introduction to the Law of the Constitution* 10th ed. (London: MacMillan, 1959)
--------------- *Law and Public Opinion in 19th Century England* (London: MacMillan Press, 1963)
Dikotter, Frank. *The Discourse of Race in Modern China* (Hong Kong Univ. Press 1992)
Dinwiddy, J.R. 'Bentham's Transition to Radicalism.' *Journal of the Hist. of Ideas* 36 (1975) 683.
Dover, Cedric. 'The Racial Philosophy of Ibn Khaldun.' *Phylon* XIII (1952) 107
------------------ 'The Racial Philosophy of Jehuda Halevi.' *Phylon* XIII (1952) 312

Drake, St. Clair. *Black Folk Here and There: An Essay in History and Anthropology* 2 vols. (Los Angeles, 1990)

Drapkin, Israel. *Crime and Punishment in the Ancient World* (Toronto: Lexington Books, 1989)

Drescher, Seymour. 'The Ending of the Slave Trade and the Evolution of European Scientific Racism.' In, *The Atlantic Slave Trade: Effects on Economies, Societies, and Peoples in Africa, the Americas, and Europe* ed. Joseph E. Inikori & Stanley L. Engerman (Duke Univ. Press, 1992).

Drury, Shadia B. *Leo Strauss and The American Right* (New York: St. Martin's Press, 1997)

-------------------- *The Political Ideas of Leo Strauss* (London: Macmillan Press, 1988)

DuBois, Page. *Centaurs and Amazons: Women and the pre-History of the Great Chain of Being* (Ann Arbor: Michigan Univ. Press, 1982)

Dumont, Louis. *Homo Hierarchicus: The Caste System and Its Implications* trans. M. Sainsburg, L. Dumont and Basia Gulati (Chicago: Univ. of Chicago Press, 1980)

------------------- 'A Modified View of our Origins: The Christian Beginnings of Modern Individualism.' *Religion* 12 (1982) 1.

Dunn, J. 'The Identity of the History of Ideas.' *Philosophy* 43 (1968) 85.

Durant, Will. *The Story of Philosophy* (New York: Simon & Schuster, 1926)

Duxbury, Neil. *Patterns of American Jurisprudence* (Oxford: Clarendon Press, 1995).

Dworkin, R. '"Natural Law" Revisited.' *Univ. of Florida L. R.* (1982)

---------------- *A Matter of Principle* (Cambridge, Mass: Harvard Univ. Press, 1985)

---------------- *Freedom's Law: The Moral Reading of the American Constitution* (Cambridge, Mass.: Harvard Univ. Press, 1996)

---------------- *Taking Rights Seriously* (Cambridge, Mass: Harvard Univ. Press, 1977)

Eastwood, David. 'Robert Southey and The Intellectual Origins of Romantic Conservatism.' *English Hist. Journal* 105 (1989) 308.

Elias, T.O. *The Nature of African Customary Law* (Manchester: Manchester Univ. Press, 1956).

Ellis, J. *Seven Against Christ: A Study of 'Essays and Reviews'* (Leiden: E.J. Brill, 1980)

Ely, R. 'Democracy and the Right to be Different.' *New York Univ. L.Rev.* 56 (1981) 397.

Emerson, Roger L. 'Conjectural History and Scottish Philosophers.' *Historical Papers* (1984)

Emery, Walter B. *Egypt in Nubia* (London: Hutchinson, 1965)

Engberg, Robert M. *The Hyksos Reconsidered* (Chicago: Univ. of Chicago Press, 1939)

Epstein, Klaus. *The Genesis of German Conservatism* (Princeton, N.J.: Princeton Univ. Press, 1966)

Eterovich, F.H. *Approaches to Natural Law* (New York: Exposition Press 1972)

Evans, Elizabeth C. 'The Study of Physiognomy in the Second Century A.D.' *Transactions of American Philological Association* 72 (1941) 96.

---------------- 'Galen, the Physician as Physiognomist.' *Transactions of American Philological Association* 76 (1945) 287

Evans, William Mckee. 'From the Land of Canaan to the Land of Guinea: The Strange Odyssey of the "Sons of Ham"'. *American Hist. Rev.* (1980) 15.

Evans-Jones, Robin. Ed. *The Civil Law Tradition in Scotland* (Edinburgh: The Stair Society, 1995).

Ewald, Janet E. *Soldiers, Traders, and Slaves: State Formation and Economic Transformation in the Greater Nile Valley, 1700-1885* (Madison: Univ. of Wisconsin Press, 1990)

Ewald, William. 'Comparative Jurisprudence (I): What Was it Like to Try a Rat?' *Univ. of Pa. L.R.* 143 (1995) 1889.

Eze, E.C. 'The Color of Reason: The Idea of 'Race' in Kant's Anthropology.' In, *Anthropology and The German Enlightenment* ed. Katherine M. Faull (Lewisburg: Bucknell Univ. Press, 1995) 200.

Farr, James & Roberts, Clayton. 'John Locke on the Glorious Revolution: A Rediscovered Document.' *Historical Journal* 28 (1985) 385.

Farrington, B. *Science and Politics in the Ancient World* (London: George Allen & Unwin 1939)

Feldman, Stephen M. 'The New Metaphysics: The Interpretive Turn in Jurisprudence.' *Iowa L.Rev.* 76 (1991)

---------------- 'Republic Revival/Interpretive Turn'. *Wisconsin L.R.* (1992) 679.

Ferry, Luc. *Political Philosophy* 2 Vols. Trans. Franklin Philip (Chicago: Univ. of Chicago Press, 1990)

Fifoot, C.H.S. *English Law and Its Background* (London: G. Bell, 1932)

Finer, S.E. *The History of Government from the Earliest Times Vol. I: Ancient Monarchies and Empires* (Oxford: Oxford Univ. Press, 1999)

Finley, M.I. 'Athenian Demagogues.' *Past and Present* 21 (1962) 3.

--------------- ed. *Slavery in Classical Antiquity* (Cambridge: W. Heffer & Sons, 1960)

-------------- *The World of Odysseus* 2nd ed. (London: Penguine Books, 1991)

Finnish, John. *Natural Law and Natural Rights* (Oxford: Clarendon Press, 1980)

Fish, Stanley. *Doing What Comes Naturally* (Duke Univ. press, 1989)

Fisher, William W. III. 'The Development of Modern American Legal Theory and the Judicial Interpretation of the Bill of Rights.' In, *A Culture of Rights: The Bill of Rights in Philosophy, Politics and Law, 1791-1991* ed. Michael J. Lacey & Knud Haskonssen (Cambridge: Cambridge Univ. Press, 1991) 266.

Flathman, Richard. 'Liberalism and the Suspect Enterprise of Political Institutionalization: The Case of the Rule of Law.' *Nomos: The Rule of Law* XXXVI (1994) 297.

Fletcher, George P. *Basic Concepts of Legal Thought* (New York: Oxford Univ. Press, 1996)

---------------------- *Loyalty: An Essay on the Morality of Relationships* (New York: Oxford Univ. Press 1993)

---------------------- *Rethinking Criminal Law* (Toronto: Little, Brown 1978)

Flew, A.G.N. 'Introduction'. In *Essays on Logic and Language*. First Series (Oxford: Basil Blackwell, 1963)

Fodor, Jerry A. *Concepts* (Oxford: Clarendon Press, 1998)

Ford, T.H. *Albert Venn Dicey: The Man and His Times* (Chichester: Barry Rose Publishers 1985)

Fowler, W. Warde. *The City-States of the Greeks and Romans* (London: Macmillan, 1913)

Frame, Grant. *Rulers of Babylonia From the Second Dynasty of Isin to the End of Assyrian Domination, 1157-612 B.C.* (Toronto: Univ. of Toronto Press, 1997)

Frankford, David M. 'The Critical Potential of the Common Law Tradition.' [Book Review] *Col. L.R.* (1994) 1076.

Frankfort, H.A. *Before Philosophy: The Intellectual Adventures of Ancient Man* (1946).

Frankfurt, H. 'Freedom of the Will and the Concept of a Person.' *Journal of Philosophy* 60 1971) 5.

Freeman, Michael. 'The Philosophical Foundations of Human Rights.' *Human Rights Quarterly* 16 (1994) 491

Frege, G. *The Foundations of Mathematics* (1884) (Illinois: Northwestern Univ. Press, 1968)

Freund, Kahn O. 'Reflections on Legal Education.' *Modern L.R.* 29 (1968) 121.

Friedman, Richard E. *Who Wrote the Bible?* (New York: Summit Books, 1987)

Friedrich, Carl J. 'The Political Thought of Neo-liberalism.' *Am. Pol .Sc. Rev*. 49 (1955) 509.

--------------------- *Philosophy of Law in Historical Perspective* 2nd ed. (Chicago & London: Univ. of Chicago Press, 1963)

Frisch, H. *Might and Right in Antiquity*, trans C.C. Martindale (Denmark, Gyldendalsk Boghandil, 1950)

Fukuyama, F. *Trust: The Social Virtues and the Creation of Prosperity* (London: Hamish Hamilton, 1995)

---------------- *The End of History and the Last Man* (New York: Free Press, 1991)

---------------- *The Great Disruption: Human Nature and the Reconstitution of Social Order* (New York: Free Press, 1999)

---------------- 'Social Capital, Civil Society, and Development.' *Third World Quarterly* 22 (2001) 7.

Fuller, Lon L. 'Positivism and Fidelity to Law: A Reply to Professor Hart.' *Harvard L.Rev.* 71 (1958) 630.

Fuller, R. Buckminster. *Critical Path* (New York: St. Martin's Press, 1981)

Gadamer, Georg. *Truth and Method* (New York: Seabury Press, 1975)

Gailbraith, J.K. *American Capitalism: The Concept of Countervailing Power* (1980 ed.)

Gairdner, William D. *The Trouble With Canada: A Citizen Speaks Out* rev. ed. (Toronto: Stoddart Publishing Co. 1994)

Gale, Susan Gaylord. 'A Very German Legal Science: Savigny and the Historical School.' *Stanford J. of International Law* 18 (1982) 123.

Gebhardt, Jurgen. 'Leo Strauss: The Quest for Truth in Times of Perplexity'. In, *Hannah Arendt & Leo Strauss: German Emigres and American Political Thought After World War II* ed. Peter Graf Kielmansegg et al (Washington, D.C.: German Historical Institute, 1995) 81.

Geetz, Clifford. *Local Knowledge: Further Essays in Interpretive Anthropology* (New York: Basic Book 1985)

------------------ 'The Uses of Diversity.' *Michigan Quarterly* 26 (1986) 105.

------------------ 'Anti-anti-Relativism.' In *Relativism: Interpretation and Confrontation* ed. Michael Krauz (Notre Dame Univ. Press, 1989)

Genevese, E. *Roll, Jordan Roll: The World the Slaves Made* (New York: Pantheon Books 1976)

Genovese, E.D. 'Critical Legal Studies as Radical Politics and World View.' *Yale Journal of Law and Humanities* 3 (1991) 131.

Gerhard, Dietrich. *Old Europe: A Study in Continuity, 1000-1800* (New York: Academic Press, 1981)

Gibbon, Edward. *The Decline and Fall of the Roman Empire*, Vol. V.

Gierke, Otto. *Natural Law and the Theory of Society*, trans. Ernest Barker (Cambridge: Cambridge Univ. Press, 1933)

Gilson, Etienne. *The Unity of Philosophical Experience* (New York: Charles Scribner's, 1965)

Ginzberg, Louis. *The Legends of the Jews*, 6 Vols. Trans. Henrietta Szold (Philadelphia: The Jewish Publication Society of America, 1909)

Glanvill, Joseph. *The Vanity of Dogmatizing: The Three Versions* (1676) ed. S. Medcalf (Sussex: Harvester Press, 1970

Goldberg, David Theo. *Racist Culture: Philosophy and the Politics of Meaning* (London: Blackwell, 1993)

Goldin, G. 'Jericho: The Archaeological Problem.' 50 *Hibbert Journal* 130.

Golding, M.P. 'Kelsen and the Concept of 'Legal System'. *Archiv fur Rechts Und Sozialphilosophie* 47 (1961) 355.

Goldstein, R.J. *Political Repression in 19th Century Europe* (London: Croom Helm, 1983)

Gomme, A.W. *The Greek Attitude to Poetry and History* (Berkeley: Univ. of California Press, 1954)

Goodman, Gordon L. 'Liberal Unionism: The Revolt of the Whigs.' *Victorian Studies* (1959) 173.

Goody, Jack. *The Domestication of the Savage Mind* (Cambridge: Cambridge Univ. Press, 1977)

---------------- *The Logic of Writing and the Organization of Society* (Cambridge: Cambridge Univ. Press, 1986)

Gordon, Cyrus H. *Before the Bible: The Common Background of Greek and Hebrew* (London: Collins Clear-Type Press, 1962)

Gower, L.C.B. *Independent Africa* (Cambridge, Mass.: Harvard Univ. Press, 1967)

Granfield, David. *The Inner Experience of Law: A Jurisprudence of Subjectivity* (Washington, D.C.: Catholic Univ. of America Press, 1988)

Grant, Mary trans. & ed. *The Myths of Hyginus, Poetica Astronomica* (Univ. of Kansas Publications, Humanistic Studies, No. 34, 1960)

Green, Leslie. '*The Concept of Law* Revisited' [Book Review] *Mich. L.R.* 94 (1994) 1682.

Greene, John C. 'The American Debate on the Negro's Place in Nature 1780-1815.' *Journal of the Hist. of Ideas* 15 (1954) 384.

Greene, Mott T. *Natural Knowledge in Pre-Classical Antiquity* (Baltimore & London: Johns Hopkins Univ. press, 1992).

Gregor, Mary. 'Kant on Welfare Legislation.' In *Poverty, Justice, and the Law: New Essays on Needs, Rights, and Obligations* ed. George R. Lucas, Jr. (Univ. Press of America, 1986) 49.

Grimke, Frederick. *The Nature and Tendency of Free Institutions* (1848) ed. J.W. Ward (Cambridge, Mass., 1968)

Gummere, Richard M. *The American Colonial Mind and The Classical Tradition: Essays in Comparative Culture* (Cambridge, Mass.: Harvard Univ. Press, 1963).

Gunn, Battiscombe & Gardiner, Alan H. 'New Renderings of Egyptian Texts.' *Journal of Egyptian Archaeology* V (1918) 36.

Guthrie, W.K.C. *The Sophists* (Cambridge: Cambridge Univ. Press, 1971)

Gyekye, Kwame. *An Essay on African Philosophical Thought: The Akan Conceptual Scheme* rev. ed. (Philadelphia: Temple Univ. Press, 1989)

Habermas, J. *The New Conservatism: Cultural Criticism and the Historians' Debate*. Ed. & trans. S. W. Nicholsen (Cambridge, Mass.: MIT Press, 1989)

Hacker, P.M.S. 'Hart's Philosophy of Law'. In, *Law, Morality, and Society: Essays in Honour of H.L.A. Hart,* ed. P.M.S. Hacker & J. Raz (Oxford: Clarendon Press, 1977) 1.

---------------- *Wittgenstein's Place in Twentieth-Century Analytic Philosophy* (Oxford: Blackwell, 1996)

---------------- *Insight and Illusion: Themes in the Philosophy of Wittgenstein,* rev. ed. (Oxford: Clarendon Press, 1989).

Hadot. P. *Philosophy as a Way of Life* (Oxford: Blackwell, 1995)

Hailsham, Lord. *Hamlyn Revisited* (London: Sweet & Maxwell, 1983)

Hale, Matthew Sir. *History of the Pleas of the Crown*

Halevy, E. *The Growth of Philosophic Radicalism*. (London: Faber & Faber, 1928)

Hall, H.R. 'Keftiu and the Peoples of the Sea', *Annual of the British School at Athens* 8 (1901-02) 157.

Hall, Jerome. *General Principles of Criminal Law*, 2nd ed. (New York: Bobbs-Merill, 1960)

--------------- *Foundations of Jurisprudence* (Indianapolis: Bobbs-Merill, 1973)

Hall, John A. *Powers and Liberties: The Causes and Consequences of the Rise of the West* (Oxford: Basil Blackwell, 1985)
---------------- *Liberalism: Politics, Ideology, and the Market* (Chapel Hill: Univ. of North Carolina Press, 1988)
Hallowell, John H. 'Plato and His Critics.' *Journal of Politics* 27 (1965) 273.
Hamburger, Max. *The Awakening of Western Legal Thought* (1942) trans. Bernard Miall (Westport, Connecticut: Greenwood Press, 1970 rep).
Hamilton, Edith. *The Greek Way* (New York: W.W. Norton 1930)
Hamilton, Mark W. 'The Past as Destiny: Historical Visions in Samal and Judah Under Assyrian Hegemony.' *Harvard Theological Rev.* 91 (1998) 215.
Harding, Sandra. 'The Curious Coincidence of Feminine and African Moralities: Challenges for Feminist Theory.' In *Women and Moray Theory*, ed. Kittay & Meyers (Ottawa: Rowmans & Littlefield, 1987).
Harrington, Anne. *Reenchanted Science: Holism in German Culture From Wilhelm II to Hitler* (Princeton, N.J.: Princeton Univ. Press, 1996)
Harris, Ian. 'Locke's Political Theory.' In, *British Philosophy and the Age of Enlightenment* ed. Stuart Brown (London & New York: Routledge, 1996) 96.
------------- *The Mind of John Locke: A Study of Political Theory in its Intellectual Setting* (Cambridge: Cambridge Univ. Press 1994)
Harrison, Ross. *Bentham* (London: Routledge & Kegal Paul, 1983)
Harris-Schan, Beverly. *Black Images in Eighteenth Century German Literature* (Stuttgert, 1981)
Hart, H.L.A. 'American Jurisprudence Through English Eyes: The Nightmare and the Noble Dream.' *Georgia L. Rev.* 11 (1977) 969.
---------------- 'Analytical Jurisprudence in Mid-20th century: A Reply to Professor Bodenheimer.' *Univ. of Penn. L.R.* 104 (1957).
---------------- 'Austin, John.' In, *International Encyclopedia of the Social Sciences*, vol. 1 (Macmillan, 1968).
---------------- 'Positivism and the Separation of Law and Morals.' *Harvard L. Rev.* 71 (1958)
---------------- *The Concept of Law* (Oxford: Clarendon Press, 1961)
Harvie, Christopher. *The Lights of Liberalism: University Liberals and the Challenge of Democracy, 1860-86* (London: Allen Lane 1976)
Hasan, Yusuf Fadl. *The Arabs and the Sudan: From the Seventh to the Early Sixteenth Century* (Edinburgh Univ. Press 1967)

Havelock, Eric A. *The Greek Concept of Justice From Its Shadow in Homer to Its Substance in Plato* (Cambridge, Mass.: Harvard Univ. Press, 1978)

---------------- *The Liberal Temper in Greek Politics* (New Haven: Yale Univ. Press, 1964)

Hay, D. 'Property, Authority and the Criminal Law.' In, *Albion's Fatal Tree*, ed. D. Hay et al (New York: Pantheon Books, 1975)

Hayek, F.A. *Law, Legislation and Liberty* 3 Vols. (Chicago: Univ. of Chicago Press,)

-------------- *The Constitution of Liberty* (London: Routledge & Kegal Paul 1960)

-------------- *The Road to Serfdom* (Chicago: Univ. of Chicago Press, 1944)

Hayes, William C. *A Papyrus of the Late Middle Kingdom in the Brooklyn Museum* (Brooklyn Museum, 1955)

Hayford, J.E. Casely. *Ethiopia Unbound* 2nd ed. (London: Frank Cass, 1969)

Hayward Fred M. ed. *Elections in Independent Africa* (London: Westview Press, 1987)

Hazard, Paul. *The European Mind 1680-1715* (London: Hollis & Carter, 1953)

Hearn, William E. *The Government of England: Its Structure and Its Development*, 2nd ed. (Melbourne: George Robertson & Co. 1886)

Heather, P.J. *Goths and Romans, 332-489* (Oxford: Clarendon Press, 1991)

Hegel, G.W.F. *The Philosophy of Right and the Philosophy of History* 46 Great Books of the Western World. Encyclopedia Britannica, Inc. 1952.

Heidegger, Martin. 'Letter on Humanism'. In *Basic Writings*, 193.

Held, David. *Models of Democracy*. (Stanford: Stanford Univ. Press, 1987)

Helgerson, Richard. *Forms of Nationhood: The Elizabethan Writing of England* (Chicago & London: Univ. of Chicago Press, 1991)

Herbst, Jurgen. *The German Historical School in American Scholarship: A Study in the Transfer of Culture* (Ithaca, N.Y.: Cornell Univ. Press, 1965)

Herm, Gerhard. *The Phoenicians: The Purple Empire of the Ancient World*, trans. Cartline Hillier (London: Victor Gollowicz, 1975)

Hermann, Donald H.J. 'Phenomenology, Structuralism, Hermeneutics, and Legal Study: Application of Contemporary Continental Thought to Legal Phenomena.' *Univ. of Miami L.R.* 36 (1982).

Hernnstein, Richard J. and Murray, Charles. *The Bell Curve: Intelligence and Class Structure in American Life* (New York: Free Press, 1994).

Herodotus. *Histories*. Trans. David Grene (Chicago: Univ. of Chicago Press, 1987)

Hershberg, James G. *James B. Conant: Harvard to Hiroshima and the Making of the Nuclear Age* (New York: Alfred A. Knopf, 1993).

Herzog, Don. *Without Foundations: Justification in Political Theory* (Ithaca & London: Cornell Univ. Press, 1985)

Hewitson, Mark. *National Identity and Political Thought in Germany: Wilhelmine Depictions of the French Third Republic, 1890-1914* (Oxford: Clarendon Press, 2000)

Hibbits, Bernard J. 'The Politics of Principle: Albert Venn Dicey and The Rule fo Law.' *Anglo-American L.Rev.* 23 (1994) 18.

Hill, H. H. 'H.L.A. Hart's Hermeneutic Positivism: On Some Methodological Difficulties in *The Concept of Law*.' *Canadian Journal of Law and Jurisprudence* 3 (1990) 113.

Himmerfarb, G. *Poverty and Compassion: The Moral Imagination of the Late Victorians* (New York: Alfred Knopf, 1991).

Hippocrates. 'Airs, Waters, Places.' In *1 Hippocrates* trans. W.H.S. Jones (London: Heinemann, 1923) Loeb Classical Library.

Hiskett, Mervyn. *The Sword of Truth: The Life and Times of the Shehu Usuman Dan Fodio* 2nd ed. (Northwestern Univ. Press, 1994)

Hobbes, Thomas. *Leviathan* ed. W.G. Pogson-Smith (Oxford: Clarendon Press, 1909)

Hobhouse, L.T. *Liberalism* (1911) (Oxford: Univ. Press, 1964)

Hoeflich, M.H. 'John Austin and Joseph Story: Two Nineteenth Century Perspectives on the Utility of the Civil Law for the Common Lawyer.' *Am. J. of Legal Hist.* 29 (1985) 36.

------------------ 'Transatlantic Friendships and the German Influence on American Law in the First Half of the 19th century.' *American J. of Comp. Law* 35 (1987) 599.

Hof, Ulrich. *The Enlightenment* (Oxford: Blackwell 1994)

Holdsworth, W.S. 'Gibbon, Blackstone and Bentham.' *Law Quarterly Rev.* 52 (1936)

Holmes, O.W. Jr. 'The Path of the Law.' *Harvard L.Rev.* 10 (1897) 457.

Hollinger, David. A. *Science, Jews and Secular Culture: Studies in Mid 20th Century American Intellectual History* (Princeton, N.J.: Princeton Univ. Press, 1996)

Homer. *The Odyssey*, trans. A.T. Murray (London: Heinemann, 1919)

Hopfl, H.M. 'From Savage to Scotman: Conjectural History in the Scottish Enlightenment.' *J. of British Studies* 17 (1978) 19.

Hourani, George F. 'The Education of the Third Class in Plato's Republic.' *Classical Quarterly* XLIII (1949) 58.

Howard, Michael. *The Lessons of History* (Oxford: Clarendon Press 1991)

Howard, Roy J. *Three Faces of Hermeneutics: An Introduction to Current Theories of Understanding* (Berkeley: Univ. of California Press, 1982)

Howard, Thomas A. *Religion and the Rise of Historicism* (Cambridge Univ. Press, 2000)

Howe, Marke DeWolfe. 'The Positivism of Mr. Justice Holmes.' *Harvard L.R.* 64 (1951) 529.

Hsing-lang, Chang. 'The Importation of Negro Slaves into China under the T'ang dynasty: A.D. 618-907.' *Bulletin of the Catholic Univ. of Peking* 7 (1930)

Hull, N.E.H. *Roscoe Pound & Karl Llewellyn: Searching for an American Jurisprudence* (Chicago & London: Univ. of Chic. Press, 1997)

---------------- 'The Romantic Realist: Art, Literature, and the Enduring Legacy of Karl Llewellyn's "Jurisprudence".' *Am. J. of Legal Hist.* 40 (1996) 115.

Hume, David. *Philosophical Works*, ed. T.H. Green & T.H. Grose.

Hunting, Claudine. 'The Philosophers and Black Slavery, 1748-1765.' *Journal of the Hist. of Ideas* 39 (1978) 405.

Hurd, Heidi M. 'Relativistic Jurisprudence: Skepticism Founded on Confusion.' *South Cal. L.R.* 161 (1988) 1417.

Husserl, Edward. *Phenomenology and the Crisis of Philosophy.* Trans. Quentin Lauer (New York: Harper & Row, 1965)

Huttenback, R.A. 'The British Empire as a "White Man's Country" – Racial Attitudes and Immigration Legislation in the Colonies of White Settlement.' *Journal of British Studies* 13 (1973) 108.

Iggers, Georg G. *The German Conception of History: The National Tradition of Historical Thought from Herder to the Present* Rev. Ed. (Middletown, Conn.: Wesleyan Univ. Press, 1983)

Immerwah, John. 'Hume's Revised Racism.' *Journal of the History of Ideas* 53 (1992) 481.

Inglis, B. *Poverty and the Industrial Revolution* (London: Hodder & Stoughton, 1971)

Irwin, I.T. 'Socrates and the Athenian Democracy.' *Philosophy and Public Affairs* 18 (1989) 184.

Issawi, Charles ed. *The Economic History of Iran, 1800-1914* (Chicago: Univ. of Chicago Press 1971)

Jacob, Margaret C. *The Radical Enlightenment: Pantheists, Freemasons and Republicans* (London: George Allen & Unwin, 1981)

---------------- *Scientific Culture and the Making of the Industrial West* (New York: Oxford Univ. Press, 1997)

Jacquette, Dale. *Wittgenstein's Thought in Transition.* (West Lafayette, Indiana: Purdue Univ. Press, 1998)

Jaffa, Harry V. *Original Intention and the Framers of the Constitution: A Disputed Question* (Washington, D.C.: Regnery Gateway, 1994)

---------------- 'The Truth About Leo Strauss.' *Chronicle of Higher Education*, December 5, 1997, B.11.

James, Lawrence. *The Savage Wars: British Campaigns in Africa, 1870-1920* (London: Robert Hale, 1985)

James, William. *Essays in Pragmatism* ed. A. Castell (New York: Hafner, 1948)_

Jameson, Fredric. *The Ideologies of Theory Essays 1971-1986* (Minneapolis: Univ. of Minnesota Press, 1988)

Janik, Allan and Toulmin, Stephen. *Wittgenstein's Vienna* (New York: Simon & Schuster, 1973).

Jarausch, Konrad. H. 'The Institutionalization of History in 18th Century Germany.' In *Aufklarund Und Geschichte Studien zur deutschen Geschitswissenschaft in 18. Jahrhundert* ed. H.E. Bodeker et al , (Vandenhoeck & Ruprecht) 625.

John, Michael. *Politics and the Law in Late Nineteenth-Century Germany: The Origins of the Civil Code* (Oxford: Clarendon Press, 1989)

Johnson, James W. *The Formation of English Neo-classical Thought* (Princeton, 1967).

Johnston, David. *The Idea of a Liberal Theory* (Princeton, N.J.: Princeton Univ. Press, 1994)

Jones, A.H.M. 'The Athenian Democracy and Its Critics.' *Cambridge Historical Journal* 11 (1953) 1.

Jordan, W.D. *White Over Black* (Chapel Hill: Univ. of Carolina Press, 1968)

Josephus. *Antiquities of the Jews.*

---------------- *The War of the Jews*

July, Robert W. *The Origins of Modern African Thought* (New York: Frederick A. Praeger, 1967)

Kahn, Charles H. 'Some Remarks on the Origins of Greek Science and Philosophy'. In *Classical Greece* ed. Alan C. Bowen (New York & London: Garland Publishing, 1991) 1.

---------------- *The Art and Thought of Heraclitus*

Kallet-Marx, Lisa. 'Institutions, Ideology, and Political Consciousness in Ancient Greece: Some Recent Books in Athenian Democracy.' *Journal of the Hist. of Ideas* 55 (1994) 307.

Kant, I. *Logic*. Trans. Robert S. Hartman & Wolfgang Schwartz (New York: Dover Publications, 1988)

---------------- 'On the Different Races of Man.' (1775) in *This is Race* ed. Earl W. Count (New York: Henry Schuman, 1950)

---------------- 'On the Forms and Principles of the Sensuous and Intellectual Worlds.' (1770) in, Gabriele Rabel, *Kant* (Oxford: Clarendon Press, 1963).

---------------- *Observations on the Feeling of the Beautiful and Sublime*, trans.J.T. Goldthwait (Berkeley: Univ. of California Press, 1960).

---------------- *Perpetual Peace and Other Essays*, trans. T. Humphrey (Indianapolis: Hackett Publishing Co. 1983)

---------------- *The Metaphysics of Morals*. Trans. Mary Gregor (Cambridge: Cambridge Univ. Press, 1991)

Kantorowicz, Herman. 'Savigny and the Historical School of Law'. *Law Quarterly Rev*. 37 (1937) 326.

Kantz, Steven. *Liberalism and Community* (Ithaca & London: Cornell Univ. Press 1995)

Kebel, Thomas E. 'Scientific Racism in the Philosophy of Science: Some Historical Examples.' *Philosophical Forum* 22 (1990) 1.

Kelley, D.R. *The Human Measure: Social Thought in the Western Legal Tradition* (Harvard Univ. Press, 1990)

---------------- '"Second Nature": The Idea of Custom in European Law, Society and Culture.' In, *The Transmission of Culture in Early Modern Europe* ed. Anthony Grafton & Ann Blair (Philadelphia: Univ. of Philadelphia Press, 1990)

---------------- 'The Old Cultural History'. *History of the Human Sciences* 9 (1996) 101

Kelley, George A. 'Veils: The Poetics of John Rawls.' *Journal of the History. of Ideas* 57 (1996) 343.

Kelsen, H. 'The Philosophy of Aristotle and the Hellenic-Macedonian Policy.' *International Journal of Ethics* XLVIII (1937) 1.

---------------- 'The Pure Theory of Law.' *Law Quarterly Rev*. 50 (1934) 474.

----------------- *General Theory of Law and State* (Cambridge, Mass.: Harvard Univ. Press, 1946)

Kerfeld, G.B. *The Sophistic Movement* (Cambridge: Cambridge Univ. Press, 1981)

Keynes, J.M. *Essays in Persuasion* (London: MacMillan, 1932)

Kinglake, A.W. *Eothen* (London: Longmans, Burne and Green, 1852)

Kingsley, C. *Lectures Delivered in America in 1874* (Philadelphia: Jos H. Coates, 1875)

Kirk, Russel. *Enemies of the Permanent Things: Observations of Abnormity in Literature and Politics* (New York: Arlington House, 1969)

----------------- *The Roots of American Order* (LaSalle, Illinois, Open Court, 1974)

Kitch, Edward W. 'The Fire of Truth: A Remembrance of Law and Economics at Chicago, 1932-1970.' *Journal of Law and Economics* 26 (1983) 163.

Kitchen, K.A. *The Third Intermediate Period in Egypt, 1100-650 B.C.*

Kitson-Clark, G.R.S. *The Critical Historian* (London: Heinemann, 1967)

Knight, F.H. 'Political Responsibility in a Democracy.' *Nomos: Responsibility* III (1960) 171.

Knowles, David. *The Evolution of Medieval Thought* (London: Longmans, 1962)

Kraeling, Emil G. *The Brooklyn Museum Aramaic Papyri: New Documents of the Fifth Century B.C. from the Jewish Colony at Elephantine* (New Haven: Yale Univ. Press 1954)

Kramer, Isaac. *History Begins at Sumer* 2nd ed. (London: Thames and Hudson, 1961)

Kramer, Samuel N. *Sumerian Mythology* rev. ed. (New York: Harper & Bros, 1961)

Kramer, Samuel N. *The Sumerians: Their History, Culture and Character* (Chicago: Univ. of Chicago Press 1963)

Krammick, Isaac. 'Eighteenth Century Science and Radical Social Theory: The Case of Joseph Priestley's Scientific Liberty.' *Journal of British Studies* 25 (1985) 1.

Kriegel, A.D. 'Liberty and Whiggery in Early 19th Century England.' *Journal of Modern History* 52 (1980) 253.

Kriegel, Blaudine. *The State and the Rule of Law*. Trans. Marc A. LePain & Jeffrey C. Cohen (Princeton, N.J.: Princeton Univ. Press, 1995).

Kristol, Irving. *Two Cheers for Capitalism* (New York: Basic Books, 1978).

Kronman, Anthony T. 'Precedent and Tradition'. *Yale L.J.* 99 (1990) 1029

Kuhn, Thomas S. *The Structure of Scientific Revolutions*, 3rd ed. (Chicago: Univ. of Chicago Press, 1996)

Kymlicka, Will. *Liberalism, Community and Culture* (Oxford: Clarendon Press, 1989)

Ladd, Barbara. *Nationalism and The Color Line in George W. Cable, Mark Twain and W. Faulkon* (Lousiana State Univ. Press, 1996)

Ladimeji, O.A. 'Nationalism, Alienation and The Crisis of Ideology.' 46 *Transition* 38.

Lambert, W.G. 'History and the Gods: A Review Article.' *Orientalia* 39 (1970) 170.

Larsen, J.A.O. 'The Origin and Significance of the Counting of Votes.' *Classical Philology* 44 (1949) 164.

Laski, H. 'The Crisis in the Theory of the State.' In *Law, A Century of Progress 1835-1935* (New York: New York Univ. Press, 1937)

Laslett, Peter. 'The English Revolution and Locke's Two Treatise of Government.' *The Cambridge Historical Journal* 12 (1956) 41

Lazare, Daniel. *The Frozen Republic: How the Constitution is Paralyzing Dem*ocracy (New York: Harcourt Brace, 1996)

Lebovics, Herman. *Social Conservatism and the Middle Classes in Germany, 1914-1933* (Princeton, N.J.: Princeton Univ. Press, 1969)

Leff, Arthur A. 'Economic Analysis of Law: Some Realism about Nominalism.' *Virginia L. Rev.* 60 (1974) 451.

Leftkowitz, Mary and Rogers, Gary Maclean ed. *Black Athena Revisited* (Chapel Hill & London: Univ. of North Carolina Press 1996)

Leftkowitz, Mary. *Not Out of Africa* (New York, 1994)

Lenoble, Jacques. 'Narrative Coherence and the Limits of the Hermeneutic Paradigm.' In *Law, Interpretation, and Reality: Essays in Epistemology, Hermeneutics, and Jurisprudence* ed. P. Nerhot (Dordrecht: Kluwer Academic Publisher, 1990). 127.

Levine, Joseph M. *Humanism and History* (Ithaca: Cornell Univ. Press, 1987)

Levine, Peter. *Nietzsche and the Modern Crisis of the Humanities* (Albany, N.Y.: State Univ. of New York Press, 1995)

Levinson, S. and Maillox, Steven ed. *Interpreting Law and Literature: A Hermeneutic Reader* (Evaston, Il: Northwestern Univ. Press, 1988)

Levitt, Norman. *Prometheus Bedevilled: Science and the Contradictions of Contemporary Culture* (New Brunswick: Rutgers Univ. Press, 1999)

Lewis, Bernard. *Race and Slavery in the Middle East: An Historical Inquiry* (New York: Oxford Univ. Press 1990)

Lewis, C.S. 'Historicism.' In *God, History and Historians* ed. C.T. MacIntire (New York: Oxford Univ. Press 1977)

Lissner, Ivar. *The Living Past.* Trans. J. Maxwell Brownjohn (New York: G.P. Putnam & Sons, 1957)

Little, K.L. *Negroes in Britain* (London: Keagan Paul, 1948)

Lo, Ping-Cheun. 'A Critical Reevaluation of the Alleged 'Empty Formalism' of Kantian Ethics'. *Ethics* 91 (1981) 181.

Lobban, Michael. 'Was There a Nineteenth Century "English School of Jurisprudence"?' *J. of Legal History* 16 (1995) 34.

----------------- *The Common Law and English Jurisprudence, 1760-1850* (Cambridge: Cambridge Univ. Press, 1991)

Locke, John. *Concerning Civil Government: Second Essay* (Great Books of the Western World, Encyclopedia Britannica, 1952)

----------------- *Essay Concerning Human Understanding*

-----------------*Questions Concerning the Law of Nature.* Trans. R. Horwitz, et al (Ithaca: Cornell Univ. Press, 1990)

Long, Douglas G. *Bentham on Liberty* (Toronto: Univ. of Toronto Press, 1977)

Loughlin, Martin. *Public Law and Political Theory* (Oxford: Clarendon Press, 1992)

Lovejoy, Arthur O. and Boas, George. *Primitivism and Related Ideas in Antiquity* (1935) (New York: Octagon Books, Inc., 1965)

Lovejoy, Arthur O. *The Great Chain of Being* (Cambridge, Mass.: Harvard Univ. Press, 1936)

Lovejoy, Paul E. *Slow Death for Slavery: The Course of Abolition in Northern Nigeria, 1897-1936* (Cambridge: Cambridge Univ. Press, 1993)

Lowith, Karl. Martin *Heidegger and European Nihilism* ed. Richard Wolin. Trans. Gary Steiner (New York: Columbia Univ. Press, 1995)

Ludovici, Anthony M. *A Defence of Aristocracy: A Text Book for Tories* rev. ed. (London: Constable & Co. 1933)

Lupoi, Maurizio. *The Origins of the European Legal Order* (Cambridge: Cambridge Univ. Press, 2000)

Lurie, Yuval. 'Culture as a Human Form of Life: A Romantic Reading of Wittgenstein.' *International Philosophical Quarterly* 32 (1992) 193.

MacCormick, D. Neil & Robert S. Summers. 'On Method and Methodology.' In, *Interpreting Statutes: A Comparative Study*, ed. D. Neil MacCormick and Robert S. Summers (Dartmouth, 1991).

MacCormick, Neil. *Legal Right and Social Democracy* (Oxford Clarendon Press, 1982)

MacDougall, Hugh A. *Racial Myth in English History* (Montreal: Harvest House 1982)

Maceboy, R. 'The Public Morality of the Rule of Law: A Critique of Ronald Dworkin.' *Harvard Journal of Law & Pub. Policy* 8 (1985) 79.

Macedo, Stephen. *Liberal Virtues: Citizenship, Virtue, and Community in Liberal Constitutionalism* (Oxford: Clarendon Press, 1990)

---------------- *The New Right v. The Constitution* (Washington: Cato Institute, 1986)

Macey, Jonathan R. and Miller, Geoffrey P. 'The End of History and the New World Order: The Triumph of Capitalism and the Competition Between Liberalism and Democracy.' *Cornell International L.J.* 25 (1992) 277.

MacIntyre, A. *After Virtue* (Notre Dame: Univ. of Notre Dame Press, 1981)

---------------- *Three Rival Versions of Moral Enquiry: Encyclopaedia, Genealogy, and Tradition* (Notre Dame: Univ. of Notre Dame Press, 1990)

---------------- *Whose Reason? Whose Justice?* (Notre Dame: Univ. of Notre Dame Press, 1988)

MacKenzie, Donald A. *Crete and Pre-Hellenic Europe* (1917) (Random House, 1995)

MacPherson, C.B. *The Political Theory of Possessive Individualism* (Oxford: Oxford Univ. Press, 1962)

Maine, Henry S. *Village Communities: East and West* 7th ed. (London: John Murray 1913)

Mama, Amina. *Beyond the Masks: Race, Gender and Subjectivity* (London & New York: Routledge, 1995).

Mann, Michael. 'The Social Cohesion of Liberal Democracy.' *Am. Sociological Rev.* 35 (1970) 423.

Mann, Susan. 'The Universe and The Library: A Critique of James Boyd White as Writer and Reader.' *Stanford L.Rev.* 41 (1989) 959.

Mannheim, *Ideology and Utopia* (New York: Harcourt Brace & World, 1968)

Manuel, Frank E. *The Eighteenth Century Confronts the Gods* (Cambridge, Mass.: Harvard Univ. Press, 1959)

Marmor, Andrei ed. *Law and Interpretation: Essays in Legal Philosophy* (Oxford: Clarendon Press, 1995)

Martin, Julian. *Francis Bacon, the State and the Reform of Natural Philosophy* (Cambridge: Cambridge Univ. Press, 1992)

Marx, Werner. *Is There a Measure on Earth? Foundations for a Nonmetaphysical Ethics*. Trans. Thomas J. Nenon and Reginald Lilly (Chicago & London: Univ. of Chicago Press, 1987)

Masonen, Pekka. 'The Negroland Revisited: Discovery and Invention of the Sudanese Middle Ages.' *Annales Academiae Scientiarum Fennica* (2000).

Mazlish, Bruce. *The Uncertain Sciences* (New Haven & London: Yale Univ. Press, 1998)

Mazor, Lester J. 'The Polarization of American Legal Theory.' *Archives for Phil. Of Law and Social Philosophy*. Supplement I, Part 2 (1982) 339.

McAllister, Ted V. *Revolt Against Modernity: Leo Strauss, Eric Voegelin, and the Search for a Post-liberal Order* (Lawrence, Kansas: Kansas Univ. Press, 1996)

McClure, Kirstie M. *Judging Rights: Lockean Polities and the Limits of Consent* (Ithaca & London: Cornell Univ. Press, 1996)

McDonald, Forrest. *Novus Ordo Seclorum* (Lawrence, Kansas: Univ. of Kansas Press, 1985)

McLaren, A. *Our Own Master Race: Eugenics in Canada, 1885-1945* (Toronto: McClelland and Stewart 1990)

Mehta, Ved. *Fly and the Fly Bottle* (Boston: Little, Brown, 1962)

Meiggs, Russel & David Lewis ed. *A Selection of Greek Historical Inscriptions to the End of the Fifth Century B.C.* (Oxford: Clarendon Press, 1969)

Mendelsohn, Isaac. *Slavery in the Ancient Near East* (New York: Oxford Univ. Press

Mill, J.S. 'Austin on Jurisprudence.' In *Collected Works of John Stuart Mill*, ed. John M. Robson (Toronto: Univ. of Toronto Press, 1984)

---------------- *On Liberty*. Ed. G. Himmelfarb (New York: Penguin Books, 1985)

---------------- *Utilitarianism*. Ed. Oskar Piest (Liberal of Arts Library, 1977)

Millar, John. *The Origin of the Distinction of Ranks* (1806 ed.) (Thoemmes: Bristol, 1990)

Miller, Charles C. 'Constitutional Law and The Rhetorics of Race.' In, *Law in American History* ed. D. Fleming & B. Bailyn (Boston & Toronto: Little, Brown 1971)

Mills, Charles W. *Blackness Visible: Essays in Philosophy and Race* (Ithaca & London: Cornell Univ. Press, 1998)

Milton, J.R. 'Dating Locke's Second Treatise.' *Hist. of Political Thought* 16 (1995) 356.

Milton, P. 'H.L.A. Hart: Jurisprudence and Linguistic Philosophy.' *Modern L.R.* 47 (1984).

Minda, Gary. *Postmodern Legal Movements: Law and Jurisprudence at Century's End* (New York: New York Univ. Press, 1995)

Minowitz, Peter. *Profits, Priests and Princes: Adam Smith's Emancipation of Economics from Politics and Religion* (Stanford: Stanford Univ. Press, 1993)

Mitchell, W.J.T. ed. *The Politics of Interpretation* (Chicago & London: Univ. of Chicago Press, 1983)

Mitzman, Arthur. 'On the Historicity of High Culture.' *Journal of the Hist. of Ideas* 55 (1994) 159.

Moles, Robert N. *Definition and Rule in Legal Theory* (London: Basil Blackwell, 1987)

Moore, Barrington, Jr. *Authority and Inequality under Capitalism and Socialism* (Oxford: Clarendon Press, 1987)

Mootz III, Francis J. 'Law in Flux: Philosophical Hermeneutics, Legal Argumentation, and the Natural Law Tradition.' *Yale J. of Law & the Humanities* 11 (1999) 311.

Moller, Astrid. *Naukratis: Trade in Archaic Greece* (Oxford Univ. Press, 2000)

Moore, Michael S. 'The Interpretive Turn in Modern Theory: A Turn for the Worse?' *Stanford L. Rev.* 41 (1989)

Monk, Ray. *Ludwig Wittgenstein: The Duty of Genius* (New York: Free Press, 1990)

Morison, W.L. *John Austin* (Stanford Univ. Press, 1982)

Mossner, Ernest C. 'Was Hume a Tory Historian? Facts and Reconsiderations.' *Journal of the Hist of Ideas* 2 (1941) 225.

Mudimbe, V.Y. and Kwame A. Appiah. 'The Impact of African Studies on Philosophy.' In *Africa and the Disciplines: The Contribution of Research in Africa to the Social Sciences and Humanities*. Ed. Robert H. Bate, et al. (Chicago & London: Univ. of Chicago Press, 1993) 113-138.

Mudimbe, V.Y. *The Invention of Africa* (Indianapolis: Indiana Univ. Press 1988)

Murphy, W.T. 'Memorizing Politics of Ancient History.' *Modern Law Rev.* 50 (1987) 384.

Mutua, Makau wa. 'The Banjul Charter and the African Cultural Fingerprint: An Evaluation of the Language of Duties.' *Virginia J. of International Law* 35 (1995) 339.

Myres, J.L. *The Dawn of History* (London: William & Norgate, 1915)

Nagel, Ernest. 'Impressions and Appraisals of Analytic Philosophy in Europe.' *Journal of Philosophy* 33 (1936) 5.

Neibuhr, R. *The Democratic Experience* (London: Pall Mall Press 1969)

Nerhot, P. *Law, Writing, Meaning: An Essay in Legal Hermeneutics*. Trans. Ian Fraser (Edinburgh: Edinburgh Univ. Press, 1992)

Newman, John H. *The Idea of a University* (1852) (London: Longmans, Green 1929)

Nibbi, Alessandra. *The Sea Peoples and Egypt* (Park Ridge, N.J.: Noyes Press 1975)

Nicholls, David. 'The English Middle Class and the Ideological Significance of Radicalism, 1760-1886.' *Journal of British Studies* 24 (1985) 415.

Nielsen, K. 'Global Justice, Capitalism and The Third World.' *Journal of Applied Philosophy* 2 (1984) 175.

Nietzsche, F. *The Use and Abuse of History*, 2nd rev. ed. trans. Adrian Collins (New York: Bobbs-Merril, 1957)

Novak, Michael. *The Spirit of Democratic Capitalism* (1982) (New York: Madison Books, 1991)

Novick, Peter. *"That Noble Dream": The Objectivity Question and the American Historical Profession* (Cambridge: Cambridge Univ. Press 1988)

Nozick, R. *Anarchy, State and Utopia* (Oxford: Oxford Univ. Press, 1974)

---------------- *The Examined Life: Philosophical Meditations* (New York: Touchstone, 1989)

Nwokeji. G. Ugo. 'The Slave Emancipation Problematic: Igbo Society and the Colonial Equation.' *Comp. Studies in Society and History* 40 (1998) 318.

O'Brien, Karen. *Narratives of Enlightenment: Cosmopolitan History from Voltaire to Gibbon* (Cambridge: Cambridge Univ. Press, 1997).

O'Hagan, Timothy. 'Gadamer, Hermeneutics and the Law.' *Archiv fur Rechts and Sozialphilosophie* 76 (1996) 197.

Oakeshott, Michael. *Rationalism in Politics* (London: Methuen 1962)

Odgen, C.K. and Richards, I.A. *The Meaning of Meaning*, 8th ed. (New York: Harcourt, Brace & World, 1923)

Odujirin. Adekemi. *The Normative Basis of Fault in Criminal Law* (Toronto: Univ. of Toronto Press, 1998)

Oesterley, W.O.E. *The Jews and Judaism During the Greek Period: The Background of Christianity* (London: S.P.C.K. 1941)

Ong, Walter J. *Orality and Literacy: The Technologizing of the Word* (London: Methuen, 1982)

Orosius, Paulus. *The Seven Books of History Against the Pagans.* Trans. J. Deferrari (Washington: The Catholic Univ. of America Press, 1964)

Orr, Susan. *Jerusalem and Athens: Reason and Revelation in the Works of Leo Strauss* (Rowman & Littlefield Publishers, 1995)

Osode, Patrick C. 'State Contracts, State Interests and International Commercial Arbitration: A Third World Perspective.' *African J. of International & Comp. Law* 9 (1997) 107.

Overin, Joanna, ed. *Reason and Morality* (London: Tavistock Publication, 1985).

Palombella, Gianluigi. 'The Cognitive Attitude: About a Structural Character in Law Interpretation.' *Archiv fur Rechts und Sozialphilosophie* 85 (1999) 151.

Pangle, Thomas L. ed. *The Roots of Political Philosophy: Ten Forgotten Socratic Dialogues* (Ithaca & London: Cornell Univ. Press, 1987)

---------------- *The Spirit of Modern Republicanism* (Chicago: Univ. of Chicago Press, 1988)

Parekh, B. 'Superior People: The Narrowness of Liberalism from Mill to Rawls.' *Times Literary Supplement* Feb. 25 (1994) 11.

Pareto, Vilfredo. *The Mind and Society: A Treatise on General Sociology*, trans. A. Bongioruo and Arthurs Livingston (New York: Dover Publications, 1963).

Parker, C.J.W. 'The Failure of Liberal Racism: The Racial Ideas of E.A. Freeman.' *Historical Journal* 24 (1981) 825.

Parkes, H.B. *Gods and Men: The Origin of Western Culture* (New York: Alfred A. Knopf, 1959)

Parry, J.H. *Europe and a Wider World 1415-1715* (London: Hutchinson Univ. Library, 1949)

Patterson, Dennis. *Law and Truth* (New York & Oxford: Oxford Univ. Press, 1996)

Pattison, Mark. 'Tendencies of Religious Thought in England, 1688-1750.' In, *Essays and Reviews* ed. Jowett 4th ed. (London: Longman & Green, 1961)

Pearson, Hearth. *Origins of Law and Economics: The Economists' New Science of Law, 1830-1930* (Cambridge: Univ. Press, 1997).

Perry, Stephen R. 'Hart's Methodological Positivism'. *Legal Theory* 4 (1998) 427.

Peters, Michael and Marshall, James. *Wittgenstein: Philosophy, Postmodernism, Pedagogy* (Westport, Conn.: Bergin & Garvey, 1999)

Pickel, Andreas. 'Never Ask Who Should Rule: Karl Popper and Political Theory.' *Canadian J. of Political Science* 22 (1989) 83.

Plato, *Laws*

---------------- *Phaedrus.*

---------------- *The Republic*

Pocock, J.G.A. *Barbarism and Religion* 2 Vols. (Cambridge: Cambridge Univ. Press, 1999)

---------------- 'The Fourth English Civil War: Dissolution, Desertion, and Alternative Histories in the Glorious Revolution.' In *The Revolution of 1688-89: Changing Perspectives* ed. Lois. G. Schwoerer (Cambridge: Cambridge Univ. Press, 1992) 52.

Polano, H. *The Talmud: Selections* (London: Fredrick Warne & Co. 1892)

Polanyi, Michael. *Personal Knowledge: Towards a Post-Critical Philosophy* (New York: Harper Tochbooks, 1964)

Pole, J.R. 'An Anatomy of the American Whig.' *The Historical Journal* 9 (1966) 229.

---------------- 'Slavery and Revolution: The Conscience of the Rich,' *Historical Journal* 20 (1977) 503

Poole, Roger. *Towards Deep Subjectivity* (London: Penguin Press 1972)

Pollock, F. & F.W. Maitland, *History of English Law*, 2nd ed. (Cambridge: Cambridge Univ. Press, 1923)

Popkin, Richard H. 'Hume's Racism.' *Philosophical Forum* 2 (1978) 211.

---------------------- 'The Philosophical Basis of 18th Century Racism.' In, *Studies in 18th Century Culture* Vol. 3, 245.

Popper, K.R. *The Open Society and Its Enemies* 5th ed. (London: Routledge & Kegan Paul, 1966)

--------------- *A World of Propensities* (Bristol: Thoemmes, 1990)

Posner, Richard A. '"Conventionalism": The Key to Law as an Autonomous Discipline?' *University of Toronto Law Journal* 30 (1988) 333.

Porter, Roy & Teich, Mikulas ed. *Romanticism in National Context* (Cambridge: Cambridge Univ. Press, 1988)

Pound, R. *The Spirit of the Common Law* (Francestown, N.H.: Marshall Jones, 1931)

Radbruch, Gustav. 'Anglo-American Jurisprudence Through Continental Eyes'. *Law Quarterly Rev.* 52 (1936) 530.

Radin, P. *The Racial Myth* (New York: Whittlesey House, 1934)

Randall, John H. Jr. 'The Development of the Scientific Method in the School of Padua.' *Journal of the History of Ideas* 1 (1940).

Rankin, H.D. *Sophists, Socratics and Cynics* (London & Totowa, New Jersey, 1983)

Rawls, J. *A Theory of Justice* (Cambridge, Mass: Harvard Univ. Press, 1971)

---------- *Political Liberalism* (New York: Columbia Univ. Press, 1993)

Rawson, Elizabeth. *The Spartan Tradition in European Thought* (Oxford: Clarendon Press, 1969)

Ray, John. 'Before the Pharaohs: The Escavation of Egyptian Pre-History.' *Times Literary Supplement* (October 1993) 27.

Raz, Joseph. *Ethics in the Public Domain: Essays in the Morality of Law and Politics* (Oxford: Clarendon Press 1994)

-------------- *The Morality of Freedom* (Oxford: Univ. Press, 1986)

Redford, D.B. 'The Hyksos Invasion in History and Tradition.' *Orientalia* (n.s.) 39 (1970) 1.

Redford, Donald B. *Egypt, Canaan, and Israel in Ancient Times* (Princeton, N.J.: Princeton Univ. Press, 1991)

Reichenbach, H. *The Rise of Scientific Philosophy* (Berkeley: Univ. of California Press, 1951)

Reimann, Mathias. 'Nineteenth Century German Legal Science'. *Boston College L. Rev.* 31 (1990) 837.

---------------- 'A Career in Itself: The German Professoriate as a Model for American Legal Academia.' In *The Reception of Continental Ideas in the Common Law World, 1820-1920* (Berlin: Duncker & Humblot, 1993) 165.

Reinbold, Meyer. *Classica Americana: The Greek and Roman Heritage in the United States* (Detroit: Wayne State Univ. 1984).

Reisner, George A. *Harvard African Studies Vol. VI (Excavations at Karma)* (Cambridge, Mass., 1923)

Resnick, David. 'Locke and The Rejection of the Ancient Constitution.' *Political Theory* 12 (1984) 97.

Rice, C. Duncan. 'Controversies Over Slavery in 18th and 19th Centuries Scotland.' In *Antislavery Reconsidered: New Perspectives on the Abolitionists*. Ed. Lewis Perry and Michael Fellman (Baton Rouge & London: Louisiana State Univ. Press, 1979) 24.

-------------------- 'Archibald Datzel, the Scottish Intelligentsia, and the Problem of Slavery.' *Scottish Historical Rev.* 62 (1983) 121.

Richards, D.A.J. 'Human Rights and the Moral Foundations of the Substantive Criminal Law.' *Georgia Law Rev.* 13 (1979) 1395.

Riley, P. Will and Political Legitimacy: *A Critical Exposition of Social Contract Theory in Hobbes, Locke, Rousseau, Kant, and Hegel* (Cambridge, Mass.: Harvard Univ. Press, 1982)

---------------- '"The Elements" of Kant's Practical Philosophy: The 'Groundwork' after 200 Years, 1795-1985.' *Political Theory* 14 (1986) 552.

Riter, Hellmut. 'Irrational Solidarity Groups: A Socio-psychological Study in Connection with Ibn Khaldun.' *Oriens* 1 (1948) 1.

Roach, John. 'Liberalism and the Victorian Intelligentsia.' *Cambridge Historical Journal* 13 (1957) 58.

Roberts, Jennifer T. *Athens on Trial: The Anti-democratic Tradition in Western Thought* (Princeton, N.J.: Princeton Univ. Press, 1994)

Robinson, James H. *Petrarch: The First Modern Scholar and Man of Letters* 2nd ed. (New York: G.P. Putnam's Sons, 1914)

Robinson, James R. 'Hermeneutics Since Barth'. In *New Frontiers in Theology: Discussions among Continental and American Theologians,* Vol. II ed. James M. Robinson & John B. Cobb, Jr. (New York: Harper & Row, 1964) 1.

Rodney, Walter. *How Europe Underdeveloped Africa* (Howard Univ. Press, 1974)

Romilly, Jacqueline. *Thucydides and Athenian Imperialism*. Trans. By Phillip Thody (Oxford: Basil Blackwell, 1963)

Root, Elihu. 'The Need for Organization in Scientific Research.' *Bulletin of the National Research Council* 1 (1919) 7.

Rorty, Richard. *Contingency, Irony and Solidarity* (Cambridge: Cambridge Univ. Press 1980)

---------------- *Philosophy and the Mirror of Nature* (Princeton, N.J.: Princeton Univ. Press, 1979)

---------------- 'Method and Morality'. In *Social Science as Moral Inquiry* ed. Norman Haan et al (New York: Columbia Univ. Press, 1983) 155.

---------------- 'A Reply to Dreyfus and Taylor'. *Review of Metaphysics* 34 (1980) 39.

Rosenberg, Alexander. *Economics – Mathematical Politics or Science of Diminishing Returns?* (Chicago & London: Univ. of Chicago Press, 1992)

Rosivach, Vincent. 'Enslaving Barbaroi and the Athenian Ideology of Slavery.' *Historia* 48 (1999) 129.

Rotunda, Ronald D. *The Politics of Language* (Iowa City: Univ. of Iowa Press, 1986)

Rousseau, Jean Jacques. *A Discourse Upon the Origin and Foundation of the Inequality and Mankind* (1761) (New York: Burt Franklin 1971 rep.)

Rumble, Wilfrid E. *The Thought of John Austin* (London: Athlone Press, 1985)

Ryerson, James. 'The Outrageous Pragmatism of Judge Richard Posner.' *Lingua Franca* 10 (2000) 26.

Ryle, G. 'Systematically Misleading Expressions.' In, *Logic and Language* (First and Second Series) ed. A. Flew (New York: Anchor Books, 1954)

Sacco, Rodolfo. 'Legal Formants: A Dynamic Approach to Comparative Law.' *Am. J. of Comp. Law* 39 (1991) 1.

Said, Edward W. *Representations of the Intellectual* (New York: Pantheon Books, 1994)

Sampson, Geoffrey. *Liberty and Language* (Oxford: Oxford Univ. Press 1979)

Samuel, Geoffrey. 'Science, Law and History: Historical Jurisprudence and Modern Legal Theory'. *Northern Ireland Law Quarterly* 41 (1990) 1.

Samuelson, Paul A. 'Economics in a Golden Age: A Personal Memoir.' In, *The Twentieth Century Sciences: Studies in the Biography of Ideas*, ed. Gerald Holton (New York: W.W. Norton, 1972) 155.

Sandars, Edith R. 'The Hamitic Hypothesis: Its Origin and Functions in Time Perspective.' *J. of African History* 10 (1969) 121.

Sandars, N.K. *The Sea Peoples: Warriors of the Ancient Meditarrenean, 1250-1150* B.C. (London: Thames & Hudson, 1985)

Sandbrook, R. 'Liberal Democracy in Africa: A Socialist-Revisionist Perspective.' *Canadian Journal of African Studies* 22 (1988) 246.

Sandel, M.J. *Democracy's Discontent: America in Search of a Public Philosophy* (Cambridge, Mass: Belknap Press, 1997)

--------------- ed. *Liberalism and Its Critics* (New York: New York Univ. Press, 1984)

---------------. *Liberalism and The Limits of Justice* (Cambridge Univ. Press, 1982)

Sarton, George. *A History of Science* (Harvard Univ. Press, 1960)

Saxonhouse, Arlene W. *Athenian Democracy: Modern Mythmakers and Ancient Theorists* (Notre Dame: Univ. of Notre Dame Press 1997)

Sayce, A.H. *The Races of the Old Testament* rev. ed. (London: Religious Tract Society, 1925)

Schafer, Peter. *Judeophobia: Attitudes toward the Jews in the Ancient World* (Cambridge, Mass.: Harvard Univ. Press, 1997)

Scheppelle, Kim Lane and Waldron, Jeremy. 'Contractarian Methods in Political and Legal Evaluation.' *Yale J. of Law & Humanities* 3 (1991) 195.

Schlesinger, Sybil. 'Working Definitions: A Critique of H.L.A. Hart's Use of Wittgenstein in The Concept of Law.' *Archiv fur Rechts und Sozialphilosophie* 83 (1997) 103.

Schmidt, Henry J. 'The Rhetoric of Survival: The Germanists in America from 1900 to 1925'. In *America and the Germans: An Assessment of a Three Hundred Year History* ed. Frank Tromurler & Joseph McVeigh, Vol. II (Philadelphia: Univ. of Pennsylvania Press, 1985) 204.

Schneider, Ulrich Johannes. 'The Teaching of Philosophy at German Universities in the 19th Century.' *Hist. of Universities* 12 (1993) 197.

Schumacker, E.F. *A Guide for the Perplexed* (New York: Harper and Row, 1977)

Schutz, Herbert. *The Prehistory of Germanic Europe* (Yale Univ. Press, 1983)

Schwartz, Andreas B. 'John Austin and the German Jurisprudence of His Time.' *Politica* (1934) 178.

Schwarzchild, B. *The Red Prussian: The Life and Legend of Karl Marx*, trans. M. Wing (New York: Charles Scribner's Sons 1947)

Schwarzchild, Maimon. 'Class, National Character and The Bar Reforms in Britain: Will There Always be an England?' *Connecticut J. of International Law* 9, 185.

Schwatz, B. *In Search of Wealth and Power* (Cambridge, Mass.: Belknap Press, 1964)

Schwebel, Stephen M. *Justice in International Law* (Grotius Publication, Cambridge Univ. Press 1994).

Scott, D.F.S. 'Growth of Classical Tradition in Germany.' *Durham University Journal* 49 (1957) 51.

Sedgwick, Sally S. 'On the Relation of Pure Reason to Content: A Reply to Hegel's Critique of Formalism in Kant's Ethics.' *Philosophy and Phenomenological Research* 49 (1988) 59.

Seipp, David J. 'The Structure of English Common Law in the Seventeenth Century.' In, *Legal History in the Making: Proceedings of the Ninth British Legal History Conference, 1989* ed. W.M. Gordon & T.D. Fergus (London: Hambledon, 1991)

Seters, John Van. *The Hyksos: A New Investigation* (New Haven: Yale Univ. Press 1966)

Shaw, W. David. *The Lucid Veil: Poetic Truth in the Victorian Age* 2nd rev. ed. (London: Athlone Press, 1987)

Sher, Richard R. *Church and University in the Scottish Enlightenment: The Moderate Literati of Edinburgh* (Princeton, N.J.: Princeton Univ. Press, 1985).

Shils, Edward. 'The Antinomies of Liberalism.' In, *The Relevance of Liberalism* (Boulder, Colorado: Westview Press, 1978) 134.

----------------- *The Intellectual Between Tradition and Modernity: The Indian Situation* (The Hague: Moutm & Co. 1961)

------------------ *Tradition* (London & Boston: Faber & Faber, 1981)

Shiner, Roger A. *Norm and Nature: The Movements of Legal Thought* (Oxford: Clarendon Press, 1992)

----------------- 'Wittgenstein and the Foundations of Knowledge'. *Proceedings of Aristotlean Society* (N.S.) 78 (1978) 78.

Shklar, Judith N. *After Utopia* (Princeton, N.J.: Princeton Univ. Press, 1957).

Shuger, Debora. 'Irishmen, Aristocrats and Other White Barbarians.' *Renaissance Quarterly* 50 (1997) 494.

Shweder, Richard A. 'Post-Nietzschian Anthropology: The Idea of Multiple Objective Worlds.' In *Relativism: Interpretation and Confrontation* ed. Michael Krauz (Notre Dame Univ. Press, 1989) 99.

Siegel, Stephen A. 'The Aristolean Basis of English Law 1450-1800.' *New York Univ. L. Rev.* 56 (1981) 18.

Simmonds, N.E. *The Decline of Juridical Reason: Doctrine and Theory in the Legal Order* (Manchester: Manchester Univ. Press, 1984)

Simpson, A.W.B. 'Legal Iconoclasts and Legal Ideals.' *Univ. of Cincinnati L.R.* 58 (1990) 819.

----------------- 'The Rise and Fall of the Legal Treatise.' *Univ. of Chicago L.R.* 48 (1981)

Skemp, J.B. 'The Permanent Importance of Greek Studies.' *Durham University Journal* LXXIII (N.S.) (1980) 1.

Skinner, Q. 'The Ideological Context of Hobbes's Political Thought.' *The Historical Journal* 9 (1966) 286.

----------------- ed. *The Return of Grand Theory in the Human Sciences.* (Cambridge: Cambridge Univ. Press, 1985)

Slattery, Brian. 'Law's Meaning'. *Osgoode Hall Law Journal* 34 (1996) 553.

----------------- 'Three Concepts of Law: The Ambiguous Legacy of H.L.A. Hart.' *Saskatchewan L. Rev.* 61 (1998) 323.

Smart, Paul. 'Some Will be More Equal Than Others: J.S. Mill on Democracy, Freedom and Meritocracy.' *Archiv fur Rechts und Sozialphilosophie* 75 (1990) 308.

Smith, Adam. *An Inquiry into the Nature and Causes of The Wealth of Nations*, ed. E. Cannan (New York: Modern Library, 1937).

----------------- *Lectures on Jurisprudence*, ed. R.L. Meek, et al (Oxford: Clarendon Press, 1978)

----------------- *The Theory of Moral Sentiments* ed. D.D. Raphael & A.L. Macfie (Oxford: Clarendon Press, 1976)

Smith, George. *The Chaldean Account of Genesis* rev. ed. A.H. Sayce (London, 1880)

----------------- *The Diffusion of Culture* (London: Watts, 1933)

Smith, John E. *The Spirit of American Philosophy* rev. ed. (Albany: State Univ. of New York Press, 1983)

Smith, R.J. *The Gothic Bequest* (Cambridge: Cambridge Univ. Press, 1987)

Smith, Steven B. *Hegel's Critique of Liberalism* (Chicago & London: Univ. of Chicago Press, 1989)

Snell, B. *The Discovery of the Mind: The Greek Origins of European Thought*, trans, by T.G. Rosenmeyer (Oxford: Basil Blackwell, 1953)

Sombart, W. *The Quintessence of Capitalism: A Study of the History and Psychology of the Modern Business man*, trans. M. Epstein (London: T. Fisher Unwin, 1915)

Sorel, Georg. *Reflections on Violence.* Trans. T.E. Hulme & J. Roth (New York: Collier Books, 1961)

Soyinka, Wole. *The Open Sore of a Continent: A Personal Narrative of the Nigerian Crisis* (New York: Oxford Univ. Press, 1996)

Speiser, E.A. 'The Biblical Idea of History and Its Common Near Eastern Setting.' In, *The Jewish Expression*, ed. Judah Goldin (New York: Bantam Books, 1970)

Spencer, H. *The Principles of Ethics*, 2 vols. (New York: D. Appleton, 1903)

Spitz, D. *Patterns of Anti-Democratic Thought* (New York: MacMillan (1949)

----------------- *The Real World of Liberalism* (Chicago & London: Univ. of Chicago Press, 1982)

Stammler, R. 'Fundamental Tendencies in Modern Jurisprudence.' *Michigan L.R.* 21 (1922-23) 623.

Standen, Jeffrey A. 'Critical Legal Studies as an Anti-Positivist Phenomenon.' *Virginia L. Rev.* 73 (1986) 983.

Starr, Chester G. *A History of the Ancient World* 4th ed. (New York: Oxford Univ. Press, 1991).

Stein, P. *Legal Evolution* (Cambridge: Cambridge Univ. Press, 1980)

----------------- *Roman Law in European History* (Cambridge: Cambridge Univ. Press, 1999)

Stephen, J.F. *History of the Criminal Law of England*, 3 vols. (London: Stevens & Sons, 1883)

Stone, Jerry H. 'Christian Praxis as Reflective Action'. In *Legal Hermeneutics: History, Theory, and Practice* ed. Gregory Leyh (Berkeley: Univ. of California Press, 1992) 103.

Strasburger, Hermann. 'The Sociology of the Homeric Epics.' In, *Homer: German Scholarship in Translation* ed. P.V. Jones and G.M. Wright (Oxford: Clarendon Press, 1997) 47.

Strauss, Leo. *Natural Right and History* (Chicago & London: Univ. of Chicago Press, 1953)

---------------- *Studies in Platonic Political Philosophy* (Chicago: Univ. of Chicago Press, 1983)

Stromholm, S. 'Legal Hermeneutics – Notes on the Early Modern Development'. *Scandinavian Studies in Law* 22 (1978) 213.

--------------- *A Short History of Legal Thinking in the West* (Stockholm: Norstedts, 1985)

Sugarman, D. 'The Legal Boundaries of Liberty: Dicey, Liberalism and Legal Science.' *Modern L. Rev.* (1983).

Sullivan, Eileen P. 'Liberalism and Imperialism: J.S. Mill's Defense of the British Empire.' *Journal of the Hist. of Ideas* 44 (1983) 599.

Sullivan, R. *The Story of Rameses* (Edwin Mellin Press, 1986)

Sullivan, R.D. 'Psammetichus I and the Foundation of Naukratis.' In, *Ancient Naukratis*, ed. William D.E. Coulson, Vol. II (Oxford: Oxbow Books, 1996).

Summers, Robert S. 'The New Analytical Jurists.' *New York Univ. L.Rev.* 41 (1966) 861.

Swain, J.S. 'What is History?' *Journal of Philosophy* 20 (1920)

Sypher, Wylie. *Guinea's Captive Kings: British Anti-Slavery Literature of the 18th Century* (Chapel Hill: Univ. of North Carolina Press, 1942)

Tacitus. *Agricola and Germania*, trans. M. Hutton

Tarlton, Charles D. '"The Rulers Now on Earth": Locke's Two Treatises, and Revolution of 1688.' *Historical Journal* 28 (1985) 279.

Tarnas, Richard. *The Passion of the Western Mind* (New York: Ballantine Books, 1991)

Taylor, Charles. 'Interpretation and the Sciences of Man'. *Review of Metaphysics* 25 (1977)

---------------- 'Understanding in Human Science.' *Review of Metaphysics* 34 (1980) 25.

Teffeteller, Annette. 'The Glory Myth.' In *The Spoils of War* ed. Jurgen Kleist & Bruce A. Butterfield (New York: Peter Lang Publishing 1997)

Tertullian. *Apology*, in, *Apologetical Works and Minucius Felis Octarius*, trans. R. Arbemann et al (New York: Fathers of the Church, 1950)

Tetsuro, Watsuji. *Climate and Culture* trans. Geoffrey Bownas (New York: Greenwood Press, 1988)
Thompson, E.P. *Whigs and Hunters: The Origin of the Black Act* (London: Penguin Books, 1975)
Thompson, Martyn P. 'Significant Silences in Locke's Two Treatises of Government: Constitutional History, Contract and Law.' *Historical Journal* 31 (1987) 275
Thomson, David. Ed. *Political Ideas* (Pelican Books, 1966)
Tillyard, E.M.W. *The Elizabethan World Picture* (New York: Vantage Books, 1967)
Tocqueville, Alexis. *Democracy in America* (New York: New American Library, 1956)
Todd, M. *The Northern Barbarians, 100 B.C. – A.D. 300* (London: Hutchinson Univ. Library, 1975)
Torok, Laszlo. 'Kush: An African State in the First Millennium B.C.' *Proceedings of the British Academy* 87 (1994) 1.
Toulmin, S. *Human Understanding* (Oxford: Clarendon Press, 1972) Vol. I.
---------------- *Cosmopolis: The Hidden Agenda of Modernity* (1990) (Chicago: Univ. of Chicago Press, 1992)
Trevor-Roper, Hugh. 'The Scottish Enlightenment.' *Studies in Voltaire and the Eighteenth Century* 58 (1967) 1635.
---------------- *The Romantic Movement and the Study of History* (London: Athlone Press, 1969)
Tuck, R. 'Grotius & Selden.' In, *The Cambridge History of Political Thought 1450-1700* ed. J.H. Burns (Cambridge Univ. Press 1991)
---------------- *Natural Rights Theories: Their Origin and Development* (Cambridge: Cambridge Univ. Press, 1979)
Tully, James. *Strange Multiplicity: Constitutionalism in an Age of Diversity* (Cambridge: Cambridge Univ. Press, 1995)
Tur, R. 'Paternalism and the Criminal Law.' *Journal of Applied Philosophy* 2 (1985) 173.
Turner, Frank M. *Contesting Cultural Authority: Essays in Victorian Intellectual Life* (Cambridge Univ. Press, 1993)
Turner, S. *The History of the Anglo-Saxons: From the Earliest Period to the Norman Conquest* 7th ed. 3 vols. (London: Longmans, 1852)
Twining, William, ed. *Legal Theory and Common Law* (Oxford: Basil Blackwell, 1986)
Ulam, Adam B. *Philosophical Foundations of English Socialism* (Cambridge, Mass.: Harvard Univ. Press, 1951)
Ulrich, Eugene. *The Dead Sea Scrolls and the Origins of the Bible* (William B. Eerdmans Publishing, 1999)

Unger, Roberto. *What Should Legal Analysis Become?* (London: Verso, 1996)

Urbina, Sebastian. *Reason, Democracy, Society: A Study on the Basis of Legal Thinking* (Dordrecht: Kluwer Academic Press, 1996)

Urmson, J.O. 'The History of Philosophical Analysis.' In, *The Linguistic Turn* ed. Richard Rorty (Chicago: Univ. of Chicago Press, 1967)

Vail, Leroy and White, Landig. *Power and The Praise Poem* (Charlottesville: Univ. Press of Virginia, 1991)

Vaughan, Frederick. 'On Being a Positivist: Does it Really Matter?' *Osgoode Hall L.J.* 29 (1991)

Vercoutter, Jean. 'Upper Egyptian Settlers in Middle Kingdom Nubia.' Kush V (1957) 61.

Vernant, Jean Pierre. *The Origins of Greek Thought* (1962) (Ithaca & New York: Cornell Univ. Press, 1982)

Vertinsky, Patricia. 'Body Matters: Race, Gender, and Perception of Physical Ability from Goethe to Weinninger.' In *Identity and Intolerance* ed. N. Finsch & B. Schirmar (Cambridge: Cambridge Univ. Press, 1998) 331.

Vidal-Naquet, Pierre. *The Black Hunter: Forms of Thought and Forms of Society in the Greek World.* Trans. Andrew Szegedy-Maszak (Baltimore: Johns Hopkins, 1986)

Viner, Jacob. 'The Intellectual History of Laissez-Faire.' *Journal of Law and Economics* 3 (1960) 45.

Virgil. *Aeneid* ed. C.H. Sisson (Carcanet Press, 1986)

Vlastos, G. 'Equality and Justice in Early Greek Cosmology.' *Classical Philology* 42 (1947) 156.

---------------- *Plato's Universe* (Seattle: Univ. of Washington Press, 1975)

Vogt, James, *Ancient Slavery and The Ideal of Man.* Trans. Thomas Wiedermann (Oxford: Blackwell, 1974)

Waismann, F. 'Ethics and Science'. In F. Waismann et al. *Ethics and the Will: Essays* ed. B. McGuinness and J. Schule. Trans Hans Kaul (Dordrecht: Kluwer Academic Publishers, 1994) 35.

Waldron, J. *Law and Disagreement* (Oxford: Clarendon Press, 1999)

-------------- 'When Justice Replaces Affection: The Need for Rights.' *Harvard Journal of Law and Pub. Policy* 11 (1988) 624.

-------------- 'Homelessness and Community.' *University of Toronto Law Journal* 50 (2000)

Walker, St. James W. *'"Race", Rights, and the Law in the Supreme Court of Canada: Historical Case Studies* (Osgoode Society & Wilfrid Laurier Univ. Press 1997)

Watkins, M.H. 'Economics as Mystification.' *Journal of Canadian Studies* 4 (1969) 55.

Watson, Alan. 'Seventeenth Century Jurists, Roman Law, and the Law of Slavery.' *Chic-Kent L. Rev.* 68 (1993) 1343.

Watson, George. *The English Ideology* (London: Allen Lane, 1973)

Weber, Max. *The Protestant Ethic and the Spirit of Capitalism*. Trans. Talcott Parson (New York: Charles Scribner's, 1955)

---------------- *Economy and Society: An Outline of Interpretive Sociology* (New York: Bedminster Press, 1968) Vol. 2.

Weiner, Michael. *Race and Migration in Imperial Japan* (New York: Routledge, 1994)

Weinre*b,* Lloyd. *Natural Law and Justice* (Cambridge, Mass.: Harvard Univ. Press, 1987)

Weinrib, Ernest J. 'Legal Formalism: On the Immanent Rationality of Law.' *Yale L.J. 97* (1988) 949.

Weiss, Robert P. 'Humanitarianism, Labour Exploitation or Social Control? A Critical Survey of Theory and Research on the Origin and Development of Prisons.*'* *Social History* 12 (1987) 331.

Welchman, Jennifer. 'Locke on Slavery and Inalienable Rights.' *Canadian Journal of Philosophy* 25 (1995) 67.

Werner, Jaeger. *Paideia: The Ideals of Greek Culture*, trans. Gilbert Highet (New York: Oxford Univ. Press, 1945)

West, Robin L. 'Liberalism Rediscovered: A Pragmatic Definition of the Liberal Vision.' *Univ. of Pitt. L.R.* 46 (1985) 673.

Weyl, Nathaniel. *Karl Marx: Racist* (New Rochelle, New York: Arlington House, 1980)

Whitehead, A.N. *Adventures of Ideas* (New York: Free Press, 1967).

Whitman, James Q. *The Legacy of Roman Law in the German Romantic Era: Historical Vision and Legal Change* (Princeton, N.J.: Princeton Univ. Press, 1990)

Whitman, James. 'From Philology to Anthropology in Mid-Nineteenth Century Germany'. In, *Functionalism Historicized: Essays on British Social Anthropology* ed. George W. Stocking, Jr. (Madison: Univ. of Wisconson Press, 1984) 214.

Wilbur, Martin. *Slavery in China During the Former Han Dynasty 206 B.C. – A.D. 25* (Chicago, 1943)

Wilford, Lt. Francis. 'On Egypt and Other Countries Adjacent to the Cali River or Nile of Ethiopia From the Ancient Books of the Hindus.' *Asiatic Researches* III (1799) 295.

Wilkinson, Doris Y. 'The 1850 Harvard Medical School Dispute and the Admission of African American Students.' *Harvard Library Bulletin* (New Series) 3 (1992) 13.

Willey, B. *The Seventeenth Century Background* (London: Chatto & Windus, 1957)

Williams, Basil. *The Whig Supremacy 1714-1760* 2nd ed. (Oxford: Clarendon Press, 1962)

Williams, Glanville. *Criminal Law: The General Part*, 2nd ed. (London: Stevens & Sons, 1961)

Williams, Patricia J. *The Rooster's Egg* (Cambridge, Mass.: Harvard Univ. Press, 1995)

Willis, John R. ed. *Slaves and Slavery in Muslim Africa* 2 Vols. (London: Frank Cass, 1985)

Wilson, P. *Second-Hand Knowledge: An Inquiry into Cognitive Authority* (Westport, Conn.: Greenwood Press, 1983)

Winch, D. *Adam Smith's Politics: An Essay in Historiographical Revision* (Cambridge: Cambridge Univ. Press 1978).

Winchell, Alexander. 'Our Remote Ancestry.' *North American Review* 139 (1884)

Windelband, Wilhelm. *A History of Philosophy*, Vol. I (Greek, Roman, and Medieval (New York: Harper & Row, 1958)

Windspear, Alban D. *The Genesis of Plato's Thought* 3rd ed. (Montreal: Harvest House, 1974)

Wiredu, K. *Philosophy and an African Culture* (Cambridge: Cambridge Univ. Press, 1980)

Wittgeinstein, L. *On Certainty* ed. G.E.M. Anscombe & G.H. von Wright (Oxford: Basil Blackwell, 1963).

---------------- *Remarks on Frazer's Golden Bough* ed. Rush Rhees (The Brynmill Press, 1979) von Wright et al, trans. G.E.M. Anscombe (Oxford: Basil Blackwell, 1956)

---------------- *Philosophical Investigations* trans. G.E.M. Anscombe (Oxford: Basil Blackwell, 1967)

Wood, Gordon S. 'The Fundamentalists and the Constitution.' *New York Rev. of Books*. 35 (No. 2) (1988) 235.

Wood, N. *The Politics of Locke's Philosophy* (Berkeley: Univ. of California Press, 1983)

---------------- 'Tabula Rasa, Social Environmentalism and the English Paradigm.' *Journal of the Hist. of Ideas* 53 (1992) 647.

Woodward, E.L. 'The Place of Lord Acton in the Liberal Movement of the Nineteenth Century.' *Politica* (1939) 248.

Wright, Bruce. *Black Robes, White Justice* (New Jersey: Lyle Stuart, 1987)

Wright, von Georg Henrik. *The Tree of Knowledge and Other Essays* (London: E.J. Brill, 1993)

---------------- *Wittgenstein* (Oxford: Blackwell, 1982)

Wright, George. 'On a General Theory of Interpretation: The Betti-Gadamer Dispute in Legal Hermeneutics'. *American J. of Jurisprudence* 32 (1987) 243.

Xenophon. *Hellenica Books I-V*. Trans. Carleton L. Brownson (London: William Heinemann, 1918).

Yntema, H.E. 'The Rational Basis of Legal Science.' *Columbia L.R.* 31 (1931) 925.

Zachernuk, Phillip S. 'Of Origins and Colonial Order: Southern Nigerian Historians and the "Hamitic Hypothesis" c.1870-1970.' *Journal of African History* 35 (1994) 427.

Zimmermann, Reinhard. 'Savigny's Legacy: Legal History, Comparative Law, and the Emergence of a European Legal Science.' *Law Quarterly Rev.* 112 (1996) 576.

Ziolkowski, Theodore. *German Romanticism and Its Institutions* (Princeton, N.J.: Princeton Univ. Press, 1990)

Zirkle, C. *Evolution, Marxian Biology and The Social Scene* (Philadelphia: Univ. of Penn. Press, 1959)

Index